CCENT® Certification

ALL-IN-ONE

FOR

DUMMIES®

D1211664

CCENT® Certification
ALL-IN-ONE
FOR
DUMMIES®

by Glen E. Clarke

WILEY

Wiley Publishing, Inc.

CCENT® Certification All-In-One For Dummies®

Published by
Wiley Publishing, Inc.
111 River Street
Hoboken, NJ 07030-5774

www.wiley.com

Copyright © 2011 by Wiley Publishing, Inc., Indianapolis, Indiana

Published by Wiley Publishing, Inc., Indianapolis, Indiana

Published simultaneously in Canada

For general information on our other products and services, please contact our Customer Care Department within the U.S. at 877-762-2974, outside the U.S. at 317-572-3993, or fax 317-572-4002.

For technical support, please visit www.wiley.com/techsupport.

Wiley also publishes its books in a variety of electronic formats. Some content that appears in print may not be available in electronic books.

Library of Congress Control Number: 2010937813

ISBN: 978-0-470-64748-6

Manufactured in the United States of America

10 9 8 7 6 5 4 3 2 1

WILEY

About the Author

Glen E. Clarke (CCENT/MCSE/MCSD/MCDBA/MCT/MCTS/CEH/CHFI/ Security+) is an independent trainer and consultant, focusing on network security and security auditing services. Glen spends most of his time delivering certified courses on A+, Network+, Windows Server, SQL Server, Exchange Server, Visual Basic .NET, and ASP.NET. Glen also teaches a number of security related courses covering topics such as ethical hacking and countermeasures, vulnerability testing, firewall design, and packet analysis.

Glen is an experienced author and technical editor who has worked on eighteen certification books. Glen designed and coauthored the award nominated *A+ Certification Bible* and has worked on certification titles involving topics such as Windows certification, CIW certification, Network+ certification, and Security+ certification. Glen is also author of *The Network+ Certification Study Guide,* 4th Edition, and coauthor of *CompTIA A+ Certification All-One For Dummies,* 2nd Edition.

When he's not working, Glen loves to spend quality time with his wife, Tanya, and their four children, Sara, Brendon, Ashlyn, and Rebecca. You can visit Glen online at www.gleneclarke.com, or contact him at glenclarke@accesswave.ca.

Dedication

To Tanya, my beautiful wife and partner in life.

Author's Acknowledgments

I want to thank the people at Wiley for their hard work and continued support. A special thank you to acquisitions editor, Katie Feltman, for her support with this project and her patience as I worked through the chapters. I also want to thank project editor Blair Pottenger for his patience and quick responses to any questions I fired his way! Katie and Blair, you are both great people to work for and I always look forward to our next project together! Much appreciation goes to copy editor Heidi Unger for an outstanding job on the editing of the chapters — thank you! I also want to thank Dan Lachance and Ed Tetz for their feedback as technical editors and a job well done! Thanks guys — love working with you both!

I also want to thank the folks at Tim Horton's for not kicking me out when I occupy a table for hours at a time and for keeping the coffee *always fresh*! I would also like to thank Bob Canning and Dan Tooke for their interest in technology and taking the time to give me a tour of their work environment — it was great, thank you!

A special thank you goes to my four children, Sara, Brendon, Ashlyn, and Rebecca, for giving me the time to sit down and participate in kids play with them — it makes me realize what is important in life. A needed thank you goes to my wife, Tanya, for all her support — you have made great sacrifices with this project as well. Thank you for all that you do!

Publisher's Acknowledgments

We're proud of this book; please send us your comments at http://dummies.custhelp.com. For other comments, please contact our Customer Care Department within the U.S. at 877-762-2974, outside the U.S. at 317-572-3993, or fax 317-572-4002.

Some of the people who helped bring this book to market include the following:

Acquisitions, Editorial, and Media Development

Project Editor: Blair J. Pottenger

Acquisitions Editor: Katie Feltman

Copy Editor: Heidi Unger

Technical Editor: Dan Lachance, Ed Tetz

Editorial Manager: Kevin Kirschner

Media Development Project Manager: Laura Moss-Hollister

Media Development Assistant Project Manager: Jenny Swisher

Media Development Associate Producer: Marilyn Hummel

Editorial Assistant: Amanda Graham

Sr. Editorial Assistant: Cherie Case

Cartoons: Rich Tennant (www.the5thwave.com)

Composition Services

Project Coordinators: Katie Crocker, Patrick Redmond

Layout and Graphics: Nikki Gately, Joyce Haughey, Christin Swinford

Special Art: Rashell Smith

Proofreaders: Melissa D. Buddendeck, Melanie Hoffman

Indexer: BIM Indexing & Proofreading Services

Publishing and Editorial for Technology Dummies

> **Richard Swadley,** Vice President and Executive Group Publisher

> **Andy Cummings,** Vice President and Publisher

> **Mary Bednarek,** Executive Acquisitions Director

> **Mary C. Corder,** Editorial Director

Publishing for Consumer Dummies

> **Diane Graves Steele,** Vice President and Publisher

Composition Services

> **Debbie Stailey,** Director of Composition Services

Contents at a Glance

Table of Contents

Introduction

The CCENT certification is a new, fast-growing certification that tests your knowledge of basic Cisco device-management and networking concepts. It is a great stepping stone to the CCNA certification and other Cisco certification tracks. The CCENT exam tests your knowledge of real-world networking concepts and Cisco features found on most networks today!

About This Book

CCENT Certification All-In-One For Dummies is designed to be a hands-on, practical guide to help you pass the CCENT certification exam. This book is written in a way that helps you not only understand complex technical content, but also prepares you to apply that knowledge to real-world scenarios.

I understand the value of a book that covers the points needed to pass the exam, but I also understand the value of ensuring that the information helps you perform IT-related tasks when you are on the job. That is what this book offers you — key points to pass the exam combined with practical information to help you in the real world, which means that you can use this book in more than one way.

+ **An exam preparation tool:** Because my goal is to help you pass the CCENT certification exam, this book is packed with exam-specific information and tips to help you with tricky exam questions. You should understand everything that is in this book before taking the exam, but to identify key points that you *must* know, look for icons named *For the Exam*. In those paragraphs, you will find helpful tips on topics you are certain to be tested on.

+ **A reference:** Rely on my extensive experience in the IT industry not only to study for (and pass) the exam, but also to help you perform common network-related tasks on the job. I hope you find this book a useful tool that you can refer to time and time again in your career as you configure networks and Cisco devices.

Conventions Used in This Book

Each chapter in this book has different elements that help you prepare to pass your CCENT, including the following features:

✦ **Quick Assessments:** Located at the beginning of each chapter is a Quick Assessment section that gives a number of questions related to the chapter content for you to assess whether you have the knowledge already in that chapter. It is highly recommended to read all chapters in the book, but if you find you are limited on study time you may want to focus on the topics you know the least about — the Quick Assessments help you determine what topics you know and what you need more work on.

✦ **Icons:** Look for the icons used in each chapter to draw your attention to information needed for the exam or in the real world. For more details on the icons I use, check out the later section, "Icons Used in This Book."

✦ **Chapter Summary:** Found at the end of each chapter, the "Chapter Summary" section covers key points you should remember for the exam.

✦ **Labs:** Lab exercises offer the opportunity to get your hands dirty with a particular topic with real-world experience performing specific tasks. In order to totally grasp the topics discussed in a chapter, be sure to perform the lab exercises. The CCENT certification has a number of simulators that will test your real-world knowledge so you really need to know how to perform the different tasks to pass the exam. Due to the fact that you may have different configurations when you do the labs, there are no lab answers within the Labs section.

✦ **Prep Test:** Following each "Chapter Summary" section, you can find questions to help review the chapter content and prepare you for the CCENT certification exam. Be sure to answer the review questions in each chapter! Then, after you finish reading the entire book and do the lab exercises, check out the practice exams on the companion CD-ROM, which is designed to function like the real exam, with the same level of difficulty.

✦ **Monofont text:** To help you distinguish commands you type or text you should see on the screen I apply the `monofont style` to the text. Examples where you see this style are on router commands, IP addresses, and names of devices.

✦ **Boldface text:** To help identify new commands that you are learning within a code listing the **boldface text style** is applied. Although you should read over all code in a code example, using the boldface text will help draw your attention to the new commands presented in a code listing.

Foolish Assumptions

I make a few assumptions about you as a reader and have written this book with these assumptions in mind:

✦ **You are interested in obtaining the CCENT Certification.** Anyone who is looking to get a solid introduction to networking and how to manage a Cisco device can use this book, but the focus of this book is concentrated on the exam objectives needed to pass the CCENT certification exam.

✦ **You have Cisco equipment to work on.** To perform the labs in the book, you will need to have two Cisco switches and two Cisco routers. If you do not have access to the Cisco hardware, you can search online for a simulator to purchase. An example simulator you can purchase is the *Network simulator for CCENT* from www.certexams.com.

✦ **You will study hard and do as much hands-on work as possible.** There is a lot of content on the CCENT exam, and you will most likely need to read over the information contained in this book a few times to ensure that you understand it. You should also experiment as much as possible on the actual devices after you read a particular topic. For example, after you read about CDP on a router, be sure to spend some time trying the commands on your router to ensure you are comfortable with what the protocol can do and what it offers as a feature.

✦ **You will read the chapters of this book in the order presented.** Although you are not required to read the chapters in order, it is highly recommended as chapters that appear later in the book assume you have read, or have the knowledge, of the previous chapters. For example, during the routing discussion I assume you have already read the subnetting and variable-length subnet mask (VLSM) chapter and use those terms within the routing chapter. It is best to read the book from cover to cover at least once and then you can jump to the chapters you need more work on.

How This Book Is Organized

Like all *All-In-One For Dummies* books, chapters are organized into minibooks. The chapters in each minibook are related by a specific theme or topic. For example, Book I — "Networking Basics" — contains all the basic networking information, including explanations of terminology and devices.

This book is designed as a study tool that you can read from cover to cover; reading the chapters in the order they are presented. I recommend that you read through the book at least once in the order it is presented and then after that pick the chapters that you need to revisit. The reason I recommend reading the chapters in order is because each chapter is written assuming you have the knowledge of the previous chapters.

The following sections outline what you can find in each minibook.

Book 1: Networking Basics

In this minibook, you discover what the CCENT certification is all about and what you will be tested on when taking the exam. You also find out about the basics of networking, starting with network types, cables, and devices, and then move on to the basics of IP addressing and the very important exam topic of subnetting.

Book 11: Cisco Device Basics

In Book II, you are introduced to Cisco devices and the basics of how they work. You first read about the physical aspects of the devices, such as the ports, and then move on to discover the Cisco operating system and the boot process. You then learn how to perform some basic configuration tasks, such as configuring interfaces and passwords before finding out how to back up your configuration, discover neighbors, and manage devices remotely with Telnet. This minibook finishes with a discussion on network services like name resolution, DHCP, and NAT.

Book 111: Routing and Switching

Book III first focuses on the routing process and how data is routed from one network to another, and then discusses static routing and dynamic routing protocols and how to control the routing process with the routing table. The minibook then changes focus to switches and talks about basic features of the switch, and I tell you how to perform basic configuration tasks on switches. The final topic in this minibook is troubleshooting, which covers basic troubleshooting steps and commands you can use on Cisco devices.

Book 1V: Advanced Topics

The final minibook starts with two chapters on network security and introduces the security best practices you need to know for the CCENT certification exam. The minibook then continues with chapters on wireless networks and introduces you to wide area networks (WANs).

Appendixes

Appendix A gives you an overview of what you can find on the CD-ROM that accompanies the book. Please have a look at this section to get the scoop on valuable resources on the book's companion CD-ROM, such the Test Engine.

Appendix B is an exam-objective mapping table that lets you know where in the book you can find details on each of the exam objectives. This is very useful when you are preparing for the exam; it can help you make sure that you know each point in the objectives.

Online Cheatsheet

To help you prepare for the CCENT certification exam, and to give you a quick listing of commands for the real world, I have created an online cheatsheet that is designed to give you some of the core facts to remember for the exam. Be sure to read and understand this book, but the online resource is there as a good refresher.

The URL for the online cheatsheet is:

```
www.dummies.com/cheatsheet/ccentcertificationaio
```

Icons Used in This Book

I use a number of icons in this book to draw your attention to pieces of useful information.

This icon gives you a heads-up on information you should absolutely know for the certification exams.

Information that would be helpful to you in the real world is indicated with a Tip icon. Expect to find shortcuts and timesavers here.

This icon flags information that may be useful to remember on the job.

Information that could cause problems to you or to the devices you are working with is indicated with a Warning icon. If you see a Warning icon, make sure you read it. The computer you save may be your own.

Detailed information that is not needed for the exams or that is a step above the knowledge you absolutely need to know for the exams is indicated with a Technical Stuff icon.

This icon lets you know when you can find accompanying information or supporting documents on the CD-ROM.

Where to Go from Here

The CCENT certification is considered an entry-level certification for candidates interested in a certification career with Cisco products. It provides a great networking foundation for other certification paths, such as these:

+ **CCNA:** The logical next step would be to take the ICND2 exam, which is exam number 640-816. The 640-816 exam combined with your CCENT certification earns you the Cisco Certified Network Associate (CCNA) certification.

+ **Other Vendors:** After receiving your CCNA certification, you could look to other certifications, such as *Microsoft Certified Technology Specialist* (MCTS), or even look to security certifications such as SCP's *Security Certified Network Professional* (SCNP) or EC-Council's *Certified Ethical Hacker* (CEH) certification.

Book I

Networking Basics

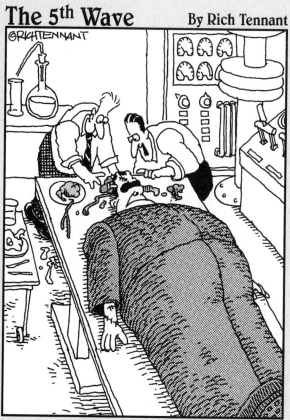

The 5th Wave   By Rich Tennant

@RICHTENNANT

"Wait! Wait! Wait! You've got a lung and two eyeballs in there! I thought you said you were CCENT Certified?"

Contents at a Glance

Chapter 1: About the CCENT Exam

In This Chapter

✔ **Mapping your Cisco certification path**

✔ **CCENT exam details**

✔ **What to expect on the CCENT exam**

✔ **Using this book to prepare for the exam**

✔ **On your test day**

Welcome to the world of Cisco certification! If you are reading this book, you have most likely decided that you are interested in furthering your career in networking by attaining your first Cisco certification — the *Cisco Certified Entry Networking Technician* (CCENT). I have to say that the CCENT certification is one of my favorite certifications because (though it is considered an entry-level certification) it ensures the exam candidate has basic networking knowledge and knows the fundamentals of Cisco device configuration.

This chapter is designed to give you information on what to expect on the CCENT certification exam and how to go about registering for it. Study hard and good luck!

The Value of CCENT Certification

For years, the first Cisco certification exam you would have taken to attain a Cisco certification was the *Cisco Certified Network Associate* (CCNA). This has changed in recent years, and now the first Cisco certification that certification candidates work toward is the CCENT. The reason for the change is that the CCNA exam topics that are now covered have expanded to the point that someone new to Cisco networking would find it very difficult to know the details of all the exam topics — so the CCNA was broken into two different exams.

Cisco decided to provide two options for someone looking to obtain a CCNA. The first option allows an individual to take two exams, known as the *Interconnecting Cisco Network Devices* (ICND) exams. The two exams are known as the ICND1 and ICND2; the ICND1 is the first exam, and after passing it, you can do your ICND2 exam to reach your CCNA certification.

The second option available to someone looking to obtain a CCNA is to take one CCNA exam — an option for those individuals who feel they are up for the challenge of taking on *all* exam topics in one exam.

Cisco also decided that if someone was to take and pass the ICND1 exam, they would earn the CCENT certification — the first Cisco certification in the many Cisco certification paths. The CCENT is a very hands-on certification exam that tests the exam-taker's networking knowledge and basic configuration and troubleshooting skills with Cisco devices.

Cisco has many different certification paths that IT professionals can take, such as the Routing and Switching path, Security path, and Wireless path. The CCENT certification is the first certification exam in all the Cisco certification paths and, as a result, has become a very popular certification.

Obtaining the CCENT certification is your way of proving to employers and customers that you have the skills to manage Cisco devices in a small network environment.

CCENT Exam Details

You earn the CCENT certification after you pass Cisco's ICND1 exam, which is exam number 640-822. You can schedule your exam appointment at any VUE testing center by calling one of the following phone numbers or by scheduling it online at www.vue.com/cisco/schedule. Pearson VUE is a company that provides computer-based testing and certification exams and is the testing provider selected by Cisco for the Cisco certification exams.

+ **United States and Canada:** 1-877-404-EXAM (1-877-404-3926)

+ **Other Countries:** For other parts of the world, check out VUE's Web site at www.vue.com/cisco/contact.

The exam is approximately 90 minutes in length, and you will be presented with 40 to 50 questions. The exam is available in a number of different languages, such as English, Japanese, Chinese, and French — to name just a few.

In order to take the CCENT certification exam, you must be 18 years old or older if you wish to take the exam without a parent's consent. If you are between 13 and 17 years old, you may still take the exam but only with a parent's consent.

If for some reason you do not pass the exam, Cisco requires that you wait six days before retaking the exam (five days from the day after your last exam). After passing the CCENT certification exam, the certification is valid for three years, at which point you will need to renew it.

The following summarizes the exam details you should know when you schedule your exam:

+ **Exam Number:** 640-822

+ **Time Limit:** 90 minutes

+ **Number of Questions:** 40–50 questions

+ **Passing Score:** 804 (based on a scale of 300–1000)

+ **Test Provider:** Pearson VUE

+ **Available Languages:** English, Japanese, Chinese, Spanish, Russian, Korean, French, Portuguese

The CCENT certification exam is a *nonadaptive* exam, meaning that you receive all 40–50 questions. Adaptive exams are shorter exams as they move on to the next topic once you answer a question in a topic area correctly — this is not the case with the CCENT certification exam! Also note that Cisco does not publish the passing score and scoring details as they are subject to change.

What to Expect on the CCENT Exam

A big part of passing any certification exam is trying to be as prepared as possible. This means knowing what to expect on the exam as far as the technical content you need to know and the style of questions on the exam.

Types of questions

The CCENT certification exam has a number of different style questions. Each style of question is designed to test you in a different way. For example, the multiple-choice questions are designed to test your knowledge level (the theory), while the simulation questions will test your hands-on skills — ensuring you can perform the task.

The following are some of the different types of question formats you will find on the CCENT certification exam:

+ **Multiple-choice, single answer:** This type of question will present you with a question and then list a number of choices as potential answers. You are required to select the best answer from the list of choices.

+ **Multiple-choice, multiple answer:** With this type of question, you are asked a question and you need to choose multiple answers from the list of choices. This type of question will normally specify "select all that apply" or may tell you how many items to select, such as "select three."

✦ **Drag-and-drop:** These questions are a little more interactive and typically involve you dragging items from the left side of the screen and dropping them in the correct place on the right side of the screen. For example, you may be given a list of definitions on the right side of the screen and you need to drop the correct term onto the proper definition.

✦ **Fill-in-the-blank:** You may receive a fill-in-the-blank question that requires you to read it and (instead of selecting the correct answer) type in the correct answer.

✦ **Testlet:** A *testlet* is a group of questions that applies (group) to the same scenario. You will first be presented with a scenario and then you will be given four or five multiple-choice questions to answer for that scenario.

✦ **Simlet:** A *simlet* is similar to testlet in the sense that you are given a scenario and have to answer multiple questions for the scenario. The difference is that the scenario is in the form of a simulation. With a simlet, you are asked multiple questions and, in order to answer the questions, you will need to use router commands to view the configuration of the router in the simulator.

✦ **Router Simulation:** Router simulations are a popular type of question in Cisco exams. With a simulation, you are given a number of tasks that need to be performed in the simulator and you are graded on how you do with your configuration within the simulation.

It is very important that you get familiar with how to answer each of the question types discussed above. I recommend visiting Cisco's Web site and go through the Cisco Certification Exam Tutorial. This exam tutorial shows you what each of the question types look like as well as how you go about answering the questions. The URL for the exam tutorial is

```
www.cisco.com/web/learning/wwtraining/certprog/training/cert_
    exam_tutorial.html
```

You can also prepare for the style of questions by taking the exam tutorial that is provided with the actual CCENT certification exam. When you actually begin your exam on test day, Cisco will ask if you would like to take the exam tutorial. I highly recommend doing the exam tutorial as it will give you a chance to see how to use the test engine. It only takes a few minutes to do the tutorial, and the time does not come off your exam time. Again, you want to be as prepared as possible!

One last point to make about the exam questions is that you cannot mark questions and go back to them at a later time like you can with Microsoft or CompTIA exams. Once you have answered a question, you cannot change the answer after moving on to the next question. Also note that it is best to select an answer to a question even if you do not know the answer because you are unable to go back to the question at a later time.

Exam objectives

The CCENT certification is very popular because it tests the exam candidate on basic networking concepts and the skills needed to configure Cisco devices in a small network environment. The following is a list of the major exam objectives that you will be tested on, with a quick description of that objective. For full detail on the exam objectives and the chapters of this book that cover each exam objective, take a look at Appendix B: CCENT Exam Reference Matrix.

✦ **Describe the operation of data networks.** This objective is designed to test your knowledge of basic networking concepts, and it includes an understanding of the OSI model, the different types of networking devices, and the pathway of communication on a network.

✦ **Implement a small switch network.** This objective tests your knowledge of the different types of connectors that exist on Cisco switches and the basic concepts of Cisco switches. You will also be tested on configuration tasks such as disabling ports and configuring port security on a switch.

✦ **Implement an IP addressing scheme and IP services to meet network requirements for a small branch office.** This objective is designed to test your knowledge of basic network services such as DHCP, DNS, and NAT. You are also tested on IP addressing and troubleshooting communication problems that are due to IP addressing issues.

✦ **Implement a small routed network.** In this objective, you are tested on the basic configuration of a router and the routing process. You are required to know how to implement static routing and dynamic routing using the RIP and RIPv2 routing protocols. This objective is also designed to cover tasks such as backing up your router configuration.

✦ **Explain and select the appropriate administrative tasks required for a WLAN.** This objective is designed to test you on basic wireless terminology and security protocols surrounding wireless. You are also tested on the purpose of wireless components such as SSID and security protocols such as WEP, WPA, and WPA2.

✦ **Identify security threats to a network and describe general methods to mitigate those threats.** This objective tests you on basic security principles with networks and networking equipment. You are also tested on best practices with router configuration and location of equipment.

✦ **Implement and verify WAN links.** The last objective tests you on basic WAN terminology and configuration of a serial link on a Cisco router.

When you have finished your exam, you will get a printout indicating your score and whether you have passed or failed. The exam results printout also gives you your score as a percentage of the objectives listed above. This lets you know what areas you need to work on to improve your knowledge when working with Cisco devices.

Using This Book to Prepare for the Exam

The Cisco CCENT certification is not a certification that you can pass by only reading the chapters in this book. It is important to make sure that after reading a chapter, you spend some time on an actual Cisco device or in a simulator practicing the topics covered in that chapter. You can download simulators from many different Web sites for a fee; for example, you can purchase the *Network simulator for CCENT* from www.certexams.com.

The best way to use this book to prepare for the exam is to first read a chapter, starting with the Quick Assessments section, to determine how much you know about the topic before you start reading. Then, read the chapter again — but this time, spend some time trying out the commands that are discussed in the chapter.

After practicing the commands as you read through the chapter, try the lab exercises at the end of the chapter. The lab exercises are designed to give you the hands-on skills you need to pass the CCENT exam.

After you have done the lab exercises for a chapter, do the review questions located in the Prep Test at the end of the chapter. These questions are designed to review the concepts presented in the chapter and give you an idea of the types of questions you may be asked on the exam.

After you have gone through the book two or three times and read and practiced the lab exercises, try the practice exams located on the book's companion CD-ROM.

I highly recommend ***not*** doing the practice tests on the CD until you have completed the entire book. I know a lot of people try the practice exams as they are reading through the book just to gauge their progress — as a result, they know all the practice test answers by the time they are done with the book. I think the practice tests will be better served if you don't try them until you have 100 percent completed the book (and labs) and then want to see how you would do if you were to take the real exam.

The CCENT certification is a hands-on, practical certification, so be sure to get as much hands-on experience as possible as you are studying each chapter.

On Your Test Day

Over the years, I have taken many different certification exams and picked up some good habits. (I am sure I have some bad habits as well, but I will keep those to myself.) This section outlines some basic steps you should take to make sure that you are prepared for your exam.

Arriving at the test site

The first thing you want to do on test day is make sure that you show up to the testing center early so that you can familiarize yourself with the facility and do things like get a drink and use the restroom before your exam starts.

Make sure that you bring two forms of ID, and one of them has to have a picture. Also, note that Cisco requires the test center take a photo of you on test day, and this photo is printed on your score card.

Getting lots of rest

Another habit I have learned over the years is that sometimes it is not best to cram any more information in my head the night before the exam. For most people, it is more effective to get a good night's sleep the night before the exam. Be sure to eat a good breakfast when you wake up in the morning before heading out to take your exam.

Also, if you are a morning person you may want to make sure that you schedule the exam earlier in the day. For me, I do not seem to do too well on an exam if I book the exam after lunchtime. I seem to think clearer in the morning, so as a result, I make sure I book all my exams around 10 a.m.

Answering questions

When you are answering questions on the exam, always read the questions thoroughly and be sure you understand the question before looking at the answer choices. When you do look at the answer choices, always eliminate the obvious choices first and then choose the best answer from those remaining. And remember that your first instinct is usually always correct, so go with your gut if you are not 100 percent sure.

Chapter 2: Introduction to Network Technologies

In This Chapter

✓ Understanding network types

✓ Identifying network topologies

✓ Looking at cable types

✓ Accessing the network with access methods

✓ Understanding network architectures

✓ Looking at the OSI model

*W*hen I took the CCENT certification exam, I was very surprised when I was presented with questions about general networking. I had spent hours preparing for the exam and learning the Cisco-specific commands, but I found that the exam not only tested me on Cisco concepts but also on the fundamentals of networking. It was a pleasant surprise!

This chapter is designed to give you the fundamentals of networking, including networking concepts and terminology, and to help you prepare for that aspect of the exam. As you progress through the next few chapters, the focus changes from networking concepts to eventually working with Cisco devices.

Quick Assessment

1 Data traveling on Cat _____ UTP cabling runs at 1 Gbps.

2 Ethernet uses _____ as its access method.

3 _____ is the 10-gigabit Ethernet standard that uses UTP cabling.

4 There are _____ layers in the OSI model.

5 The _____ layer is responsible for reliable and unreliable delivery.

6 A(n) _____ cable is used to connect to a router to change the configuration.

Answers

1 *5e.* See "Looking at Cable Types."

2 *CSMA/CD.* Review "Understanding Network Architectures."

3 *10GBaseTX.* Check out "Understanding Network Architectures."

4 *Seven.* Peruse "Looking at the OSI Model."

5 *Transport.* Take a look at "Looking at the OSI Model."

6 *Rollover.* Peek at "Looking at Cable Types."

Understanding Network Types

The purpose of a network is to allow a number of systems to share resources such as files and printers, or services such as an Internet connection. Networks come in all different shapes and sizes, and there are different terms for the different-size networks. In the most basic network setup, you will have a few systems connected to a central device such as a switch. The switch acts as a connection point for all systems on this small network. (See Figure 2-1.) When WorkstationA sends data to WorkstationB, the data leaves WorkstationA and travels along the cable that reaches the switch. The switch is then responsible for sending that data on to WorkstationB. (There is a lot more to say about a switch, but let's save that for the switch discussion; see Book I, Chapter 3, and Book III, Chapters 3 and 4).

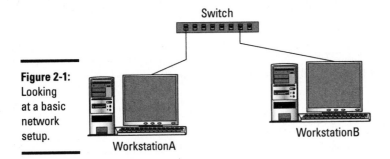

Figure 2-1: Looking at a basic network setup.

There are two major categories of networks — you can have a *local area network* (LAN), which is a network in a single location, or you can have a *wide area network* (WAN) that spans multiple locations. The following sections discuss LANs and WANs.

Local area network

The term that we use in the networking world for systems that are connected in a small network environment, such as a home network or an office network in a building, is *local area network* (LAN). A LAN is a network environment where all systems and devices are physically located in close proximity to one another, like in an office building.

LANs use LAN-type networking devices such as workstations, servers, printers, and switches to make up the network. If the LAN is made up of a number of workstations that are sharing resources with one another, it is called a *peer-to-peer* network; if there is a central server that the workstations connect to, it is called a *client-server* network.

Wide area network

A *wide area network* (WAN) is a type of network where there is a large distance between network devices. For example, if your company has a LAN in New York and you want it to connect to your company's other LAN in Toronto, this is considered a WAN because of the distance between the two offices.

WAN environments use what we call WAN-type devices, such as routers and telecommunication links. Figure 2-2 shows a typical WAN environment where there is distance between the network devices.

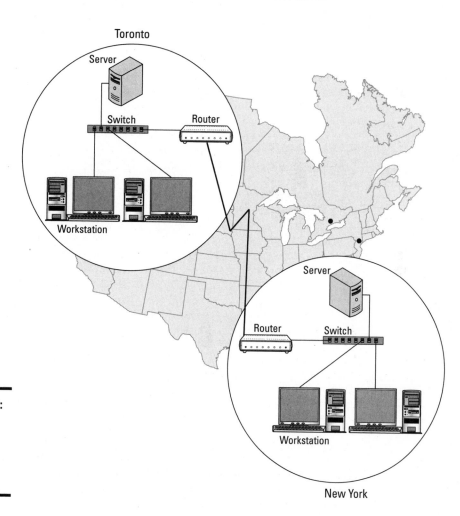

Figure 2-2:
A WAN
connects
multiple
LANs
together.

Before I get too much into LAN and WAN devices, I first define some basic networking components, such as topologies, cable types, and access methods. I then piece these components together to help define some of the very popular network architectures found in network environments today.

Identifying Network Topologies

The term *topology* means "layout," so a *network topology* defines the network layout — meaning how the network devices are positioned on the network. There are three major network topologies: the bus, ring, and star topologies. This section outlines these topologies and also discusses a fourth topology known as a hybrid topology.

Bus topology

The bus topology was popular years ago when networking began. It involved having a main cable (known as a *trunk*) that all systems would connect to. (See Figure 2-3.)

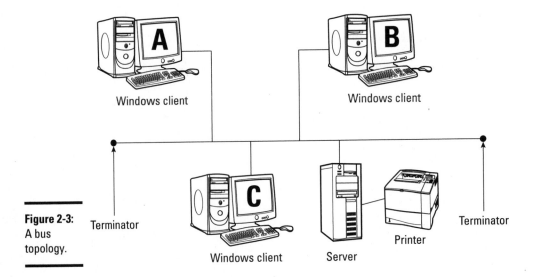

Figure 2-3: A bus topology.

When looking at Figure 2-3, you notice that there are terminators at either end of the trunk. The terminators at either end of the trunk are designed to absorb the electrical signal off the network. If there were no terminators to absorb the signal, then the signal would bounce back and collide with other data on the cable.

When WorkstationA sends data to WorkstationB, that data leaves WorkstationA and reaches the trunk in the bus topology. The electrical signal then travels the length of the trunk in both directions before it reaches the terminators and is absorbed off the main cable. Note that the data is seen by all systems on the network, but only WorkstationB processes the information, as it is the only intended recipient of the information.

One of the major drawbacks to a bus topology is that if there is a break in the trunk, the entire network fails. This is because the break in the main cable creates a nonterminated end that causes the signal to bounce back and eventually collide with other data. When the data collides, it is destroyed and needs to be retransmitted.

Ring topology

The ring topology (shown in Figure 2-4) has all systems connected in a circle, or ring. The data travels around the ring with each system regenerating the signal so that it can move to the next system (also known as a *node* on the network; a node is a system or device that exists on the network) in the ring. Like a bus topology, if there is a break in the ring the entire network will go down.

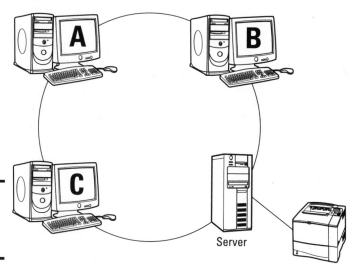

Figure 2-4:
Looking at a ring topology.

Server

Most ring topologies implement fault tolerance by providing two rings. When the primary ring fails the secondary ring is used to carry the data.

Star topology

The star topology is a network layout that involves using a central device such as a switch as the connection point for all systems on the network. When looking at Figure 2-5, you notice that when WorkstationA wants to send data to WorkstationD, the data travels from WorkstationA to the switch, which then sends the data on to WorkstationD.

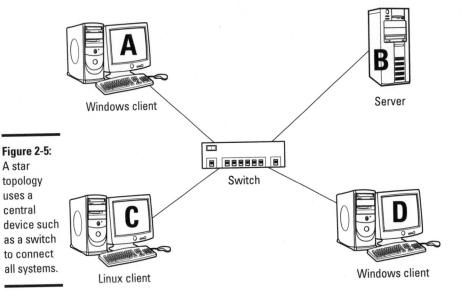

Windows client

Server

Figure 2-5:
A star topology uses a central device such as a switch to connect all systems.

Switch

Linux client

Windows client

Star topologies are popular today, and one of the reasons is that a break in the cable affects only the system connected to that cable — the rest of the network still functions.

Hybrid topology

Although a star topology is very popular today, many companies use a hybrid topology, which is a combination of bus, ring, and star topologies. For example, many companies use a main cable to cover the distance (known as a *bus topology*) between two switches, which create their own star topologies. (See Figure 2-6.) Some network professionals call this specific hybrid topology a star-bus topology.

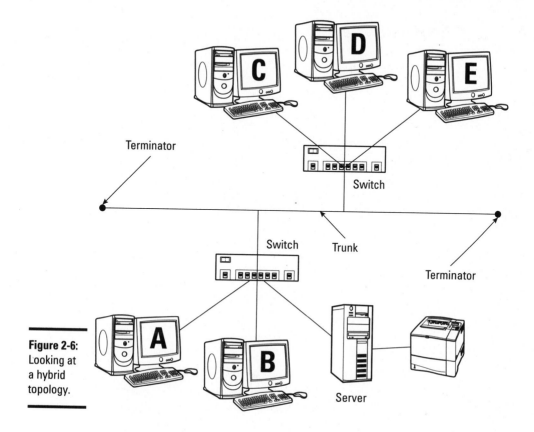

Figure 2-6:
Looking at
a hybrid
topology.

Looking at Cable Types

To add to your networking terminology, not only do you need to be familiar
with topologies (network layouts), but you also need to be familiar with the
different types of network cables that connect all the systems together.

This section discusses the popular network cable types and identifies the
key concepts you need to be familiar with as far as cables go with the CCENT
certification exam.

Coaxial cable

The first type of network cabling to discuss is coaxial cabling. Coaxial cable, also known as *coax,* was very popular in the early years of networking and is still seen today with your TV's cable hookup. Coax cable is more rigid than other cable types and is sometimes hard to work with.

Coax cable has a copper wire at the core that carries the data in the form of an electrical signal. This copper wire is surrounded by insulation, which is made up of a braided wire and metal foil that helps protect the signal from outside interference.

Networking with coax cabling started with two types of coaxial cabling — Thinnet (see Figure 2-7) and Thicknet. Thinnet and Thicknet get their names for obvious reasons: Thinnet is the thinner cable type and Thicknet is the thicker cable type.

Thinnet is one-quarter-inch thick and is known as the *RG-58 grade* coax cable. Thinnet has a maximum distance of 185 meters (606 feet) and a transfer rate of 10 Mbps. Thinnet uses a BNC connector to connect systems to the cable.

Figure 2-7:
Looking at a coaxial cable and a BNC connector.

For the CCENT exam know the lengths of the different cable types in meters, as that is what the exam will test you on.

As mentioned, Thicknet is the thicker of the two cable types, as it is one-half-inch thick. Thicknet gets its extra thickness by having an extra layer of insulation to help protect the signal traveling along the copper wire from outside interference. This protection and a thicker-diameter copper core allow the signal to travel farther, so Thicknet has a maximum distance of 500 meters (1,640 feet). Thicknet has a transfer rate of 10 Mbps and is known as the *RG-8 grade* cabling. Table 2-1 summarizes coax cabling.

Table 2-1		Types of Coax Cabling		
Type	*Coax Type*	*Maximum Cable Length*	*Diameter*	*Speed*
Thinnet	RG-58	185 meters (606 feet)	¼"	10 Mbps
Thicknet	RG-8	500 meters (1,640 feet)	½"	10 Mbps

Thicknet uses a different connector than Thinnet's BNC connector; it uses what is known as a *vampire tap* to connect stations to the Thicknet cable. The term vampire tap comes from the fact that the vampire tap is a device that connects to the coax cable by having "teeth" that cut through the outer layers of the cable and make contact with the copper core.

Twisted-pair cabling

You are not likely to see a lot of coax cable on networks today — a more popular cable type to discuss is twisted-pair cabling. Twisted-pair cabling gets its name by having eight wires divided into four pairs of wires, with each wire in a pair being twisted around one another throughout the length of the cable. (See Figure 2-8.) The purpose of the twist is to help protect against interference.

There are two types of twisted-pair cabling — *shielded twisted pair* (STP) and *unshielded twisted pair* (UTP) cable. Both types of cabling use eight wires that are placed inside a jacket to cover the wires, but STP has an extra layer of shielding in the jacket to help protect against interference.

Twisted-pair cabling has a maximum distance of 100 meters (328 feet) and uses what is known as an *RJ-45 connector* (see Figure 2-9) to connect the cable to a system. The transfer rate supported by twisted pair depends on the category of the cable — Table 2-2 displays the different categories and their transfer rates.

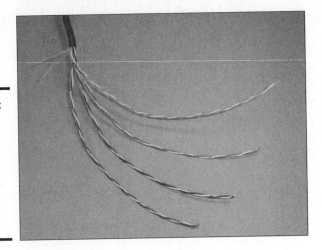

Figure 2-8:
A twisted-pair cable has eight wires divided into four different pairs.

The telephone also uses twisted pair cabling, but there are only four wires in the cable instead of the eight wires found in a network cable. The phone cable uses an RJ-11 connector, which is similar to an RJ-45 connector but smaller.

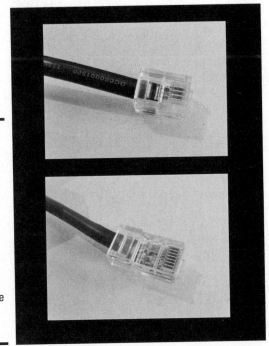

Figure 2-9:
Comparing an RJ-11 connector (top) used on a telephone cable and an RJ-45 connector (bottom) used for the network cable.

For the CCENT exam, be sure to know the different categories of UTP cabling! You should focus on CAT 5, 5e, and CAT 6 for the exam.

Table 2-2	UTP Category Cables	
Category	*Purpose*	*Speed*
Category 1 (Cat 1)	Voice only	
Category 2 (Cat 2)	Data	4 Mbps
Category 3 (Cat 3)	Data	10 Mbps
Category 4 (Cat 4)	Data	16 Mbps
Category 5 (Cat 5)	Data	100 Mbps
Category 5e (Cat 5e)	Data	1 Gbps
Category 6 (Cat 6)	Data	10 Gbps

Today's popular category of twisted-pair cabling is Cat 5e (which has a transfer rate of 1 Gbps) and Cat 6 (which has a transfer rate of 10 Gbps).

Fiber-optic cabling

The final type of network cabling to discuss is fiber-optic cabling. As shown in Figure 2-10, fiber-optic cabling is totally different than coax and twisted pair, as it has a glass or plastic core instead of a copper core, and it sends pulses of light that travel through the core as opposed to an electrical signal that travels through the copper.

Figure 2-10: Fiber-optic cabling uses a glass or plastic core to carry signals of light.

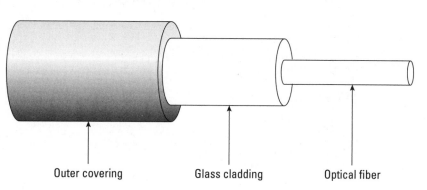

Outer covering Glass cladding Optical fiber

Just as there are different types of coax and twisted-pair cabling, there are different types of fiber-optic cabling. The two types of fiber-optic cabling are *single-mode fiber* (SMF) and *multimode fiber* (MMF).

SMF uses a single ray of light to transmit the data. The ray of light is known as a *mode* — hence the term single-mode fiber-optic cabling! SMF is the fiber-optic cable type used for long distances, such as 40 kilometers (131,233 feet).

MMF sends multiple rays of light at a time, with each ray of light running on different reflection angles. MMF is the fiber-optic cable type used for short distances, such as 2 kilometers (6,561 feet).

Fiber-optic cabling has a number of different types of connectors that are used to connect a system to the cable media. Three popular connector types for fiber-optic cabling are the SC, ST, and the LC connectors. (See Figure 2-11.)

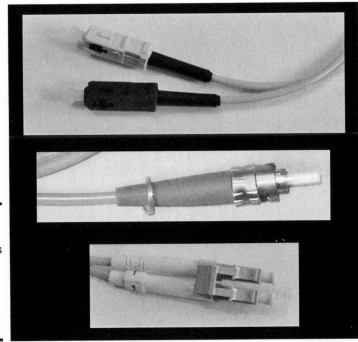

Figure 2-11:
Fiber-optic cabling uses the SC (top), ST (middle), and LC (bottom) connectors.

Before leaving the topic of network cabling, it may be useful to summarize some of the characteristics of the different cable types for the exam. Table 2-3 summarizes the different network cable types.

Table 2-3		Network Cable Summary	
Cable	*Transfer Rate*	*Maximum Cable Length*	*Connector Used*
Thinnet	10 Mbps	185 meters (606 feet)	BNC
Thicknet	10 Mbps	500 meters (1640 feet)	vampire tap
Cat 3 UTP	10 Mbps	100 meters (328 feet)	RJ-45
Cat 5 UTP	100 Mbps	100 meters (328 feet)	RJ-45
Cat 5e UTP	1000 Mbps	100 meters (328 feet)	RJ-45
Cat 6 UTP	10 Gbps	100 meters (328 feet)	RJ-45
Fiber	1+ Gbps	Over 2 km (6561 feet)	SC, ST, and LC

Connecting devices to one another

For the CCENT certification exam, you need to know the details of when to use different types of cabling, such as the straight-through cable, the crossover cable, and the rollover cable. This section discusses when to use each of those cable types.

Straight-through cable

The *straight-through cable* is the techie term for a normal twisted-pair network cable that connects a system to a switch. The straight-through cable gets its name because each of the eight wires in the cable retains its position within the cable from one end to another. For example, the third wire is the third wire at both ends.

Let's look at why positioning of the wires in the connector is important. When you plug the RJ-45 connector of a UTP cable into a computer, the wires make contact with pins in the RJ-45 port of the network card. For RJ-45 ports on a computer, the important pins are pins 1, 2, 3, and 6.

Pins 1 and 2 are the *transmit pins* (TX) for sending data, while pins 3 and 6 are the *receive pins* (RX) for receiving data. When connecting the system to a switch on the network, the transmit and receive pins are reversed on the switch (as shown in Figure 2-12).

The + and the - found with the TX and RX represent the positive (+) and negative (-) wires within each pair that are used to carry the positive and negative voltages.

Figure 2-12:
Using a straight-through cable to connect a workstation to a switch.

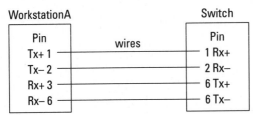

When you use a straight-through cable to connect to a switch, you see that the transmit pins on one end of the cable (wires in the cable) are connected to the receive pins on the other end of the cable. This allows for data being sent (transmitted) from one end to be received on the other end.

If the transmit and receive pins on the switch had not been "switched," then you would be sending out the transmit pins on one system, but the data could not be received — the wire would be connecting a transmit pin to a transmit pin.

Remember that the straight-through cable is used to connect dissimilar devices together. For example, you use a straight-through cable to connect a system to a switch or a router to a switch.

Crossover cable

From time to time, you will want to connect similar devices together in a network situation. For example, you may want to connect two computers together or even two switches together.

If you want to connect two systems to one another via a direct connection from one network card to another, you will not be able to use a straight-through cable, as it will connect the transmit pins on one system to the transmit pins on another system. (See Figure 2-13.)

Looking at Figure 2-13, you can see that the two workstations will not be able to communicate because the transmit pins are not making contact with the receive pins on the other end. To fix this, we need to change the order of the wires on one end of the twisted-pair cable. On one end of the cable, you will put wires 1 and 2 in the position of wires 3 and 6 and place wires 3 and 6 in the position of 1 and 2, thus creating what is known as a *crossover cable*. This will allow WorkstationA and WorkstationB to be able to send and receive data directly with one another without using a hub or switch. (See Figure 2-14.)

Figure 2-13:
Making the mistake of using a straight-through cable to connect two systems together.

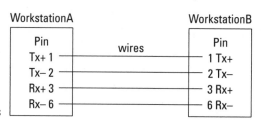

Figure 2-14:
Using a crossover cable to connect similar devices together, such as two computer systems.

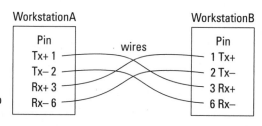

Remember that crossover cables are used to connect similar devices together — such as two systems, two switches, or a system to a router. (They are both considered hosts on the network.)

The last thing I want to mention about crossover cables is that most companies make it a policy that a crossover cable that is purchased or created must be a different color than a straight-through cable. The reason is you do not want to accidentally use the wrong cable, thinking it is the right cable — you could be troubleshooting why a system cannot communicate on the network for hours only to find out that the problem is you are using the wrong type of cable. Most companies will ensure that all crossover cables are yellow or red, while the straight-through cables are grey or blue.

Rollover cable

The final type of cable to discuss is a rollover cable. The *rollover cable* (also known as a *console cable*) is used to connect the serial port on your system to a router or switch so you can configure the router or switch. Note that your system will still have a network connection to the switch using a straight-through cable, but for management purposes, we use a rollover cable.

The rollover cable (see Figure 2-15) is normally a light-blue cable (I have also seen black rollovers) and is flat instead of rounded like a twisted-pair cable. The reason they call it a rollover is that all of the wires in the cable change positions from one end to another. For example, wire 1 on one end of the cable would be wire 8 on the other end of the cable.

Figure 2-15:
A rollover cable is used to connect your system to the router or switch in order to configure the device.

Accessing the Network with Access Methods

A big part of networking environments is not only the network layout (the topology) and the types of cables that are being used, but also how data is placed on the network. Data is placed on the network using what is known as an *access method*.

This section discusses the different access methods that different network environments use. This topic will help you understand how communication occurs on the network.

CSMA/CD

The first — and probably most popular — access method to discuss is *Carrier Sense Multiple Access/Collision Detection* (CSMA/CD). Here is how CSMA/CD works: When a system wants to send data on the network, it first senses the wire to see if there is already data on the wire (see Figure 2-16) — if there is already data on the wire, it waits until the wire is free, but if the wire is free of traffic, the system goes ahead and sends the data.

As mentioned, if the wire is already busy transmitting a signal, the system waits until the wire is free — once the wire is free, the system sends the data. If, at the time the data was sent, another system happened to send data at the same time, we would have what is called a collision. A *collision* is when two pieces of data traveling on the wire meet — they collide and the data is destroyed. If that data collides because another system sent data at the same time, then the systems involved in the collision will wait a variable length of time before resending the data. The variable length of time is determined by an algorithm that is built into CSMA/CD and ensures the two systems do not try to retransmit at the same time.

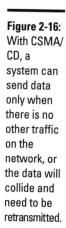

Figure 2-16:
With CSMA/CD, a system can send data only when there is no other traffic on the network, or the data will collide and need to be retransmitted.

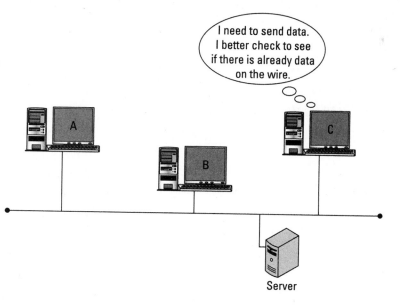

Token passing

Token passing is a different approach to how systems can send data on the network. With *token passing,* there is an empty packet (the *token*) that circulates through the network thousands of times a second. When a system wants to send data on the network, the system has to wait for the token to reach the system.

Once the token reaches the system, the system fills the token with data and flags the token as being in use. The token is then submitted back on the network (with data in it) and is headed to the destination system.

The benefit of token passing is that in order to send data you need to have the token — because there is only one token on the network, it is impossible to have collisions in a token-passing environment.

CSMA/CA

Another access method (though it has become less and less popular over the years) is Carrier Sense Multiple Access/Collision Avoidance (CSMA/CA). When a system wants to send data on the wire, it first senses the wire to see if any data is already on it. If the wire is free, the system sends an announcement on the wire letting everyone know it is about to send data in hopes that no other system will send data when they see the announcement. After the announcement is sent, then the system sends the real data. This is a method of trying to avoid collisions.

Wireless networks use CSMA/CA as their method of placing data on the network.

Understanding Network Architectures

If you have been reading this chapter from the beginning, you understand that the network topology is the layout of the network, that there are three major types of network cabling, and you know the different types of access methods. Now it is time to put it all together to create what is known as network architectures.

A *network architecture* is a standard that defines how the network works in terms of how data is placed on the wire, the types of cabling used, and the network topology being employed. The standards are defined by the *Institute of Electrical and Electronics Engineers* (IEEE).

This section is designed to give you background on two of the major types of network architectures, Ethernet and Token Ring, and the details on what makes each network architecture special. Note that I discuss some of the older architectures to make the discussion more complete, as well as some of the newer architectures that you will need to know for the exam.

Ethernet architectures

Ethernet architectures are very popular network architectures of the past and the present. There are a number of different Ethernet architectures, with the difference primarily being the cabling that is used with that network architecture.

Before I get into the details of each of the network architectures, I want to give you a breakdown of the architecture name. When you look at Figure 2-17, you see an example of a network architecture divided into three parts.

Figure 2-17: Breaking down the name of network architectures.

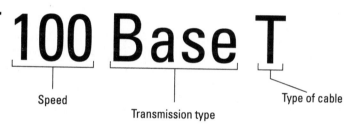

Speed

Transmission type

Type of cable

The first part of the name indicates the speed of the network. In the example network architecture shown in Figure 2-17, the speed is 100 Mbps.

The second part of the architecture name specifies whether baseband or broadband communication is used. *Baseband* communication uses the entire bandwidth for the communication, while *broadband* uses a portion of the bandwidth for the communication. In my example, the network architecture is using baseband transmission.

The third part of the architecture name identifies the type of cable that is being used. In our example, the "T" indicates twisted-pair cabling and — because we know the speed of the architecture is 100 Mbps — we can deduce that the type of twisted-pair cabling is Cat 5. You will also notice some architectures use a "C" for coaxial cable and an "F" for fiber-optic cabling.

It is important to note that all Ethernet environments use CSMA/CD as the access method.

Let's have a look at some of the Ethernet architectures.

10Base2

The first Ethernet standard to mention is an older network architecture, but I want to mention it along with a few of the older ones to help practice picking apart the architecture name to identify its meaning. Remember that with a network architecture we need to choose a topology, cable, and access method.

Looking at the 10Base2 name, we can see that the architecture runs at 10 Mbps and uses baseband transmission. The type of cable is indicated with the number 2, which is used in this case to remind you of a distance of 200 meters. Do we know of any cables that are limited in length to approximately 200 meters? The Thinnet coax cable uses 185 meters as a maximum distance.

10Base2 uses a bus topology and CSMA/CD as a method of placing data on the wire.

10Base5

Another example of an older Ethernet architecture is the 10Base5 architecture. 10Base5 runs at 10 Mbps and also uses baseband transmission. The difference between 10Base5 and 10Base2 is the type of cabling used — 10Base5 uses Thicknet cabling, which has a maximum distance of 500 meters, while 10Base2 uses Thinnet coaxial cable.

10Base5 also uses a bus topology and, like all other Ethernet architectures, uses CSMA/CD as the access method.

10BaseT

The 10BaseT architecture changes things up a little by using a different cable type and a different topology. 10BaseT uses Cat 3 UTP cabling, which runs at 10 Mbps, and uses a star topology. 10BaseT uses baseband transmission and CSMA/CD as the access method.

Fast Ethernet standards

The big jump in network speed after 10 Mbps was to the 100 Mbps networking standards, known as the *Fast Ethernet standards* — all of which run at 100 Mbps, use CSMA/CD as the access method, use baseband transmission, and use a star topology. The difference between these Fast Ethernet standards is the type of cabling used.

The two popular forms of fast Ethernet are 100BaseTX and 100BaseFX. 100BaseTX uses Cat 5 UTP cable, while 100BaseFX uses fiber-optic cabling.

Gigabit Ethernet standards

Today's new networking devices are looking at transferring data at 1000 Mbps (1 Gbps). Network architectures that transfer information at 1 Gbps are known to follow the *Gigabit Ethernet standards* and use a star topology, baseband transmission, and the access method of CSMA/CD.

IEEE has created a number of standards for Gigabit Ethernet, with each using a different type of cable to reach the transfer rate of 1 Gbps. The following are the Gigabit Ethernet standards:

✦ **1000BaseCX:** Uses coaxial cable to reach a maximum distance of 25 meters (82 feet).

✦ **1000BaseLX:** Uses single-mode fiber-optic cabling to reach a maximum distance of 3 kilometers (9,842 feet).

✦ **1000BaseSX:** Uses multimode fiber-optic cabling to reach a maximum distance of 550 meters (1,804 feet).

✦ **1000BaseTX:** This Gigabit Ethernet standard reaches 1000 Mbps but uses Cat 5e UTP cable instead of fiber-optic cabling. The difference between 100BaseT and 1000BaseTX is that 1000BaseTX uses all eight wires while 100BaseT only uses four.

10 Gigabit Ethernet standards

The next level of Ethernet standards is to reach transfer rates of 10 Gbps. The 10 Gigabit Ethernet standards use a star topology, baseband transmission, and an access method of CSMA/CD. Like the Gigabit Ethernet standards, there are different versions of the 10 Gigabit Ethernet standards.

The standards include 10GBaseLR, 10GBaseSR, and 10GBaseER, which all use fiber-optic cabling. The difference among them is 10GBaseSR uses multimode fiber-optic cable to reach short distances (100 meters), while 10GBaseLR uses single-mode fiber-optic cabling to reach a longer range of 10 kilometers. 10GBaseER can reach extra-long ranges (40 kilometers) using single-mode fiber-optic cabling.

A way to remember the difference between 10GBaseSR, 10GBaseLR, and 10GBaseER is that the "S" stands for short range, the "L" stands for long range, and the "E" stands for extra long range.

There is also a 10 Gigabit Ethernet standard that uses Cat 6 UTP cabling; it's known as 10GBaseTX. With this standard, the maximum cable distance is 100 meters.

Table 2-4 summarizes some of the Ethernet architectures and their key points to know for the exam.

Table 2-4		Ethernet Architectures		
Name	*Topology*	*Access Method*	*Cable Type*	*Transfer Rate*
10Base2	bus	CSMA/CD	Thinnet	10 Mbps
100BaseT	star	CSMA/CD	Cat 5 UTP	100 Mbps
1000BaseTX	star	CSMA/CD	Cat 5e UTP	1000 Mbps
1000BaseSX	star	CSMA/CD	multimode fiber	1000 Mbps
1000BaseLX	star	CSMA/CD	single-mode fiber	1000 Mbps
10GBaseSR	star	CSMA/CD	multimode fiber	10 Gbps
10GBaseLR	star	CSMA/CD	single-mode fiber	10 Gbps

Token Ring

Over the years, there have been network architectures outside of Ethernet that have been developed and used, but they have not been as popular as Ethernet. One of the biggest competitors to Ethernet in the early years was Token Ring, which was developed by IBM.

Token Ring uses a ring topology and token passing as the access method. Remember, with token passing a system needs to have the token to submit data on the wire.

Over the years, Token Ring has used many different cable types, from its own proprietary IBM cable types to using UTP cabling. Token Ring networks use a central device such as a switch to connect all the systems, but the device is called a *multistation access unit* (MAU) instead of a switch. (See Figure 2-18.) The reason for the name change is the device operates a little bit differently — it creates a ring internally.

Figure 2-18:
An IBM data
connector
and a Token
Ring MAU.

Looking at the OSI Model

When manufacturers develop networking components, they must follow
the conceptual model called the *Open Systems Interconnection* (OSI) model.
This model defines the rules for networking components to communicate
with one another and was developed by the International Organization for
Standardization (ISO).

The OSI model is a seven-layer model, with each layer depicting a specific
role in the concept of network communication. The seven layers of the OSI
model are application, presentation, session, transport, network, data link,
and, finally, the physical layer.

It is important to understand the function of each layer of the OSI model,
so be sure to study this topic well. The CCENT certification exam will have
questions that test your knowledge of the OSI model, so you need to be
familiar with the different layers of it. Also note that as I progress through
the chapters of this minibook, I reference this model as much as possible.

When learning the OSI model, it is best to visualize that the OSI is present on both the sending and receiving system (as shown in Figure 2-19). In this example, you can visualize someone surfing a Web site as I discuss the layers of the OSI model.

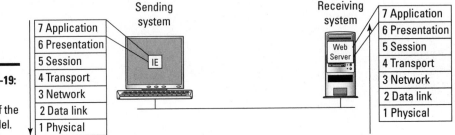

Figure 2-19: Seven layers of the OSI model.

+ **Layer 7 – Application:** The application layer of the OSI model is responsible for sending the network request on the sending computer, but servicing the request on the receiving system. For example, when the network user is surfing a Web site, the Web browser uses HTTP to send a request to the Web server. The Web server then services the request by sending the desired Web page back to the client.

+ **Layer 6 – Presentation:** The presentation layer is responsible for formatting the information so that it is understood at the other end of the communication. Examples of presentation layer functions are character coding, such as ASCII and Unicode (these are character code standards that define what characters can be used by a system), but depending on the example, you could also have compression and encryption at this layer as well.

In my Web surfing example, the client may choose to compress the information before sending the request to the Web server. At the presentation layer on the Web server, the system would then have to decompress the information before passing it up to the Web site (application).

+ **Layer 5 – Session:** The session layer is responsible for establishing the communication dialog between the two systems and maintaining that dialog.

+ **Layer 4 – Transport:** The transport layer is responsible for reliable and unreliable delivery. *Reliable delivery* means that if information is sent, the transport layer will ensure the data reaches the destination and, if the data does not reach the destination, the information is re-sent. *Unreliable delivery* means that the information is sent but no effort is made to ensure the data reaches the destination. The transport layer is also responsible for breaking the data into smaller, more manageable chunks, called *segments*. Each segment is then sent to the destination and will need to be reassembled at the transport layer on the receiving system.

✦ **Layer 3 – Network:** The network layer is responsible for logical addressing and routing functions. A *logical address* is an address that you can assign to the system such as an IP address. *Routing* is the concept of delivering the data to the destination — which is one of the main roles of the network layer. I talk a lot more about logical addressing in Book I, Chapter 4.

In my Web surfing example, after the transport layer on the sending system breaks the data into smaller segments they are then passed down to the network layer so the network layer can add a source and destination IP address to each segment. The source and destination IP address are applied so that it is known where the segment came from and where it is headed. It is also important to note that once the segment reaches the network layer the segment is now known as a *packet*.

✦ **Layer 2 – Data link:** The data link layer is responsible for physical addressing as opposed to logical addressing. The *physical address* is burned into the network card of the system or device by the manufacturer and is used to address where the information is headed and where it is coming from. The data link layer is responsible for converting the packet to a pattern of bits that will be placed on the wire in the form of an electrical signal. On the receiving end, the opposite occurs — the electrical signals are received and converted to a packet and passed up to the network layer. Note that the data link layer is where your access methods such as CSMA/CD run.

When the packet is passed down to the data link layer and the MAC address is added to the packet, the packet then becomes known as a *frame*. The MAC address is the physical address burned into the network card that is a unique identifier for the network card.

✦ **Layer 1 – Physical:** The physical layer of the OSI model is responsible for working with the electrical signal — as a result, anything that works with the electrical signal runs at this layer. Examples of components that run at this layer are cables and connectors used to connect the systems together and carry the electrical signal.

You will notice that network professionals sometimes use the term *packet*, and other times they use the term *frame*. When the data is at layer 4 (the transport layer), it is called a segment. After the logical addressing has been assigned to each segment at layer 3 (the network layer), it is then known as a packet. After the physical addresses are added to the packet at layer 2 (the data link layer), it is then known as a frame.

Chapter Summary

This chapter discusses some key networking terminology that you need to be familiar with for the CCENT certification exam. The following are some key points to remember when thinking about networking basics:

✦ Network *topology* refers to the layout of the network. There are three major topologies — bus, star, and ring.

✦ There are three major cable types — coaxial, twisted-pair, and fiber-optic cabling.

✦ To support Gigabit Ethernet networking, you use UTP Cat 5e and Cat 6 cabling or fiber-optic cabling.

✦ *Crossover cables* are used to connect two similar devices, such as connecting two systems directly together or two switches directly together.

✦ A *straight-through cable* is used to connect dissimilar devices, such as a computer to a switch or a router to a switch.

✦ An *access method* is how information is placed on the wire. All Ethernet environments use CSMA/CD as their access method.

✦ A *network architecture* is a network standard that uses a specific topology, cable type, and access method.

✦ The *OSI model* is a seven-layer model with each layer having a specific network function.

✦ From a network-professional point of view, you need to be familiar with layers 4, 3, 2, and 1 of the OSI model.

Lab Exercises

This chapter introduces you to a number of networking terms and concepts that you need to be familiar with for the CCENT certification exam. The following labs are designed to help you practice associating the terminology with meaning.

Lab 2-1: Identifying network architectures

In this lab, match the network architecture to the appropriate definition by placing the letter of the definition beside the term.

____ 10GBaseLR	**A.** A Gigabit Ethernet standard that uses coaxial cable to reach a maximum distance of 25 meters.
____ Token Ring	**B.** A Fast Ethernet standard that uses Cat 5 UTP cabling.
____ 1000BaseCX	**C.** A 10 Gigabit Ethernet standard that uses multimode fiber-optic cable to reach short distances (100 meters).
____ 100BaseT	**D.** A Gigabit Ethernet standard that reaches 1000 Mbps using unshielded twisted-pair cable.
____ 1000BaseSX	**E.** A 10 Gigabit Ethernet standard that can reach extra-long ranges (40 kilometers) using single-mode fiber-optic cabling.
____ 1000BaseTX	**F.** A Gigabit Ethernet standard that uses single-mode fiber-optic cabling to reach a maximum distance of 3 kilometers.
____ 10GBaseSR	**G.** A network architecture that uses token passing as the access method.
____ 1000BaseLX	**H.** A 10 Gigabit Ethernet standard that uses single-mode fiber-optic cabling to reach a longer range of 10 kilometers.
____ 10GBaseER	**I.** A Gigabit Ethernet standard that uses multimode fiber-optic cabling to reach a maximum distance of 550 meters.

Lab 2-2: Remembering cable specifications

For this lab, fill out the missing parts of the table to help review the different types of cables and their specifications.

Cable	Transfer Rate	Maximum Cable Length	Connector Used
Thinnet	10 Mbps		
Thicknet		500 meters	
Cat 3 UTP		100 meters	RJ-45
Cat 5 UTP			RJ-45
Cat 5e UTP		100 meters	
Cat 6 UTP		100 meters	
Fiber		Over 2 km	

Lab 2-3: OSI model terminology

In this lab, review the OSI model by placing the letter of the definition beside the correct layer.

Layer	Description
___ Application	A. Responsible for routing of information and logical addressing.
___ Session	B. Provides the physical addressing and prepares the information for the wire.
___ Presentation	C. Responsible for making or receiving a network request and is typically the networking software.
___ Data link	D. Responsible for formatting the information so that the information is understood on the receiving system.
___ Network	E. Deals with the components, such as cabling and connectors, that work with the electrical signal.
___ Physical	F. Responsible for breaking the information into smaller segments.
___ Transport	G. Responsible for managing the communication dialog between two systems.

Prep Test

1 Which of the following is considered a layer-2 address?

A ○ 192.168.2.200

B ○ www.gleneclarke.com

C ○ COMPUTER1

D ○ 00-AB-0F-2B-3C-4E

2 You connect a workstation to the switch and notice a link light. What layer of the OSI model are you troubleshooting when looking at a link light?

A ○ Application

B ○ Physical

C ○ Network

D ○ Data link

3 You wish to connect a workstation to an RJ-45 port on a switch. What type of cable will you use?

A ○ Fiber

B ○ Crossover

C ○ Straight-through

D ○ Thinnet

4 Which Gigabit Ethernet standard uses UTP cabling to reach 1000 Mbps?

A ○ 1000BaseTX

B ○ 1000BaseSX

C ○ 1000BaseCX

D ○ 1000BaseLX

5 What cable type would you use to connect an RJ-45 port on a router to a workstation?

A ○ Fiber

B ○ Crossover

C ○ Straight-through

D ○ Thinnet

6 **What layer of the OSI model is responsible for breaking the data into smaller segments?**

A ○ Data link

B ○ Physical

C ○ Network

D ○ Transport

7 **Which of the following is considered a layer-3 address?**

A ○ 192.168.2.200

B ○ www.gleneclarke.com

C ○ COMPUTER1

D ○ 00-AB-0F-2B-3C-4E

8 **You wish to connect a computer to a computer. Which type of cable would you use?**

A ○ Fiber

B ○ Crossover

C ○ Straight-through

D ○ Thinnet

9 **Which 10 Gigabit Ethernet standard uses multimode fiber-optic cabling?**

A ○ 10GBaseLR

B ○ 10GBaseER

C ○ 10GBaseSR

D ○ 1000BaseSX

10 **What layer of the OSI model is responsible for routing and logical addressing?**

A ○ Network

B ○ Physical

C ○ Data link

D ○ Transport

Answers

1 **D.** A layer-2 address is the physical address, also known as the MAC address of the system. *See "Looking at the OSI Model."*

2 **B.** The physical layer of the OSI model deals with physical aspects of the network such as the cables and connectors. The link light displaying simply means that there is a connection. *Review "Looking at the OSI Model."*

3 **C.** Straight-through cables are used to connect dissimilar devices such as a computer to a switch or a router to a switch. *Check out "Connecting devices to one another."*

4 **A.** The Gigabit Ethernet standard that uses UTP cabling is 1000BaseTX. *Peruse "Ethernet architectures."*

5 **B.** This is a strange question because you typically would not do this — but it is on the exam. In this example, the router and workstation are both "hosts" on the network, so you can consider them similar devices — similar devices are connected with a crossover cable. *Take a look at "Connecting devices to one another."*

6 **D.** The transport layer is responsible for breaking the data into smaller chunks called segments. *Peek at "Looking at the OSI Model."*

7 **A.** A layer-3 address is a logical address that is assigned to the system. An example of a logical address is an IP address. *Look over "Looking at the OSI Model."*

8 **B.** To connect two systems directly together, you use a crossover cable. *Study "Connecting devices to one another."*

9 **C.** The 10 Gbps standard that uses multimode fiber-optic cabling is 10GbaseSR. Remember that the *S* stands for short range, and multimode fiber-optic cabling is used for short distances. *Refer to "Ethernet architectures."*

10 **A.** The network layer is responsible for logical addressing and routing. *Examine "Looking at the OSI Model."*

Chapter 3: Network Devices and Services

In This Chapter

✔ Understanding network devices

✔ Identifying network services

✔ Traffic management concepts

A huge part of being able to manage and troubleshoot networking environments is being familiar with the role of the different network devices and services that can exist on the network. The CCENT certification exam not only focuses on Cisco routers and switches but also tests your knowledge on the purpose of the different network devices, such as hubs, switches, and routers. The exam also tests your knowledge of network services such as DHCP, DNS, and NAT.

This chapter is designed to give you the background on these networking devices and services so that you are prepared to answer the related exam questions. Note that there is not a lot of detail of switches and routers in this chapter because they are the focus of the rest of this book.

Quick Assessment

1   (True/False). The Web server uses SMTP to deliver a Web page to a client.

2   A(n) _____ server is used to control whether someone gets access to the network.

3   A switch is an example of a layer-_____ device.

4   (True/False). NAT is responsible for translating the name to an IP address.

5   A(n) _____ server is responsible for assigning IP addresses.

6   _____ is responsible for converting the FQDN to an IP address.

Answers

1 *False.* See "Web servers."

2 *Authentication.* Review "Authentication servers."

3 *2.* Check out "Switches."

4 *False.* Peruse "Network Address Translation."

5 *DHCP.* Take a look at "DHCP servers."

6 *DNS.* Peek at "DNS servers."

Building Networks with Network Devices

When working with networks — and especially when troubleshooting communication problems — it is important to be familiar with the role of the different network devices that exist on a network. This section describes the purpose of different network devices.

Hubs and repeaters

The first network device to take a look at is the network hub. Hubs are used as central devices to connect all the hosts on the network to one another. A *host* is a workstation, server, printer, or any other object that plugs into the network. The term I use often in this book for something that connects to the network is a *system* — which could be a workstation or server. Figure 3-1 shows a 5-port hub that is used to connect five systems to a network.

Figure 3-1:
A five-port hub used to connect five systems together.

How hubs work

The important thing to note about a hub is that it is a layer-1 device, and not a very intelligent device. It simply acts as a connection point for all the systems. Also note that if a system wants to send data to another system, the data leaves the first system and reaches the hub, and then the hub sends the data to all other ports on the hub even though the data is destined for only one other system. All systems receive the data; systems that are not the intended recipients discard the data, while the intended recipient receives and processes the data.

The reason I stress how a hub works is that this leads to performance and security issues. The performance problem is the fact that bandwidth is being used — data is sent to all ports on the hub — when it doesn't really need to be. The security issue is that all systems receive a copy of the data even though they are not the intended recipient. If any of these systems has a network sniffer running (such as Wireshark; www.wireshark.org), it can capture and read all data on the network! Both of these issues go away when you use a switch instead of a hub (more on that in a bit).

Repeaters

The other device to make a note about at this point is the repeater. In Book I, Chapter 2, you find out that each cable type has a maximum distance associated with it — if the signal travels farther than that distance, the data is unreadable. The unreadable data is due to signal degradation over distance and interference from other sources.

If you want (or need) to exceed the maximum length of a cable, you need to use a repeater (see Figure 3-2) to connect the cable lengths together. The *repeater* not only acts as a connection point for the two cables, but it is also responsible for regenerating the signal so that it can travel from one cable to the other — and thus travel a greater distance.

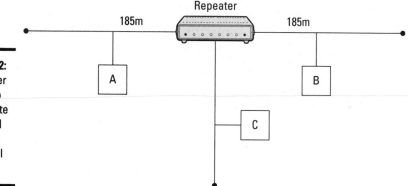

Figure 3-2: A repeater is used to regenerate the signal so that it can travel farther.

Remember that hubs and repeaters are examples of layer-1 devices. An easy way to remember this is layer-1 components work with the electrical signal. Because a hub simply passes the electrical signal on to all other ports, it is considered a layer-1 device. Because a repeater amplifies the signal, it, too, is considered a layer-1 device.

Network interface card

The *network interface card* (NIC) is present in your system and allows you to connect to the network cable. Some systems have network cards built into the motherboard of the system, while others have the network card installed in the system as its own component.

Physical address

The network card has its own address assigned to it, and this address is burned into the ROM chip of the card. This address is known as the *physical address,* as it is burned into the network card (also known as an *interface*) and cannot be changed unless a special program is used. Another popular term for the physical address is the *Media Access Control* (MAC) address.

The MAC address is a 48-bit address that uses hexadecimal values. An example of a MAC address is 00-01-80-35-00-7B. As shown in Figure 3-3, the MAC address is divided into two parts — the first part is the manufacturer ID, and the second part is the unique ID that identifies that card made by the manufacturer.

Figure 3-3:
A MAC address is divided into two parts — the manufacturer ID and the unique card ID.

Each manufacturer of network cards is assigned a number of manufacturer IDs that the manufacturer can use as the first half of all MAC addresses for network cards it builds. This helps ensure that MAC addresses are unique.

How MAC addresses are used

From a networking point of view, it is important to understand how the MAC addresses are used. The data you send on the network is called a *frame,* and the frame has three parts to it — the header, the data portion, and the trailer portion of the frame, as shown in Figure 3-4.

Figure 3-4:
The three parts of a frame.

Header	Data	Trailer
Source MAC		
Destination MAC		

The *header* contains information about the frame itself, such as where the frame is coming from (the source) and where it is headed (the destination). These are known as the *source* and *destination addresses* and are the MAC addresses of the sender and the intended recipient of the frame.

In the classroom, I have a lot of students ask why the source address is in the header — they understand that the destination address is in the header because it is needed for the data to reach the correct system, but they don't understand why the source address is included. The answer is simple; the source address is included so that whatever system receives the data knows who to send a reply to.

The *data* portion of the frame contains the information that is actually being sent, and the *trailer* contains *checksum information* that is used to verify that the frame has not been altered in transit.

Bridges

Back when hubs were the popular devices on networks, we would eventually encounter performance issues because one hub was usually connected to another hub to allow for more systems to connect to the network. Figure 3-5 shows why this is such a big issue. The hub acts as one big cable — data that reaches the hub is sent to every port on the hub. This means all data is seen by all systems on the network when using a hub.

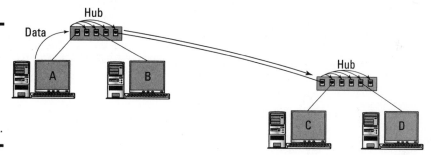

Figure 3-5: When you use a hub, all data is seen by all systems on the network.

The problem with connecting one hub to another (and then to another) as you have more users that need to connect to the network is this: When WorkstationA sends data to WorkstationB, the data reaches the hub that WorkstationA is connected to, and then that hub sends the data to *all* of its ports. This causes the data to go to the second hub that then sends the data to *all* of its ports. The traffic continues on like this for as many hubs that you have.

When 10Base2 and 10Base5 networks were popular — and when hubs are used on a network — you must follow the 5-4-3 rule. This rule states that you are only allowed to have 5 networks segments, joined by 4 repeaters or hubs, and only 3 of those segments can be populated with systems. The reason for the rule is to limit the size of the network so that data can reach the end of the network in a reasonable amount of time.

This is a problem because Ethernet environments use CSMA/CD (meaning that all systems are waiting for the line to be free before they can send data), which is slowing the network down. Remember, if someone sends data while traffic is traveling through this network, the data will collide and need to be retransmitted.

Also, this type of setup means that you have more systems "sensing" the wire, waiting for the wire to be free so they can send their data. Unfortunately, so is everyone else! In this situation, when the network is free of traffic you have multiple systems trying to send data at the same time, which means the data will collide and need to be retransmitted. Bottom line: A lot of data is being sent that is not reaching anyone.

The *bridge* offers a solution to the performance issue by breaking the network down into multiple network segments. The bridge has a MAC address table that keeps track of each system's MAC address and the network segment a system is on. When a frame reaches the bridge, the bridge looks at the destination address in the frame and then locates that address in the MAC address table. Once the address is found in the MAC address table, the bridge sends the data only to the network segment that the destination system resides on (see Figure 3-6), thus conserving bandwidth on the other network segments. In Figure 3-6, for example, when WorkstationA sends information to WorkstationC the bridge forwards the information only to segment 3, after finding out (from the MAC address table) that WorkstationC exists on segment 3.

Using a bridge is different from using a bunch of hubs, as a hub will always send the data to all other ports on the hub — essentially sending the data across the entire network. Bridges are used to filter this traffic so the data will not travel across the entire network.

Switches

If you understand the concept of a bridge, then you will have no problem understanding what a switch does. Why is that? Because a switch does the exact same thing as a bridge — the only difference is that each port on the switch (see Figure 3-7) acts as its own network segment. As a result, if you plug a workstation into each port on the switch, each workstation is on its own network segment.

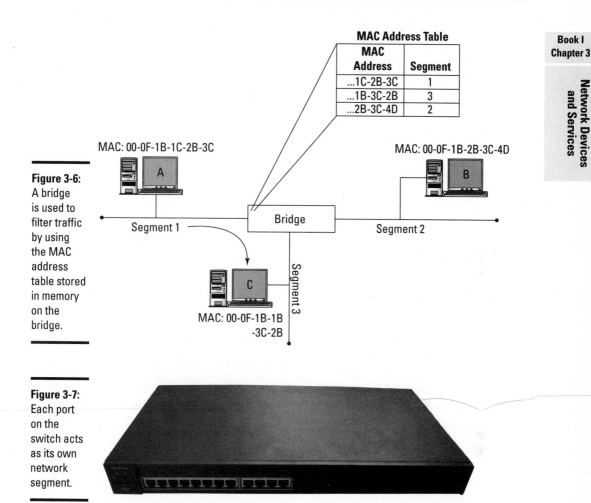

MAC Address Table

MAC Address	Segment
...1C-2B-3C	1
...1B-3C-2B	3
...2B-3C-4D	2

MAC: 00-0F-1B-1C-2B-3C

MAC: 00-0F-1B-2B-3C-4D

A

B

Bridge

Segment 1

Segment 2

Segment 3

C

MAC: 00-0F-1B-1B
-3C-2B

Figure 3-6:
A bridge
is used to
filter traffic
by using
the MAC
address
table stored
in memory
on the
bridge.

Figure 3-7:
Each port
on the
switch acts
as its own
network
segment.

Let's look at an example of how a switch works. Figure 3-8 displays a typical
network setup with a switch having multiple systems connected. Like a
bridge, the switch has a MAC address table that records each system's
MAC address and what port on the switch that system can be found at.
When WorkstationA sends data to WorkstationC, the data travels from
WorkstationA to the switch. The switch then looks at the destination MAC
address that is stored in the header of the frame to find out where the frame
is headed. Once the switch knows the destination MAC address, it then
locates that MAC address in the MAC address table and sends the frame
to the associated port on the switch (in this case, port 7). The destination
system then receives the frame.

TIP

There is a lot more to say about network switches, as they are a big part of your CCENT exam, but I will save the in-depth discussions for the switching chapters in Book III.

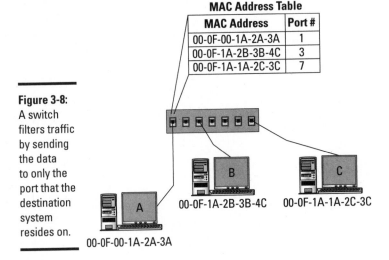

MAC Address Table

MAC Address	Port #
00-0F-00-1A-2A-3A	1
00-0F-1A-2B-3B-4C	3
00-0F-1A-1A-2C-3C	7

Figure 3-8:
A switch filters traffic by sending the data to only the port that the destination system resides on.

FOR THE EXAM

Remember, because bridges and switches work with physical addresses (the MAC address), they are considered layer-2 devices, as that is the layer that handles physical addressing.

Routers

The *router* is responsible for sending data from one network to another router on a different network. (See Figure 3-9.) The router does this by storing a routing table in memory, and the routing table has a listing of what networks exist and what router to send the data to in order to reach that network.

Once a router receives a packet from another router, it looks at the destination address in the packet and then sends the packet to the system on its network that the packet is destined for.

REMEMBER

You will need to know a lot more about routers and switches in order to prepare you for the CCENT certification exam. The purpose of the discussion of routers and switches in this chapter is to give a brief description of the different devices — there is more detail to come on routers and switches as you progress through the book!

Remember, routers are layer-3 devices and, as a result, work with layer-3 addresses (IP addresses) and not the physical address. A physical address is a layer-2 address, and only layer-2 devices (such as a switch or bridge) work with layer-2 addresses.

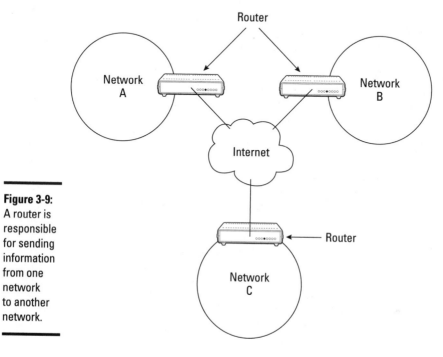

Figure 3-9:
A router is responsible for sending information from one network to another network.

Identifying Network Services

While it is very important for the CCENT certification exam that you know the different devices that can exist on the network, you also need to be familiar with the different network services that are available on the network. This section outlines popular network services you need to be familiar with for the exam — be sure to study these!

Web servers

The first service to be familiar with is a Web server. A *Web server* is responsible for hosting Web pages and delivering those Web pages to a Web client, also known as a *Web browser.* A Web server can be used to host a company intranet site or even a company's public Web site.

The Web site's pages are designed in a language called *Hypertext Markup Language* (HTML), while the actual protocol that is responsible for delivering the page from the server to the client is *Hypertext Transfer Protocol* (HTTP).

E-mail servers

An *e-mail server* is responsible for sending and receiving e-mail on a network. Two different protocols are used by e-mail servers — one protocol for sending e-mail and one protocol for receiving e-mail.

The Internet protocol for sending an e-mail is *Simple Mail Transfer Protocol* (SMTP), which is used by the e-mail client to send the e-mail to their server, which then uses SMTP to send the e-mail to the recipient's e-mail server.

Once the e-mail has been delivered to the recipient's mail server, the client uses an Internet protocol to read the e-mail off the server. *Post Office Protocol version 3* (POP3) is an example of an Internet protocol for reading e-mail and so is Internet Message Access Protocol version 4 (IMAP4).

DNS servers

A very critical service to networking and networking applications is that provided by the *domain name system* (DNS) servers. DNS is responsible for converting the friendly names such as www.gleneclarke.com to IP addresses. (IP addresses are discussed in the next chapter.) The friendly names are called *fully qualified domain names,* or FQDN for short.

A DNS server has a database of FQDNs and their corresponding IP addresses so that clients on the network can query the DNS server to find out the IP address of the system (workstation or server) they are trying to contact. The hook with DNS is that it is impossible for one DNS server to hold all of the friendly names and IP addresses for all the systems in the world. Because of this, a protocol was originally created in 1983 by Paul Mockapetris, where each company hosts its own DNS server. If a DNS server does not know the IP address of a FQDN, it forwards the request out to DNS servers on the Internet. Figure 3-10 displays how this works.

Looking at Figure 3-10, you see that the first step your system uses to find out the IP address of a Web site is to send a query to the DNS server in your office — essentially your system is saying, "Do you have the IP address for www.wiley.com?" Your DNS server will most likely not have the answer, as no one has programmed the address into the server. (Remember, each company is responsible for its own addresses in the database.) So your DNS sends the query out to the DNS root servers that start the hierarchy of the DNS system.

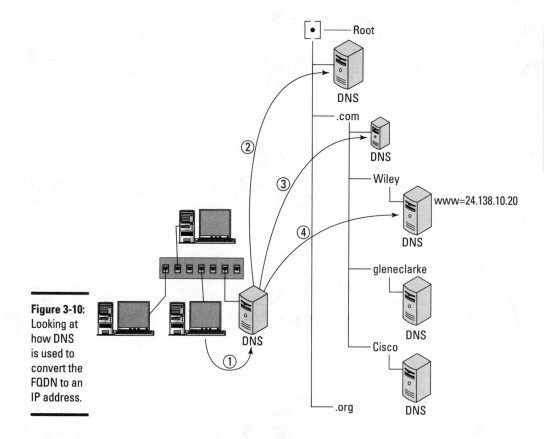

Figure 3-10:
Looking at
how DNS
is used to
convert the
FQDN to an
IP address.

The root server receives the request and looks in its database for an entry called www.wiley.com. It will not have an entry for www.wiley.com, so it looks at the last part in the name and says, "I don't know who www.wiley.com is, but why don't you check with the .com DNS server — he may know who www.wiley.com is?"

Your system then sends the query to the .com name server, which then sends you down to the next level by saying, "No, I don't know who www.wiley.com is, but why don't you check with the wiley.com DNS server?"

Finally, your DNS server queries the wiley.com DNS server and says, "Do you have an IP address for www.wiley.com?" The wiley.com DNS server does have an entry for www, so it sends back the answer of 24.138.10.20 to your company DNS server. Your company DNS server then sends that answer (the IP address) to the system that sent the query.

Authentication servers

Most networking environments limit who is allowed to access the network by making people authenticate to the network. *Authentication* is the process of identifying yourself, typically with a username and password, and then having that verified against a database of usernames and passwords that are allowed to access the network. If you present a valid username and password, you will be authenticated and given access to the network.

There are many different examples of authentication servers out there. Microsoft has an authentication server, known as a *domain controller,* that runs the Active Directory database. Novell has an authentication database known as *eDirectory,* and there is also an industry standard authentication service known as *Remote Authentication Dial-In User Service* (RADIUS), which is a central authentication service that can be used by a number of technologies, such as wireless authentication and remote access.

DHCP servers

Another important service on the network (and one you can be sure you will be tested on in the CCENT exam) is that provided by a Dynamic Host Configuration Protocol (DHCP) server. A *DHCP server* is responsible for assigning IP addresses to systems on the network when those systems start up. There are four phases to a system obtaining an IP address from a DHCP server. (See Figure 3-11.)

+ **DHCP discover:** When a client boots up, it sends out a broadcast message to all systems on the network that says, "If there are any DHCP servers out there, I need an IP address." A *broadcast message* is a frame that is destined for all systems and has a destination MAC address of FF-FF-FF-FF-FF-FF. All systems on the local LAN segment process this message.

+ **DHCP offer:** Any systems receiving the DHCP discover message that are not DHCP servers discard the message, but the DHCP servers send out a message to the system offering an IP address for that system to use. The address is actually leased to the system and, like all leases, expires.

+ **DHCP request:** Because it is possible that multiple DHCP servers will answer a broadcast message with IP address offers, the client sends a request for the first offer that is received. All other offers are then retracted.

✦ **DHCP acknowledge:** The DHCP server that has the IP address offer requested then sends a final acknowledgement that states the client has the address leased for a certain period of time.

Figure 3-11: DHCP is a service that automatically assigns IP addresses to computers.

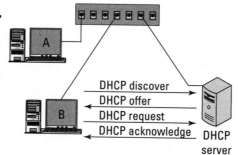

DHCP discover
DHCP offer
DHCP request
DHCP acknowledge

DHCP server

Note that many products can serve as DHCP servers on your network. A Windows server or Linux server can act as a DHCP server, or you can configure your Cisco router to be a DHCP server as well. (See Book II, Chapter 4.) Another point worth noting is that a system that receives an IP address from a DHCP server is known as a *DHCP client.*

For the CCENT certification exam, remember that DHCP is responsible for automatically assigning IP addresses to systems when they first boot up. If there is no DHCP service, you have to manually configure each system with TCP/IP settings. You find out more about TCP/IP and IP addresses in Book I, Chapter 4.

Network Address Translation

The last service that I want to discuss in this chapter is *Network Address Translation,* or NAT. NAT is a service on the network that is responsible for converting the source IP address that is in the header of an outbound packet to the public IP address used by the NAT device. That is a lot to consume, so let's look at an example!

Looking at Figure 3-12, you see that our router has been configured as a NAT device. You also notice that there are two network cards, known as *interfaces,* on the router. One of the interfaces is an Ethernet card (or interface) known as E0. The other interface is a serial interface that is normally connected to your Internet connection (if you are not using a different interface for that). The serial interface in this diagram is known as S0.

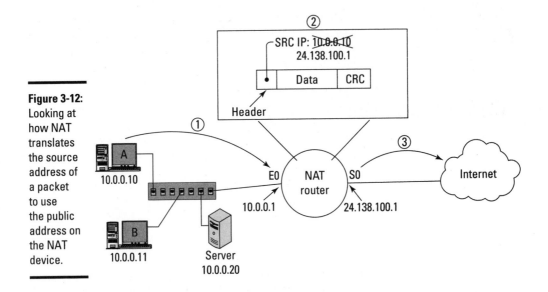

Figure 3-12:
Looking at how NAT translates the source address of a packet to use the public address on the NAT device.

The two other things I want you to notice in Figure 3-12 are that the serial interface has the IP address of 24.138.100.1, and it is the interface connected to the Internet. Any interface connected to the Internet is known as the *public interface,* while in this example the Ethernet interface is known as *private interface,* as it is connected to the private LAN.

Now I will talk about how NAT works. When WorkstationA surfs the Internet, the packet is sent from WorkstationA to the NAT device (in this case, the NAT–enabled router). In step 2, the NAT device strips out the source IP address of WorkstationA from the header of the packet and places the public IP address of the NAT device in its place. The NAT device then records an entry in a translation table so that the NAT device knows when a reply comes back to convert the address back to the address of WorkstationA. Then in step 3, the packet is sent out to the Internet.

The benefit of NAT is that it is a method of sharing one IP address and having a number of systems surf the Internet using that one IP address (which equates to a cost benefit because you would normally need to purchase an IP address for each system to access the Internet). The other benefit is security — if anyone on the Internet captures the packet and looks at where it came from, they will notice the IP address of the NAT device. If they decide to attack that address, they will be attacking the NAT device and not your systems inside the network. You definitely want to use a firewall as well — and most firewalls are NAT devices. I know that some of you have those home routers at home — do not worry because they are NAT devices and firewalls all packaged in one!

For the CCENT certification exam, you need to know that NAT translates a private address to a public address. You also need to know that NAT essentially hides your internal systems from the Internet. You read more about NAT in Book II, Chapter 4.

Traffic Management Concepts

Now that you understand some of the different services and networking devices that make up the network, I want to discuss some other networking concepts you need to be familiar with for the exam. This section discusses network concepts that deal with managing network traffic. In this section, you find out about duplexing, types of communication, and the very important concepts of collision domains and broadcast domains.

To duplex or not to duplex

Most networking devices today (such as network cards and switches) support the concept of duplexing. *Duplexing* is having the capability for a signal to flow between two points in both directions. There are different forms of duplexing terms you need to be familiar with, and I outline them in the following list:

+ **Simplex:** A device that supports simplex communication can communicate in only one direction. It can either send or receive, but it does not support both.

+ **Half-duplex:** A device that supports half-duplex communication can both send and receive, but not at the same time. This is similar to how walkie-talkies work — you cannot talk and listen at the same time.

+ **Full-duplex:** A device that supports full-duplex communication can send and receive information at the same time! This means that as a full-duplex device is receiving data, it can send information to another device.

When hubs were used on Ethernet networks (you might still have some floating around the office), understand that those are half-duplex devices, but a switch is an example of a full-duplex device. The interfaces (also known as *ports*) on the older switches defaulted to half-duplex, and it was up to the administrator to configure the ports for full-duplex. The interfaces on the newer switches default to full-duplex. You read more about configuring duplexing on switches in Book III, Chapter 4.

Types of communication

There are three major types of network communication that you need to be familiar with for the CCENT certification exam — unicast, broadcast, and multicast. The following outlines the differences in the three types:

✦ **Unicast:** One-on-one communication between two systems. Unicast communication has a specific host set as the destination address, and only that host will receive that information. The layer-2 destination address for unicast communication is set to the MAC address of the destination system, while the layer-3 destination address in the packet is set to the IP address of the destination system.

✦ **Broadcast:** A communication that is sent to all systems on the network. The layer-2 destination address for broadcast traffic is FF-FF-FF-FF-FF-FF, while the layer-3 representation of a broadcast address is all bits set to 1, which gives you the broadcast address of 255.255.255.255. The broadcast address of 255.255.255.255 is known as an internetwork broadcast address (refers to all networks), while each subnet also has a broadcast with all host bits set to 1 (known as a subnet broadcast address). For example, 12.255.255.255 would be the layer-3 subnet broadcast address of the 12.0.0.0 network.

✦ **Multicast:** A communication that is not sent to *all* systems, but is sent to a *group* of systems. This allows an application to send data to a multicast address, and anyone who has subscribed, so to speak, to the address (typically through an application) will be part of that grouping and thus receive the information.

Also note that there are some predefined multicast addresses. For example, 224.0.0.2 is an address that means all routers on the network, whereas 224.0.0.5 is a multicast address for all routers running a popular routing protocol known as OSPF (which I discuss in more detail in Book III, Chapter 2).

Broadcast domains versus collision domains

A very important concept to be familiar with for the CCENT certification exam is the concept of broadcast domains and collision domains. Let's take a look at each of these.

Broadcast domain

A *broadcast domain* is a group of systems that receive each other's broadcast messages. Looking at Figure 3-13, you see three systems connected to a hub. When ComputerA sends a broadcast message to everyone, the message reaches the hub, which forwards the message to all systems connected to the hub. Each system receives the broadcast message — therefore, all of these systems are part of the same broadcast domain.

Looking at Figure 3-13, if you were using a switch to connect all the systems together, you would still have one broadcast domain, as the switch would forward the broadcast message to all ports on the switch.

Regarding traffic management, as the network administrator you need to be aware of broadcast domains because, at some point, you will say to yourself, "I do not want ComputerC to receive any broadcast messages from ComputerA or ComputerB." In this case, you need to ensure that ComputerC is placed in its own broadcast domain by using a router. Broadcast messages do not cross routers, so as a result, you create multiple broadcast domains when using a router. (See Figure 3-14.)

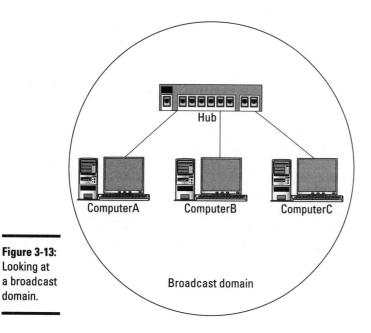

Figure 3-13:
Looking at a broadcast domain.

Figure 3-14:
Routers create multiple broadcast domains.

Note that the grouping in Figure 3-14 uses a hub as a central device to connect all systems, but the resulting number of broadcast domains would be the same if switches were used instead of hubs — broadcast domains are created by adding routers to the network.

You can actually create multiple broadcast domains on a switch using the VLANs feature, but I save that information for the VLAN discussion in Book III, Chapter 4.

Collision domain

A collision domain is different from a broadcast domain, as a *collision domain* is a group of systems in which data can collide (which is not a good thing). Let's look back to Figure 3-13 to find out about collision domains.

Since a hub sends any data it receives to all other ports on the hub, it is possible for the data to collide with any other data sent at the same time. This means that all of the systems in Figure 3-13 exist in a single collision domain.

With a switch, each port acts as its own dedicated network segment, which means that when ComputerA sends data to ComputerC, the information travels up the cable from ComputerA to the switch. Because no other systems are connected to that cable, there is no possibility for collisions. This means that each port on the switch creates a separate collision domain.

For the CCENT certification exam, remember that a network using a hub creates one collision domain and one broadcast domain, while a switch creates a collision domain per port on the switch, and one broadcast domain. The only way an additional broadcast domain is created is with a router or VLAN.

Managing traffic

It is important to understand the different network devices presented in this chapter, as they will help you manage network traffic. For example, you want to ensure that you are using switches instead of hubs, as the switch filters traffic by sending the data to only the port that the destination system resides on. A hub wastes bandwidth, as it sends the data to all ports, even though the destination systems do not reside on those ports.

You should also be familiar with how to create broadcast domains on the network. A number of applications send broadcast traffic on the network, and you may want to limit how far a broadcast message can travel on your network. Remember when looking at your network documentation that you can add routers to the network to divide the network into different broadcast domains!

There are a number of other steps you can take to manage traffic. For example, you can take advantage of quality of service (QoS) functions on your network devices. *QoS* allows you to place priority on traffic from different applications to ensure that each application has adequate bandwidth available. This is a popular solution for *Voice over IP (VoIP)* — a technology that encapsulates your telephone traffic over a TCP/IP network.

Chapter Summary

This chapter illustrates the importance of networking devices and services. The following are some key points to remember for the CCENT exam:

✦ *Hubs* and *repeaters* are layer-1 devices that work with the electrical signal.

✦ A *hub* passes the electrical signal to all ports on the hub.

✦ A *repeater* regenerates a signal so the signal can travel farther.

✦ Bridges and switches are layer-2 devices that filter traffic based off the destination MAC address.

✦ A *switch* filters traffic by sending the data to only the port that the destination address of the frame resides on.

✦ *Routers* are layer-3 devices that send data from one network to another network.

✦ *SMTP* is the Internet protocol for sending e-mail, while *POP3* is the Internet protocol for receiving e-mail.

✦ *DNS* is a network service that is responsible for converting Internet-style names, known as *FQDNs,* to IP addresses.

✦ *NAT* is responsible for translating the source address of a packet to use the public address of the NAT device. *NAT devices* allow all users on the network to connect to the Internet using the same IP address.

✦ *DHCP* is a service that is responsible for assigning IP addresses to systems on the network.

Lab Exercises

This chapter introduces you to a number of networking devices and services that you need to be familiar with for the CCENT certification exam. The following labs are designed to help you practice associating the terminology with meaning.

Lab 3-1: Network devices

In this lab, read the description and then match the description to the appropriate network device.

___ Network interface card	**A.** A network device that is responsible for sending information from one network to another network.
___ Switch	**B.** A layer-2 device that filters traffic by sending the data to only the network segment that the destination system resides on.
___ Router	**C.** A layer-1 device that allows systems to connect to the network.
___ Repeater	**D.** The component of a network device that has a MAC address associated with it.
___ Hub	**E.** A layer-2 device that filters traffic by sending the data to only the port that the destination system resides on.
___ Bridge	**F.** A layer-1 device that regenerates the signal.

Lab 3-2: Remembering network services

In this lab, read the description of the network service and then associate it with the appropriate term.

___ Web server	**A.** Responsible for assigning IP addresses to systems on the network.
___ Authentication server	**B.** Translates the source address of a packet to use the public interface of the device.
___ DHCP	**C.** Responsible for translating the friendly name of a system to an IP address.
___ DNS	**D.** Delivers Web pages to a Web browser client.
___ NAT	**E.** Responsible for validating logon requests in order to control access to the network.

Prep Test

1 Which of the following are considered layer-2 devices? (Choose two.)

A ❑ Bridge

B ❑ Router

C ❑ Repeater

D ❑ Switch

E ❑ Hub

2 Which of the following services is responsible for translating the source IP address of a packet to the IP of the public interface on the device?

A ○ DHCP

B ○ NAT

C ○ DNS

D ○ HTTP

3 What device is responsible for regenerating the signal so that the signal can travel a greater distance?

A ○ Bridge

B ○ Router

C ○ Repeater

D ○ Switch

E ○ Hub

4 Which of the following are considered layer-1 devices? (Choose two.)

A ❑ Bridge

B ❑ Router

C ❑ Repeater

D ❑ Switch

E ❑ Hub

5 Which device filters traffic by looking at the destination address of the frame and then forwards the frame to the port that the destination system resides on?

A ○ Hub

B ○ Router

C ○ Repeater

D ○ Switch

6 **Which of the following identifies the destination address of the DHCP discover message?**

A ○ 0F-1B-3C-2F-3C-2A

B ○ FF-FF-FF-FF-FF-FF

C ○ 192.168.4.5

D ○ 192.168.0.0

7 **You are troubleshooting a communication problem. You seem to be able to communicate with Glen's Web site by IP address, but not by the fully qualified domain name (`www.gleneclarke.com`). What is most likely the problem?**

A ○ DHCP

B ○ NAT

C ○ DNS

D ○ HTTP

8 **Which network service is responsible for assigning IP addresses to systems on the network?**

A ○ DHCP

B ○ NAT

C ○ DNS

D ○ HTTP

9 **Which of the following is a layer-3 device?**

A ○ Bridge

B ○ Router

C ○ Repeater

D ○ Switch

E ○ Hub

10 **Which of the following addresses does a router use to determine where a packet needs to be delivered? (Choose two.)**

A ❑ 24.56.78.10

B ❑ 00-3B-4C-2B-00-AF

C ❑ A layer-3 address

D ❑ A layer-2 address

Answers

1 **A, D.** Both bridges and switches run at layer 2 and are devices that filter traffic by the MAC address. *See "Building Networks with Network Devices."*

2 **B.** NAT is responsible for translating the source IP address of a packet to use the IP of the public interface on the NAT device. *Review "Network Address Translation."*

3 **C.** A repeater is a layer-1 device that is responsible for regenerating the signal. *Check out "Repeaters."*

4 **C, E.** A hub and a repeater are examples of layer-1 devices. Remember that a layer-1 device works with the electrical signal. *Peruse "Building Networks with Network Devices."*

5 **D.** A switch is a layer-2 device that filters traffic based off the destination MAC address of the frame. *Take a look at "Switches."*

6 **B.** The DHCP discover message is a broadcast message which is used to locate the DHCP server on the network. `FF-FF-FF-FF-FF-FF` is the layer-2 representation of a broadcast address. *Peek at "DHCP servers."*

7 **C.** If you can communicate with a system by the IP address but not the FQDN, that is a classic indication that the name is not able to convert to an IP address. This is a sign that there is a problem with DNS. *Look over "DNS servers."*

8 **A.** The DHCP service is responsible for assigning IP addresses automatically to systems on the network. *Study "DHCP servers."*

9 **B.** A router is an example of a layer-3 device and is responsible for sending or receiving information to and from the network. *Refer to "Routers."*

10 **A, C.** Routers use layer-3 address to determine where to send a packet. *Examine "Routers."*

Chapter 4: Introduction to TCP/IP

In This Chapter

✔ The basics of TCP/IP

✔ IP address classes

✔ Public versus private addresses

✔ Assigning IP addresses

✔ The TCP/IP Internet model

Regardless of the kind of networking environment you work in these days, all of the networks today run TCP/IP and, as a result, the CCENT certification exam requires anyone who passes the exam to have extensive knowledge of the protocol suite.

As a network professional, you have to be familiar with the basic concepts of TCP/IP. You also need to have advanced knowledge of how all of the protocols in the protocol suite work together to allow communication to occur.

This chapter is designed to introduce you to the basics of TCP/IP and sets the foundation for the next chapter, which covers the more in-depth addressing topics. Be sure to be very comfortable with this chapter before moving on to other chapters in the book, as this chapter sets the TCP/IP foundation!

Quick Assessment

1   (True/False). The IP protocol is responsible for converting the IP address to a MAC address.

2   The _____ protocol is the connection-oriented protocol within TCP/IP.

3   `156.78.92.10` is an example of a class _____ address.

4   (True/False). `131.107.10.20` is an example of a private address.

5   The acknowledgement number is a field in the _____ header.

6   An IP address is a _____-bit address.

Answers

1   *False.* See "Internet Protocol (IP)."

2   *TCP.* Review "Transport layer protocols."

3   *B.* Check out "Class B."

4   *False.* Peruse "Public versus private addresses."

5   *TCP.* Take a look at "The TCP header."

6   *32.* Peek at "IP address."

The Basics of TCP/IP

A *protocol* is a language used by computers or applications to communicate, and the *Transmission Control Protocol/Internet Protocol* (TCP/IP) is the hot protocol on the market these days because it is the protocol of the Internet and Internet-based technologies. TCP/IP has become the protocol of choice for Windows, Linux, and Novell networks, and for devices from vendors such as Cisco, because of its ability to communicate in heterogeneous environments. *Heterogeneous* is the term we use for an environment that is made up of different systems. The bottom line is this: It doesn't matter what kind of OS you are running — if you're running TCP/IP, you can communicate globally.

TCP/IP is a protocol suite. *Protocol suites* are like application suites in the sense that there is more than one protocol in the group. For example, if you purchase the Microsoft Office suite, you purchase an entire group of applications, or an entire *suite* of applications. TCP/IP is a group of protocols that make up the protocol suite, and some of these protocols are used day in and day out. For example, the TCP/IP protocol suite has protocols to remotely connect and manage a system or device, and it has a protocol for downloading files from another computer.

This section is designed to give you the basics of TCP/IP version 4 (IPv4), including information on the required settings for TCP/IP to work. The CCENT exam requires you to have sound knowledge of IPv4, while the CCNA exam tests you on IPv6.

IP addressing

Every system and device (a printer, router, or switch) running the TCP/IP protocol has two basic configuration settings that need to be configured — three if you intend to communicate off the network.

The two required settings are the IP address and the subnet mask; these are required values for TCP/IP to work on a system. The third, optional, setting — which is required only if you wish to communicate off the network — is the default gateway setting. Let's look at each of these settings!

IP address

The *IP address* is a unique address assigned to a workstation, server, or device. This unique address is used to identify the system or device on the network or even within the world!

The IP address is a 32-bit value that is typically represented in the decimal format. The decimal format is displayed similar to 145.25.10.100. Notice that the decimal format is represented with four sets of numbers, and each set is separated with a period (.) — this is actually known as the *dotted*

Introduction to TCP/IP

decimal notation. The reason for the dotted decimal notation is it is easier to remember an address of `145.25.10.100` than it is to remember thirty two 1s and 0s (such as 10010001 00011001 00001010 01100100) to identify the system.

Each set of numbers in the IP address is known as an *octet* because each number is made up of 8 bits — the term *oct* meaning eight. Because there are four octets, each containing 8 bits, we have a 32-bit address.

The next important point to make about the IP address is that it is logically divided into two parts. The first part is known as the network ID, and the second part is known as the host ID. (See Figure 4-1.)

Figure 4-1:
The IP address is divided into two parts — the network ID and the host ID.

145.25.10.100

Network ID   Host ID

The network ID portion of the IP address is the same for your entire network and unique in the world. All hosts (computers, servers, or devices) on the same network will have the same network ID assigned and then have unique numbers assigned to the host ID portion of the IP address to make the IP address unique as a whole. For example, if we look at the address `145.25.10.100` in Figure 4-1, the network ID portion is `145.25.x.y`. This means that every system on this network must start with `145.25.x.y` and then have any valid numbers in the x and y portion of the address. The x and y portion in this example is the host ID portion, and the network administrator for the network will decide what the host ID portion is (or have the DHCP server give the host IDs out automatically).

The relevance of the network ID is that (unless you are using NAT) every network has a unique network ID, and your IP address identifies the network you are on. Plus, it is a unique identifier for your system on that network. The routers use the network ID of the destination address in a packet to decide where to send the information.

I know what you are asking yourself right now: "Is it always the first two octets that make up the network ID?" The answer is no; sometimes it is the first octet, and other times it is the first two octets or even the first three octets. Well, how do you know what portion of an IP address is the network ID and what portion is the host ID? The answer is simple — the subnet mask tells you this!

Subnet mask

The *subnet mask* is an IP setting on the system used to identify the network ID portion of an IP address. For right now, let's keep things simple and just discuss the default way that TCP/IP works. If the subnet mask has a 255 in an octet, the corresponding octet in the IP address is part of the network ID. If there is a 0 in an octet within the subnet mask, then the corresponding octet in the IP address is part of the host ID portion. For example, see the bold text in the table that follows:

	Octet 1	Octet 2	Octet 3	Octet 4
IP Address	**145**	**25**	10	100
Subnet Mask	**255**	**255**	0	0
Result	Network ID	Network ID	Host ID	Host ID

Looking at the example, you see that the system has an IP address of 145.25.10.100 and a subnet mask of 255.255.0.0. The subnet mask tells you that the first two octets are the network ID (because they have a 255), and the last two octets are the host ID portion (because they have a 0).

In Book I, Chapter 5, you find out how the subnet mask can be customized by subnetting the network. This chapter focuses on the basics of TCP/IP before customizing the addresses.

The next big point to make is the relevance of identifying the network ID portion of the IP address. When a system tries to communicate with another system, the first thing TCP/IP does (actually the IP protocol, but more on that later) is determine if the system you are trying to communicate with exists on the same network. If it does, your computer can send the data directly to that system. If the system you are trying to communicate with exists on a different network, your system will pass the information to the router so that the router can send the data off the network to the destination.

Figure 4-2 displays an example of how the subnet mask is used to determine if a system is on the same network as your own system. For Figure 4-2, assume that WorkstationA has the IP address of 12.0.0.10 with a subnet mask of 255.0.0.0.

When WorkstationA tries to communicate with WorkstationC by its IP address, WorkstationA first compares his own IP against his subnet mask to find out what his network ID is. In this example, WorkstationA identifies the first octet as being his network ID. He then compares the first octet against the first octet of the system he is trying to communicate with to see if the system is on the same network or not. The logic here is if the systems are on the same network, they will have the same network ID. WorkstationA sees that the network IDs are different, so he knows that the systems are not on the same network.

Figure 4-2:
How the
subnet
identifies
whether a
system is
on the same
network as
your own
system.

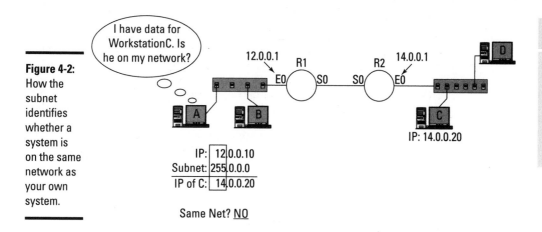

Once WorkstationA determines that the system he is trying to communicate with is on a different network, he knows to send the information to the router so the router can route the data off the network and to its destination. The next logical question is this: "How does a system know what router to send the information to?" The answer is simple — the default gateway setting!

Default gateway

The *default gateway setting* of a device points to the IP address of the router that the system or device is to use in order to send information off the network. In my example from Figure 4-2, WorkstationA and WorkstationB need to be configured with a default gateway of 12.0.0.1 as that is the IP address of the device they must send data to in order to send data off the network. In this case, when you configure the IP address on those systems you will also configure 12.0.0.1 as the default gateway of those systems with the default gateway setting in the TCP/IP configuration.

WorkstationC and WorkstationD need to be configured to use the default gateway of 14.0.0.1, as that is the router connected to their network. Notice that the default gateway address is an address on the system's network — it would be hard to send the data to the router if the router wasn't on your network because you would have to route to get to the router. That doesn't make much sense.

Converting decimal to binary

Before we continue into the remaining topics of this chapter and the subnetting discussion in the next chapter, it is important to know how to convert binary values to decimal and decimal values to binary as the rest of this chapter and the next chapter depends on that knowledge. Let's take a look at how an octet gets its decimal value from the eight bits that are in the octet.

In the "IP address" section earlier in this chapter, you found out that there are eight bits in an octet. Each of these bits have a decimal value associated with them, as shown in Figure 4-3. Starting on the right side of Figure 4-3, the eighth bit has a value of one (1), which then doubles for the next bit moving to the left. The value of each bit is double the value of the previous bit when moving from right to left. As you can see, the first bit on the left side has a decimal value of 128. Because the first bit (on the left) has the highest value associated with it, it is considered the *most significant bit* (MSB); because the eighth bit has the lowest value, it is considered the *least significant bit* (LSB).

Figure 4-3:
Looking at the values of the eight bits in an octet.

	MSB							LSB
Bit	1	2	3	4	5	6	7	8
Value	128	64	32	16	8	4	2	1

You can calculate the eight bits when you know the decimal value by enabling the bits (setting the bit to a 1) that mathematically add up to the decimal value of the octet. Let's look at the example IP address of 145.25.10.100 and focus on the first octet, which has a decimal value of 145. To convert the number 145 to the binary (1s and 0s) representation, you enable (set to 1) the bits that have the value 128, 16, and 1 (128 + 16 + 1 = 145) as shown below.

Bit	1	2	3	4	5	6	7	8
Value	128	64	32	16	8	4	2	1
State	1			1				1

Once you enable all of the bits that mathematically add up to the number you are looking for, you disable (turn off) all the other bits by setting them to zero (0), as shown below.

Bit	1	2	3	4	5	6	7	8
Value	128	64	32	16	8	4	2	1
State	1	0	0	1	0	0	0	1

So the eight bits that make the value of 145 are 10010001. Now you calculate the eight bits for the second octet of the IP address 145.25.10.100, which is 25. Again, use our chart to enable the bits that make the value 25 and then turn all other bits off. You should have the bits that have the value 16, 8, and 1 enabled (16 + 8 + 1 equals the decimal value of 25) and the remaining bits should be turned off, as shown below.

Bit	1	2	3	4	5	6	7	8
Value	128	64	32	16	8	4	2	1
State	0	0	0	1	1	0	0	1

The decimal value of the third octet in our `145.25.10.100` IP address example is 10, which, when converted to binary, has the binary value of 00001010. When the decimal value of 100 in the fourth octet is converted to binary, we get a binary value of 01100100.

It is important that you are able to convert decimal values to binary and binary values to decimal for the exam. You have to practice it and be able to do it very quickly if you want to pass the CCENT certification exam. Be sure to check out the labs at the end of this chapter to practice converting decimal to binary and vice versa.

To practice converting numbers to binary feel free to check out the number of games on the Cisco Games Arcade site at `https://learningnetwork.cisco.com/community/connections/games`!

IP Address Classes

Let's summarize what we know about IP addresses so far. You know that an IP address is a unique 32-bit address assigned to each system or device and is used to communicate with the system. The address is made up of four, 8-bit octets and is divided into two parts, the network ID portion and the host ID portion. You also know that the subnet mask is used to determine which part of an IP address is the network ID and which part is the host ID portion. If the subnet mask has 255 in an octet, the corresponding octet in the IP address is part of the network ID. If there is a zero (0) in an octet of the subnet mask, the corresponding octet in the IP address is part of the host ID portion.

The next issue for us to tackle is figuring out what the subnet mask of a system is so you can determine what part of the IP address is the network ID. To determine what the subnet mask of a system is, you have to understand the different address classes in TCP/IP because they determine the default subnet mask of a system.

The *Internet Assigned Numbers Authority* (IANA) is responsible for designing the IP addressing schemes.

Class A

The first class address to discuss is a class A address, which has a default subnet mask of `255.0.0.0`, meaning the first octet is the network ID portion and the last three octets are the host ID portion of the address. This allows for 16,777,214 hosts on the network — a very big network! To calculate how many hosts can exist on the network, you use the formula of 2<*# of host bits*>.

For example, 12.x.y.z is a class A address with a subnet mask of 255.0.0.0. This means there are 24 bits (the last 3 octets) that make up the host ID portion, so the formula is 2^{24} = 16,777,216. But I said there were 16,777,214 hosts on the network. Is my math wrong? No, after you use the formula to calculate the number of hosts you subtract 2 from it because there are two addresses on every network that you are not allowed to use. You are not allowed to use the address with all host bits set to 0, as that is reserved for the network ID, and you are not allowed to use the address with all host bits set to 1 because that is reserved for the *broadcast address,* which is the address that a system sends data to when it wants everyone on the network to receive the information.

It is imperative for the exam that you are familiar with converting binary to decimal. An example of when this ability is important is when you are identifying illegal addresses — the rules to remember are you are not allowed to assign a system the address with all host bits set to 0 (reserved for the network ID itself) and you are not allowed to assign a system the address with all host bits set to 1 (reserved for the broadcast address).

Now that we have this knowledge, we need to modify our formula for calculating the number of hosts that can exist on the network. Our modified formula is now 2<*# of host bits*> – 2.

In the example of the 12.x.y.z class A address, the two illegal addresses are 12.0.0.0 (reserved for the actual network ID) and 12.255.255.255 (reserved for the broadcast address). The *broadcast address* is the address that a system sends data to when it wants everyone on the network to receive the information.

The final point to make about class A addresses is that they always have a number between 1 and 127 in the first octet. So if an IP address has a number between 1 and 127 in the first octet, you know that it has a default subnet mask of 255.0.0.0, which means the first octet is the network ID.

Why the range 1 to 127? Well, when IANA designed the addressing for TCP/IP, they defined class A addresses as having the first bit in the first octet as always off — this gives you the following binary ranges **00000001** (decimal value 1) to **01111111** (decimal value 127).

It is important to note that — even though class A addresses have the value of the first octet range between 1 and 127 — you will never see a system use 127 in the first octet because it is already reserved for the *loopback address,* which is an address that always refers to the TCP/IP software installed on *your* system. Typically, the loopback address is referred to as 127.0.0.1, but you could use any address that starts with 127 as the loopback address. The most common use of the loopback address is as a quick way to make sure that TCP/IP has been installed on your system and that it is functioning properly. You can test your own system by typing the following in a command prompt:

```
Ping 127.0.0.1
```

If TCP/IP has been installed and is functioning correctly you will receive replies to the `ping 127.0.0.1` command. If there are any issues with the protocol you will receive an error message as a result of the ping stating the problem.

A system's IP address cannot start with 127, but it can have the number 127 in the second, third, or fourth octets.

Table 4-1 summarizes what you need to know about Class A addresses.

Book I
Chapter 4

Introduction
to TCP/IP

Table 4-1	Class A Addresses
Feature	*Value*
First octet range	1 to 127
Default subnet mask	`255.0.0.0`
IP address breakdown	`n.h.h.h`*
Number of class A networks	126
Number of hosts per network	16,777,214 ($2^{24} - 2$)

*n = network, h = host

Class B

A class B address is an address that has the first octet ranging from 128 to 191. The IANA states that a *class B* address will always have the first two bits of the first octet take a 10 state. This means that the possible values for the first octet in a class B address would range from **10**000000 (128) to **10**111111 (191).

A class B address has a default subnet mask of `255.255.0.0`. This means that the first two octets are part of the network ID, and the last two octets make up the host ID. Using the formula of $2^{<\text{\# of host bits}>} - 2$, you see that a class B address supports 65,534 hosts on the network ($2^{16} - 2$). Class B networks are considered medium-sized networks.

An example of a class B network is `129.65.x.y`, with `129.65.0.0` being the network ID (all host bits set to 0) and `129.65.255.255` being the broadcast address (all host bits set to 1).

Table 4-2 summarizes what you need to know about Class B addresses.

Table 4-2	Class B Addresses
Feature	*Value*
First octet range	128 to 191
Default subnet mask	255.255.0.0
IP address breakdown	*n.n.h.h**
Number of class B networks	16,384
Number of hosts per network	65,534 ($2^{16} - 2$)

*n = network, h = host

Class C

The next class address is a class C address, which has an IP address with the first octet ranging from 192 to 223. Again, the numbers are derived from binary. When the addressing was defined, class C addresses were defined as always having 110 as the first three bits of the first octet. This means that a class C address will range between **110**00000 (192) to **110**11111 (223).

The subnet mask for a class C address is 255.255.255.0, which means that the first three octets are part of the network ID, and the last octet makes up the host ID portion. This means that you can have 254 hosts ($2^8 - 2$) on a class C network — a fairly small network compared to a class A network.

Table 4-3 summarizes what you need to know about Class C addresses.

Table 4-3	Class C Addresses
Feature	*Value*
First octet range	192 to 223
Default subnet mask	255.255.255.0
IP address breakdown	*n.n.n.h**
Number of class C networks	2,097,152
Number of hosts per network	254 ($2^8 - 2$)

*n = network, h = host

Classes D and E

There are two class addresses that remain: class D and class E addresses. *Class D* addresses are used by multicasting applications (*multicasting* means sending information to multiple systems at the same time) and *class E* addresses are not used in production environments because they are for experimental purposes.

Class D addresses have a value in the first octet that ranges from 224 to 239, while class E addresses have a first octet that ranges between 240 and 247. You do not need to be familiar with class D and E addresses for the CCENT certification exam; I only mention them here so that you know there are more than class A, B, and C addresses.

For the CCENT certification exam, you need to be very familiar with IP addressing, starting with identifying class A, B, and C addresses.

Looking at Special Addresses

For the CCENT certification exam, it is important to be familiar with special address types such as private addresses and automatic private IP addresses. This section is designed to identify these special address types.

Public versus private addresses

A *private address* is an address that is not routable on the Internet. So, if you are using a private address, your systems cannot use the Internet without a device such as NAT to translate the address to a *public address* (an address that is routable on the Internet).

There are three private address ranges, one range per class address, that you will work with on networks. (For more on the class addresses, see the "IP Address Classes" section earlier in this chapter.) The three private IP address ranges are

✦ Class A: `10.0.0.0` to `10.255.255.255`

✦ Class B: `172.16.0.0` to `172.31.255.255`

✦ Class C: `192.168.0.0` to `192.168.255.255`

For the CCENT certification exam, be sure to know the three private address ranges. Note that the private addresses are made up of one class A network ID, sixteen class B network ranges, and 256 class C network ranges. Remember that addresses that are not private are routable on the Internet and are considered public addresses that are registered to a specific owner.

Automatic Private IP Addressing (APIPA)

Another important address to be able to identify is an *Automatic Private IP Address* (APIPA). It is a feature of today's operating systems and allows a client to assign itself an IP address if a DHCP server does not respond to the DHCP request. (I discuss DHCP servers in Book I, Chapter 3.) The address that the client assigns to itself is within the $169.254.x.y$ network range. The system will also configure itself with a subnet mask of $255.255.0.0$, but will not configure the default gateway entry. This means that if the DHCP server is down and your network clients boot up, they will all have an address in the $169.254.x.y$ range and will be able to communicate with one another. Because they are not configured for a default gateway entry, they will not be able to communicate with systems off the network or with the Internet.

When troubleshooting networking connectivity, use the `ipconfig` command on a Windows machine or `ifconfig` on a Linux system (some newer Linux systems use the `ip addr` command) to view the TCP/IP settings of a system. If the IP address is $169.254.x.y$, that means the client cannot communicate with the DHCP server. Make sure that the client is connected to the network correctly and then verify that the DHCP server is functioning!

Assigning IP Addresses

In Book II, Chapter 2, you discover how to configure the different network cards, known as *interfaces,* on a Cisco router. But for now, I just want to discuss how the addresses are assigned on the client (also known as a *workstation*).

Identifying invalid addresses

Before we see how to assign IP addresses to the client systems, it is important to understand what an invalid address is. An *invalid address* is an address that is illegal to assign to a system or a device.

Be sure to remember these rules for the exam and for the real world:

+ **An address cannot start with 127.** Any address that starts with 127 reserved for the loopback address and is used to reference your own system.

+ **An address cannot have all host bits set to 1.** All host bits set to 1 are reserved as the broadcast address for any given network ID.

+ **An address cannot have all host bits set to 0.** All host bits set to 0 are reserved to reference the actual network ID. The network ID is used to program the routing tables on routers.

+ **An octet cannot contain a number over 255.** If you add the values of all eight bits in an octet, you get the number 255; therefore, it is impossible to have a number higher than 255 in an octet.

+ **You cannot duplicate an address.** You cannot duplicate any other address on the network or Internet. If you try to use an address already in use, you will receive a duplicate IP address error.

Static addressing versus dynamic addressing

When assigning IP addresses to systems on the network, you will have to decide if you use static addressing or dynamic addressing. *Static addressing* means that you manually assign the IP address to the system or device, while *dynamic addressing* means that the address is assigned through DHCP. The term *static* means that the address does not change (unless you manually change it), whereas a dynamic address could be different each time your power on the workstation.

Normally, you will statically assign IP addresses to the following:

✦ **Servers:** In networking environments, you normally do not want the address of a server to change, so you statically assign it an IP address. This way, you always know the IP address of the server.

✦ **Routers:** A router is another example of a device that you do not want the IP address to change on. You will need to configure all your clients' default gateway settings to point to the router. As a result, you do not want the router's IP address to change.

✦ **Switches:** You do not need to assign your switch an IP address for it to filter and forward traffic to the destination system. You need to assign an IP address to your switch only if you intend to remotely manage the switch from a Telnet session, ssh session, or a Web browser. If you want your switch to have an IP address, you will configure it with a static address.

✦ **Printers:** A printer is another example of a device that should not have its IP address change, as clients and servers will be configured to point to the printer by its IP address. If the IP address changes on the printer, you will need to reconfigure each client to print to the new address.

After you have manually configured the IP addresses on routers, switches, printers, and servers, it is then time to configure IP addresses on your client systems. As mentioned earlier in the book, most network administrators will create a DHCP server on the network so that the IP addresses are assigned to systems automatically. Book II, Chapter 4 shows you how to configure your Cisco router as a DHCP server, so I save that discussion for then.

Configuring TCP/IP on a client

Before I leave the discussion of IP addresses, I want to outline the steps to configure a Windows and Linux system for an IP address. Configuring IP addresses on a client is not required knowledge for your CCENT certification exam, as the exam focuses on the router configuration, but I think it is important to discuss this because it is part of configuring a network.

To configure TCP/IP on a Windows system, access your local area connection properties and configure the TCP/IP protocol. Be aware that all Microsoft operating systems have TCP/IP installed by default. You simply need to configure the IP address on the system if you are statically configuring addresses. To configure TCP/IP on a Windows system, follow these steps:

1. **Locate the network connections.**

- *Windows XP/2003:* Choose Start⇨Control Panel⇨Network and Internet Connections⇨Network Connections.

- *Windows 2008/Vista/7:* Click Start. Right-click Network and choose Properties. Click the Manage Network Connections link on the left.

2. **Right-click your local area connection and choose Properties.**

3. **In the list of items used by the connection, do one of the following:**

- *Windows XP/2003:* Select TCP/IP and then choose Properties.

- *Windows 2008/Vista/7:* Select Internet Protocol version 4 (TCP/IPv4) and then click Properties.

4. **To assign a static address, select Use the Following IP Address (as shown in Figure 4-4) and then type your computer's IP address, subnet mask, and default gateway in the corresponding text boxes.**

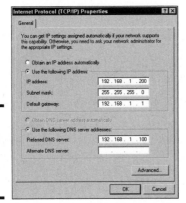

Figure 4-4:
Configuring
TCP/IP on
a Windows
client.

5. **To configure the system to send DNS queries to a specific DNS server, type the address of your DNS server in the Preferred DNS Server text box.**

6. **Click OK and then click OK again.**

The steps are very similar to configure a Linux system for a static address. The steps that you take will differ depending on the Linux distribution you are using. The following steps are how to configure Linux Fedora with a static IP address:

1. **Choose System⇨Administration⇨Network.**

2. **Once inside the Network Configuration dialog, select the Eth0 network card and click the Edit button.**

3. **Choose the option Statically Set IP Address and then type the desired IP address, subnet mask, and default gateway you want the system to use.**

4. **Click OK.**

If you decide to configure TCP/IP on your Windows or Linux systems dynamically through a DHCP server, you typically do not need to do anything at the client, as being a DHCP client is normally the default. If you want to verify that you are configured to be a DHCP client, you follow the same steps listed above, but you select the Obtain an IP Address Automatically option in Step 4 for a Windows system, or choose the Automatically Obtain IP Address Settings with DHCP option in Step 3 for the Linux system.

The TCP/IP Internet Model

A very important topic we need to discuss is the TCP/IP Internet model, which is a four-layer model that defines the functionality of different network components that run at the different layers. If you understand the OSI model (which I explain in Book I, Chapter 2), you will have no problem understanding the TCP/IP Internet model because essentially what the designers of TCP/IP did was simplify the OSI model to become the TCP/IP Internet model.

The four layers

The TCP/IP Internet model is a four-layer model (see Figure 4-5), as opposed to the seven layers in the OSI model. When the TCP/IP Internet model was designed, it was decided that the top three layers of the OSI model would be handled by the software applications — so the functionality of those three layers were grouped together to create the application layer of the TCP/IP Internet model.

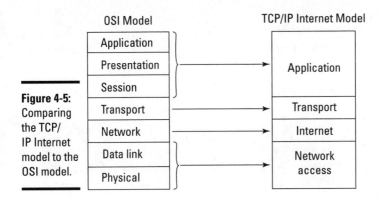

Figure 4-5:
Comparing
the TCP/
IP Internet
model to the
OSI model.

The name and functionality of the transport layer stays the same in the
TCP/IP Internet model. The network layer of the OSI model becomes the
Internet layer in the TCP/IP Internet model — the functionality of this layer
stays the same in spite of the layer's name change. Finally, the data link and the
physical layers are grouped together to create the network access layer in
the TCP/IP Internet model.

The following summarizes the purpose of each layer of the TCP/IP Internet
model:

✦ **Application:** Responsible for initiating the request on the sending
computer and servicing the request on the receiving system. On the
sending system, once the request has been created it is then passed
down to the transport layer.

✦ **Transport:** Responsible for reliable and unreliable delivery. When the
request is passed down to the transport layer, a transport layer protocol
is selected based on whether reliable delivery or unreliable delivery
is required. With *reliable delivery,* the system delivers the data and
ensures the information reaches the destination. If the data does not
reach the destination, the information is retransmitted. If an *unreliable
delivery* protocol is used, the information is sent to the destination but
not monitored to ensure that it reaches the destination. I talk more
about reliable and unreliable protocols in the "Transport layer protocols"
section later in this chapter.

✦ **Internet:** Responsible for routing and logical addressing, just as the
network layer of the OSI model is responsible for logical addressing and
routing.

✦ **Network access:** Responsible for tasks such as physical addressing and
the physical aspects of the network, including placing the bits on the
wire.

Data encapsulation

Like the OSI model, as the information flows down the TCP/IP Internet model there is header information for each layer that is added to the packet — appending header information at each layer is known as *encapsulation*. For example, looking at Figure 4-6, you can see that when information travels from the sending system it is first created by the application and then passed down to the transport layer. At the transport layer, a protocol is selected for delivery, and then the transport layer information is appended to the data as a header — the transport layer header. The data is then passed down to the Internet layer.

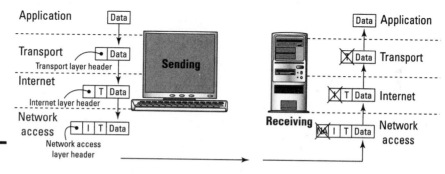

Figure 4-6:
Header information is added to the data at each layer.

Legend

| T = Transport layer header |
| I = Internet layer header |
| NA = Network access layer |

The Internet protocol header is then added to the packet (typically containing the source and destination IP addresses) and the information is then passed down to the network access layer, where network access layer information, such as the MAC address, is placed in a header and appended to the packet.

The packet is then sent on to the destination, and as the information is passed through the layers on the receiving system, the appropriate header is stripped off and read. For example, when looking at Figure 4-6, you see that at the Internet layer on the receiving system the system strips off the Internet layer header and reads the header (in this case, the destination IP address, to verify that the packet is destined for the system).

The term for the process of adding header information at each layer is called *encapsulation* — be sure to be familiar with this term for your exam!

Application layer protocols

The *application layer* is responsible for initiating the request — or servicing the request, depending on whether you look at it from the sending or receiving system's point of view. There are many different application layer protocols in the TCP/IP protocol suite, and chances are you have used many of the different protocols in your day-to-day activities.

The following is a listing of popular application layer protocols used in the TCP/IP protocol suite:

✦ **HTTP:** The *Hypertext Transfer Protocol* (HTTP) is responsible for delivering Web pages from the Web server to the Web browser. Do not confuse HTTP with HTML; HTML is the language used to create the page while HTTP is the protocol that delivers the page to the client.

✦ **HTTPS:** The *Hypertext Transfer Protocol Secure* (HTTPS) is responsible for delivering Web traffic between the Web client and Web server in an encrypted format.

✦ **Telnet:** Telnet is an application protocol that is responsible for allowing you to remotely run an application that resides on a Telnet server. For example, you can Telnet into a Cisco router from across the Internet and administer the router as if you were sitting at it.

✦ **FTP:** The *File Transfer Protocol* (FTP) is an application protocol that allows you to connect to an FTP server and download files from that server.

✦ **SMTP:** The *Simple Mail Transfer Protocol* (SMTP) is the Internet protocol for sending an e-mail message. Your computer at home sends an e-mail message out on the Internet using SMTP. Here's how this works: Your e-mail software connects to your Internet service provider's SMTP server and then sends the message. When your ISP's mail server receives the message, it sends the message to the SMTP server of the person you are sending the mail message to. That SMTP server then deposits the e-mail in the user's mailbox until the message is downloaded.

✦ **POP3:** *Post Office Protocol version 3* (POP3) is the Internet protocol for reading, or downloading, e-mail. For example, in order for you to read your personal e-mail from your ISP, your ISP installs POP3 on the e-mail server that holds your e-mail. You then use your e-mail software (POP3 client) which connects to that mail server and downloads the e-mail.

✦ **IMAP4:** *Internet Message Access Protocol 4* (IMAP4) is another example of an Internet protocol used to read e-mail over the Internet. IMAP4 has additional features beyond what POP3 offers, such as being able to filter messages that are downloaded and having a copy of the messages left on the server with a synchronized copy stored on the client. IMAP4 also supports more folders than the typical inbox, outbox, sent items, and deleted items.

✦ **SNMP:** The *Simple Network Management Protocol* (SNMP) is a protocol used to remotely manage a network device over a TCP/IP network, as long as that device has SNMP running.

✦ **LDAP:** The *Lightweight Directory Access Protocol* (LDAP) is an industry standard protocol for accessing a network directory that contains objects such as user accounts, printers, or folders on the network. This protocol is typically used to search a directory listing of objects across a TCP/IP network.

✦ **NTP:** The *Network Time Protocol* (NTP) is an industry standard protocol for synchronizing time on systems across a TCP/IP network or the Internet.

It is important to understand that when an application initiates the request on the sending system, the application request travels down the model to the transport layer, where a transport layer protocol is selected by the application, and then onto the Internet layer where an Internet layer protocol is selected. The information is then passed on to the network access layer, which is the physical aspect of the network. Remember that at each of the layers the information passes through, data encapsulation occurs where specific header information that relates to that layer is appended to the packet. (Refer to Figure 4-6.)

Transport layer protocols

The *transport layer* is responsible for reliable and unreliable delivery. As you read earlier in this chapter, *reliable delivery* means that when information is sent from one system to another, a tracking mechanism verifies that the information has reached the destination. If the information does not reach the destination, the information is retransmitted.

Unreliable delivery means that there is no tracking of the information to ensure it reaches the destination. The concept of unreliable communication is that you simply send the information and hope it reaches the destination. Unreliable delivery exists because of its performance — because it doesn't track data sent, unreliable delivery is more efficient, as it has less overhead.

In the TCP/IP protocol suite, the *Transmission Control Protocol* (TCP) is the reliable protocol and *User Datagram Protocol* (UDP) is the unreliable protocol in the protocol suite.

Another term for reliable delivery is *connection-oriented communication,* and another term for unreliable delivery is *connectionless communication.* TCP is the connection-oriented protocol in TCP/IP, while UDP is the connectionless communication protocol!

Transmission Control Protocol (TCP)

The TCP transport layer protocol is responsible for reliable delivery, and it accomplishes this by using sequence and acknowledgement numbers. A *sequence number* is a large number assigned to the packet being sent. When the receiving system receives the packet, the receiving system sends back an acknowledgement that uses the original sequence number as an acknowledgement. This is TCP's way of saying, "I received packet number 1065438." (See Figure 4-7.)

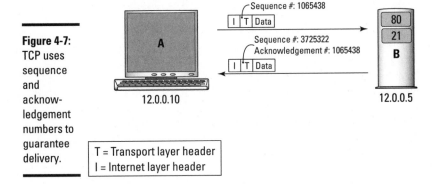

Figure 4-7: TCP uses sequence and acknowledgement numbers to guarantee delivery.

In Figure 4-7, notice that ComputerA is sending data to ComputerB, and the transport layer header has a field for the sequence number. In this example, the sequence number assigned to the packet is 1065438. Also notice that when ComputerB sends a reply, the transport layer header contains an *acknowledgement number* field, which is the packet that the system is confirming has been received. It is also important to note that when ComputerB sends the reply with the acknowledgement number, the reply message is its own packet that requires its own sequence number. Also note that the two sequence numbers are totally unrelated — ComputerA has a set of sequence numbers it uses for each packet sent by that system, and ComputerB has its own set of sequence numbers that it uses.

TCP ports

The TCP protocol uses port numbers to identify the different applications that run on a system, and as a result, each application must have a unique port number. (See Figure 4-8.) Examples of applications that use port numbers are Web servers, FTP servers, or any TCP/IP application, including client software such as your Web browser.

Introduction
to TCP/IP

Figure 4-8:
Source and
destination
ports
numbers
are used to
identify the
applications
that are
sending and
receiving
the
information.

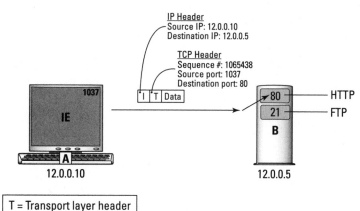

IP Header
Source IP: 12.0.0.10
Destination IP: 12.0.0.5

TCP Header
Sequence #: 1065438
Source port: 1037
Destination port: 80

| I | T | Data |

1037

IE

A

12.0.0.10

80 — HTTP
21 — FTP

B

12.0.0.5

T = Transport layer header
I = Internet layer header

Looking at Figure 4-8, you can see that the IP header contains the source and destination IP address (more on the IP header later in the chapter, in the section "Internet Protocol (IP)"). This information is important because it has to be known where the packet is headed and where it came from. When ComputerB receives the packet, it checks the destination address to verify that it is the intended recipient. Once it verifies that it is the intended recipient, the packet is then passed to the transport layer, where the transport layer header is read. Upon reading the transport layer header, the system knows which port number the packet is destined for, and it sends the packet to the application using that port number. Once the application receives the packet, it reads the request and generates a reply.

In this example, when the reply is sent back, the original source and destination fields are swapped. (See Figure 4-9.) For example, in the reply message, the source IP address is 12.0.0.5, and the destination IP is 12.0.0.10. Likewise, the source port and destination ports are swapped: The new source port is 80 (the Web site), and the new destination port is 1037 (the Web browser on the client). This is because the message (in this case, a Web page) is coming from the Web site and headed to the client's Web browser.

It is important for the CCENT certification exam that you memorize some of the popular TCP port numbers that applications use. Table 4-4 displays a listing of the popular port numbers that you need to be familiar with.

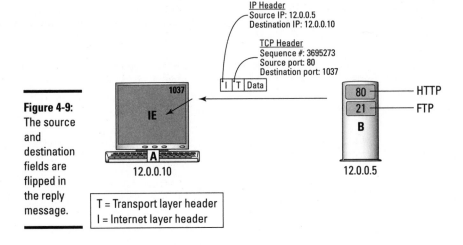

Figure 4-9:
The source and destination fields are flipped in the reply message.

T = Transport layer header
I = Internet layer header

Table 4-4		Popular TCP Ports
Port Number	*Protocol*	*Purpose*
21	TCP	The FTP control port. FTP commands sent from the FTP client to the FTP server use this port.
20	TCP	The FTP data port. You download data from the FTP server through this port.
23	TCP	Telnet uses this port.
25	TCP	SMTP uses this port.
53	TCP	DNS uses this port. *DNS zone transfers,* which happen when the DNS data is copied from one server to another, occur through TCP 53.
80	TCP	HTTP uses this port for what is known as unsecured Web traffic.
110	TCP	POP3 uses this port.
143	TCP	IMAP4 uses this port.
443	TCP	Web sites that have the traffic encrypted (HTTPS) use this port.

Three-way handshake

We know that TCP uses sequence and acknowledgement numbers in order to guarantee delivery. (See the previous section for more on TCP.) It is important to note that the sequence numbers assigned to each packet do not start at the value of 1 for each conversation. The initial sequence number (the sequence number in the first packet sent) is a randomly generated number and communicated to the other system via the three-way handshake.

The *three-way handshake* is a three-step process that creates a TCP connection. After the connection is established with the three-way handshake, the data between the client and server is then exchanged, with each packet having a sequence number, and each packet needing to be acknowledged.

Figure 4-10 displays the three-way handshake. The first step in the three-way handshake is known as the *synchronization (SYN) phase*. In this phase, the client is sending the initial sequence number to the server. In the second phase of the three-way handshake, the server replies by acknowledging (ACK) that it has received the SYN message, but at the same time communicates its initial sequence number to the client — this is why the second phase is called the *ACK/SYN phase*. The final phase of the three-way handshake is the client acknowledging that it has received the server's ACK/SYN message by sending a final acknowledgement message — this in known as the *ACK phase*.

Figure 4-10:
The three phases of the TCP three-way handshake.

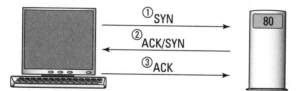

Once the three-way handshake occurs, the data is exchanged between the two systems involved in the dialog. After the data is exchanged, one of the systems decides that it wants to end the conversation, so it sends a signal to the other system indicating that it is done with the conversation. This signal is sent by sending a finish message (FIN) to the system. For example, ComputerA sends a FIN message to ComputerB to let it know that it is ready to end the conversation. (See Figure 4-11.)

Figure 4-11:
Disconnecting from a TCP session involves four steps.

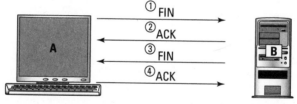

Once ComputerB receives the FIN message, it sends an acknowledgement that it has received the FIN message and, then, in the third step, sends its own FIN message. This is similar to talking on the phone; when someone says, "goodbye," you respond with "goodbye."

After ComputerB sends its FIN message in the third step, the fourth step to end a TCP conversation is a final message sent by ComputerA to acknowledge that the previous message (the FIN) has been received.

TCP flags

In the previous section, you see how the three-way handshake that starts a TCP connection and the four-phase process that ends the TCP connection are very important processes in the dialog, and the packets involved are very special types of packets. In order to identify these special types of packets, TCP has what are called TCP flags. A *TCP flag* is an indicator in the packet (actually, it is a bit) that can be turned on or off to identify that type of packet. For example, if a system acknowledges that a previous packet has been received, it then sends a packet with the ACK bit turned on. (It has a 1 value.)

Table 4-5 is a listing of popular TCP flags that you need to be familiar with for the CCENT certification exam.

Table 4-5	TCP Flags
Flag	**Purpose**
ACK	The ACK bit is set on any packet that is acknowledging a previous packet.
SYN	The SYN bit is set on a packet that is in the first or second phase of the three-way handshake.
FIN	The FIN flag is set when a system is trying to say goodbye to another system. This is how TCP applications end a conversation politely.
RST	An application can end a conversation impolitely by simply dropping the connection with the reset flag (RST).
PSH	The push flag (PSH) is used to force information on a system.
URG	The urgent flag (URG) is how a TCP application flags a piece of information as highly important.

The TCP header

You have been reading that the TCP protocol is used for reliable delivery and places information such as source and destination ports in the header of the packet — which is actually known as the *TCP header* in this case.

There are a number of pieces of information (called *fields*) that are stored in the TCP header, so I want to take a few minutes to outline the TCP header. Figure 4-12 displays the fields that exist in the TCP header, with each row in the header being a total of 32 bits in length.

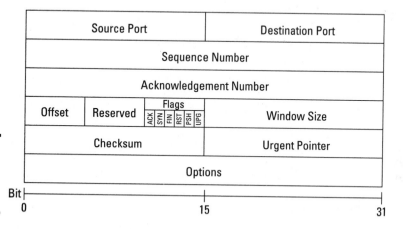

Figure 4-12:
Fields found
in the TCP
header.

The following is a quick description of the important fields in the TCP header:

✦ **Source Port (16 bits):** The port number used by the application sending the information.

✦ **Destination Port (16 bits):** The port number of the application that is to receive the information on the destination system.

✦ **Sequence Number (32 bits):** The number assigned to this packet.

✦ **Acknowledgement Number (32 bits):** A packet number that this packet is acknowledging.

✦ **Offset (4 bits):** Specifies where the data begins.

✦ **Reserved (6 bits):** This field is always set to 0 and is for future use.

✦ **Flags (6 bits):** This is where the bits for ACK, SYN, FIN, RST, PSH, and URG are stored.

✦ **Window Size (16 bits):** The amount of information that can be sent before an acknowledgement is received.

✦ **Checksum (16 bits):** A checksum field that is used to verify the integrity of the TCP header.

✦ **Urgent Pointer (16 bits):** The urgent pointer is used if the URG flag is set and points to the last piece of data that is considered urgent.

+ **Options (variable length):** Any additional options that need to be specified in the TCP header.

For the CCENT certification exam, be sure to know about the source port, destination port, sequence number, acknowledgement number, and flags found in the TCP header.

User Datagram Protocol (UDP)

The *User Datagram Protocol* (UDP) is the connectionless transport layer protocol in the TCP/IP protocol suite. Because the UDP protocol is connectionless, or *unreliable,* it has no three-way handshake to start a conversation, and no sequence and acknowledgement numbers — because it doesn't have a tracking mechanism to ensure delivery.

UDP is a very simple protocol with less overhead than TCP, so if an application developer wants a network application to perform quickly and he does not care if data is lost (or is willing to make delivery verification part of the application layer) he uses the UDP protocol instead of TCP. UDP is the protocol of choice when sending small bits of information such as DNS lookups or DHCP traffic where you do not want to have the overhead of establishing a session when data needs to be delivered.

Due to the simplicity of the UDP protocol, the UDP header is much smaller and more basic than the TCP header. Figure 4-13 displays the UDP header and identifies the fields that exist in the UDP header.

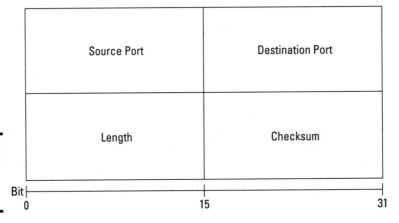

Figure 4-13: Fields found in the UDP header.

It is important to understand that UDP is like TCP in the sense that it uses source and destination ports to identify the application sending the information, and the application on the destination system that is to receive the information.

The following is a quick description of the fields that exist in the UDP header:

+ **Source Port (16 bits):** The port number of the application sending the information.

+ **Destination Port (16 bits):** The port number of the application on the destination system that is to receive the information.

+ **Length (16 bits):** The length of the UDP header in bytes.

+ **Checksum (16 bits):** Verifies the integrity of the UDP header.

Most applications today use TCP as the transport layer protocol because they want to guarantee that the information reaches the destination, but here are a few examples of applications that use UDP:

+ **DHCP:** When a system's or device's TCP/IP settings are retrieved from a DHCP server, the traffic uses UDP as the transport layer protocol. There are two ports used; when packets are sent from the DHCP server to the DHCP client, they use UDP port 67, while packets from the client to the DHCP server use UDP port 68.

+ **DNS:** UDP is used when a client queries a DNS server for the IP address of an FQDN. In this example, the packet is destined for UDP port 53.

+ **SNMP:** The SNMP protocol uses UDP port 161.

+ **Streaming and multicast applications:** Most streaming applications, including Voice Over IP (VoIP), and multicast applications use UDP as the transport layer protocol to deliver the data.

For the CCENT certification exam, you need to be able to identify the UDP header and also know examples of applications that use UDP, such as DHCP, DNS, and SNMP. Be sure to know that DHCP uses ports 67/68 and DNS uses port 53.

Internet layer protocols

After a transport layer protocol (TCP or UDP) is selected for the traffic, the data is passed down to the Internet layer, where an Internet layer protocol is selected. A number of different protocols run at the Internet layer, three of which you need to be familiar with for the CCENT certification exam. The sections that follow tell you about those three layers (IP, ICMP, and ARP).

Internet Protocol (IP)

The *Internet Protocol* (IP) protocol is responsible for routing and logical addressing. I talk about routing later in Book III, but the concept of routing is that the IP protocol looks at the destination address in a packet and then decides where to send the packet.

Logical addressing deals with all the topics discussed in this chapter, such as IP addressing, and how a system mathematically calculates whether the destination system resides on the same network (using the subnet mask) — this is all handled by the IP protocol running on the device or system.

When the data is passed down from the transport layer to the Internet layer, the IP header — containing IP-related information such as the source IP address and the destination IP address — is added. You can see in Figure 4-14 that more fields than just the source and destination IP address are stored in the IP header.

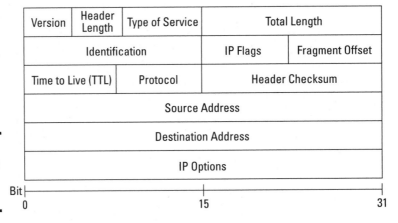

Figure 4-14: Fields found in the IP header.

The following is a description of each field found in the IP header:

✦ **Version (4 bits):** The version of IP being used, either 4 or 6. The CCENT certification exam is focused on IP version 4.

✦ **Header Length (4 bits):** Specifies the size of the header.

✦ **Type of Service (8 bits):** Specifies how a system should handle the packet. The bits in this field indicate certain communication settings. For example, *low delay* means that the information should be dealt with right away.

✦ **Total Length (16 bits):** Specifies the size of the packet, including the header and data portion.

✦ **Identification (16 bits):** The packet can be broken into smaller chunks called *fragments* due to the fact that the network can send only so much data at one time — known as the *maximum transmission unit* (MTU). This field can be used to uniquely identify the fragment.

✦ **IP Flags (3 bits):** There are three IP flags; the first is the reserved bit, which is always set to zero. The second is the *Don't Fragment* (DF) bit, which means that this data is not allowed to be fragmented. The final bit is a flag that states there are *More Fragments* (MF) — meaning that the data has been broken down into smaller fragments and the system can expect more pieces to come.

✦ **Fragment Offset (13 bits):** The fragment offset is a value specifying which piece of the puzzle this fragment is. This field is used to specify the order that the packet fragments are to be assembled in on the receiving end.

✦ **Time To Live (8 bits):** The *Time to Live* (TTL) field specifies how many routers this packet can pass through before the packet is expired. Each time the packet hits a router, the TTL is decremented by 1. Windows operating systems set the initial value of a TTL to 128, while most Linux operating systems set the TTL to 64.

✦ **Protocol (8 bits):** This field specifies other protocols that are to be used with this data. For example, this field specifies whether TCP or UDP should be used as the transport layer protocol.

✦ **Header Checksum (16 bits):** A checksum field that is used to verify the integrity of the IP header.

✦ **Source Address (32 bits):** The IP address of the system that is sending the data. The receiving system sends a reply to the address specified here.

✦ **Destination Address (32 bits):** The IP address of the system where this packet is delivered.

✦ **IP Options (Variable):** Any additional information that an application may want to specify in the IP header.

Internet Control Message Protocol (ICMP)

Another example of a protocol in the TCP/IP protocol suite that runs at the Internet layer is the *Internet Control Message Protocol* (ICMP). ICMP is the error- and status-reporting protocol built into TCP/IP. For example, when you ping a system, you receive status information indicating whether the system you have pinged is up and running. ("Request timed out" in the code that follows indicating that the system cannot be found.) For more information on troubleshooting commands such as ping, check out Book III, Chapter 5.

```
H:\>ping 192.168.1.50
Pinging 192.168.1.50 with 32 bytes of data:
Request timed out.
Request timed out.
Request timed out.
Request timed out.
Ping statistics for 192.168.1.50:
 Packets: Sent = 4, Received = 0, Lost = 4 (100% loss),
H:\>
```

The `ping` command is an example of a program that uses ICMP as the underlying protocol to display this status information. It is important to understand that there are different types of ICMP messages. Looking at Figure 4-15, when you ping a system, your system sends what is called an ICMP echo request message. If the system you are pinging is available, it sends an ICMP echo reply message.

Figure 4-15: ICMP is the underlying protocol used by the ping command.

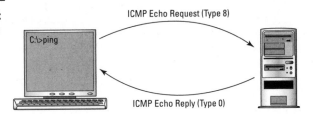

Notice in the figure that the echo request message is known as *type 8,* while the echo reply message is known as *type 0.* The ICMP type indicates each different status or error message with ICMP; be sure to be familiar with ICMP types 8 and 0 for the CCENT certification exam. Some of the popular ICMP types are shown in Table 4-6.

Table 4-6	Popular ICMP Types	
Type	*Code*	*Purpose*
0 – Echo Reply	0	Echo reply
3 – Destination Unreachable	0	Destination network unreachable
	1	Destination host unreachable
	2	Destination protocol unreachable
	3	Destination port unreachable
8 – Echo Request	0	Echo request
11 – Time Exceeded	0	TTL expired in transit
	1	Fragment reassembly time exceeded

You will notice in Table 4-6 that I have added a code column; the purpose of the code is that some of the different types need more of a breakdown explaining in more detail why a message is occurring. For example, ICMP type 3 is destination unreachable, but there are many reasons why a destination may be unreachable. So type 3 has many codes — type 3, code 0 means the destination is unreachable because the entire network is not available, while type 3, code 3 means that the destination is not available because the port you are trying to communicate with is unreachable.

Some of the ICMP types do not have multiple reasons why the message is occurring, so you do not see multiple codes. For example, ICMP type 8 is an echo request message, and because an echo request has only one code, the code is always zero. The following code displays what the `ping` command shows when an echo reply message is received from a `ping` command. (This means that the system you are communicating with is up and running.) Notice that you do not see any indication that ping is using ICMP as the underlying protocol or the ICMP types being used. If you were to monitor the traffic with a traffic analyzer you would see the ICMP protocol and types.

```
H:\>ping 192.168.1.3
Pinging 192.168.1.3 with 32 bytes of data:
Reply from 192.168.1.3: bytes=32 time<1ms TTL=128
Reply from 192.168.1.3: bytes=32 time<1ms TTL=128
Reply from 192.168.1.3: bytes=32 time<1ms TTL=128
Reply from 192.168.1.3: bytes=32 time<1ms TTL=128
Ping statistics for 192.168.1.3:
 Packets: Sent = 4, Received = 4, Lost = 0 (0% loss),
Approximate round trip times in milli-seconds:
 Minimum = 0ms, Maximum = 0ms, Average = 0ms
H:\>
```

ICMP is a very simple protocol that has only a few fields in its header (see Figure 4-16), but keep in mind that ICMP traffic is placed in an IP packet and uses IP for delivery of the data.

Figure 4-16:
The ICMP header.

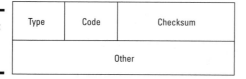

In Figure 4-16, notice that the major fields in the ICMP header are the Type field (8 bits) and the Code field (8 bits), which are used to indicate the type of ICMP message. For example, if we were looking at an echo request packet, the Type field would have an 8 in it, while the Code field would have a 0 in it. There is also a 16-bit Checksum field in the header, which verifies the integrity of the header and ensures it has not been altered in transit. The field labeled *other* is also known as the *data field* and contains any additional data to go with the ICMP message. For example, the ICMP echo request message that is generated by a Microsoft operating system places part of the alphabet in the data (other) field.

For the CCENT certification exam, remember that ICMP is an Internet layer protocol that is responsible for error reporting and status information. Also be familiar with ICMP type 8 and ICMP type 0.

Address Resolution Protocol (ARP)

The final Internet layer protocol to discuss is the *Address Resolution Protocol,* also known as *ARP,* which is a very important protocol because it is responsible for converting the logical address we are trying to communicate with to the physical address.

Let's look at an example. In Figure 4-17, you are sitting at ComputerA, and you want to communicate with ComputerB. Normally, when you communicate with a system you use the IP address of that system (the logical address). When you try to send data to that system, the first thing that needs to happen is your system needs to figure out the MAC address of ComputerB (the physical address) because at the lowest level all communication is sent using the physical address.

At this point, ComputerA sends an ARP message out on the network. The *ARP message* is a packet destined for all systems (a broadcast message). This message is known as an *ARP request,* and it says, "Whoever has the 12.0.0.6 IP address, please send me your MAC address." This message is received by all systems on the network, but only ComputerB replies because that is the IP address of ComputerB. ComputerB replies by sending its MAC address in what is known as the *ARP reply* message.

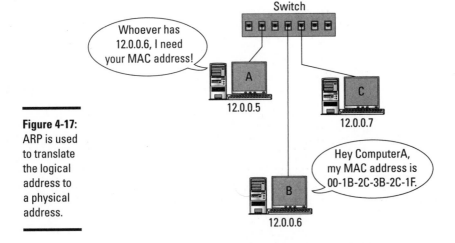

Figure 4-17:
ARP is used to translate the logical address to a physical address.

It is important to note that when ComputerA receives the ARP reply, it then stores the IP address of ComputerB and the MAC address for that system in an area of memory known as the *ARP cache.* The ARP cache is then used in the future to prevent future broadcast messages for the same address, as it stores the address already.

Another important note to make is that when a system on your network communicates with a system on another network or the Internet, your system will ARP the default gateway (the router) because that is who your system sends the data to so that it can be delivered off the network.

Once your system ARPs the router on your network, your router then ARPs the next router that the information is passed on to. It is important to note that any system or device running TCP/IP has an ARP cache, and if any destination IP address does not exist in the ARP cache, the device will ARP the destination IP address.

Now that you understand the core protocols that run at the Internet layer, let's take a look at the four-layer TCP/IP model one more time and place the different protocols discussed in this chapter at the appropriate layers. (See Figure 4-18.)

Figure 4-18:
The core protocols in the TCP/IP Internet model.

Application
HTTP, SMTP, DNS, FTP, POP3

Transport
TCP   UDP

Internet
IP   ICMP   ARP

Network access

Remember for the CCENT certification exam that ARP is responsible for converting the logical address to the physical address. Also remember that the ARP request is a broadcast message that has a destination MAC address of FF-FF-FF-FF-FF-FF.

Chapter Summary

This chapter discusses the basics of TCP/IP, and this is something you will need to master for the CCENT certification exam. The following lists some key points to remember about TCP/IP:

✦ An *IP address* is a 32-bit value that uniquely identifies the system.

✦ The IP address is made up of four octets that are divided into two parts — the network ID and the host ID.

✦ The octets that correspond to the network ID are determined by the subnet mask.

✦ There are three major classes of IP address: class A, class B, and class C.

✦ Class A networks have a default subnet mask of 255.0.0.0 and support 16,777,214 hosts on the network.

✦ Class B networks have a default subnet mask of 255.255.0.0 and support 65,534 hosts on the network.

✦ Class C networks have a default subnet mask of 255.255.255.0 and support 254 hosts on the network.

✦ Some IP addresses do not allow you to assign to systems or devices on the network; they are the network ID and the broadcast address, and you are not allowed to use an IP address that has 127 in the first octet, as it is reserved for loopback testing.

✦ There are four layers in the TCP/IP Internet model: the application layer, the transport layer, the Internet layer, and the network access layer.

✦ At the transport layer, TCP is responsible for reliable, connection-oriented communication, while UDP is responsible for unreliable, connectionless communication.

✦ At the Internet layer, IP is responsible for logical addressing and routing, ICMP is responsible for error and status reporting, and ARP is responsible for converting the logical address to the physical address.

Lab Exercises

This chapter introduces you to a number of concepts relating to IP addressing and the protocols that exist in the TCP/IP protocol suite. The following labs help you digest this information and put the concepts into practice.

Lab 4-1: Identifying address classes

In this lab, you practice identifying the different address classes by filling-in the table that follows:

IP Address	Address Class	Subnet Mask
12.34.56.7	Class A	255.0.0.0
129.45.76.200		
38.99.87.56		
131.107.2.200		
195.34.56.78		
190.52.98.74		
222.23.38.10		
10.24.58.100		
192.168.0.100		

Lab 4-2: Converting decimal to binary

Before you jump into the next chapter (which discusses subnetting), it is important to practice converting decimal to binary. In this lab, practice converting decimal to binary by filling in the table below:

Decimal	Binary
156	
87	
205	
131.107.2.200	
195.34.56.78	
190.52.98.74	
222.23.38.10	
10.24.58.100	
192.168.0.100	

Lab 4-3: Converting binary to decimal

In this lab, you practice converting binary values to decimal. Again, this is important practice before moving into the subnetting discussion in the next chapter. Take some time to fill out the table below:

Binary	Decimal
00101010	
10101010	
10010010	
01011011	
01011010.01011010.11010101.11111110	
00001010.00000000.00101011.00000001	
11111111.11111111.11000000.00000000	
01111111.00101010.11010101.00101011	
00110011	

Lab 4-4: Identifying invalid addresses

A very important practice is to take some time to look at different IP addresses and decide if the addresses are valid to assign to a system, or a device on the network, such as a router. An invalid address is an address that is illegal to assign to a system. Fill in the following table by identifying if the address is valid and, if not, specify why it is not valid.

IP Address	Valid?	Why not?
216.83.11.255		
10.78.34.5		
14.56.10.0		
127.45.67.10		
100.15.78.255		
192.168.45.10		
131.107.258.10		
187.34.10.20		
222.45.67.0		

Lab 4-5: Match the protocol

In this lab, you practice identifying the different TCP/IP protocols by matching the protocol to its definition.

Protocol	Definition
___ IP	**A.** An application layer protocol used to send e-mail
___ UDP	**B.** The connection-oriented protocol in the TCP/IP protocol suite
___ FTP	**C.** The protocol within TCP/IP that is responsible for logical addressing and routing
___ SMTP	**D.** An application layer protocol that is responsible for transferring Web pages to the client
___ ARP	**E.** The error reporting protocol in TCP/IP
___ TCP	**F.** The transport layer protocol responsible for connectionless communication
___ ICMP	**G.** Responsible for converting the logical address to a physical address
___ HTTP	**H.** The application layer protocol that is responsible for transferring files

Prep Test

1 Which of the following are considered class A addresses? (Select all that apply.)

A ❑ 129.45.10.15
B ❑ 10.35.87.5
C ❑ 131.15.10.12
D ❑ 192.156.8.34
E ❑ 121.59.87.32
F ❑ 210.45.10.112

2 What ICMP type is used in an echo request message?

A ○ 0
B ○ 8
C ○ 3
D ○ 11

3 Which of the following is considered a class A private address?

A ○ 24.56.10.12
B ○ 192.168.0.5
C ○ 172.16.45.10
D ○ 10.55.67.99

4 Your system has an IP address of 131.107.45.10. Which of the following systems is on the same network as you?

A ○ 131.56.10.12
B ○ 130.107.45.10
C ○ 131.107.22.15
D ○ 113.107.45.11

5 The ARP request is sent to which of the following layer-2 destination addresses?

A ○ FF-FF-FF-FF-FF-FF
B ○ 192.168.0.255
C ○ 00-FF-00-FF-00-FF
D ○ 00-00-00-00-00-00

6 Which of the following are true statements about TCP ports? (Select all that apply.)

A ❏ FTP uses TCP port 21 and 20
B ❏ FTP uses TCP port 11 and 12
C ❏ HTTP uses TCP port 53
D ❏ HTTP uses TCP port 80
E ❏ SMTP uses TCP port 53
F ❏ SMTP uses TCP port 25

7 What are the three phases of the TCP three-way handshake?

A ○ ACK/SYN, SYN, ACK
B ○ SYN, ACK/SYN, ACK
C ○ ACK/SYN, ACK, SYN
D ○ SYN, ACK, SYN/ACK

8 Which TCP flag is responsible for dropping a connection at any point in time?

A ○ PSH
B ○ FIN
C ○ ACK
D ○ RST

9 Which of the following are true statements about ports? (Select all that apply.)

A ❏ DHCP uses UDP 67/68
B ❏ DHCP uses TCP 67/68
C ❏ SNMP uses UDP 161
D ❏ DNS uses UDP 25
E ❏ SNMP uses TCP 161
F ❏ DNS uses UDP 53

10 Which of the following are fields found in the IP header? (Select all that apply.)

A ❏ Sequence number
B ❏ Destination port
C ❏ Source IP address
D ❏ Type
E ❏ Time to Live
F ❏ SYN flag

Answers

1 **B, E.** Class A addresses have a value in the first octet that ranges between 1 and 127. *See "IP Address Classes."*

2 **B.** The echo request message uses ICMP type 8. *Review "Internet layer protocols."*

3 **D.** The class A private address range is `10.0.0.0` to `10.255.255.255`. *Check out "Public versus private addresses."*

4 **C.** Because `131.107.45.10` is a class B address, it means that the first two octets are the network ID. Anyone with the same first two octets would be on the same network. *Peruse "IP Address Classes."*

5 **A.** The ARP request message is sent to all systems on the network, which means that the destination address is `FF-FF-FF-FF-FF-FF` (the broadcast address). *Take a look at "Address Resolution Protocol (ARP)."*

6 **A,D,F.** It is important to know the popular TCP and UDP ports for the exam. FTP uses TCP 21 and 20, HTTP uses TCP 80, and SMTP uses TCP port 25. *Peek at "Transmission Control Protocol (TCP)."*

7 **B.** The three phases of the TCP three-way handshake are SYN, ACK/SYN, and then ACK. *Look over "Transmission Control Protocol (TCP)."*

8 **D.** The reset flag (RST) is how you can drop a connection at any point in time. The FIN flag is used to finalize a conversation, but it must go through the four steps and doesn't just drop the connection. *Study "Transmission Control Protocol (TCP)."*

9 **A, C, F.** It is important to know the popular TCP and UDP ports for the exam. *Refer to "Transport layer protocols."*

10 **C, E.** The only fields listed that are IP header fields are the source IP address and the TTL. *Examine "Internet layer protocols."*

Chapter 5: Subnetting and VLSM

In This Chapter

✔ Identifying the reasons to subnet

✔ Subnetting a network

✔ Understanding variable-length subnet masks (VLSM)

This chapter is *the* critical chapter to understanding IP addressing, and it will help you prepare for questions related to IP addressing on the CCENT certification exam. This chapter focuses on the concept of subnetting, including why you want to subnet, and how to subnet an address range! A great topic, and an exciting one at that! This chapter also introduces you to variable-length subnet masks (VLSM); a topic you find out more about when you look to your CCNA certification. VLSM is a feature designed to make better use of the addresses when subnetting a network.

The CCENT certification exam heavily tests your knowledge of IP addressing and subnetting, so it is important to make sure that you are very comfortable with this chapter. Not only do you have to read this chapter and do the examples on your own with a pen and paper, but you must practice the math so much that it becomes second nature! The reason is you have a limited amount of time on the exam and doing long calculations for subnetting scenarios will use up too much time on the clock.

Quick Assessment

1 (True/False). IP Subnet Zero is a feature that allows you to use the first and last subnets when subnetting.

2 You can use _____ to create different-size subnets on the network.

3 There are _____ subnetted bits in this address: `192.168.2.0/27`.

Answers

1 *True*. See "IP Subnet Zero."

2 *VLSM*. Review "Understanding Variable-Length Subnet Masks."

3 *Three*. Check out *"Subnetting a class C network."*

Identifying Reasons to Subnet

Subnetting is the concept of dividing your IP address block into multiple smaller IP address blocks. Before I dive into the exciting concepts of subnetting and the brain-numbing calculations (it's actually not that bad) required to subnet network ranges, it is important to focus on why you need to subnet. When teaching subnetting in the classroom, I find that students are so focused on the math that they forget why network designers implement subnetting in the first place. This section is designed to give you the background to understand why you might want to subnet.

For this discussion, let us assume that you have the IP range of 24.0.0.0, which is a class A network range that supports over 16 million addresses. You decide that you want to divide this network into multiple broadcast domains within your office to cut down on the broadcast traffic that goes from one end of the network to the other. You divide the network into two broadcast domains by placing a router (NY-RI) in the middle of the network and connecting two switches to the router, as shown in Figure 5-1.

The labels F0/0 and F0/1 are unique identifiers for each of the Fast Ethernet interfaces on the routers. You find out more about interfaces and their unique IDs in Book II, Chapter 1.

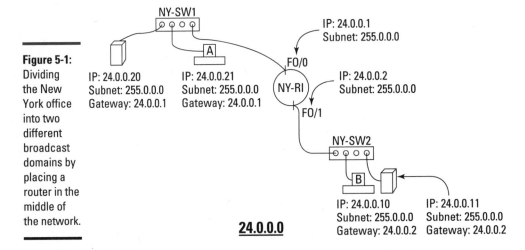

Figure 5-1: Dividing the New York office into two different broadcast domains by placing a router in the middle of the network.

NY-SW1

IP: 24.0.0.20
Subnet: 255.0.0.0
Gateway: 24.0.0.1

IP: 24.0.0.21
Subnet: 255.0.0.0
Gateway: 24.0.0.1

A

F0/0

IP: 24.0.0.1
Subnet: 255.0.0.0

NY-RI

IP: 24.0.0.2
Subnet: 255.0.0.0

F0/1

NY-SW2

B

IP: 24.0.0.10
Subnet: 255.0.0.0
Gateway: 24.0.0.2

IP: 24.0.0.11
Subnet: 255.0.0.0
Gateway: 24.0.0.2

24.0.0.0

After placing the router in the middle of the network, you then connect it to the two network switches, NY-SW1 and NY-SW2. After the switches are connected, the systems are then plugged into the switches and assigned IP addresses within the network range of 24.0.0.0. Each system is assigned a subnet mask of 255.0.0.0, and the default gateway is configured for the router interface closest to the system.

The question to answer is this: After assigning all the IP addresses, subnet masks, and default gateway settings to each of the systems, can ComputerA ping ComputerB (and why or why not)?

The answer to the question is no, ComputerA cannot ping ComputerB. The reason is the IP protocol running on the system believes the computers are on the same network, so the computer never forwards the packet to the router. Why would it? As far as the system is concerned, all IP addresses that start with 24.0.0.0 are on the same network.

Let's take a look at how this works. When ComputerA goes to ping ComputerB, the IP protocol on ComputerA looks at its IP address and subnet mask to determine which octets in the address correspond to the network ID. With a subnet mask of 255.0.0.0, the system determines that the network ID is 24.0.0.0. The system then compares the network ID to the corresponding octet of the system it is trying to communicate with. If the network IDs are the same, the systems believe they are logically on the same network, so there is no need to send the data to the router. (See Figure 5-2.) This is a problem!

Figure 5-2:
The IP
protocol
compares
its network
ID to the
network ID
of another
system to
determine if
the systems
are on
the same
network.

IP Address: 24.0.0.21
Subnet Mask: 255.0.0.0

Computer B
IP Address: 24.0.0.10

n.h.h.h

Same Network?: **Yes**

What you need to do is modify the subnet mask so that the logical address corresponds to the physical network structure, which means that the physical network has two network segments. So you need to divide the logical address into two networks as well. This is the purpose of subnetting — to manipulate the subnet mask of an address so that more bits are allocated to the network ID, which as a result, increases the number of networks. Once you calculate the different networks, you can then assign a network ID to each network segment in the diagram.

Let's get to work!

Understanding ANDing

The term used to describe how the IP protocol compares two addresses against one another to determine if the two addresses are on the same network is *anding,* and it is done at the bit level. Let's look at an example of how anding is performed.

When ComputerA sends data to ComputerB, the IP protocol first performs a mathematical operation on the binary values of the IP address against the binary value of the subnet mask to create a result. Then the IP protocol performs the same mathematical operation on the binary value of ComputerB's IP address against ComputerA's subnet mask to create another result. Once both results are calculated they are compared — and if they are equal the two systems exist on the same network.

As mentioned, the actual mathematical operation is performed at the bit level — meaning that the first bit in the IP address is calculated against the first bit in the subnet mask to create the first bit in the result, then IP moves to the second bit and performs the same operation. The mathematical operation for anding is if the two bits have a one value then a 1 is generated in the result for that bit position. If any other combination of bits are compared (for example 0 and 1, 1 and 0, 0 and 0) then a 0 bit is generated in the result set. Here is an example of how anding looks:

```
ComputerA IP:       11000000.10100000.00000000.00001010
ComputerA Subnet:   11111111.11111111.11111111.00000000
Result:             11000000.10100000.00000000.00000000

ComputerB IP:       11000000.10100000.00000000.00001011
ComputerA Subnet:   11111111.11111111.11111111.00000000
Result:             11000000.10100000.00000000.00000000
```

When looking at the two results, you see they have generated the same answer which means that both systems are part of the same network. This is anding!

Subnetting a Network

There are a number of different subnetting calculators online and a number of different quick ways to subnet. However, I want to make sure that you know how to subnet the long and hard way, as it ensures you understand where all the numbers are coming from. In this section, you find out how to subnet class A, class B, and class C networks before discovering how to subnet the quick way.

Subnetting a class A network

The first example to go over with you is subnetting a class A address. Use the example from Figure 5-1 — you need to subnet the 24.0.0.0 class A address range. Let's assume that you want to divide it into four networks instead of two, though — perhaps for future growth reasons.

Get a few blank pieces of paper and walk through the calculations with me.

The idea behind subnetting is to take some of the host bits in a subnet mask and convert them to network bits (also called *subnet bits*), by turning the bit on. Before you find out how to do that, you first need to determine how many bits to convert from host bits to subnet bits. The formula to figure this out is

$2^{<\text{\# of bits}>}$ = number of subnets

For example, if you are looking for two subnets (also known as *networks*), you use this formula:

2^1 = 2 subnets

This creates two subnets. If you want four subnets, as in my example, the formula of $2^{\text{number of bits}}$ = number of subnets would need to be

2^2 = 4 subnets

For the CCENT certification exam, you need to be able to calculate how many bits are needed for a given number of subnets.

Now that you know to manipulate two bits in the subnet mask to create four subnets, the next step is to write out the starting IP address information. In my example, the network address `24.0.0.0` is the IP you start with and end up manipulating to get the two network IDs. The default subnet mask is `255.0.0.0` for this network address. I personally recommend writing that out on paper as the following:

	Octet 1	Octet 2	Octet 3	Octet 4
IP Address	24	0	0	0
Subnet Mask	255	0	0	0
Subnet Mask (binary)	11111111	00000000	00000000	00000000

Notice that, right now, the focus is the subnet mask because it is responsible for determining the network ID portion of an address. When subnetting, I write out all the binary for the subnet mask, as that will become your work area to calculate the new network addresses for the four new networks! The *work area* is where you are going to do all of the pen work to calculate the addresses in a subnet.

Once you have written out the starting network addresses and have the subnet mask in binary, you can then convert two of the left-most host bits to network bits by changing the bits from zeros to ones.

	Octet 1	Octet 2	Octet 3	Octet 4
IP Address	24	0	0	0
Subnet Mask	255	0	0	0
Subnet Mask (binary)	11111111	**11**000000	00000000	00000000

When you convert host bits from 0s to 1s, they are known as *subnet bits*. You now have three types of bits in the example above. You have the original bits set to 1 (which are known as *network ID bits*) in the subnet mask, you have the *host bits* (which are set to 0) in the subnet mask, and now you have the bits you converted to 1s (known as the *subnet bits*) in order to subnet.

After stealing two of the host bits for subnet bits, you now have fewer hosts available because there are fewer bits assigned to the host ID portion of the IP address — but you now have more networks available. At this point, you should verify the math and calculate how many subnets are available and how many hosts can exist on each subnet. The following formulas are used to calculate the number of subnets and number of hosts on each subnet:

✦ **Number of subnets:** To calculate the number of subnets, take $2^{\text{subnetted bits}}$, which in this example is 2; you can calculate the number of subnets in the example as $2^2 = 4$ subnets.

✦ **Number of hosts per subnet:** To calculate the number of hosts per subnet, the formula is $2^{<\text{\# of bits}>} - 2$. In the example, you can calculate the number of hosts per subnet: $2^{22} = 4{,}194{,}304 - 2 = 4{,}194{,}302$ hosts per subnet! You subtract 2 from the number of hosts because there are two addresses that you cannot use: the network ID for the subnet (all host bits set to 0) and the broadcast address for the subnet (all host bits set to 1).

The CCENT certification exam gives you requirements of how many subnets (or networks) are needed and how many hosts per subnet need to be supported. With this information, you can use the formulas presented here to calculate how many bits are needed as subnet bits in order to answer the questions.

Going back to my subnetting example, you have taken two bits away from the host ID port and are using them as subnet bits to increase the number of subnets that exist on the network. Because you have modified the subnet mask, all four subnets in the example have a new subnet mask. I recommend calculating the subnet mask next. To calculate your new subnet mask, convert the modified subnet mask from binary to decimal, as shown below.

	Octet 1	Octet 2	Octet 3	Octet 4
IP Address	24	0	0	0
Subnet Mask	255	0	0	0
Subnet Mask (binary)	11111111	**11**000000	00000000	00000000
New Subnet Mask	**255**	**192**	0	0

A very popular method of indicating the subnet mask is to use the *Classless Inter-Domain Routing* (CIDR) notation. With the CIDR notation, you simply place a / (forward slash) and then the number of bits that are enabled in the subnet mask. In this example, the CIDR notation for each of the new subnets is /10.

I recommend writing the new subnet mask down, as you will need it later when you fill in the subnetting table. You are almost done with this subnetting example, but before you can say it is complete, you must have the following information about each of the four subnets:

✦ **Network ID:** The network ID is calculated by having all host bits for the subnet set to 0.

✦ **First valid address:** The first valid address is calculated by having all host bits set to 0 except for the host bit on the far-right side — it is enabled by setting it to 1. The bit on the far-right side is known as the *least significant bit* because it has the lowest value associated with it.

✦ **Last valid address:** The last valid address is calculated by having all host bits enabled (set to 1) except for the lease significant bit (the bit on the far-right side) — it takes a value of 0.

✦ **Broadcast address:** The broadcast address is calculated by having all host bits set to 1.

✦ **Subnet mask:** The subnet mask is calculated after converting host bits to subnet bits. You have this value already; it is 255.192.0.0 in this example.

In order to calculate each of these pieces of information for the four subnets, you need to calculate all of the possible on/off states that the two subnet bits could create. The following is a listing of all the on/off states that the two bits can create:

✦ **00:** Both bits are off.

✦ **01:** The far-right bit is on, but the left bit is off.

✦ **10:** The far-right bit is off, but the left bit is on.

✦ **11:** Both bits are on.

Each of these combinations will eventually work out to be the four new subnets. (I know that seems weird, but hang in there.) What I would do next is write out the original network ID before it is subnetted, and then write out your new subnet mask below it in binary. The subnet mask is your work area! Next, list the on/off combinations that the two subnet bits create in the second octet. After doing that, finally place the host bits in each octet with each host bit being off (set to 0).

	Octet 1	Octet 2	Octet 3	Octet 4
Original IP Address	24	0	0	0
New Subnet Mask (binary)	11111111	**11**000000	00000000	00000000
		00000000	00000000	00000000
		01000000	00000000	00000000
		10000000	00000000	00000000
		11000000	00000000	00000000

On paper, you should have a chart like the one here. Notice that I do not have anything filled into the first octet for each of the entries. This is because you always use the original network ID when subnetting — it is the octets after the original value that you manipulate. Just so you do not forget that the first octet has a 24 in it, I recommend listing the 24 in each of the octets as follows:

	Octet 1	Octet 2	Octet 3	Octet 4	Decimal Value
Original IP Address	24	0	0	0	
New Subnet Mask (binary)	11111111	**11**000000	00000000	00000000	
Subnet #1	24	**00**000000	00000000	00000000	
Subnet #2	24	**01**000000	00000000	00000000	
Subnet #3	24	**10**000000	00000000	00000000	
Subnet #4	24	**11**000000	00000000	00000000	

Calculating the network IDs

Now it is time to calculate the network IDs — actually, the network IDs for each of the networks are pretty much already calculated in the work area. To calculate the network ID, set each of the host bits to 0, and then convert all the octets to decimal, as shown in the chart that follows.

	Octet 1	Octet 2	Octet 3	Octet 4	Decimal Value
Original IP Address	24	0	0	0	
New Subnet Mask (binary)	11111111	**11**000000	00000000	00000000	
Subnet #1	24	**00**000000	00000000	00000000	24.0.0.0
Subnet #2	24	**01**000000	00000000	00000000	24.64.0.0
Subnet #3	24	**10**000000	00000000	00000000	24.128.0.0
Subnet #4	24	**11**000000	00000000	00000000	24.192.0.0

To calculate the value of each octet, use the values associated with each bit that you read about in Book I, Chapter 4. For example, the first subnet has a first octet of 24 (you do not need to convert that to decimal, as it was already in decimal format), and the second octet of the first subnet has a binary of 00000000, which is the decimal value of 0. The remaining octets in the first subnet equal 0 as well, making the network ID of the first subnet 24.0.0.0.

Looking at the second subnet, the first octet is again 24, but the second octet has a binary value of 01000000, which equals 64 in decimal. The remaining octets in the second subnet have a decimal value of 0 because no host bits are enabled in those octets. This gives the second subnet a network ID of 24.64.0.0.

Looking at the third subnet, the first octet is 24, while the second octet has a binary value of 10000000, which has a decimal value of 128. The third and fourth octet for the third subnet have a decimal value of 0, as there are no bits enabled. This means that the network ID for the third subnet is 24.128.0.0.

Finally, continue this process with the fourth subnet, which has a first octet of 24, while the binary value of the second octet is 11000000, which equals 192 (128+64). The third and fourth octets have a decimal value of 0, as there are no bits enabled. This means that the fourth subnet has a network ID of 24.192.0.0.

Remember for the CCENT exam that the network ID can be determined by having all host bits in the host ID portion of the address set to 0.

Calculating the first valid address

Now that you have the network ID for each of the subnets, you can calculate the first valid address by enabling the least significant host bit. The following chart displays the results of enabling the least significant host bit, and it calculates it in the decimal format.

	Octet 1	Octet 2	Octet 3	Octet 4	Decimal Value
Original IP Address	24	0	0	0	
New Subnet Mask (binary)	11111111	**11**000000	00000000	00000000	
Subnet #1	24	**00**000000	00000000	00000001	24.0.0.1
Subnet #2	24	**01**000000	00000000	00000001	24.64.0.1
Subnet #3	24	**10**000000	00000000	00000001	24.128.0.1
Subnet #4	24	**11**000000	00000000	00000001	24.192.0.1

Notice in the chart that the least significant host bit is the one on the far-right side. This bit has a decimal value of 1, which makes the first valid address of the first subnet 24.0.0.1. The second subnet has a first valid address of 24.64.0.1, the third subnet has a first valid address of 24.128.0.1, and finally, the fourth subnet has a first valid address of 24.192.0.1.

Remember that after manipulating the bits, you always convert each of the octets to binary in their entirety. I see many people make the mistake of not including the first two bits of the second octet when converting from binary to decimal!

Calculating the broadcast address

The next piece of information to calculate for each of the subnets is the broadcast address. To calculate the broadcast address, you enable each of the host bits by setting them to 1.

	Octet 1	Octet 2	Octet 3	Octet 4	Decimal Value
Original IP Address	24	0	0	0	
New Subnet Mask (binary)	11111111	**11**000000	00000000	00000000	
Subnet #1	24	**00**111111	11111111	11111111	24.63.255.255
Subnet #2	24	**01**111111	11111111	11111111	24.127.255.255
Subnet #3	24	**10**111111	11111111	11111111	24.191.255.255
Subnet #4	24	**11**111111	11111111	11111111	24.255.255.255

The host bits are all the bits past the subnet bits, so I have converted all the host bits to 1. Once you convert the host bits, you then convert each of the octets to decimals to come up with the broadcast address. Once you have the broadcast address calculated for each of the subnets, you can then write the subnet addresses down.

Remember for the CCENT exam that the broadcast address can be calculated by having all bits in the host ID portion of the address set to 1.

Calculating the last valid address

The final piece of information you need to calculate is the last valid address of each subnet. To calculate the last valid address, after calculating the broadcast address, simply turn off the least significant bit, as shown in the table that follows.

	Octet 1	Octet 2	Octet 3	Octet 4	Decimal Value
Original IP Address	24	0	0	0	
New Subnet Mask (binary)	11111111	**11**000000	00000000	00000000	
Subnet #1	24	**00**111111	11111111	1111111**0**	24.63.255.254
Subnet #2	24	**01**111111	11111111	1111111**0**	24.127.255.254
Subnet #3	24	**10**111111	11111111	1111111**0**	24.191.255.254
Subnet #4	24	**11**111111	11111111	1111111**0**	24.255.255.254

The reason you calculate the first valid address and the last valid address is because you can input that information into a DHCP server and have the DHCP server give the valid addresses out to clients on the network. You may also want to know the valid address ranges if you are manually assigning addresses — you do not want to assign an address out of the range because it will cause communication errors.

You are done! You have calculated all relevant information for each of the four subnets in this example. The following summarizes the values for each of the subnets that you have calculated.

	Network ID	First Valid	Broadcast	Last Valid	Subnet Mask
Subnet #1	24.0.0.0	24.0.0.1	24.63.255.255	24.63.255.254	255.192.0.0
Subnet #2	24.64.0.0	24.64.0.1	24.127.255.255	24.127.255.254	255.192.0.0
Subnet #3	24.128.0.0	24.128.0.1	24.191.255.255	24.191.255.254	255.192.0.0
Subnet #4	24.192.0.0	24.192.0.1	24.255.255.255	24.255.255.254	255.192.0.0

With this information, you can now configure the IP addresses on each of the devices in the two subnets of Figure 5-1. To see an example of what to do with this subnetted information, take a look at Figure 5-3 — notice that I am using the first and second subnet, and I will save the third and fourth subnets for networks that the company plans to have in the future.

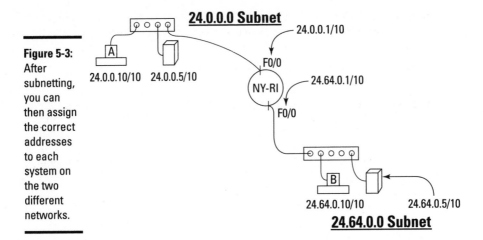

Figure 5-3:
After
subnetting,
you can
then assign
the correct
addresses
to each
system on
the two
different
networks.

Subnetting a class B network

Now that you have walked through an example of subnetting a class A address range, let's walk through an example of subnetting a class B network range.

In this scenario, you have the 131.107.0.0 network range, and it needs to be divided into six subnets. Remember that your first step is to decide how many bits you need to take from the host ID portion of the subnet mask and convert them to subnet bits. Run through the following calculations until you reach six subnets:

$2^{1 \text{ bit}}$ = 2 subnets

$2^{2 \text{ bits}}$ = 4 subnets

$2^{3 \text{ bits}}$ = 8 subnets

In this example, you need only six subnets, but you are going to have to take three bits because using two bits gives you only four subnets. This means you will have two subnets that are unused.

So you need to use three bits! Next, grab a piece of paper and calculate all of the subnets and determine each of the pieces of information listed below for each subnet:

✦ **Network ID:** The network ID is calculated by having all host bits for the subnet set to 0.

✦ **First valid address:** The first valid address is calculated by having all host bits set to 0 except for the host bit on the far-right side — it is enabled by setting it to 1. The bit on the far-right side is known as the *least significant bit* because it has the lowest value associated with it.

✦ **Last valid address:** The last valid address is calculated by having all host bits enabled (set to 1) except for the least significant bit (the bit on the far-right side) — it takes a value of 0.

✦ **Broadcast address:** The broadcast address is calculated by having all host bits set to 1.

✦ **Subnet mask:** The subnet mask is calculated after converting host bits to subnet bits.

Before reading any further, try to calculate everything on your own with the information you gained from the example in the previous section. Once you have calculated everything — or if you get stuck — read on to see the steps I would take to complete this example.

The first thing to do is to write down the original IP address and the subnet mask in binary. Remember that the subnet mask in binary is your work area. After writing out the subnet mask in binary, convert the first three host bits from the left side to subnet bits by setting them to 1.

	Octet 1	Octet 2	Octet 3	Octet 4
Original IP Address	131	107	0	0
New Subnet Mask (binary)	11111111	11111111	**111**00000	00000000

Notice that in this example we are working in the third octet because that is where the host ID portion starts. When you convert the first three host bits to subnet bits, you get the new subnet mask for all eight subnets right off the bat. The new subnet mask is 255.255.224.0.

After that, list all the possible on/off states that three bits could make. Each of these combinations represents one of the subnets of the eight subnets. The following are the on/off states of three bits:

000

001

010

011

100

101

110

111

Next, list the on/off states below your new subnet mask in the work area, as shown in the chart below:

	Octet 1	Octet 2	Octet 3	Octet 4
Original IP Address	131	107	0	0
New Subnet Mask (binary)	11111111	11111111	**111**00000	00000000
Subnet #1			**000**00000	00000000
Subnet #2			**001**00000	00000000
Subnet #3			**010**00000	00000000
Subnet #4			**011**00000	00000000
Subnet #5			**100**00000	00000000
Subnet #6			**101**00000	00000000
Subnet #7			**110**00000	00000000
Subnet #8			**111**00000	00000000

Once you list all the combinations that three bits make (there are eight of them), list the remaining host bits — the five remaining host bits in the third octet and the eight in the fourth octet (as shown in the chart).

I recommend doing two other things to the table before moving on. The first two octets still use the original IP range of 131.107, so I would fill that into the table so you do not forget that every calculation starts with 131.107. Second, I would add a column to the right, showing the decimal value of whatever we are calculating. (See the chart.)

	Octet 1	Octet 2	Octet 3	Octet 4	Decimal Value
Original IP Address	131	107	0	0	
New Subnet Mask (binary)	11111111	11111111	**111**00000	00000000	
Subnet #1	131	107	**000**00000	00000000	
Subnet #2	131	107	**001**00000	00000000	
Subnet #3	131	107	**010**00000	00000000	
Subnet #4	131	107	**011**00000	00000000	
Subnet #5	131	107	**100**00000	00000000	
Subnet #6	131	107	**101**00000	00000000	
Subnet #7	131	107	**110**00000	00000000	
Subnet #8	131	107	**111**00000	00000000	

We can now start calculating all the information required for each subnet, starting with the network ID. Remember that the network ID is all host bits set to 0 (which is actually what you get when you fill out all the host bits with zeros in the chart). The following shows the network IDs in decimal format for each of the subnets — be sure to look at the binary and make sure you agree with my calculation.

	Octet 1	Octet 2	Octet 3	Octet 4	Decimal Value
Original IP Address	131	107	0	0	
New Subnet Mask (binary)	11111111	11111111	**111**00000	00000000	
Subnet #1	131	107	**000**00000	00000000	131.107.0.0
Subnet #2	131	107	**001**00000	00000000	131.107.32.0
Subnet #3	131	107	**010**00000	00000000	131.107.64.0
Subnet #4	131	107	**011**00000	00000000	131.107.96.0
Subnet #5	131	107	**100**00000	00000000	131.107.128.0
Subnet #6	131	107	**101**00000	00000000	131.107.160.0
Subnet #7	131	107	**110**00000	00000000	131.107.192.0
Subnet #8	131	107	**111**00000	00000000	131.107.224.0

After calculating the network ID, you can move on to calculating the first valid address for each of the subnets. To calculate the first valid address, convert the least significant host bit to a 1.

	Octet 1	Octet 2	Octet 3	Octet 4	Decimal Value
Original IP Address	131	107	0	0	
New Subnet Mask (binary)	11111111	11111111	**111**00000	00000000	
Subnet #1	131	107	**000**00000	00000001	131.107.0.1
Subnet #2	131	107	**001**00000	00000001	131.107.32.1
Subnet #3	131	107	**010**00000	00000001	131.107.64.1
Subnet #4	131	107	**011**00000	00000001	131.107.96.1
Subnet #5	131	107	**100**00000	00000001	131.107.128.1
Subnet #6	131	107	**101**00000	00000001	131.107.160.1
Subnet #7	131	107	**110**00000	00000001	131.107.192.1
Subnet #8	131	107	**111**00000	00000001	131.107.224.1

The next thing to calculate is the broadcast address for each of the subnets. Remember that the broadcast address is all host bits set to 1. After converting all host bits to 1, convert the octets from binary to decimal format.

	Octet 1	Octet 2	Octet 3	Octet 4	Decimal Value
Original IP Address	131	107	0	0	
New Subnet Mask (binary)	11111111	11111111	**111**00000	00000000	
Subnet #1	131	107	**000**11111	11111111	131.107.31.255
Subnet #2	131	107	**001**11111	11111111	131.107.63.255
Subnet #3	131	107	**010**11111	11111111	131.107.95.255
Subnet #4	131	107	**011**11111	11111111	131.107.127.255
Subnet #5	131	107	**100**11111	11111111	131.107.159.255
Subnet #6	131	107	**101**11111	11111111	131.107.191.255
Subnet #7	131	107	**110**11111	11111111	131.107.223.255
Subnet #8	131	107	**111**11111	11111111	131.107.255.255

Once you have calculated the broadcast address for each subnet, you can then move on to calculate the last valid address. The last valid address is calculated by having all host bits set to 1 except for the least significant bit — it needs to be turned off by setting it to 0. Remember the least significant bit is the one on the far-right side.

	Octet 1	Octet 2	Octet 3	Octet 4	Decimal Value
Original IP Address	131	107	0	0	
New Subnet Mask (binary)	11111111	11111111	**111**00000	00000000	
Subnet #1	131	107	**000**11111	11111110	131.107.31.254
Subnet #2	131	107	**001**11111	11111110	131.107.63.254
Subnet #3	131	107	**010**11111	11111110	131.107.95.254
Subnet #4	131	107	**011**11111	11111110	131.107.127.254
Subnet #5	131	107	**100**11111	11111110	131.107.159.254
Subnet #6	131	107	**101**11111	11111110	131.107.191.254
Subnet #7	131	107	**110**11111	11111110	131.107.223.254
Subnet #8	131	107	**111**11111	11111110	131.107.255.254

You now have calculated all relevant information for each of the subnets, so the next thing I recommend doing is filling out a final chart — if your work area looks anything like mine, it is now messy from all the changes! The following is the final result of subnetting the 131.107.0.0 into six subnets. (Remember, we actually had to do eight.)

	Network ID	First Valid	Broadcast	Last Valid	Subnet Mask
Subnet #1	131.107.0.0	131.107.0.1	131.107.31.255	131.107.31.254	255.255.224.0
Subnet #2	131.107.32.0	131.107.32.1	131.107.63.255	131.107.63.254	255.255.224.0
Subnet #3	131.107.64.0	131.107.64.1	131.107.95.255	131.107.95.254	255.255.224.0
Subnet #4	131.107.96.0	131.107.96.1	131.107.127.255	131.107.127.254	255.255.224.0
Subnet #5	131.107.128.0	131.107.128.1	131.107.159.255	131.107.159.254	255.255.224.0
Subnet #6	131.107.160.0	131.107.160.1	131.107.191.255	131.107.191.254	255.255.224.0
Subnet #7	131.107.192.0	131.107.192.1	131.107.223.255	131.107.223.254	255.255.224.0
Subnet #8	131.107.224.0	131.107.224.1	131.107.255.255	131.107.255.254	255.255.224.0

Subnetting a class C network

Now let's do one more example, subnetting a class C address. Most people find subnetting a class C address hard because you do not see a lot of the same numbers you see when subnetting class A and class B addresses. For example, with class A and class B addresses, the broadcast addresses end with 255. Bottom line is if you are calculating everything in binary you cannot go wrong.

For the class C example, we need to have the 216.83.11.0 network divided into four networks. In order to subnet the 216.83.11.0 network into four networks, how many bits do we need to steal from the host ID portion of the subnet mask? I hope you came up with the answer of two bits ($2^2 = 4$ subnets)!

So the first step is to write out the original network ID and the subnet mask in binary. Then, take two of the host bits in the subnet mask (starting on the left side) and convert them to subnet bits by changing them to a 1.

	Octet 1	Octet 2	Octet 3	Octet 4
Original IP Address	216	83	11	0
New Subnet Mask (binary)	11111111	11111111	11111111	**11**000000

Now when you convert the subnet mask to decimal, the new subnet mask is 255.255.255.192. This allows you to have 4 subnets (2^2 = 4) with each subnet supporting $2^{6 \text{ host bits}}$ = 64 – 2 illegal addresses (the network ID and broadcast address) = 62 hosts.

After stealing the two bits, you can list all the on/off states that two bits create. You should have the following on/off bit combinations with two bits:

00

01

10

11

After filling out all of the combinations that two bits create and listing them in the chart, I would then fill in the other six bits that are host bits with 0s. You should have something like the following:

	Octet 1	Octet 2	Octet 3	Octet 4	Decimal Value
Original IP Address	216	83	11	0	
New Subnet Mask (binary)	11111111	11111111	11111111	**11**000000	
Subnet #1				**00**000000	
Subnet #2				**01**000000	
Subnet #3				**10**000000	
Subnet #4				**11**000000	

So that you don't forget that you are working in the fourth octet, I recommend filling in the first three octets of each subnet with the beginning network ID that you are subnetting — the 216.83.11.0 network.

	Octet 1	Octet 2	Octet 3	Octet 4	Decimal Value
Original IP Address	216	83	11	0	
New Subnet Mask (binary)	11111111	11111111	11111111	**11**000000	
Subnet #1	216	83	11	**00**000000	
Subnet #2	216	83	11	**01**000000	
Subnet #3	216	83	11	**10**000000	
Subnet #4	216	83	11	**11**000000	

With each of the six host bits set to 0 (you know they are host bits by looking at the subnet mask) in the fourth octet, you have now calculated the first piece of information — the network ID of each subnet. Notice in the chart that follows that the network ID for the first subnet is 216.83.11.0, the second subnet is 216.83.11.64, the third network ID is 216.83.11.128, and finally the fourth network ID is 216.83.11.192. These are strange-looking network IDs, but they are correct, as the host bits are all set to 0 — the rule to calculating the network ID.

	Octet 1	Octet 2	Octet 3	Octet 4	Decimal Value
Original IP Address	216	83	11	0	
New Subnet Mask (binary)	11111111	11111111	11111111	**11**000000	
Subnet #1	216	83	11	**00**000000	216.83.11.0
Subnet #2	216	83	11	**01**000000	216.83.11.64
Subnet #3	216	83	11	**10**000000	216.83.11.128
Subnet #4	216	83	11	**11**000000	216.83.11.192

After calculating the network ID, you are ready to calculate the first valid address. To calculate the first valid address, you simply enable the least significant host bit on the right side. The following chart shows the first valid address of each of those subnets.

	Octet 1	Octet 2	Octet 3	Octet 4	Decimal Value
Original IP Address	216	83	11	0	
New Subnet Mask (binary)	11111111	11111111	11111111	**11**000000	
Subnet #1	216	83	11	**00**000001	216.83.11.1
Subnet #2	216	83	11	**01**000001	216.83.11.65
Subnet #3	216	83	11	**10**000001	216.83.11.129
Subnet #4	216	83	11	**11**000001	216.83.11.193

After calculating the first valid address of each subnet, I recommend calculating the broadcast address, which is all host bits set to 1. The following chart shows all host bits set to 1 and calculates the decimal representation of the broadcast address for each subnet.

	Octet 1	Octet 2	Octet 3	Octet 4	Decimal Value
Original IP Address	216	83	11	0	
New Subnet Mask (binary)	11111111	11111111	11111111	**11**000000	
Subnet #1	216	83	11	**00**111111	216.83.11.63
Subnet #2	216	83	11	**01**111111	216.83.11.127
Subnet #3	216	83	11	**10**111111	216.83.11.191
Subnet #4	216	83	11	**11**111111	216.83.11.255

Now that you have calculated the broadcast address, the final calculation is to turn off the least significant bit to calculate the last valid address for each subnet. The following chart shows the least significant bit being set to 0 and then converts the value to decimal.

	Octet 1	Octet 2	Octet 3	Octet 4	Decimal Value
Original IP Address	216	83	11	0	
New Subnet Mask (binary)	11111111	11111111	11111111	**11**000000	
Subnet #1	216	83	11	**00**111110	216.83.11.62
Subnet #2	216	83	11	**01**111110	216.83.11.126
Subnet #3	216	83	11	**10**111110	216.83.11.190
Subnet #4	216	83	11	**11**111110	216.83.11.254

The following chart summarizes the details of the subnetted 216.83.11.0 address:

	Network ID	First Valid	Broadcast	Last Valid	Subnet Mask
Subnet #1	216.83.11.0	216.83.11.1	216.83.11.63	216.83.11.62	255.255.255.192
Subnet #2	216.83.11.64	216.83.11.65	216.83.11.127	216.83.11.126	255.255.255.192
Subnet #3	216.83.11.128	216.83.11.129	216.83.11.191	216.83.11.190	255.255.255.192
Subnet #4	216.83.11.192	216.83.11.193	216.83.11.255	216.83.11.254	255.255.255.192

Now that you know how to subnet a class A, class B, and class C address the long way, it is time to show you a shortcut.

Keep in mind that I am not a fan of using shortcuts, as I find people never understand the theory behind the actual numbers that way. It is important to know the binary.

Subnetting the quick way

From an exam point of view, you may not have the time to write out all the binary the way that I show you in the example scenarios in this chapter. It is very important to practice the binary calculations with a mix of class A, class B, and class C addresses. Once you have that down, look to speed things up with some shortcuts!

There are many shortcuts you can use to perform subnetting. When you look back at each of the examples you did earlier in this chapter, I want you to notice that the network IDs always increment by the same values in each example. For example, the class C network range you just finished subnetting has the following network IDs:

    216.83.11.0
    216.83.11.64
    216.83.11.128
    216.83.11.192

Notice that each of the values increment by 64. I am going to show you how you can fill out the subnetting details by using the "increment" shortcut!

The first thing to do when subnetting using the increment shortcut method is determine how many bits to subtract from the host ID portion of the subnet mask in order to create the desired number of subnets. I use the same example I used for the class C address scenario in the previous section and say that we want to subnet the 216.83.11.0 network into four subnets. This requires two bits to be converted from host bits to subnet bits:

	Octet 1	Octet 2	Octet 3	Octet 4
Original IP Address	216	83	11	0
New Subnet Mask (binary)	11111111	11111111	11111111	**11**000000

Before we go any further, make note that your new subnet mask is 255.255.255.192.

Now look at the value of the last bit that you stole from the host bits (from left to right), and then look at the value of that bit. In this example, the last bit from left to right that was enabled as a subnet bit has a value of 64. This becomes your increment value! You are home free now because you simply create the list of network IDs, starting with the original network ID and then incrementing by 64 for each one. In this case, the network IDs are

> 216.83.11.0
>
> 216.83.11.64
>
> 216.83.11.128
>
> 216.83.11.192

Once you have the network IDs, you can then fill in the first valid address of each subnet because it is one more than the network ID. The following chart has the first valid address filled in.

	Network ID	First Valid	Broadcast	Last Valid	Subnet Mask
Subnet #1	216.83.11.0	216.83.11.1			255.255.255.192
Subnet #2	216.83.11.64	216.83.11.65			255.255.255.192
Subnet #3	216.83.11.128	216.83.11.129			255.255.255.192
Subnet #4	216.83.11.192	216.83.11.193			255.255.255.192

You now need to calculate the broadcast address of each subnet. This is a little trickier, as the broadcast address is one address less the next network ID. For example, the second subnet has a network ID of 216.83.11.64, so the previous subnet should have a broadcast address one number less, which is 216.83.11.63. The following chart shows the broadcast address filled in for each subnet — notice they are one less than the next subnet's network ID.

	Network ID	First Valid	Broadcast	Last Valid	Subnet Mask
Subnet #1	216.83.11.0	216.83.11.1	216.83.11.63		255.255.255.192
Subnet #2	216.83.11.64	216.83.11.65	216.83.11.127		255.255.255.192
Subnet #3	216.83.11.128	216.83.11.129	216.83.11.191		255.255.255.192
Subnet #4	216.83.11.192	216.83.11.193	216.83.11.255		255.255.255.192

The only issue with calculating the broadcast address this way arises when you get to the last broadcast address — how do you know what it should be? The last broadcast address will be whatever the normal network broadcast address was before you subnetted (all host bits set to 1).

To fill in the last valid address, simply take one number minus the broadcast address, and you have the last valid address for that subnet. The chart now looks like the following:

	Network ID	First Valid	Broadcast	Last Valid	Subnet Mask
Subnet #1	216.83.11.0	216.83.11.1	216.83.11.63	216.83.11.62	255.255.255.192
Subnet #2	216.83.11.64	216.83.11.65	216.83.11.127	216.83.11.126	255.255.255.192
Subnet #3	216.83.11.128	216.83.11.129	216.83.11.191	216.83.11.190	255.255.255.192
Subnet #4	216.83.11.192	216.83.11.193	216.83.11.255	216.83.11.254	255.255.255.192

Because of the CCENT exam's time limit, you need to be able to use the increment shortcut method to figure out your IP address for each subnet — be sure to practice it a lot before taking the exam. It is really easy to make a mistake using the shortcut method, and because each number is based on you figuring out the previous number, making one mistake can throw all your answers off.

IP Subnet Zero

The last topic I want to mention before moving on to variable-length subnet masks is the IP Subnet Zero feature. In the past, a number of different devices could not use the first and last subnet that was calculated. For example, in the previous class C example, you would not be allowed to use subnet #1 and subnet #4. This meant that if you actually had to have four subnets, then you would need to accommodate for that in your calculation and ensure you calculated at least six subnets (which actually meant you needed to calculate eight subnets).

The reason for not supporting the first and last subnets is that the older routing protocols did not send subnet mask information along with the route, so the receiving router would have no way of knowing if the first subnet of 216.83.11.0 is intended as the entire network or a subnetted network.

The `ip subnet-zero` command is used to configure your Cisco router to use the first and last subnets and is a default command as of Cisco IOS 12.0 and greater. (I tell you about Cisco IOS in Book II, Chapter 1.) If the command on the router was `no ip subnet-zero`, you would not be able to use the first and last subnet.

If a question on the CCENT certification exam asks you to subnet and implies that the `no ip subnet-zero` is set, you will have to subtract the first and last subnets from your results. If `no ip subnet-zero` is not mentioned at all, your routers support the first and last subnets.

Understanding Variable-Length Subnet Masks

One of the problems with the subnetting examples in this chapter is that each subnet has the same subnet mask and supports the same number of hosts on the network. Realistically, you may require a different number of hosts on each network. For example, looking at Figure 5-4, you see a network with two routers (NY-R1 and BOS-R1) connected to the WAN link via the serial ports (labeled S0/0). The two routers create three different networks that I call networks A, B, and C.

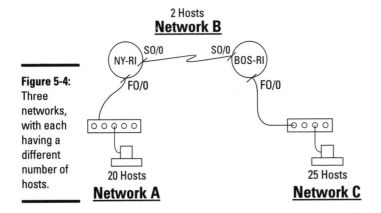

Figure 5-4: Three networks, with each having a different number of hosts.

Notice that Network A requires only 20 hosts (or addresses), Network B requires only two hosts (one address for each serial port on the WAN link), and Network C requires 25 hosts.

Let's assume that we have a class C range such as `216.83.11.0`. If you subnet this network the normal way, you would be required to create four subnets by borrowing two bits from the host ID portion of the subnet mask. This would allow each network to have $2^{6 \text{ host bits}}$ = 64 – 2 illegal addresses = 62 hosts for each subnet. This is a waste of addresses on the WAN link. Also note that you may require more than 62 addresses on one of the subnets — so what can you do? *Variable-length subnet masks* (VLSM) allows you to make better use of your address space by supporting subnets of different sizes. This is possible by allowing you to have different subnet masks for each subnet, which gives you the flexibility to use only two addresses on the WAN link and keep more addresses available for the other networks.

The CCENT certification exam does not test you on VLSM, so I give you only an overview here. I do believe it is important for you to be familiar with the concepts. One of the main reasons I want to make sure you are familiar with VLSM is because when considering different routing protocols, some of the protocols support VLSM and some do not.

You find out more about routing protocols in Book III, Chapter 2, but for now, you need to know that RIPv1 and IGRP do not support VLSM, while RIPv2, EIGRP, and OSPF do support VLSM.

I want to give you a quick walk-through on a shortcut method you can use to implement variable-length subnet masks. I use the class C address `216.83.11.0` and calculate the variable-length subnet masks for each subnet on the network.

The first thing to expose you to is a summary table of different calculations (see Figure 5-5). The benefit of using a table like this is that you only have to do the math once — when you actually create the table. Once the table is created there is no math involved — you simply reference the table!

Figure 5-5:
Creating
a table of
subnet sizes
to aid in the
calculations.

# of Hosts	Subnet Size	CIDR	Subnet Mask
126	128	/25	128
62	64	/26	192
30	32	/27	224
14	16	/28	240
6	8	/29	248
2	4	/30	252

Let's review what I did in Figure 5-5. The first column displays the number of desired hosts on the network. For example, I said that Network A needs 20 hosts. Looking at the table, you have to accept the fact that you have 30 supported hosts on the network as the closest match to the 20-host requirement.

Once you identify that you are going to support 30 hosts, the next column (Subnet Size) shows the actual size of the subnet. In this case, the size is 32. The reason you have 30 hosts (or addresses) available to you but the actual subnet supports 32 is because there are two addresses in the range that you are not allowed to use — the network ID and the broadcast address. The subnet size is also referred to as the *block size* — the block of addresses assigned to that subnet.

The next column shows the CIDR notation for the subnet mask you will use to attain that number of hosts. In the example of 30 hosts, the CIDR notation is /27, meaning that you have taken three bits from the host ID portion of the class C subnet mask. (Remember, there are 24 bits in a class C subnet mask already being used for network ID.) This means that there are 5 host bits remaining, so if you use the formula $2^{5 \text{ host bits}} = 32$, you can verify that the block size is correct.

The final column (Subnet Mask) displays what that subnet mask is in decimal for the fourth octet of this class range. For example, the decimal format for the 30 hosts supported subnet is 255.255.255.224.

The next thing you want to do is create a plotting area for your different subnets to ensure you do not use more addresses than an actual class C address range provides. Figure 5-6 displays a scale you can use to plot these different subnets.

Now, plot Network A in the plotting area. In order to select a range of addresses, you take the subnet size for that network. Remember that Network A has a subnet size of 32, so you take 32 addresses in the plotting area. The hook is you cannot take just any 32 addresses — the range has to start on an address that falls into the increment of your subnet size. For example, the subnet size (or block size) for Network A is 32, so you can start that network block on 0, 32, 64, 96, 128, 160, 192, or 224. If the block size was 16, that would be your increment on starting values — with a block size of 16, you could start on 0, 16, 32, 48, 64, and so on.

So for Network A, take the 32-address block that starts with address 32 and goes to 63, and plot that in the plotting area so that you know those addresses are used up. (See Figure 5-7.) Do not forget that the subnet mask that gave you that address block is 255.255.255.224, or /27 in CIDR.

Figure 5-6:
Create a
plotting area
showing
the range of
addresses
that can be
assigned.
This
ensures
you do not
duplicate
address
assignment.

Figure 5-7 displays Network A added to the plotting area; notice that the actual network ID for this subnet is 216.83.11.32/27.

Figure 5-7:
Plotting Network A on the plotting area.

Now, plot Network C. Looking back at the network diagram (refer to Figure 5-4), Network C requires 25 hosts, so it, too, will use a 32-address block. Remember that you have to start network C on increments of 32, so I start on address 64 and go to 95. (See Figure 5-8.)

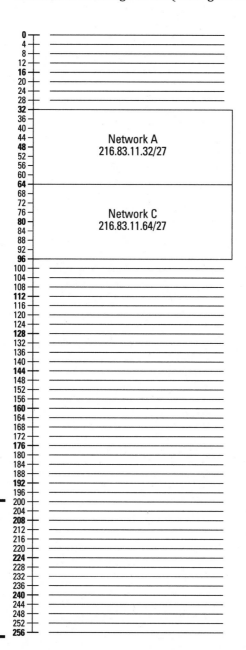

Figure 5-8:
Adding
Network
C to the
216.83.
11.64/27
network
block.

Finally, plot Network B, which requires only two addresses, but you need to accommodate for the network ID and the broadcast as well. So it is actually a subnet size of 4 — 4 is the increment, so you can start this network on addresses 0, 4, 8, 12, and so on. I plot Network B right after Network C using the 216.83.11.96 address block. (See Figure 5-9.)

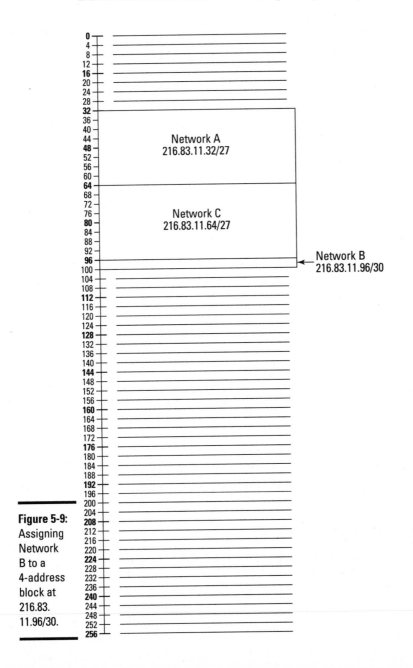

Figure 5-9: Assigning Network B to a 4-address block at 216.83.11.96/30.

Network A
216.83.11.32/27

Network C
216.83.11.64/27

Network B
216.83.11.96/30

The benefit of VLSM is that it allows you to create a network design that makes better use of address space. Keep in mind that I do not expect you to receive any VLSM questions on the CCENT certification exam, as it is more of a CCNA topic, but you should know what VLSM is.

Chapter Summary

This chapter illustrates the concepts related to subnetting and the need for variable-length subnet masks. This chapter is critical to you passing the CCENT certification exam, so be sure to review it many times and practice different subnetting examples. Remember the following key points about subnetting:

✦ You need to subnet so you can configure the logical address to match the physical network structure.

✦ *CIDR notation* is a method of specifying the subnet mask. For example, 192.168.2.0/24 indicates that this is a class C network.

✦ The network ID is calculated by having all host bits set to 0.

✦ The broadcast address is calculated by having all host bits set to 1.

✦ In order to calculate the number of hosts that are supported on the subnet, the calculation is $2^{\text{\# of host bits}} - 2$.

✦ In order to determine how many subnets are supported, use the formula $2^{\text{\# of subnetted bits}}$.

✦ In order to support different-size networks, you implement *variable-length subnet masks* (VLSM), which allow each network to have a different subnet mask and support a different number of hosts.

✦ Most Cisco devices have the ip subnet-zero command, which allows you to use the first and last subnets that are calculated when subnetting.

Lab Exercises

This chapter introduces you to the concepts of subnetting a network to ensure that the logical address scheme corresponds to the physical network structures. The following labs help you practice those concepts.

Lab 5-1: Subnetting class A

In this lab, practice subnetting a class A network range. It is very important to use scratch paper and calculate all information in binary to ensure the accuracy of your numbers.

1. You have the 120.0.0.0 network range and are responsible for subnetting it into eight subnets. For each of the subnets, be sure to calculate the following information:

   - Network ID
   - First valid address
   - Broadcast address
   - Last valid address
   - New subnet mask

2. After completing the exercise, answer the following questions:

   a. How many bits did you borrow from the host ID?

   b. How many networks are supported?

   c. How many hosts per network are supported?

Lab 5-2: Subnetting class B

In this lab, practice subnetting a class B network range. It is very important to use scratch paper and calculate all information in binary to ensure the accuracy of your numbers.

1. You have the 129.15.0.0 network range and are responsible for subnetting it into four subnets. For each of the subnets, be sure to calculate the following information:

   - Network ID
   - First valid address
   - Broadcast address
   - Last valid address
   - New subnet mask

2. After completing the exercise answer the following questions:

   a. How many bits did you borrow from the host ID?

   b. How many networks are supported?

   c. How many hosts per network are supported?

Lab 5-3: Subnetting class C

In this lab, practice subnetting a class C network range. It is very important to use scratch paper and calculate all information in binary to ensure the accuracy of your numbers.

1. **You have the** `220.15.10.0` **network range and you are responsible for subnetting it into eight subnets. For each of the subnets, be sure to calculate the following information:**

- Network ID
- First valid address
- Broadcast address
- Last valid address
- New subnet mask

2. **After completing the exercise, answer the following questions:**

a. How many bits did you borrow from the host ID?

b. How many networks are supported?

c. How many hosts per network are supported?

Lab 5-4: Subnetting class B using the shortcut

In this lab, practice subnetting a class B network range using the increment concept.

1. **You have the** `130.10.0.0` **network range and you are responsible for subnetting it into four subnets. For each of the subnets, be sure to calculate the following information, but start by calculating all network IDs using the increment shortcut:**

- Network ID
- First valid address
- Broadcast address
- Last valid address
- New subnet mask

2. **After completing the exercise, answer the following questions:**

a. How many bits did you borrow from the host ID?

b. How many networks are supported?

c. How many hosts per network are supported?

Prep Test

1 How do you calculate the broadcast address of a subnet?

  A ○ Set all host bits to 0
  B ○ Set all host bits to 1
  C ○ Set all network bits to 0
  D ○ Set all subnet bits to 1

2 You want to assign your serial interface the third valid IP address in the second subnet of `192.168.2.0/26`. Which command would you use?

  A ○ `192.168.2.3`
  B ○ `192.168.2.35`
  C ○ `192.168.2.64`
  D ○ `192.168.2.67`

3 The `24.60.32.20/11` address is located in which of the following subnets?

  A ○ `24.32.0.0`
  B ○ `24.64.0.0`
  C ○ `24.96.0.0`
  D ○ `24.16.0.0`

4 Your manager would like you to subnet the `129.65.0.0` network into six different networks. What is your new subnet mask?

  A ○ `255.224.0.0`
  B ○ `255.255.192.0`
  C ○ `255.255.224.0`
  D ○ `255.255.255.224`

5 How do you calculate the network ID of a subnet?

  A ○ Set all host bits to 0
  B ○ Set all host bits to 1
  C ○ Set all network bits to 1
  D ○ Set all subnet bits to 0

6 What is the network ID for the third subnet of 220.55.66.0/27?

A ○ 220.55.66.32

B ○ 220.55.66.96

C ○ 220.55.66.60

D ○ 220.55.66.64

7 What is the last valid address for the subnet of 220.55.66.64/27?

A ○ 220.55.66.32

B ○ 220.55.66.94

C ○ 220.55.66.62

D ○ 220.55.66.64

8 Which IP feature allows you to use different subnet masks on different subnets within the network?

A ○ IP Subnet Zero

B ○ RIPv1

C ○ VLSM

D ○ RIPv2

9 Which option on the Cisco router indicates that you can use the first and last subnets of a subnetted network?

A ○ VLSM

B ○ ip subnet-zero

C ○ RIPv1

D ○ RIPv2

10 You wish to subnet 137.15.0.0 in order to support 8,190 hosts on each of the networks. You wish to use the smallest subnet size to support this number of hosts. What will be the new subnet mask?

A ○ 255.255.255.224

B ○ 255.255.192.0

C ○ 255.255.240.0

D ○ 255.255.224.0

Answers

Subnetting and VLSM

1 **B.** In order to calculate the broadcast address of a subnet, you set all host bits to 1 and then convert to decimal. *See "Subnetting a class A network."*

2 **D.** The second subnet is the 192.168.2.64 subnet, with the third valid address being 192.168.2.67. Remember that the first address (64) is the network ID, so the first valid address is 65, then 66, and the third valid address is 67. *Review "Subnetting a class C network."*

3 **A.** The 24.60.32.20/11 address is located in the 24.32.0.0 network range. A quick way to figure these questions out is to look at the /11 and ask yourself what is the increment value supplied by the last bit used to subnet — it is 32! This means that the network IDs increment by 32, starting with 24.0.0.0, then 24.32.0.0, and then 24.64.0.0. In this question, the address 24.60.32.20 is less than 24.64.0.0, so it must be on the 24.32.0.0 network. *Check out "Subnetting a class A network."*

4 **C.** To create six new subnets, you need to actually create eight subnets by borrowing three bits from the host ID portion of the subnet mask and converting them to subnet bits. *Peruse "Subnetting a class A network."*

5 **A.** The network ID for a subnet can be calculated by having all host bits set to 0 and then converting to decimal. *Take a look at "Subnetting a class A network."*

6 **D.** 220.55.66.64 is the network ID of the third subnet. A quick way to figure this out is to determine the increment value of the last bit used to subnet — in this example, it is 32, so the increments are 0, 32, 64, 96, and so on. The third network ID is 64, so you simply add that to 220.55.66.0 to get 220.55.66.64. *Peek at "Subnetting a class C network."*

7 **B.** The last valid address of the 64 subnet in this example is 94. An easy way to figure this out is the next network ID would have 96 as a value and the number before that would be the broadcast address (95), which leaves the last valid address to be 94. *Look over "Subnetting a class A network."*

8 **C.** The variable-length subnet masks feature allows you to use different subnet masks for different subnets within your organization. *Study "Understanding Variable-Length Subnet Masks."*

9 **B.** The ip subnet-zero command is a default command on today's Cisco routers, which allows you to use the first and last subnets when subnetting. *Refer to "IP Subnet Zero."*

10 **D.** Because you need to borrow three bits from the third octet in order to have each subnet support 8,190 hosts, the new subnet mask is 255.255.224.0. *Examine "Subnetting a class B network."*

Book II

Cisco Device Basics

The 5th Wave   By Rich Tennant

"Here's a little tip on disassembly that you won't find on the CCENT Certification test."

Contents at a Glance

Chapter 1: Introduction to the Cisco IOS

In This Chapter

✔ Introducing the Cisco IOS

✔ Identifying ports on Cisco devices

✔ Ways to configure the IOS

✔ Identifying types of memory

✔ Powering on your Cisco device

✔ Understanding Cisco configuration modes

✔ Looking at IOS versions

*T*he previous minibook exposes you to a number of networking concepts, such as network devices and services, the OSI model, the TCP/IP Internet model, IP addressing, and subnetting. Now that you have the basics of networking down, you can focus on the specifics of Cisco devices such as routers and switches.

This chapter is designed to introduce you to those Cisco devices by discussing the operating system that resides on them, the different types of ports and memory, and some fundamental concepts, including the important discussion of configuration modes. All of these topics are extremely important basics that you must be familiar with before you take a look at how to configure the devices in the next chapter.

Quick Assessment

1   (True/False). The POST verifies that the hardware in the device is functioning.

2   _____ stores the running configuration.

3   The startup configuration is stored in _____ memory.

4   (True/False). The console port is typically connected to a modem.

5   The _____ is a command-line interface used to manage the Cisco device.

Answers

1 *True*. See "The boot process."

2 *VRAM*. Review "Volatile RAM (VRAM)."

3 *NVRAM*. Check out "Nonvolatile RAM (NVRAM)."

4 *False*. Peruse "Console port."

5 *CLI*. Take a look at "Using the CLI."

Introducing the Cisco IOS

Cisco devices run an operating system known as the *Internetwork Operating System* (IOS). The IOS is responsible for the features of Cisco devices such as routing, switching, and even security features. It enables you to interact with a Cisco device by exposing a number of commands to you that you can use in the *command-line interface* (CLI). The IOS is responsible for offering the feature set on the device — features that are different from one IOS version to another.

One of the most important points to understand regarding how to manage a Cisco device is that different IOS versions have different features available. For example, a Cisco router IOS prior to version 11.3 does not have the *Network Address Translation* (NAT) feature. Cisco IOS versions above 11.3 have the Network Address Translation feature. When troubleshooting why a command is not working on your Cisco device, one thing to verify is that you have a version of the IOS that the command you are trying to use works on.

In the classroom, two things that I stress to students who are new to Cisco devices is (1) get familiar with the different ports and connectors so that you have an idea of what needs to be configured on the device, and (2) know how to use the help system within the Cisco IOS. If you can get comfortable with the help system and you know your way around the IOS, you can figure out how to manage any Cisco device — even if the model is new to you!

Identifying Ports on the Cisco Device

There are so many different models of Cisco routers and switches that the most important thing to understand when working with these devices is there are a number of different configuration settings, such as configuring ports, that are consistent with each model Cisco device. One of the consistent features of all Cisco devices is configuring the different ports.

This section is designed to inform you of the different ports — console, auxiliary, Ethernet, and serial — and it can help you understand what each port is used for. You also discover the different unique port IDs that are assigned to each port and how to work with the different ports.

Cisco router ports

There are a number of different types of ports that can appear on your Cisco routers. Let's start by taking a look at some older routers and then work our way into some newer routers. Figure 1-1 displays a Cisco 2501 router and the different ports that exist on it.

Figure 1-1:
Looking at
the ports on
a Cisco 2501
router.

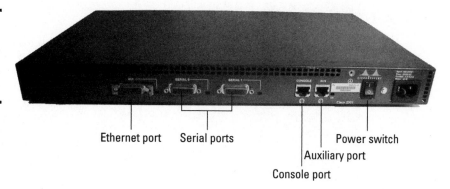

Ethernet port   Serial ports   Power switch

Auxiliary port

Console port

Console port

Looking at Figure 1-1, you can see a console port on the back of the Cisco router. The *console port* allows you to connect to and administer the router and change its configuration. You connect your workstation to the console port with a *console cable* (also known as a *rollover cable*).

Connecting to the console port on the router to change the settings on the device is called connecting *locally* to the router because you have to be physically with the router in order to make the connection. The opposite of connecting locally is to connect *remotely* — meaning you connect across the network or Internet using TCP/IP to manage the device. An example of connecting remotely to the router is when you Telnet into the router to make configuration changes to the router. You find out how to Telnet into the router in Book II, Chapter 3.

When connecting locally to the router, the console cable typically connects from your computer's serial port to the console port on the Cisco device, as shown in Figure 1-2.

All port types are referenced by a unique ID that is made up of the type of port and an index number specifying which port of that type you are referencing. For example, the console port is referenced as *console 0*, or *con 0* for short, because it is the first (and only) console port on the router.

Auxiliary port

The *auxiliary port* is used exactly as a console port in the sense that you connect locally to the auxiliary port using a console cable. The original reason the auxiliary port was created was so you could connect a modem to the auxiliary port (see Figure 1-3) and then dial into the modem from a remote location to perform your administration. This meant that you did not have to be physically in front of the router to do your administration.

Figure 1-2:
Connecting
a work-
station to
the console
port to
perform
local
admini-
stration.

Because most networks are connected to the Internet, today's network administrators do not use the auxiliary port as much — normally they remotely administer the Cisco device by Telneting into the router or using a secure connection such as SSH.

The auxiliary port is referenced with an ID of *auxiliary 0,* or *aux 0* for short.

Figure 1-3:
Using the
auxiliary
port to
remotely
manage the
network
over the
phone lines.

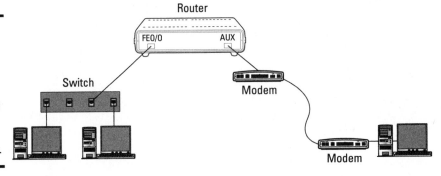

Cisco Ethernet ports

Most routers today have multiple Ethernet (10 Mbps), Fast Ethernet (100 Mbps), or even Gigabit Ethernet (1000 Mbps) ports on them. For example, the Cisco 2501 router has only one Ethernet port (labeled AUI) and it uses the *Attachment Unit Interface* (AUI) port instead of a typical RJ-45 port. The benefit of the AUI port is that you can connect a transceiver (shown in Figure 1-4) to the AUI port; on the other end of the transceiver, there may be different types of connectors that allow different types of cabling to be used to connect to the Ethernet port. The AUI port provides a way to attach a transceiver that may have any of the many different cable types that can connect to the transceiver.

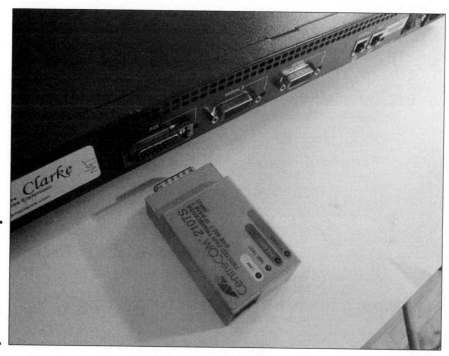

Figure 1-4:
A transceiver connects to the AUI port on the Cisco router.

Most newer routers today have the Ethernet, Fast Ethernet, and Gigabit Ethernet ports using an RJ-45 port (see Figure 1-5) or even fiber connectors, so it is unlikely that you will see an AUI connector if you are dealing with newer hardware.

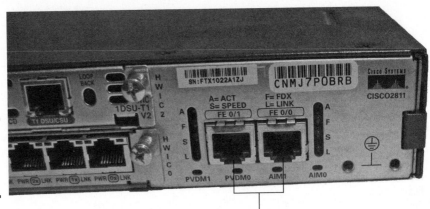

Figure 1-5:
Newer
routers use
RJ-45 ports.

RJ-45 ports

When you configure aspects of the network interfaces, you must reference the different types of Ethernet interfaces by their IDs. Table 1-1 lists the IDs used by the different types of Ethernet interfaces.

Table 1-1	Network Interface IDs
Port Type	*Example ID*
Ethernet (10 Mbps)	Ethernet0 or Ethernet1
Fast Ethernet (100 Mbps)	FastEthernet0/0 or FastEthernet0/1
Gigabit Ethernet (1000 Mbps)	GigabitEthernet0/0 or GigabitEthernet0/1
10 Gigabit (10 Gbps)	TenGigabitEthernet0/0 or TenGigabitEthernet0/1

Looking at Table 1-1, you see that the Ethernet ports are referenced by Ethernet0 or Ethernet1. The 0 and the 1 are the port numbers on the Cisco device, with the first port starting at index 0, the second port being index 1, and so on.

The Fast Ethernet ports are identified a little bit differently. With Fast Ethernet ports, the port identifier starts with the word *FastEthernet,* but then there are two numbers that follow (instead of the one number used with Ethernet). The two numbers that follow the words *FastEthernet* use the syntax of *slot/port.* Ports are added to Cisco devices by placing *cards,* or *modules,* into slots — so a single slot can have multiple ports on it. Looking at Figure 1-6, you see a Cisco device with three slots; each slot has a module

placed in it, and each module has multiple ports. To reference the fourth
Fast Ethernet port on the first module, the ID of that port is *FastEthernet1/4*
(or you can abbreviate it as fa1/4 or even f1/4).

Figure 1-6:
A
conceptual
diagram
displaying
how to
reference
Fast
Ethernet
ports by
their IDs.

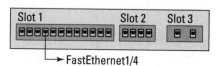

Sometimes the index numbers of ports start with 0, and sometimes they
start with 1. For example, my Cisco 2811 router has two Fast Ethernet
interfaces, with the first interface being FastEthernet0/0 and the second
being FastEthernet0/1. But on my Cisco 2950 switch, the first Fast Ethernet
port has an ID of FastEthernet0/1. If you are unsure of the port ID, take a look
at the device because a lot of times the ports are labeled. (Refer to Figure 1-5,
and you see the two ports labeled as FE0/0 and FE0/1).

Serial ports

Looking back at Figure 1-1, you see two serial ports labeled Serial 0 and
Serial 1. *Serial ports* are typically used to connect your Cisco router to your
WAN environment; they can also be used to create a direct point-to-point
link between two routers. A *point-to-point link* means that you connect one
router directly to another router using a special cable known as a *back-to-
back serial cable.*

I talk more about WANs in Book IV, Chapter 4, but I want to give you a quick
rundown on how routers are typically connected in a WAN environment.
Remember that a *WAN* is created when you connect multiple offices, such as
when you connect your office in New York to your office in Toronto.

In order to create the connection between two offices that are seperated
over distance, you subscribe to a monthly service from your *telco,* or *service
provider,* that provides the physical links between the two office locations.
All you need to do is get a connection to the service provider's network
infrastructure, which is what the serial port is typically used for.

The serial port on your router connects to an external WAN device, such as a *Channel Service Unit/Data Service Unit* (CSU/DSU), that offers a T1 or T3 connection to the service provider (more on T1 and T3 in the WAN chapter; Book IV, Chapter 4). Once you connect the serial port on the router to the CSU/DSU, you then take the line that the service provider installed (typically in your wiring closet) and plug it into the CSU/DSU. (See Figure 1-7.)

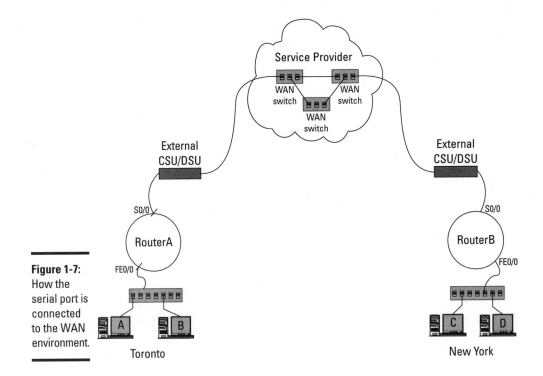

Figure 1-7: How the serial port is connected to the WAN environment.

In Figure 1-7, your router in Toronto is connected to the WAN (the service provider's network) via serial port Serial0/0 (S0/0). This serial port is connected to the *external* CSU/DSU device, which is then connected to your service provider's network — typically into what is called a *WAN switch*. Your office in New York has the same setup, but it may be connected to a different part of the service provider's network.

The reason I stress the term *external CSU/DSU device* is that it is possible to install a CSU/DSU module into an available slot in your router so you can connect the line from your service provider directly into the port on the router — this is known as an *internal CSU/DSU device*. (It is integrated into the router.) Figure 1-8 displays an integrated CSU/DSU on a Cisco 2811 router.

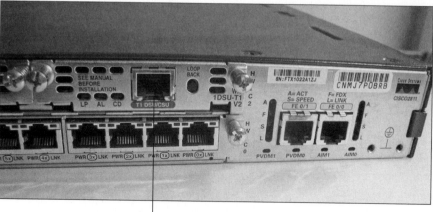

Figure 1-8:
An integrated CSU/DSU port on a Cisco 2811 router.

Internal CSU/DSU port

Looking at Figure 1-8 you see that the CSU/DSU port has been added to the router as a *Wan Interface Card* (WIC) module (notice the screws on either side of the port. Cisco has started to use WICs as a method to add any type of port by inserting a card, or module, to the newer routers. WICs are not only used for WAN ports, they are used to add many other types of ports — you can see in Figure 1-8 that the Fast Ethernet ports below the CSU/DSU are a module that was added. The use of WICs has added greater flexibility in what types of ports can exist in your routers over the older fixed port routers.

Identifying 1604 router ports

A number of other ports can exist on a Cisco router, or can be added by inserting a module into one of the available slots in the router. Looking at Figure 1-9, you see an older Cisco 1604 router that has the following ports:

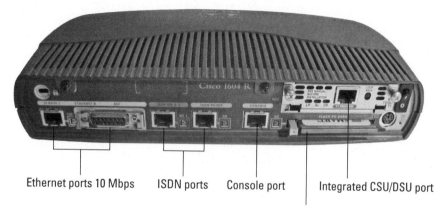

Figure 1-9:
Identifying the ports on a Cisco 1604 router.

Ethernet ports 10 Mbps   ISDN ports   Console port   Integrated CSU/DSU port

Flash memory

✦ **Ethernet0:** One of the reasons I want to show you this older router is so you can see the two Ethernet ports on the left side of the router. One of the Ethernet ports is an RJ-45 port, and the other is an AUI connector. The hook with this router is both ports are known as Ethernet0, and you are allowed to use only one of them at a time. The benefit is that instead of having to purchase a transceiver to connect UTP cable to the router, you can use the built-in RJ-45 port that is supplied.

✦ **ISDN ports:** ISDN is another example of a WAN technology that you can use to connect to a remote office. I discuss ISDN as a WAN technology in Book IV, Chapter 4, but I want you to notice in the figure that this router has some ISDN ports built in.

✦ **Console port:** You connect your computer to the local console port so you can administer the router.

✦ **Flash memory:** This router has flash memory installed via a flash card that can be removed and replaced at any time. The flash memory stores the IOS.

✦ **Integrated CSU/DSU:** Notice that this router has an integrated CSU/DSU that you can use to connect the router to a WAN link such as a T1 link.

Identifying 2811 router ports

Cisco 1604 is an older router, so you will not be tested on it for the CCENT certification exam — I show it to you because I want you to see some different variations of ports that appear on Cisco devices. Figure 1-10 displays a Cisco 2811 router and identifies the ports on the router.

Figure 1-10 displays two images; the top image shows ports on the front of the router, and the bottom image displays ports on the back of the router.

The front of the router has a flash card, which stores the IOS. The front also includes the console port and the auxiliary port to connect to the router and make changes to the configuration. Notice that the front of the router also has USB ports (for security and storage purposes) that can be referenced with the USB0 or USB1 IDs.

The back of the 2811 router has two Fast Ethernet ports for connecting to Ethernet networks, and an integrated CSU/DSU to connect a T1 line to the router. You will notice in this router that a number of switch ports (Fast Ethernet) also exist for you to connect systems to the network. This device is acting as a multifunctional device — a router and a switch.

Cisco switch ports

Ports on a Cisco switch are referenced in the same way that ports on a router are referenced. The difference is the number of ports that exist on a device. A Cisco router connects networks and, as a result, has only a few interfaces (maybe a few serial and a few Fast Ethernet interfaces), but a switch is designed to allow systems to connect to the network and, as a result, has more ports available. Switches do not have an auxiliary port; auxiliary ports are present only on routers.

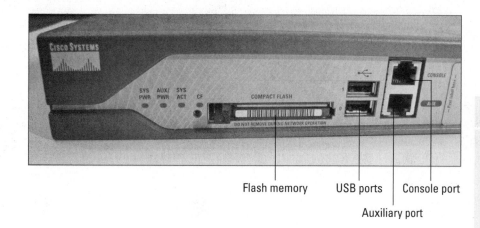

Flash memory   USB ports   Console port

Auxiliary port

Figure 1-10:
Identifying
the ports
on the
front (top)
and back
(bottom) of
a Cisco 2811
router.

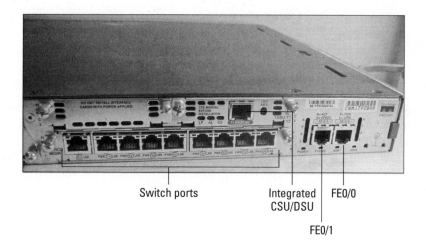

Switch ports   Integrated   FE0/0
                   CSU/DSU

FE0/1

Console port

A Cisco switch has a console port that is referenced as console 0, or con 0, and is used to locally connect to the switch to administer the changes to the switch.

Ethernet ports

Switches normally have a number of Ethernet, Fast Ethernet, or Gigabit Ethernet ports on the switch. (See Figure 1-11.) Most switches have 12, 24, or even 48 ports that are used to connect systems to the network. When configuring the switch and applying settings to these ports, you reference the ports by the *slot/port* syntax discussed in the "Cisco Ethernet ports" section earlier in the chapter. For example, to reference the third Fast Ethernet port in slot 1, use *FastEthernet1/3* to refer to it.

Figure 1-11:
Fast
Ethernet
ports on
a Cisco
switch.

Ethernet ports

Ways to Configure the Cisco Device

There are a number of different ways that you can configure the Cisco device — you can use the *command-line interface* (CLI), *Security Device Manager* (SDM), or a graphical program such as *Cisco Network Assistant* (CNA), which you can download from Cisco's Web site.

Using the CLI

The command-line interface (CLI) is the main method for configuring a Cisco device because all Cisco devices (at least all Cisco devices I know of) support you connecting to the console port and using HyperTerminal (or connecting remotely using Telnet or SSH) to connect to the command-line interface of the device. When you are in the CLI, you can then issue any number of commands to administer the device. The following sample code is an example of how to use the CLI to change the name of the router.

```
R1>enable
R1#config term
Enter configuration commands, one per line.  End with CNTL/Z.
R1(config)#hostname NY-R1
NY-R1(config)#
```

Most people who are new to the Cisco world find the CLI frustrating to use, but it is a very intuitive interface once you get used to it.

The CCENT certification exam tests your knowledge of the CLI exclusively, so you need to be comfortable with this method of configuring the Cisco device. As you progress through the chapters of this book you will find out how to perform many tasks in the CLI.

Locally

You can use the CLI to configure a switch or router *locally*. This means that you are physically in the same room with the router or switch and you connect your computer to the console port or auxiliary port on the device. This is known as *locally connecting* to the device. Once you are connected, you can then use the different CLI commands to manage the device.

Remotely

You can also use the CLI by connecting to the router or switch remotely using an application such as Telnet or SSH, which allows you to connect to the router via its IP address. When you're connected, the command-line interface is presented to you, and then you can issue the same configuration commands you would if you were locally connected to the device.

```
C:\>telnet 24.0.0.1
Trying 24.0.0.1 ...
User Access Verification
Password:

NY-R1>enable
Password:
NY-R1#
```

Notice in the sample code that after Telneting into the device from my computer, I am then placed in the CLI of the router — so I can then administer the device.

Security Device Manager (SDM)

Over the years, there have been graphical tools created to help you manage your Cisco devices. One of the popular graphical tools you can use is Security Device Manager, or SDM, which is a piece of software installed on newer Cisco device models by default, but you can install it on other devices if needed.

SDM is a Java application that offers a graphical interface that connects to the router's IP address through a browser. Once you have connected to the router, the SDM appears, offering you configuration options to modify the settings on the Cisco device. (See Figure 1-12.)

**Book II
Chapter 1**

Introduction to
the Cisco IOS

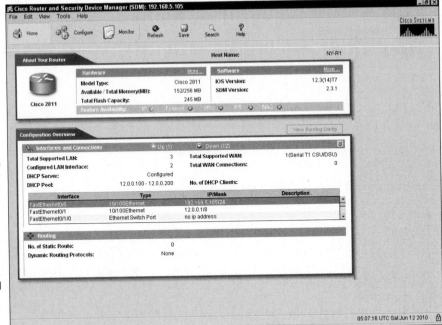

Figure 1-12:
Utilize
Security
Device
Manager
to manage
the Cisco
device using
a graphical
interface.

The following is a description of some of the buttons available at the top of the main screen of SDM:

✦ **Home:** Displays the status of the Cisco router and includes information such as what features have been configured on your Cisco device.

✦ **Configure:** Lets you configure a number of settings on your Cisco device, such as the settings for interfaces, NAT, routing protocols, and DHCP, to name a few.

✦ **Monitor:** Displays statistics on your router, such as CPU usage, memory usage, and the status of the different network interfaces.

If you are running the Cisco IOS 12.4 and would like to use SDM to configure your router, you can download it from the Cisco Web site at www.cisco. com/pcgi-bin/tablebuild.pl/sdm. If you do not have a router to run SDM, on you can download a demo router to use the SDM feature with at www.cisco.com/pcgi-bin/tablebuild.pl/sdm-tool-demo. There are instructions with the download on how to set up the demo.

Cisco Network Assistant

Cisco Network Assistant (CNA) is another free application that you can download and install from the Cisco Web site (www.cisco.com/go/cna). It allows you to manage devices such as routers and switches using a graphical interface.

Cisco Network Assistant (see Figure 1-13) has been around longer than SDM, and you will find that you may be able to use it on devices that you cannot install the SDM software on. CNA can be used to manage a wealth of different features, including port configuration and VLANs on a switch.

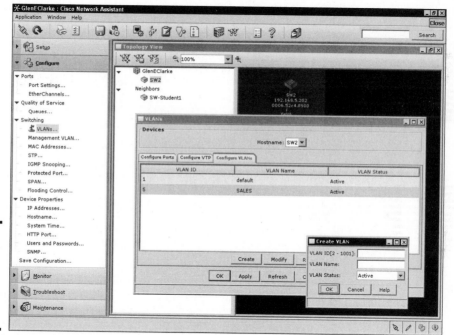

Figure 1-13: Using Cisco Network Assistant to configure a switch.

Because the CCENT certification exam tests your knowledge of the CLI and not SDM or CNA, this book focuses on the commands within the CLI you need to know to configure a Cisco router and switch. You need to be familiar with SDM when you take your CCNA exam — not the CCENT certification exam.

Identifying Types of Memory

The first really important aspect of Cisco devices to understand is that there are different types of memory — including ROM, flash, VRAM, and NVRAM — installed on the Cisco device. Each type of memory has a specific purpose, and you will be tested on these memory types on your CCENT certification exam.

ROM

The first type of memory to discuss is the read-only memory (ROM) that is stored on the Cisco device. *ROM* on a Cisco device takes the role of ROM on a computer — it contains the low-level code that is responsible for the startup operations of the device. *Startup operations* is a general term for what happens when you boot, or power-on, the device.

ROM stores important components that are critical to the startup of the Cisco device. The following list outlines components that are stored in ROM:

✦ **POST:** The Power-On Self-Test (POST) is a set of routines located in ROM that are executed on startup to verify the hardware in the Cisco device.

✦ **Bootstrap:** The bootstrap program, also known as the *boot loader program,* is also located in ROM and is executed after the POST. The purpose of the bootstrap program is to locate the IOS in flash memory and then load it into memory.

✦ **RX-boot:** A mini-IOS located in ROM that you can use if you have no IOS in flash memory. This mini-IOS is limited in functionality and is normally used to enable an interface so that an IOS can be downloaded from a TFTP server on the network.

✦ **ROM Monitor:** The ROM Monitor (ROMMON) troubleshoots configuration issues with the Cisco device. For example, if you forget the password on your Cisco device, you can boot to ROMMON to bypass the password request. You can access ROMMON by using a Ctrl-Break keystroke while the Cisco device is booting.

Flash memory

Flash memory on a Cisco device is used to store the Cisco IOS. The reason Cisco stores the IOS in flash memory and not in ROM is because the IOS is upgraded from time to time — if the IOS were stored in ROM memory, you would not be able to write to it.

You can install flash memory on the actual system board in the Cisco device or by inserting a flash memory card, as shown in Figure 1-14.

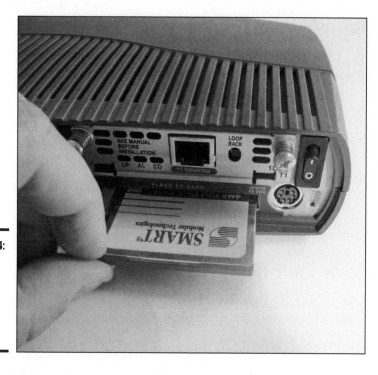

Figure 1-14:
Installing
a flash
memory
card on
a Cisco
router.

Volatile RAM (VRAM)

Volatile RAM (VRAM), also known as just *RAM,* is a type of memory that loses its information when power is lost or the device is turned off. VRAM stores what is known as the *running configuration,* which is the current setup of the device. For example, if you were to start your router and then change the name of the router, the new name is stored in VRAM. If you were to shut down the Cisco device, you would lose the new name you applied because the contents of VRAM are erased when the system is powered off. (That is why they call it volatile.)

In order for you to store the configuration permanently, you need to copy the running configuration to nonvolatile RAM (see the next section for more about nonvolatile RAM) before turning off the device so that the information is retained.

A number of additional items are stored in memory along with the running configuration. VRAM stores items such as your ARP cache, routing table (if your device is a router), and MAC address table (if your device is a switch).

Nonvolatile RAM (NVRAM)

Nonvolatile RAM, also known as *NVRAM,* stores information permanently, even when the device is powered off. When you are a Cisco administrator, you will need to get used to copying your running configuration (which is stored in VRAM) to more permanent storage — NVRAM — in order to maintain your change when the device is shut down. The configuration that is stored in NVRAM is known as the *startup configuration* and is applied to your device each time it starts up. To copy the changes you make in VRAM (running-config) to NVRAM (startup-config), use the `copy running-config startup-config` command. You read more about making changes to your Cisco device in the next chapter.

For the CCENT certification exam, know that the running configuration is stored in VRAM, while the startup configuration is stored in nonvolatile RAM.

Powering On Your Cisco Device

Now that you are familiar with the different types of memory on the Cisco device (if you are not familiar with them, read the previous section before continuing), you are now ready to find out what occurs when you boot a Cisco router or switch.

This section introduces you to the Cisco boot process and the events that occur during the boot process. This section also discusses the initial configuration dialog — a wizard that appears on your screen the first time you power on your Cisco device or anytime that you do not have a startup configuration.

Understand that the boot process may be a little different from one model to another, but the general idea stays the same.

The boot process

When you first boot your router or switch, the device starts the boot process by performing a hardware test known as the *Power-On Self-Test* (POST). As mentioned earlier in this chapter, the POST is a routine built into the ROM chip that tests all the hardware components (including the different ports) on the device to ensure they are working.

On a Cisco switch, if there is an error during the POST, the switch displays an amber light on the system LED. For more information on the different LEDs on a switch, check out Book III, Chapter 3.

After the POST verifies the hardware, control of the boot process is then passed on to the bootstrap program. The bootstrap program, also known as the *boot loader,* is stored in ROM and its job is to locate an IOS in flash memory and load it into RAM.

Once the IOS is loaded into memory, the bootstrap program then tries to locate a startup configuration from NVRAM that it can apply to the device. If the startup configuration does not exist, the device will try to locate a TFTP server on the network and load a configuration file from the TFTP server.

If there is not a startup configuration in NVRAM and a TFTP server cannot be found, the Cisco device will then display the *initial configuration dialog,* which prompts you for the configuration of the device one setting at a time. The initial configuration does not ask you to configure all settings, but enough settings to get the device up and running. After the initial configuration dialog completes, the configuration becomes the running configuration.

If the Cisco device does contain the startup configuration, the configuration is applied to the device upon startup to become the running configuration stored in VRAM. The startup configuration retains your router and switch configuration through reboots. Figure 1-15 summarizes the boot process of a Cisco device.

**Book II
Chapter 1**

Introduction to
the Cisco IOS

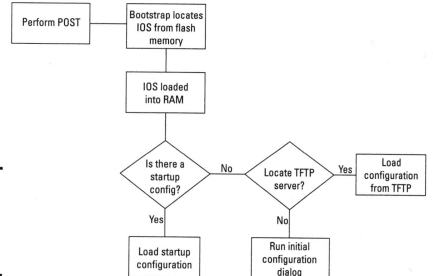

Figure 1-15:
Identifying
the steps in
the Cisco
device boot
process.

Configuration changes are stored in the current configuration, which is located in NVRAM. In order to retain any changes to the router or switch after a reboot, you must copy the running configuration to the startup configuration (NVRAM) by using the `copy running-config startup-config` command.

Initial configuration dialog

The initial configuration dialog is the closest thing the CLI has to a wizard that prompts you for configuration information one question at a time. The initial configuration dialog appears anytime there is no startup configuration when the Cisco device boots up. It also appears when you type the `setup` command at the CLI.

Once the initial configuration dialog launches, you can use it to quickly create a basic configuration on your Cisco device without needing to know all of the commands. Listing 1-1 displays the initial configuration dialog that appears on bootup if there is no startup configuration or if you use the `setup` command at any time. My responses to the questions that the initial configuration dialog asks are shown in bolded text.

Once the initial configuration dialog starts, you can terminate it at any time by using the Ctrl-C keystroke.

Listing 1-1:   The Initial Configuration Dialog

```
    --- System Configuration Dialog ---

Continue with configuration dialog? [yes/no]: yes

At any point you may enter a question mark '?' for help.
Use ctrl-c to abort configuration dialog at any prompt.
Default settings are in square brackets '[]'.

Basic management setup configures only enough connectivity
for management of the system, extended setup will ask you
to configure each interface on the system

Would you like to enter basic management setup? [yes/no]
Configuring global parameters:

  Enter host name [NY-R1]: NY-R2

  The enable secret is a password used to protect access to
  privileged EXEC and configuration modes. This password,
   after
```

entered, becomes encrypted in the configuration.
Enter enable secret [<Use current secret>]: **secret**

The enable password is used when you do not specify an
enable secret password, with some older software versions,
and some boot images.
Enter enable password [password]: **password**

The virtual terminal password is used to
access to the router over a network interface.
Enter virtual terminal password [telnet]: **telnet**
Configure SNMP Network Management? [no]: **no**

Current interface summary

Book II
Chapter 1

Interface	IP-Address	OK?	Method	Status
FastEthernet0/0	192.168.5.105	YES	manual	up
FastEthernet0/1	12.0.0.1	YES	TFTP	up

Enter interface name used to connect to the
management network from the above interface summary:
  fastethernet0/0

Configuring interface FastEthernet0/0:
  Use the 100 Base-TX (RJ-45) connector? [yes]:
  Operate in full-duplex mode? [no]: **yes**
  Configure IP on this interface? [yes]: **yes**
    IP address for this interface [192.168.5.105]:
    Subnet mask for this interface [255.255.255.0] :
    Class C network is 192.168.5.0, 24 subnet bits; mask is
    /24

!
(output cut for briefness)
!
end

[0] Go to the IOS command prompt without saving this config.
[1] Return back to the setup without saving this config.
[2] Save this configuration to nvram

Enter your selection [2]: **2**

Building configuration...
[OK]

NY-R2#

In Listing 1-1, notice that you are prompted for the name of the device, some passwords, and eventually the settings on the interfaces, such as the speed, duplex settings, and IP address. At the end of the dialog, you are asked if you wish to discard the settings or if you want to save them. I choose option 2 to save the setting to NVRAM (the startup configuration). This means that the next time my Cisco device boots I will not be prompted for the configuration as it will be applied from NVRAM (the startup configuration).

The last thing I want to mention before leaving the topic of the boot process and the initial configuration dialog is that there are two related commands you can use in priv exec mode that you should be familiar with. The first command is the `reload` command, which is the command to reboot the router at any point in time. Also, if you ever want to start the initial configuration dialog you can use the `setup` command — which is why some techs also refer to the initial configuration dialog as *setup mode*.

Understanding Cisco Configuration Modes

Now that you understand the boot process of a Cisco device (if you do not understand it, see the previous section before proceeding), you next need to be familiar with the different configuration modes on a Cisco device. Each configuration mode — user exec mode, priv exec mode, and global configuration — is responsible for allowing you to execute different types of commands on the Cisco device. When reading about each of these modes, use Figure 1-16 to help you understand the relationships between the different modes.

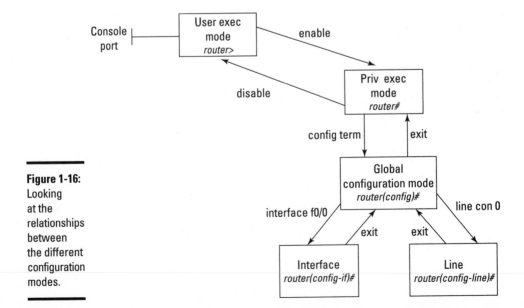

Figure 1-16:
Looking at the relationships between the different configuration modes.

User exec mode

The first configuration mode is known as *user exec mode,* which is a read-only-type mode that does not allow you to make changes to the device configuration. In user exec mode, you can view the configuration using some of the show commands, but again, you cannot modify the configuration.

In order to get to user exec mode, you typically Telnet into the router or connect through the console port. Once you connect through the console port or Telnet in, you will notice that your prompt displays with a > at the end of the prompt, which indicates you are in user exec mode.

When using the CLI you will notice there is a prompt waiting for you to issue a command. The default prompt is `router>`, which is made up of the name of your router and the symbol indicating what configuration mode you are in. The default name of a router is "router," which is why the prompt displays as `router>`, but as you find out in the next chapter you can change the name of the router — which will change the text in the prompt. The symbol that follows the prompt (for example > or #) is important to note as it indicates the configuration mode you are in and the types of changes you can make.

Book II
Chapter 1

Introduction to
the Cisco IOS

Priv exec mode

If you need to make changes to the Cisco router or switch, you need to move into *priv exec mode,* also known as *privilege exec mode.* To get to privilege exec mode, you type the `enable` command. Once you are in priv exec mode, you will notice that your prompt changes from a > to a # at the end of the prompt — this indicates you are in priv exec mode and can make changes.

If you decide you want to move back to user exec mode, you can use the `disable` command. This will place you back in the user exec mode prompt, which displays with a >.

Priv exec mode is also known as *enable* mode, as that is the command you used to navigate to that mode.

Global configuration

The strange thing about the Cisco IOS is that although, in theory, you can modify your configuration in priv exec mode, there actually are not any commands that I can think of that allow you to change a setting directly from priv exec mode. For most of the settings that you need to change, you need to navigate one step deeper in the configuration modes. Most changes need to be made from global configuration mode. *Global configuration mode* allows you to change a setting that affects the entire router and not just a single interface or port.

In order to navigate to global configuration mode, you use the `configure terminal` command, or `config term` for short. When you're in global configuration mode, you will notice that your prompt changes to display `(config)#` at the end of the prompt. Notice that # symbol still exists in the prompt, indicating that you have reached this point by going to priv exec mode.

If you wish to move backward from global configuration to priv exec mode, you can use the `exit` command. An example configuration change you can make from global configuration is changing the name of the router with the `hostname` command (more on the changes you can make in the coming chapters).

Interface prompt

Once you reach global configuration mode, you can make changes that affect the entire device (such as the hostname), but you can also move into the prompt hierarchy a bit deeper by navigating to a particular interface. Moving into the interface prompt, which displays with a `(config-if)#` at the end of the prompt, allows you to configure settings on an interface such as an IP address.

To move to a specific interface from global configuration, you use the `interface` command and specify the interface ID you would like to configure. For example, the `interface f0/0` or `interface fa0/0` commands navigate to the first Fast Ethernet port on the router. You know that you are at the interface prompt because your prompt changes to `(config-if)#`.

In order to move backward from the interface prompt to global configuration, you use the `exit` command to go one step back.

Line prompt

There are a number of other prompts you can navigate to from global configuration. An example is the line prompt, which is used to configure different ports, such as the console port, Telnet ports, and auxiliary ports. To navigate to the console port, you use the `line con 0` command from global configuration mode. When you're at the console prompt of `(config-line)#`, you can then configure settings that affect the console.

To go back to global configuration mode from the line console prompt, you can use the `exit` command just as you do to move from the interface prompt back to global configuration.

The CCENT certification exam will not test your knowledge directly on these configuration modes, but you need to be comfortable with them and know how to move through the prompts in your simulations. You also need to know what commands can be used within which prompts — something you will get more comfortable with as you continue through this book!

Cisco IOS Features

Before leaving this chapter and diving into the configuration of your Cisco devices, there are two other topics I want to cover. I first want to ensure that you know how to locate the version of the IOS you are running, and I also want to make sure you understand how to use the help features in the Cisco IOS.

Looking at IOS versions

Each Cisco device will most likely run a different version of the IOS, or operating system. This is no different from supporting systems on a network where each computer could potentially run a different version of the operating system.

The important thing to know about the different IOS versions is that a command available with one IOS version may not be available with another version, or it may be available but work differently.

When your Cisco device boots up and loads the IOS from flash memory, it displays the IOS version information, along with some device summary information such as the number of interfaces that exist. The following code is displayed on startup. (The boldface text is relevant for this discussion.)

```
System Bootstrap, Version 12.1(3r)T2, RELEASE SOFTWARE (fc1)
Copyright (c) 2000 by Cisco Systems, Inc.
Cisco 2811 (MPC860) processor (revision 0x200) with
    60416K/5120K bytes of memory

Self decompressing the image :
######################### [OK]
```

The initial output displayed when you start up your Cisco device indicates the version of the bootstrap program running in ROM. In this example, it's 12.1. Also notice that you can identify that this device is a Cisco 2811 router. You can also see the IOS expanding into memory and then the Cisco copyright message displays this:

```
                  Restricted Rights Legend

Use, duplication, or disclosure by the Government is
subject to restrictions as set forth in subparagraph
(c) of the Commercial Computer Software - Restricted
Rights clause at FAR sec. 52.227-19 and subparagraph
(c) (1) (ii) of the Rights in Technical Data and Computer
Software clause at DFARS sec. 252.227-7013.

            Cisco Systems, Inc.
            170 West Tasman Drive
            San Jose, California 95134-1706
```

After the copyright information is displayed, you see information on the IOS as the system continues to boot, as shown in the example that follows. On the screen, you should notice the version of the IOS software — in this example, I am running version 12.4. You can also see the name of the IOS image file that was loaded from memory — in this example, it is C2800NM-ADVIPSERVICESK9-M, as shown in the code below:

```
Cisco IOS Software, 2800 Software (C2800NM-
    ADVIPSERVICESK9-M), Version 12.4(15)T1, RELEASE SOFTWARE
    (fc2)
Technical Support: http://www.cisco.com/techsupport
Copyright (c) 1986-2007 by Cisco Systems, Inc.
Compiled Wed 18-Jul-07 06:21 by pt_rel_team
Image text-base: 0x400A925C, data-base: 0x4372CE20

(output cut for briefness)
```

After the IOS version is displayed, the device continues to display additional information, such as the amount of memory installed, the processor, and the different ports, as shown here:

```
Cisco 2811 (MPC860) processor (revision 0x200) with
    60416K/5120K bytes of memory
Processor board ID JAD05190MTZ (4292891495)
M860 processor: part number 0, mask 49
2 FastEthernet/IEEE 802.3 interface(s)
2 Low-speed serial(sync/async) network interface(s)
239K bytes of non-volatile configuration memory.
62720K bytes of  ATA CompactFlash (Read/Write)
Cisco IOS Software, 2800 Software (C2800NM-
    ADVIPSERVICESK9-M), Version 12.4(15)T1, RELEASE SOFTWARE
    (fc2)
(output cut for briefness)
```

The router then displays the state of your different network connections before presenting you with a message to press Enter to get a prompt used to configure the device:

```
%LINK-5-CHANGED: Interface FastEthernet0/1, changed state to
    up
%LINK-5-CHANGED: Interface FastEthernet0/1, changed state to
    administratively down
Press RETURN to get started!
```

It is very difficult to read all this information as the router or switch boots up because the screen scrolls past the information very quickly. At any point in time, you can display the version information of your device by using the show version command from user exec mode:

```
R1>show version
Cisco IOS Software, 2800 Software (C2800NM-
    ADVIPSERVICESK9-M), Version 12.4(15)T1, RELEASE SOFTWARE
    (fc2)
Technical Support: http://www.cisco.com/techsupport
Copyright (c) 1986-2007 by Cisco Systems, Inc.
Compiled Wed 18-Jul-07 06:21 by pt_rel_team
```

(output cut for briefness)

You find out more about the IOS commands as you progress through this book.

Using the help system

It is important to get comfortable with using the help system in the IOS, as it is very difficult to memorize every command and every option on every command. To prepare for the CCENT exam, you want to practice the commands discussed in this book over and over again so that you know them well, but from a real-world point of view, it is more important for you to know how to use the help system so you can discover new commands that are required to complete a task.

After you boot your router or switch, you are sitting in user exec mode. It is important to understand that the modes that I discuss earlier in this chapter (user exec, priv exec, and global configuration) each have their own commands that you can use within them. You definitely do not want to memorize all the commands, all the options with each command, and the mode you need to be in for each command — this is the purpose of the help system!

When you are at a prompt on the router or switch, you can use ? command at any time to see a list of commands that you can use at that prompt. For example, if you are in user exec mode and you use the ? command, you will notice in the list of commands that appear that you can use the enable command:

```
R1>?
Exec commands:
  <1-99>      Session number to resume
  connect     Open a terminal connection
  disconnect  Disconnect an existing network connection
  enable      Turn on privileged commands
  exit        Exit from the EXEC
  ipv6        ipv6
  logout      Exit from the EXEC
  ping        Send echo messages
  resume      Resume an active network connection
```

**Book II
Chapter 1**

Introduction to
the Cisco IOS

```
show       Show running system information
ssh        Open a secure shell client connection
telnet     Open a telnet connection
terminal   Set terminal line parameters
traceroute Trace route to destination
```

Once you have viewed the list of available commands, you can then type the name of the command with a ? at the end to see which options, known as *parameters*, the command needs to perform its purpose. For example, notice that the `ping` command is in the output; if you type `ping ?`, you find out which parameters the ping command needs:

```
R1>ping ?
  WORD  Ping destination address or hostname
R1>ping
```

Notice that after the parameters are listed, the IOS retypes the command you asked for help with; the IOS does this so you do not have to type it again once you get a list of parameters. Also notice in the code shown here that when you use the ? after the `ping` command, it displays the help that states you need to give a "word" where the question mark is located — and that the word is a destination address or hostname. So then you use the `ping 24.0.0.1 ?` command to see a list of parameters after the address:

```
R1>ping 24.0.0.1 ?
  <cr>
```

In the code that you see here, help displays a <cr> as a parameter to use in place of the ?. The <cr> means that you can press the Enter key on the keyboard (known as a *carriage return*) to end the command. So the final command to do a ping operation is

```
R1>ping 24.0.0.1
```

Ensure that you spend some time practicing using the help system. The best thing I can recommend is use help on commands that you are already familiar with — this way, you can better understand how to read the results of the help screen.

To see a demonstration of how to use the help system on Cisco devices, check out the demonstration video on the accompanying CD for this book!

Chapter Summary

This chapter creates the groundwork for future chapters by outlining the different ports and connectors found on Cisco routers and switches. You also find out about the different types of memory and the boot process that Cisco devices use. The following are some key points to remember about this chapter when preparing for the CCENT certification exam:

✦ Routers and switches have a console port on the back of the device that is used to locally connect to the device and change its settings.

✦ The auxiliary port is present on most routers and is typically used to remotely connect to the router over the phone lines by plugging a modem into the auxiliary port.

✦ Most routers have one or more Fast Ethernet ports that are usually referenced as F0/0 and F0/1.

✦ Most routers have one or more serial ports that are used to connect to your WAN environment. The serial ports are normally referenced with IDs such as S0/0 and S0/1.

✦ Know the different memory types for Cisco devices! The IOS is stored in flash memory on the Cisco device, VRAM stores the running configuration, and NVRAM stores the startup configuration.

✦ Know the boot process for Cisco devices — you are sure to get a question on it! The boot process is summarized as POST, bootstrap locates IOS, IOS is loaded in memory, and startup configuration is applied.

✦ Know the different configuration modes — user exec mode is a read-only mode used to view the configuration of the device, while priv exec mode is used to make changes. Most changes occur from within global configuration mode, which is an extension of priv exec mode.

✦ Use the IOS help feature (the ? command) to help you locate the correct syntax to perform a specific task.

✦ You can use the `show version` command to display the IOS version you are using on the device.

Lab Exercises

This chapter covers the basic concepts related to the physical aspects of the router, such as the different ports and connectors. It also discusses the basics of working with the IOS. The following labs are designed to give you some practice working with these concepts.

Lab 1-1: Identifying ports

In this lab, review the different ports displayed on a Cisco 2811 router, and identify which ports are used for what purpose. Use Figure 1-17 to identify each of the ports:

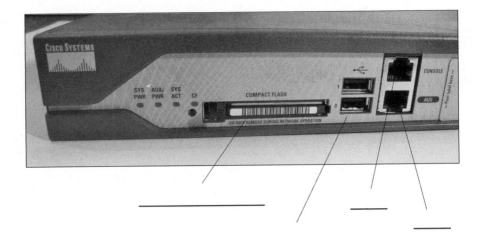

Figure 1-17: Identify the ports on the front (top) and back (bottom) of a Cisco 2811 router.

Lab 1-2: Identifying terminology

In this lab, review Cisco device configuration terms by associating the term with the definition.

Definition	Term
___ The first step in the boot process that verifies the hardware is functioning.	**A.** Console port
___ Location of the running configuration.	**B.** Nonvolatile RAM
___ A port used to locally administer the device.	**C.** Serial port
___ A program stored in ROM that is responsible for locating and loading the IOS into memory.	**D.** Flash memory
___ A port used to connect to a WAN environment.	**E.** Auxiliary port
___ Location of the startup configuration.	**F.** POST
___ A port used to remotely administer the device by connecting a modem to the port.	**G.** Volatile RAM
___ Location of the IOS image.	**H.** Bootstrap program

Lab 1-3: Identifying IOS configuration modes

In the following lab, use Figure 1-18 and fill out the flowchart indicating the missing configuration mode information and commands to navigate to the configuration modes.

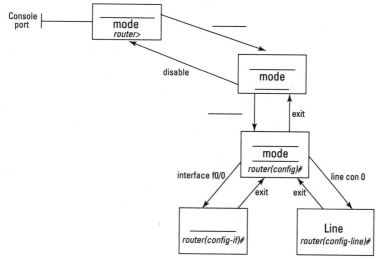

Figure 1-18:
Identifying
configuration
modes.

Lab 1-4: Identifying the boot process

In this lab, identify the steps that occur during the startup of a Cisco router. Fill in the information in the uncompleted steps below:

1. Upon startup, the router first runs the _____, which _____.

2. The _____ program, which resides in _____, locates the IOS image from _____ memory.

3. The IOS is then loaded into memory.

4. The _____ configuration is retrieved from _____ and applied to the device's _____ configuration.

Lab 1-5: Using help

In this lab, explore the help feature on your Cisco router or switch.

1. On your Cisco router, type the ? command when at user exec mode. Do you see the hostname command (which is used to change the name of your router)?

   Answer: _____.

2. List three of the commands that appear.

   Answer: _____, _____, and _____.

3. Navigate to priv exec mode by typing the enable command. How does your prompt change?

   Answer: _____.

4. Once in priv exec mode, use the ? command to display a list of commands. Do you have the hostname command in the list of available commands?

   Answer: _____.

5. In the available commands list that appears, list two commands that are different from the commands available in user exec mode.

   Answer: _____ and _____.

6. Type the config term command to navigate to global configuration mode.

7. Use the ? command to display a list of commands. Can you see the hostname command?

   Answer: _____.

8. To see if there are any parameters required on the hostname command, type `hostname ?`. What parameters are listed?

Answer: _____.

9. To change the name of your router, type `hostname lab15`. Did your router name change?

Answer: _____.

Prep Test

1 **Where is the running configuration stored?**

A ○ NVRAM

B ○ VRAM

C ○ ROM

D ○ Flash

2 **Which of the following best identifies the boot order of a Cisco device?**

A ○ Bootstrap loads IOS from flash; POST; apply startup configuration to running config.

B ○ Bootstrap loads IOS from flash; apply startup configuration to running config; POST.

C ○ POST; apply startup configuration to running config; bootstrap loads IOS from flash.

D ○ POST; bootstrap loads IOS from flash; apply startup configuration to running config.

3 **What is the purpose of the POST?**

A ○ Locate the IOS in flash memory.

B ○ Locate the IOS in ROM.

C ○ Verify that hardware is functioning.

D ○ Apply the startup configuration.

4 **What is the command to move to priv exec mode?**

A ○ router>enable

B ○ router#enable

C ○ router(config)#enable

D ○ router#disable

5 **Which of the following prompts represents global configuration mode?**

A ○ router#

B ○ router(config)#

C ○ router>

D ○ router(global)#

6 Which command can you use to save the running configuration to the startup configuration?

A ○ `copy startup-config running-config`
B ○ `save running-config startup-config`
C ○ `save running-config`
D ○ `copy running-config startup-config`

7 Where is the startup configuration stored?

A ○ NVRAM
B ○ VRAM
C ○ ROM
D ○ Flash

8 What type of memory stores the Cisco IOS?

A ○ NVRAM
B ○ VRAM
C ○ ROM
D ○ Flash

9 Which of the following IDs are used to reference a Fast Ethernet port? (Select two.)

A ❏ s0/0
B ❏ f0/0
C ❏ con 0
D ❏ aux 0
E ❏ fa0/0

10 What type of cable is used to connect to the console port?

A ○ Crossover
B ○ Straight-through
C ○ Null modem
D ○ Rollover

Answers

1 **B.** The running configuration is stored in volatile RAM (VRAM). *See "Volatile RAM (VRAM)."*

2 **D.** When a device boots up, the POST first verifies the hardware, and then the bootstrap program loads the IOS image file from flash memory. Once the IOS has been loaded, the startup configuration is read from NVRAM and copied to the running configuration. *Review "The boot process."*

3 **C.** The POST is the first step performed in the boot process and is responsible for verifying that the hardware is functioning. *Check out "The boot process."*

4 **A.** In order to move to priv exec mode, you use the `enable` command from user exec mode. *Peruse "Priv exec mode."*

5 **B.** Global configuration mode is identified with `(config)#` in the prompt. *Take a look at "Global configuration."*

6 **D.** In order to save the running configuration to more permanent memory, use the `copy running-config startup-config` command. *Peek at "The boot process."*

7 **A.** The startup configuration is stored in permanent memory known as nonvolatile RAM (NVRAM). *Look over "Nonvolatile RAM (NVRAM)."*

8 **D.** The IOS image file is stored in flash memory and is loaded from flash memory into RAM during the bootup process. *Study "Flash memory."*

9 **B, E.** When working on a router or switch, you can refer to a Fast Ethernet port by using an interface ID such as f0/0 or fa0/0. *Refer to "Cisco Ethernet ports."*

10 **D.** The rollover cable, also known as a *console cable,* is used to connect a system to the console port. *Examine "Console port."*

Chapter 2: Basic Router Configuration

In This Chapter

✔ Basic configuration of a Cisco router

✔ Configuring Ethernet interfaces

✔ Configuring serial interfaces

✔ Configuring passwords

✔ Configuring users

✔ Configuring banners

✔ Verifying your configuration

*T*he previous chapter introduces you to the basics of a Cisco device, such as the different types of memory and what happens when you power on your Cisco device. Now it is time to take a look at some basic configuration settings that are normally applied to Cisco routers.

In this chapter, you discover how to configure popular settings on the Cisco router, such as the name of the router and the IP addresses on the interfaces, and how to configure passwords. This chapter also explores how to verify your configuration with a number of show commands that are critical to your CCENT certification exam!

Quick Assessment

1   (True/False). Routers use interfaces to send and receive information.

2   A(n) _____ interface is typically used for a point-to-point link or to connect to a service provider.

3   A router is an example of a layer-_____ device.

4   (True/False). PPP is an example of a serial link protocol.

5   The `show` _____ command is used to view the interfaces and their settings.

Answers

1 *True*. See "Configuring Ethernet Interfaces."

2 *Serial*. Review "Configuring Serial Interfaces"

3 *3*. Check out "Basic Configuration of a Cisco Router."

4 *True*. Peruse "Encapsulation protocol."

5 `interfaces`. Take a look at "The show interfaces command."

Basic Configuration of a Cisco Router

The network router is a layer-3 device that provides routing functions on the network. In this section, you discover the basic configuration steps needed to get your Cisco router up and running. This includes the steps you must take to connect to the router for the first time through the console port, and changing the device hostname which is a way to uniquely identify your router.

The most interesting way to understand this stuff is to look at an example network topology and walk through the configuration of the routers in the example. Figure 2-1 shows the example network that I have created. This example has two routers, labeled R1 and R2, that are connected to one another via their serial ports. Each router is also connected to a switch that has one workstation connected to it. This chapter focuses on the router configuration.

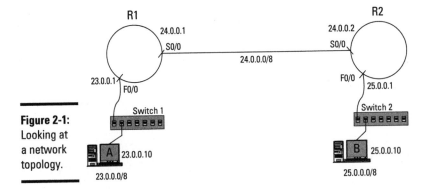

Figure 2-1: Looking at a network topology.

Connecting to your Cisco device

The first thing you want to do is connect to the router via the console port so you can configure the router. To connect to the console port on the router, you connect one end of the console cable (normally a blue cable) to your administrative system's serial port, and then connect the other end to the console port on the router. (See Figure 2-2.) The sections that follow explain in more detail what you see in this figure.

Once you have physically connected your system to the router's console port, you are ready to launch *HyperTerminal* — an application that allows you to administer the router via the command-line interface (CLI). You can launch HyperTerminal on your Windows system by choosing Start⇨ All Programs⇨Accessories⇨Communications⇨HyperTerminal.

Figure 2-2:
A console
cable is
used to
connect to
the router
so that
you can
administer
the device.

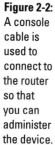

HyperTerminal was removed from Windows Vista and Windows 7. If you are running those operating systems, or another operating system that does not have a HyperTerminal application, you need to download third-party software. You can download and install TeraTerm as a replacment product from `http://ttssh2.sourceforge.jp/`.

When you select HyperTerminal, it asks you how you are going to connect to the Cisco device. Two popular options are to connect to the local console port using the serial port on your computer (COM1), or you can Telnet into the router by its IP address once the router has been configured. If you have not configured the IP address on the router, you need to connect via COM1.

The following are the steps to connect to your Cisco router using HyperTerminal:

1. **Choose Start➪All Programs➪Accessories➪Communications➪ HyperTerminal.**

The Connection Description dialog box appears.

2. **In the Connection Description dialog box, type the name of this connection (for example, R1), and then click OK.**

   The Connect To dialog box opens.

3. **Select COM1 from the Connect Using drop-down list (see Figure 2-3), and then click OK.**

Figure 2-3:
When connecting to a console port on a router from the serial port on your computer, choose COM1.

4. **In the COM1 Properties dialog box that appears, set the Bits per Second to 9600 and change the Flow Control to None. All other options are left at the defaults.**

   Figure 2-4 displays what your COM1 settings should be.

Figure 2-4:
Configuring COM1 properties to support a connection to the Cisco device.

5. **Click OK.**

6. **After you click OK, you should be connected, but you need to press the Enter key once.**

   This creates activity in the HyperTerminal window and causes the router prompt to come up.

Changing the hostname

After you connect to the router, the first thing you want to do is configure the name (also known as the *hostname*). All Cisco routers have a default hostname of *router,* so changing the name of the router is a great first change to make so that you know which router you are connected to at any point in time. Also, most companies design relevant naming conventions to use on network devices, conventions that indicate the location of the device and maybe its purpose. For example, you might use NY-R01 or NY-R-Acct1 as the name of your router for the New York office.

Look back at Figure 2-1, and you see that, in this example, the first router will have the name R1 and the second router will have the name R2.

Configuring router R1

To change the name of router R1, the first thing you have to do is move from user exec mode to privilege (priv) exec mode by typing enable. You should notice that your prompt now ends with a # instead of a >, as shown in the following code example:

```
Router>enable
Router#
```

Once you are in priv exec mode, the name of the device is a global change — remember that changes that affect the router as a whole are modified in global configuration mode. To move to global configuration mode, type the configure terminal command — or config term for short.

When you're in global configuration mode, your prompt displays as router(config)#. To change the name of the router from global configuration, you can use the hostname command where you pass in a value as a parameter to use as the hostname. The following is the complete code sample to change your hostname for router R1:

```
Router>enable
Router#config term
Router(config)#hostname R1
R1(config)#
```

Configuring router R2

You change the name of router R2 the exact same way you changed the name of router R1. You will need to connect to the console port on router R2 and then use HyperTerminal to connect to the device. Once you are connected, you should be in user exec mode and be able to use the same commands to configure the name of router R2:

```
Router>enable
Router#config term
Router(config)#hostname R2
R2(config)#
```

When you are configuring multiple Cisco devices by connecting to the console port on each device, you do not need to close and open HyperTerminal each time. To switch from one device to another, simply take the console cable out of one device and plug it into the second device — then press the enter key on the keyboard while in HyperTerminal!

Configuring Ethernet Interfaces

Once you have configured the names of the routers, the next step is to configure the network interfaces on the router. Each network interface is similar to the network card in your computer — it is used to send and receive information. If you intend to use the interface to connect to another device or network, you have to configure it with the correct protocol information and then enable the interface so that it is up and running. Let's look at how to configure the Ethernet interfaces first!

You can connect the Ethernet interfaces on your router to local network devices, such as a switch, using a straight-through cable, but you can also use the Ethernet port to connect to another router or a computer if you use a crossover cable.

Once you connect the Ethernet port on the router to the switch, you then have to configure the settings on the interface. Example settings you may configure on the Ethernet card are IP settings, a description, a speed, and maybe duplex settings. I tell you how to configure those settings in the paragraphs that follow.

Configure IP settings for the Ethernet interface

In order to configure your Ethernet interface for an IP address, you need to navigate to the interface prompt. You can navigate to the Ethernet prompt a number of different ways depending on the type of interface. If you are dealing with an older router, such as a 2501, you simply use the `interface` ethernet0 command to navigate to the first interface. If you are dealing with a router that has Fast Ethernet ports (100 Mbps), you use the interface fastethernet 0/0 syntax to connect to the first Fast Ethernet port, or interface fastethernet 0/1 to connect to the second Fast Ethernet port.

```
R1>enable
R1#config term
R1(config)#interface f0/0
```

Notice in the code example that you use the interface command from global configuration mode. Also notice that I have used the abbreviation for the Fast Ethernet port; f0/0. Using the abbreviation of fa0/0 is also very common.

Book II
Chapter 2

Basic Router
Configuration

You will notice that the Cisco devices and documentation label the Fast Ethernet ports using the FE identifier, for example, FE0/1. However, when you configure the port you must use f0/1 or fa0/1 instead of fe0/1 as the FE label is not used in a command and will not work.

Once you have navigated to the Ethernet port, you can assign an IP address to the interface. To assign an IP address to an interface on the router, you use the ip address command, as shown here.

```
R1(config-if)#ip address 23.0.0.1 255.0.0.0
```

Most router interfaces will have a static address assigned to them, but from time to time you may want to configure the interface to obtain an IP address from a DHCP server on the network. (I tell you about DHCP servers in Book I, Chapter 3.) The following code sample is used to configure the interface to obtain an IP address from a DHCP server:

```
R1(config-if)#ip address dhcp
```

Again, this is not overly popular, as assigning a static address is normally what we do with routers — you do not want the IP address of the router to change.

To remove the IP address from an interface, you use the no ip address command once in the interface prompt.

Configure a description for the Ethernet interface

Once you assign an IP address to the Ethernet interface, you may want to assign a description. The purpose of the description on an interface is to allow you to add a quick comment (up to 240 characters) about the purpose of the port. In my example in this chapter, I configure the Ethernet port on router R1 for a description of "Private LAN," as shown here:

```
R1>enable
R1#config term
R1(config)#interface f0/0
R1(config-if)#description Private LAN
```

The benefit of adding a description is that when you troubleshoot later on down the road, you will see the description of the interface as you use some of the different show commands — extremely valuable when you cannot remember the purpose of all the different network connections!

Configure other settings for the Ethernet interface

Before you enable the interface, you may want to configure other settings on the Ethernet interface. The first setting you may want to configure, in addition to an IP address, is the duplex setting, such as setting the interface to half- or full-duplex. In the code example that follows, I configure the interface for full-duplex (allows the port to send and receive at the same time):

```
R1>enable
R1#config term
R1(config)#interface f0/0
R1(config-if)#duplex full
```

You can use the full-duplex setting when making direct connections between two devices such as connecting two devices with a crossover cable, or when connecting a device to a switch. You use half-duplex when connecting the device to a hub.

You can also set the speed of the network link with the speed command, which indicates what speed to run the interface at, as most interfaces today support multiple speeds. You normally have a choice of 10 Mbps, 100 Mbps, or 1000 Mbps (depending on the interface) and you should choose a speed for the interface that matches the speed at the other end of the link. For example, if you are connecting your router to a 10 Mbps hub then you set the speed on your router's interface to 10 Mbps. The following code example sets the speed of the interface to 100 Mbps:

```
R1>enable
R1#config term
R1(config)#interface f0/0
R1(config-if)#speed 100
```

Enabling and disabling the interface

Once the interface is configured, you can then enable the interface with the no shutdown command. I know that the no shutdown command is a strange command to enable an interface, but it makes sense when you find out where it came from. To understand the no shutdown command, it is probably best to find out how to disable an interface with the shutdown command.

A lot of my students ask why you use the `shutdown` command to disable an interface, instead of something like "disable." The reason is that the `disable` command is already used for exiting from priv exec mode to user exec mode, so Cisco had to come up with a different command to disable the interface — so `shutdown` is the command.

With most Cisco commands, if you want to do the opposite action or negate a command, you put the word `no` at the beginning of the command. For example, if `shutdown` disables an interface, `no shutdown` enables the interface.

After configuring the interface, use the following command to enable it and bring it online (meaning the interface is active and up and running):

```
R1(config-if)#no shutdown
```

After using the `no shutdown` command, you see a status message, indicating that the state of the link has changed. This message tells you which interface is changing state and what that new state is — either up or down. The following is a sample of the status message you should receive:

```
%LINK-5-CHANGED: Interface FastEthernet0/0, changed state to up
```

If the Cisco device reports back a state change of *down* it means the interface is offline and not running. If the state of the interface is *up,* it means the interface is online and is running.

Configuring router R2 for the Ethernet interface

After you configure the Ethernet interface on router R1, you can configure similar settings on router R2 from the sample network diagram. Looking back at Figure 2-1, note that the Fast Ethernet port is used to connect to the LAN and you see that the Fast Ethernet port on router R2 should be assigned the IP address of 25.0.0.1. Use the following commands to configure router R2:

```
Router>enable
Router#config term
Router(config)#hostname R2
R2(config)#interface f0/0
R2(config-if)#ip address 25.0.0.1 255.0.0.0
R2(config-if)#description Private LAN
R2(config-if)#speed 100
R2(config-if)#duplex full
R2(config-if)#no shutdown

%LINK-5-CHANGED: Interface FastEthernet0/0, changed state to
    up
R2(config-if)#
```

Once you have configured router R2, you can navigate backward in your prompts using the `exit` command. The first time you type `exit`, it takes you back to global configuration mode, but the second `exit` command takes you back to priv exec mode. Here's what that looks like:

```
R2(config-if)#exit
R2(config)#exit
%SYS-5-CONFIG_I: Configured from console by console
R2#
```

Configuring Serial Interfaces

After you configure the Ethernet interface, you can look at configuring the serial interface. In the previous chapter, you found out that the serial interface is typically used to connect to a WAN device, such as a CSU/DSU, which is connected to your service provider's WAN link (remember that the WAN is used to connect multiple LANs together over great distances).

You can also use the serial port to connect two routers directly together (a point-to-point link) using a special cable known as a *back-to-back serial cable*. This is very popular in test labs and training environments as you do not actually need to have a real WAN (multiple LANs connected over great distances) to practice using serial port commands.

Configure IP settings for the serial interface

You can configure the IP address on the serial port the same way you configure an IP address on an Ethernet port, which I cover earlier in the chapter. The following commands demonstrate how to configure router R1's serial interface from Figure 2-1:

```
R1>enable
R1#config term
R1(config)#interface serial 0/0
R1(config-if)#ip address 24.0.0.1 255.0.0.0
```

In the example here, you notice that the serial port is from slot 0, port 0 (0/0). When you navigate to the interface, you use the `ip address` command just as you do on an Ethernet port. (See the "Configure IP settings for the Ethernet interface" section earlier in the chapter for details.

If you are unsure of the different port numbers on your Cisco device, you can normally view the running configuration to see each interface and its configuration. To view the running configuration on your Cisco device you use the `show running-config` command. You find out more about working with your configuration files in the "Verifying Your Configuration" section later in this chapter.

Configure a description for the serial interface

After configuring an IP address on the serial port, you may want to add a description to the port as well. You use the `description` command just as you do on the Ethernet interface to add a description:

```
R1(config-if)#description WAN-To-ISP
```

Like setting a description on your Ethernet port for the LAN connection, it may be useful to label the interface that is connecting to your service provider with the `description` command. This helps you identify the purpose of the connection to that interface when you view the configuration.

Configure other settings for the serial interface

There are some unique settings you are required to configure on the serial port in order for it to send and receive data across the link such as the encapsulation protocol and the clock rate (if it is a DCE device). Some of the additional optional settings you may want to configure are settings such as the description (which you have already seen) and the bandwidth setting. This section shows you how to configure these required and optional settings on your serial interface.

Encapsulation protocol

When sending data across a serial link, you must send the data using a serial link protocol. This works by placing the data you are sending inside a layer-2 frame using a serial link protocol, known as an *encapsulation protocol.* (See Figure 2-5.) The paragraphs that follow explain in greater detail how this works.

Figure 2-5: Serial link protocols encapsulate the packet inside a frame to send across the serial link.

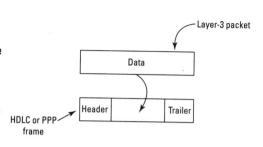

The serial port is typically used to connect to your service provider allowing you access to the WAN. You find out more about WANs and configuring WAN interfaces in Book IV, Chapter 4, but for a now, take a look at two main serial link protocols — HDLC and PPP.

The *High-Level Data Link Control* (HDLC) protocol is a layer-2 protocol that is designed to send information over a serial link from one point to another. Cisco devices use a Cisco proprietary version of the HDLC protocol, meaning that a Cisco router running HDLC on one side of the link cannot communicate with a different vendor running HDLC on the other side of the link. If the serial link has a Cisco router on both ends of the link, you can use the HDLC protocol to allow communication across the link.

To enable the HDLC protocol on the serial port, you use the encapsulation command followed by the protocol you want to use. The following are the commands to enable the HDLC protocol on a serial port:

```
R1>enable
R1#config term
R1(config)#interface serial 0/0
R1(config-if)#encapsulation hdlc
```

If you are using different types of routers on the ends of the serial link, you may be unable to use the HDLC protocol, and you may have to use an industry-standard serial link protocol such as the *Point-to-Point Protocol* (PPP), which has been a popular serial link protocol for many years. Computers with dialup connections have been using it to connect from computer to ISP for over a decade now.

If you wish to configure your router to use the PPP protocol as its encapsulation protocol, use the encapsulation command as follows:

```
R1>enable
R1#config term
R1(config)#interface serial 0/0
R1(config-if)#encapsulation ppp
```

Remember that you must use the same protocol at either end of the serial link in order for communication to occur! In my example, if you configure the serial port on router R1 for PPP, the serial port on router R2 must also use PPP.

The following code example configures both router R1 and router R2 for the HDLC protocol:

On router R1:

```
R1>enable
R1#config term
R1(config)#interface serial 0/0
R1(config-if)#encapsulation hdlc
```

On router R2:

```
R2>enable
```

```
R2#config term
R2(config)#interface serial 0/0
R2(config-if)#encapsulation hdlc
```

Clock rate

After you configure the encapsulation protocol on the serial link, you may have to set the clock rate, which sets the clocking speed, or timing, for the link itself. It is typically set by the service provider if your serial port connects to the service provider. However, if you are not connecting the serial port to the WAN service provider — for example, you are creating a point-to-point connection between the two routers using a back-to-back serial cable — then you are required to configure one end of the link as the end that provides the speed of the link.

In a point-to-point configuration, the end that provides the speed uses the *Data Communication Equipment* (DCE) end of the cable — the other end of the cable is the *Data Terminal Equipment* (DTE), which does not provide clocking information. Figure 2-6 shows the label on the end of a back-to-back cable, which indicates whether you are using the DCE or DTE end of the link.

Once you connect the serial ports with a back-to-back cable, you then go to the router that has the DCE end of the cable to set the clock rate. In my example, connect the DCE end of the cable to router R1 so that router R1 has to provide the clocking information. The following code sample demonstrates how to set the clocking speed in *bits per second* (bps):

```
R1>enable
R1#config term
R1(config)#interface serial 0/0
R1(config-if)#clock rate 64000
```

In the example code here, the clock rate, or speed of the link, is set to 64000 bits per second; essentially, it is a 64 Kbps link. If you want to see the different speeds that can be set with the clock rate command, you can use the help system within the Cisco IOS by typing a ? where the speed would be supplied:

```
R1(config-if)#clock rate ?
Speed (bits per second
  1200
  2400
  4800
  9600
  19200
  38400
  56000
  64000
  72000
(output has been cut for briefness)
R1(config-if)#
```

Book II
Chapter 2

Basic Router
Configuration

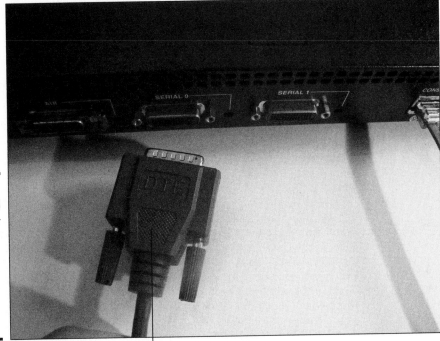

Figure 2-6:
The DTE end
of a back-to-
back serial
cable used
to connect
two Cisco
devices
directly
together.

The DTE label

Bandwidth

Another setting you can specify on your different interfaces is the bandwidth
of the link. The *bandwidth* is different from the clock rate in the sense that
the bandwidth setting does not control the actual speed of the link — it is
just a setting that different routing protocols use to determine the best route
to a destination network. Bandwidth will make more sense to you once you
understand routing and routing protocols, which is covered in Book III, but
the key point is the links with higher bandwidth become the more preferred
routes to a destination.

Setting the bandwidth is optional, and the default bandwidth on a serial
link is 1.544 Mbps. To set a different bandwidth on an interface, you use the
`bandwidth` command, which is measured in kilobits:

```
R1>enable
R1#config term
R1(config)#interface serial 0/0
R1(config-if)#bandwidth 1000
```

The following summarizes the commands that we will use to configure the serial ports on router R1 and router R2:

For router R1:

```
R1>enable
R1#config term
R1(config)#interface serial 0/0
R1(config-if)#ip address 24.0.0.1 255.0.0.0
R1(config-if)#clock rate 64000
R1(config-if)#encapsulation hdlc
R1(config-if)#bandwidth 1000
R1(config-if)#no shutdown
```

For router R2:

```
R2>enable
R2#config term
R2(config)#interface serial 0/0
R2(config-if)#ip address 24.0.0.2 255.0.0.0
R2(config-if)#encapsulation hdlc
R2(config-if)#bandwidth 1000
R2(config-if)#no shutdown
```

Notice in the above code examples that the clock rate is set only on router R1, as it is the DCE device — the clock rate does not need to be set on the DTE device because it receives the clocking information from the DCE device.

Also notice that at the end of the code for both serial interfaces, there is a no shutdown command, which is used to enable the serial interface. If you do not use the no shutdown command, the interface will default to being disabled.

Configuring Passwords

Cisco devices support many different types of passwords. You want to make sure you set a password for when an administrator tries to enter privilege exec mode, but you also want to set passwords on each of the connection types, such as a console port connection, auxiliary port connection, and a Telnet connection.

This section introduces you to configuring passwords on your Cisco device, and the topic is revisited again in Book IV, Chapter 2.

You can configure your Cisco router or switch to prompt for a password when someone tries to move from user exec mode to priv exec mode on the router or switch by setting an *enable password*. An enable password kicks in when someone tries to use the `enable` command to go to priv exec mode.

```
R1>enable
R1#config term
R1(config)#enable password mypass
```

The problem with the `enable password` command is that the password is stored in the router configuration in clear text — anyone who can view the configuration can see the password! To countermeasure this, Cisco has created what it calls the *enable secret* — it is a password for enable mode, but the password is encrypted in the configuration file. If you configure an enable password and an enable secret, the secret is the one that takes precedence and will need to be used to enter privilege exec mode.

Use the following commands to configure both the enable password and the enable secret on your Cisco router:

```
R1>enable
R1#config term
R1(config)#enable password mypass
R1(config)#enable secret mysecret
```

It is important to remember the difference between the `enable password` command and the `enable secret` command — the enable password is stored in an unencrypted format in the device configuration files, while the enable secret is encrypted in the configuration. Note that it is a best practice to use the enable secret over the enable password.

Let's take a look at the configuration after the enable password and the enable secret are set on the router. To view the current configuration, you can use the `show running-config` command:

```
R1(config)#exit
R1#show running-config

Building configuration...
(output omitted for briefness)
!
enable secret 5 $1$u76B$IOFVJ7VxfVXYVpGDrFTcI0
enable password mypass
!
(output omitted for briefness)
!
```

Notice in the above output that the secret has been encrypted, but the enable password is stored in clear text.

For the CCENT certification exam, remember that the enable secret is encrypted in the configuration and takes precedence over the `enable password` command when both are used.

After setting a password to enter privilege exec mode, you should also set a password on each of the different ports that someone may use to make a connection to your router; these ports are the console port, the auxiliary port, and the Telnet ports used for remote connections.

**Book II
Chapter 2**

**Basic Router
Configuration**

Console password

In order to set a password on the console port — which you need to do so that someone can make a connection through that port — you use the following commands:

```
R1>enable
R1#config term

R1(config)#line con 0
R1(config-line)#password conpass
R1(config-line)#login
```

Looking at the commands in this example, you see that you first move to global configuration to make the change. Then you use the `line con 0` command to move into the configuration of the console port. When you are in the `line` prompt, you can specify the password you want for this port. Then you use the `login` command to turn on authentication for that port and have the Cisco device ask for a password. If you forget the `login` command, the Cisco device will never prompt for the password.

Remember for the CCENT certification exam that the `login` command is needed in order to enable authentication. If the `login` command is missing, your router will not prompt for passwords on the port you are connecting through!

Auxiliary port password

Configuring a password on the auxiliary port is similar to configuring the console port for a password. In order to configure the auxiliary port for a password, use the following commands:

```
R1>enable
R1#config term

R1(config)#line aux 0
R1(config-line)#password auxpass
R1(config-line)#login
```

You can see that the only difference between setting a password on the console port and the auxiliary port is the `line aux 0` command. Notice that the `login` command is supplied once again and is used to enable authentication on that port.

Telnet password

The purpose of setting the console and auxiliary port passwords on the router is to control who can physically connect to those ports and manage the device. Administrators can also Telnet into the router in order to administer the device from a remote location. You need to configure your router for Telnet passwords if someone is going to Telnet into the router. The following commands are used to configure passwords on the Telnet ports:

```
R1>enable
R1#config term

R1(config)#line vty 0 15
R1(config-line)#password vtypass
R1(config-line)#login
```

Cisco devices require a Telnet password and a password when entering privilege exec mode to be configured on the router in order to be able to remotely connect to the router. The Cisco devices do not allow you to do remote administration without these passwords set.

Notice in the preceding code example that to set Telnet passwords you use the `line vty` command. `vty` is the code used for Telnet ports, and it stands for *virtual teletype*. The other key point is that there are multiple Telnet ports; each port allows a Telnet connection, and in order to require a password for each connection, you specify 0 and then the maximum number of Telnet ports.

To find out how many Telnet ports your router supports, use the following command:

```
R1>enable
R1#config term
R1(config)#line vty 0 ?
  <1-15>  Last Line number
  <cr>
```

Notice in the preceding code example that my router supports up to 15 Telnet ports.

Let's take a look at what the configuration looks like with all the passwords configured on each of the different ports. In order to view the current configuration, you use the `show running-config` command again:

```
R1#show running-config
Building configuration...
!
(output omitted for briefness)
!
enable secret 5 $1$u76B$IOFVJ7VxfVXYVpGDrFTcI0
enable password mypass
!
(output omitted for briefness)
!
line con 0
  password conpass
  login
line aux 0
  password auxpass
  login
line vty 0 4
  password vtypass
  login
line vty 0 15
  password vtypass
  login
!
(output omitted for briefness)
```

 Configuring passwords is revisited in the security best practices chapter, Book IV, Chapter 2. There you find out that storing the passwords in clear text within the configuration is not a good practice, so you should use the `service password-encryption` command to encrypt all passwords that are stored in the configuration file.

Creating Users

If you want to require more than just a password in order for an administrator to connect to your router, you can create usernames and passwords on your Cisco router.

In order to create a user on your Cisco router, you use the `username` command in global configuration mode, as shown here:

```
R1>enable
R1#config term
R1(config)#username dan password danpass
R1(config)#username glen password glenpass
```

Once you have created the usernames and passwords, you can then force the router to prompt for those local usernames (*local* meaning the accounts in the current device) when an administrator tries to log in to the different ports; use the `login local` command to do so. The following shows how to enable login access on the console port using the local user accounts that you have configured:

```
R1(config)#line con 0
R1(config-line)#login local
```

If you want the router to ask for those usernames when someone tries to connect to the Telnet ports, you use the following commands after creating the usernames:

```
R1(config)#line vty 0 15
R1(config-line)#login local
```

Again, notice that the `login local` command (instead of just `login`) is used — it tells the Cisco device to enable authentication but to use the local usernames configured on the device. You configure the auxiliary port the same way but navigate to the aux 0 port instead of con 0.

Configuring Banners

A *banner* is a message you wish to display to an administrator when he connects to the Cisco router. Depending on the type of banner you create, this message could appear before or after login. The purpose of the banner is to show critical information to the administrator, and in this day and age, it is also used to display a legal notice that unauthorized access to the device is strictly prohibited.

I discuss banners in more detail in Book IV, Chapter 2.

Types of banners

Before I show you how to configure banners on a Cisco router or switch, it is important to know that there are different types of banners that you can configure. Each type of banner is designed for a specific purpose and appears at a different time during the logon process.

+ **Message of the day (MOTD):** Displays before the administrator is asked to log in. The initial purpose of the MOTD banner was to show a temporary notice that could change from time to time to the person connecting. Network administrators are now using the MOTD banner to display legal notices that unauthorized access to the device is prohibited.

+ **Login:** Displays before the administrator is asked to log in but appears after the MOTD banner (if one is set) displays. The login banner is designed to display a more permanent message, something that will not change from day to day, to the person connecting.

✦ **Exec:** The exec banner, or what I like to refer to as the *user exec banner* (not an official term, by the way), displays after an administrator logs on and enters user exec mode. Use this type of banner to display only those messages that you want to display to an administrator who has authenticated to the system. Because the MOTD and login banner appear before a login, anyone who connects to the system can view them; the exec banner, however, is visible only after an administrator logs on — so you know that whoever sees the message is an authorized person.

Configuring a banner

When you are comfortable with the different types of banners (if you are not now, see the previous section), take a look at how to configure the banners on a Cisco router. Keep in mind that you configure banners on a switch the exact same way.

The following code configures a MOTD banner on your Cisco device.

```
R1(config)#banner motd #
Enter TEXT message. End with the character '#'.
This device is for authorized personnel only.
Please disconnect at once if you have not been given
    permission to access this device.
#
R1(config)#
```

Notice that you set the MOTD banner from global configuration mode with the banner motd # command. The # symbol serves as the *delimiter* and indicates what character ends the message when you type the message out. Notice that I have two lines of text set as the message of the day and a third line with the #, indicating that I am done setting the message of the day.

You can use whichever character you like as the delimiter, as long as you specify it in the banner command.

The following code example specifies the login banner. Notice that it is very similar to setting the MOTD banner, but you use the login keyword instead of motd in the banner command.

```
R1(config)#banner login #
Enter TEXT message. End with the character '#'.
*** Login Required. Unauthorized use is prohibited ***
#
R1(config)#
```

You are not required to set the MOTD banner and the login banner, and most companies usually set one or the other. If you find that you have the need to show a unique message on different days, you may set your normal "unauthorized access is prohibited" message as the login banner so that you can have a MOTD banner as well when it is needed.

Notice in the following output that when someone connects to the router or switch the MOTD is displayed before the login banner:

```
R1 Con0 is now available
Press RETURN to get started!

This device is for authorized personnel only.  Please
    disconnect at once if you have not been given permission
    to access this device

*** Login Required.  Unauthorized use is prohibited ***

User Access Verification

Password:
```

If you wish to set a user exec password, you can use the banner exec command. Remember, this message shows after login as the individual enters user exec mode:

```
R1(config)#banner exec #
Enter TEXT message.  End with the character '#'.
*** Be sure to update the change log after any changes ***
#
R1(config)#
```

Other Useful Commands

Before you discover how to view your configuration, I want to mention a few other commands that I think are useful to know when working with Cisco routers.

Saving configuration changes

The first command I want to review is how to save your changes. You find out in the previous chapter that there are two main configuration files — the running-config and the startup-config. The running-config file is stored in volatile memory (RAM) and is lost when you power down or reboot the router. The startup-config file is nonvolatile RAM (NVRAM), which maintains its data even when the power is lost or the router is rebooted.

As you make your changes, they are stored in the `running-config` file, and if you wish to permanently store the changes, you must copy the changes to the `startup-config` file. The following command copies your running configuration to the startup configuration for permanent storage:

```
R1#copy running-config startup-config
Destination filename [startup-config]?
Building configuration...
[OK]
```

Notice in the code example that after typing the `copy` command, the Cisco IOS prompts for confirmation by asking what the destination filename is. Notice that Cisco provides a default response in the square brackets, and if you wish to use that default response, you can press the Enter key instead of typing a response. You can't see it in the output, but I pressed Enter to accept the default.

The `copy` command has been around in the Cisco world for a long time, and in the next chapter, you find out how to use it to store your configuration on a TFTP server. Because saving your changes to the `startup-config` file is so popular, Cisco came up with a shorter command that you can use to perform the same task — the `write` command.

```
R1#write
Building configuration...
[OK]
```

What I like about the `write` command is that it does not prompt for a destination — it always writes to the `startup-config` file. One less prompt is always a good thing!

The `write` command is short for `write memory`, which is also a valid command and can be used. There is a rumor that Cisco will be dropping the `write` command in favor of the `copy` command as the `copy` command is more flexible and supports different memory types as the source and destination of the copy operation. You find out more about the `copy` command in Book II, Chapter 3.

Deleting the configuration

You can delete your router's configuration, also known as *erasing the configuration,* by erasing the startup configuration and then rebooting the router. Because there is no startup configuration present, the Cisco device will ask if you want to use the initial configuration dialog to apply basic settings.

If you answer yes, the initial configuration dialog prompts you for basic password information and interface configuration. If you answer no, the initial configuration dialog is skipped and you are given a default configuration for the device, which has a hostname of router and no settings applied to the interfaces.

To erase the configuration on your Cisco router, use the following commands:

```
R1>enable
R1#erase startup-config
Erasing the nvram filesystem will remove all configuration
    files! Continue? [confirm]
[OK]
Erase of nvram: complete

R1#reload
Proceed with reload? [confirm]
```

If you want to save this default configuration after the reload is complete, simply use the write command to save the running configuration to the startup configuration.

Looking at the most recently used commands

One of the great things about the Cisco IOS is it keeps a history of the commands that you type so you can navigate to a command at a later time without having to type it again! You can navigate through the history of commands by using the up and down arrow keys on the keyboard.

You can view the list of commands stored in the history by using the show history command as shown here:

```
R1#show history
  enable
  show history
  config terminal
  show history
  show interfaces
  show history
  show running-config
  show history
```

The maximum number of commands stored in the history is ten, but you can change that setting. To view the history size setting, you can use the show terminal command as follows:

```
R1#show terminal
(Output cut for briefness)
Modem type is unknown.
Session limit is not set.
```

```
Time since activation: 00:03:04
Editing is enabled.
History is enabled, history size is 10.
DNS resolution in show commands is enabled
Full user help is disabled
Allowed input transports are All.
Allowed output transports are pad telnet rlogin.
Preferred transport is telnet.
(Output cut for briefness)
```

In order to change the history size, you use the `terminal history` command to increase the number of commands stored in the history:

```
R1#terminal history size 30
R1#show terminal
(Output cut for briefness)
Session limit is not set.
Time since activation: 00:03:04
Editing is enabled.
History is enabled, history size is 30.
DNS resolution in show commands is enabled
Full user help is disabled
Allowed input transports are All.
Allowed output transports are pad telnet rlogin.
Preferred transport is telnet.
(Output cut for briefness)
```

Domain lookups and console timeout

When working on a Cisco router there are two things that may annoy you — having an incorrect command trying to be resolved through DNS and having the console timeout when working. This section discusses both of these annoyances and how to disable both features.

Domain lookups

When you type a command incorrectly, the Cisco device thinks you are trying to connect to another system by name so it tries to resolve the incorrect command to an IP address by sending the query to a DNS server. A great feature, right? Well the problem is it takes time for the reply to come back for a name (or command, in this case) you know will not have an associated IP address in DNS, and you will get tired of waiting — especially if you are like me and have a typo in every second command you type!

To disable DNS lookups use the following command:

```
R1>enable
R1#config term
R1(config)#no ip domain-lookup
```

Console Timeout

You may want to have the console timeout within a certain amount of time of inactivity. This means if you leave the system for a few minutes and get tied up, you have the confidence of knowing that the console connection will timeout and you will be automatically disconnected — no one will be able to sit at the console and execute commands because you have been automatically disconnected!

To configure the console to timeout you can use the following commands:

```
R1>enable
R1#config term
R1(config)#line con 0
R1(config-line)#exec-timeout 1 45
```

In the code above, the timeout is set to 1 minute and 45 seconds. You can also disable the console timeout feature by setting the exec-timeout to 0 minutes and 0 seconds as shown below:

```
R1(config-line)#exec-timeout 0 0
```

Verifying Your Configuration

After you complete the basic configuration of your routers, you want to verify the configuration to ensure that the router is configured properly. This section introduces you to a number of different commands that you should be familiar with to verify your configuration.

Viewing the configuration files

I am sure you are familiar with the first command by now — it is the show running-config command, which displays the current configuration in volatile memory. You use this command to verify the commands you have used to configure the passwords, banners, and the configuration of the different interfaces.

```
R1>enable
R1#show running-config
Building configuration...
(Output cut for briefness)
version 12.4
no service password-encryption
hostname R1
!
!
interface FastEthernet0/0
 ip address 23.0.0.1 255.0.0.0
 duplex auto
```

```
 speed auto
!
interface Serial0/2/0
 bandwidth 1000
 ip address 24.0.0.1 255.0.0.0
 clock rate 64000
!
line con 0
 password conpass
 login
 history size 30
line vty 0 15
 password vtypass
 login
!
(output cut for briefness)
```

You use the `show running-config` command to display settings such as the IP address on an interface or the password on a specific port, but it is also a great way to understand commands from an already configured router!

Remember that the `running-config` is not permanent memory, so if you want to ensure that your configuration settings will come back after a reboot, you may want to verify the settings in the `startup-config`. You can view the `startup-config` file by using the `show startup-config` command, which displays similar results as the running configuration.

In the code above, notice that the interface in the `show running-config` command is identified as serial0/2/0. This interface identifier is different than the slot/port syntax you read about in the previous chapter. In this example, the first 0 is an index number for the device (router or switch) in a pool of devices. So the full syntax is device/slot/port, and you may see this from time to time.

Viewing interface configuration

Not only do you need to view the `running-config` to verify the configuration of your router (see the previous section), but it is also important for you to know how to view the status of the interfaces by using a number of `show` commands.

The CCENT certification exam will give you a number of *simlets* (a scenario-based question that uses a simulator) where you are allowed to use the `show running-config` command, but you will also have simlets where that command is disabled because Cisco wants to test your knowledge of other `show` commands. This section is designed to expose you to those commands.

The show interfaces command

The first command to view the status of your interfaces is the show interfaces command. This command has a lot of output, as it displays information about every interface on the router. You are presented with one screenful of information at a time, and you need to press the spacebar to continue viewing the next screen of information. To cancel viewing the information at any time, you press the Esc key. The following shows sample output from the show interfaces command:

```
R1>show interfaces
FastEthernet0/0 is up, line protocol is up
  Hardware is Lance, address is 00d0.bc99.1801 (bia 00d0.
  bc99.1801)
  Internet address is 23.0.0.1/8
  MTU 1500 bytes, BW 100000 Kbit, DLY 100 usec, rely 255/255,
  load 1/255
  Encapsulation ARPA, loopback not set
(Output cut for briefness)
Serial0/2/0 is up, line protocol is up
  Hardware is HD64570
  Internet address is 24.0.0.1/8
  MTU 1500 bytes, BW 1000 Kbit, DLY 20000 usec, rely 255/255,
  load 1/255
  Encapsulation HDLC, loopback not set, keepalive set (10 sec)
(Output cut for briefness)
```

The first thing I want you to notice in the output is that there are two statuses on each port; in this example, the interface is up and the line protocol is up. This status message (which is shown in bold type in the output here) is important because the first part (FastEthernet0/0 is up) indicates that there is a physical link between the interface and the line you connected to the interface, and the second part (line protocol is up) indicates that the protocol has been configured properly.

There may be a different status displayed on the interface as summarized below; you find out more on troubleshooting interfaces in Book III, Chapter 5:

✦ **Serial0/2/0 is up:** As mentioned, if the interface displays as up it means there is a physical link between the interface and the other end of the cable you are connecting to the interface. A status of up is a good thing as it indicates everything is up and running.

✦ **Serial0/2/0 is down:** A status of down indicates there is a problem with the connection or you have misconfigured the interface. In order to fix the problem review your configuration.

✦ **Serial 0/2/0 is administratively down:** When you see a status of administratively down it means an administrator has purposely disabled the interface. In order to bring the interface up you use the no shutdown command on the interface.

Assuming the interface is up, there are two statuses that can display with the line protocol — up or down. If the line protocol is up then you have configured the protocol for the interfaces at either end of the link properly. If the line protocol is down, you should verify the configuration on both ends of the link as there is most likely a mistake in the configuration if the protocol cannot come online. The most common mistake is to load the wrong encapsulation protocol or to not set the clock rate on the DCE end of the cable.

For the CCENT certification exam, remember that the first part of the status message (FastEthernet0/0 is up) indicates a layer-1 status, while the second part of the status message (line protocol is up) is an indication that the layer-2 protocol is fine.

Also notice that you can see the MAC address and the IP address assigned to each of the ports when using the show interfaces command.

Book II
Chapter 2

Basic Router
Configuration

The show interface f0/0 command

If you find there is too much information displayed on the screen when you use the show interfaces command, you can use the show interface (note that "interface" is singular, not plural) command and then supply the ID of a specific interface to see status information on just that one interface.

```
R1>show interface f0/0
FastEthernet0/0 is up, line protocol is up
  Hardware is Lance, address is 00d0.bc99.1801
  Internet address is 23.0.0.1/8
  MTU 1500 bytes, BW 100000 Kbit, DLY 100 usec, rely 255/255,
    load 1/255
  Encapsulation ARPA, loopback not set
(Output cut for briefness)
```

The output is nearly the same as the show interfaces command, but again you see the status of only the one interface. The show interface command is great if you are troubleshooting a specific link or interface.

The show ip interface command

Another show command (one that is probably more important for your CCNA exam than the CCENT but is still worth mentioning) is the show ip interface command. When you use this command, it displays each interface and tells you whether that interface is up and running. It also displays protocol information such as the IP address on the interface and things like whether an access list is applied. *Access lists* (an in-depth discussion of them is outside the scope of this book) are lists of rules that allow or deny traffic through the interface.

```
R1>show ip interface
FastEthernet0/0 is up, line protocol is up
  Internet address is 23.0.0.1/8
```

```
Broadcast address is 255.255.255.255
Address determined by setup command
MTU is 1500 bytes
Helper address is not set
Directed broadcast forwarding is disabled
Outgoing access list is not set
Inbound  access list is not set
Proxy ARP is enabled
Security level is default
Split horizon is enabled
ICMP redirects are always sent
ICMP unreachables are always sent
ICMP mask replies are never sent
(Output cut for briefness)
```

The show ip interface brief command

A more relevant command for the CCENT certification exam is the show ip interface brief command, which displays a nice listing of status information for all the ports on your router:

```
R1>show ip interface brief
Interface       IP-Address   OK? Method Status Protocol
FastEthernet0/0 23.0.0.1     YES manual up     up
FastEthernet0/1 unassigned   YES manual up     down
Serial0/2/0     24.0.0.1     YES manual up     up
```

Notice that you can see the IP address assigned to the interface, what method is used to assign that IP address (either manual or through DHCP), the status of the link (layer-1), and the status of the layer-2 protocol.

The show controller command

The final command to mention is the show controller command, where you supply the interface as a parameter. This command is valuable to use on serial ports because it shows the clock rate that is set on the port and displays whether the serial port is the DCE device or the DTE device.

```
R1>show controller serial0/1
Interface Serial0/2/0
Hardware is PowerQUICC MPC860
DCE V.35, clock rate 64000
(Output cut for briefness)
```

Notice in the output above that the serial port is the DCE device and has a clock rate of 64000 bps.

Be sure to know the different show commands for the CCENT certification exam, as you will need to use them in simulators to troubleshoot problems. The best way to get comfortable with them is to practice using them before taking the exam!

Chapter Summary

This chapter introduces you to basic configuration settings on a Cisco router, with the focus on configuring the interfaces on the router. The following are some key points to remember regarding basic configuration:

✦ Settings are stored in volatile RAM (running-config) until you use the write command to save the settings to the startup-config.

✦ The Cisco IOS stores your recent commands in the history, so you can access previously typed commands using the arrow keys on your keyboard.

✦ You change the history size using the terminal history size command in priv exec mode.

✦ You must set an encapsulation protocol on your serial port to carry data over the serial link. Two popular serial link protocols are HDLC and PPP.

✦ The speed of the WAN link is normally determined by the service provider, but if you connect to another Cisco router using a back-to-back serial cable, the DCE device needs to specify the speed of the link with the clock rate command.

✦ You negate most commands with the keyword no at the beginning of the command.

✦ There are a number of commands you can use to view your current configuration when troubleshooting. You can start with the show running-config command to view a list of configuration commands applied to the router.

✦ You use the show interfaces command to view the status of each of the network interfaces.

✦ You use the show ip interface brief command to display a table-like view that summarizes the status of the interfaces.

✦ The show controller serial0/1 command determines the clock rate set on the interface and whether the interface is the DCE or DTE device. You can use this show controllers command on any serial interface by its interface ID.

Lab Exercises

Now that you have some basic understanding of how to configure settings on a Cisco router, you can practice the configuration steps by looking at some network diagrams and applying the configuration. These labs build off of each other, so be sure to complete the labs in order.

Lab 2-1: Configuring router interfaces

In this lab, look at Figure 2-7 and configure each of the interfaces as instructed. At the end of each interface configuration, the code is provided for you to check your work.

✦ You will need two routers connected by a back-to-back serial cable for this lab and a switch connected to each of the Ethernet ports.

✦ Using Figure 2-7 as a guideline, connect all the devices and configure the interfaces on router NY-R1 and BOS-R1.

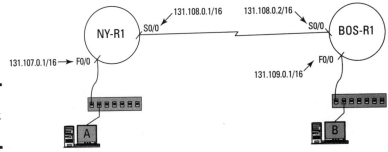

Figure 2-7:
Lab network diagram.

Router NY-R1 configuration

1. **Change the hostname of the router to NY-R1.**

2. **Configure the serial port as a DCE device by setting the clock rate to 64000 and the encapsulation protocol of HDLC. Also assign an IP address to the interface of 131.108.0.1/16. Ensure that you enable the interface.**

3. **Configure the Ethernet port by assigning the IP address of 131.107.0.1/16, a description of Private LAN, and then enable the card.**

4. **Double-check your work by verifying it against the following code:**

```
Router>enable
Router#config term
Router(config)#hostname NY-R1
NY-R1(config)#interface f0/0
NY-R1(config-if)#ip address 131.107.0.1 255.255.0.0
NY-R1(config-if)#description Private LAN
NY-R1(config-if)#no shutdown

NY-R1(config-if)#interface serial 0/0
NY-R1(config-if)#ip address 131.108.0.1 255.255.0.0
NY-R1(config-if)#clock rate 64000
NY-R1(config-if)#encapsulation hdlc
NY-R1(config-if)#no shutdown
```

Router BOS-R1 Configuration

1. Change the hostname of the second router to BOS-R1.

2. Configure the serial port as a DTE device by *not* setting the clock rate. Set the encapsulation protocol to HDLC and assign an IP address to the interface of 131.108.0.2/16. Ensure that you enable the interface.

3. Configure the Ethernet port by assigning the IP address of 131.109.0.1/16, set the description to Private LAN, and enable the card.

4. Double-check your work by verifying it against the following code:

```
Router>enable
Router#config term
Router(config)#hostname BOS-R1
BOS-R1(config)#interface f0/0
BOS-R1(config-if)#ip address 131.109.0.1 255.255.0.0
BOS-R1(config-if)#description Private LAN
BOS-R1(config-if)#no shutdown

BOS-R1(config-if)#interface serial 0/0
BOS-R1(config-if)#ip address 131.108.0.2 255.255.0.0
BOS-R1(config-if)#encapsulation hdlc
BOS-R1(config-if)#no shutdown
```

Lab 2-2: Configuring passwords

In this exercise, configure passwords and a banner on the NY-R1 Cisco router.

1. Configure an enable password of "mypass" and a secret password of "mysecret."

2. Configure a console password of "con."

3. Configure an auxiliary password of "aux."

4. Configure a password of "telnet" for all the Telnet ports.

5. Set a message of the day banner that says, "This device is for authorized personnel only."

6. The following is the code you should have come up with to set these passwords:

```
NY-R1>enable
NY-R1#config term
NY-R1(config)#enable password mypass
NY-R1(config)#enable secret mysecret

NY-R1(config)#line con 0
NY-R1(config-line)#password con
NY-R1(config-line)#login
```

```
NY-R1(config)#line aux 0
NY-R1(config-line)#password aux
NY-R1(config-line)#login

NY-R1(config)#line vty 0 15
NY-R1(config-line)#password telnet
NY-R1(config-line)#login

NY-R1(config)#banner motd #
Enter TEXT message.  End with the character '#'.
This device is for authorized personnel only.
```

7. **Save the configuration on both routers with a `write` command.**

Lab 2-3: Viewing the configuration

In this lab, practice viewing the configuration of the NY-R1 router.

1. **On router NY-R1, use the `show interfaces` command to verify the configuration of the serial and Fast Ethernet ports.**

   a. *Can you determine the IP address of each interface?*

   b. *Can you verify that each interface is up and running?*

   c. *Can you determine the MAC address of the Ethernet port?*

2. **Use the `show ip interface brief` command to get a summary of each interface.**

   a. *Can you determine the IP address of each interface?*

   b. *Can you verify that each interface is up and running?*

3. **Use the `show controller serial0/0` command to view whether NY-R1 is the DCE or DTE device.**

   a. *Can you verify that NY-R1 is the DCE device?*

   b. *Can you verify that each interface is up and running?*

   c. *Can you determine the MAC address of the Ethernet port?*

Prep Test

1 When looking at the `interface fastethernet 0/1` command, what is the port number for the interface?

A ○ 0

B ○ 1

C ○ 2

D ○ 3

2 What command do you use on the interface to assign an IP address to the interface automatically via DHCP?

A ○ `R1(config)#ip address dhcp`

B ○ `R1(config)#ip dhcp address`

C ○ `R1(config-if)#ip dhcp address`

D ○ `R1(config-if)#ip address dhcp`

3 Which of the following are additional commands needed to configure a serial interface over what is needed when configuring an Ethernet interface? You are configuring the DCE device on a serial link. (Select all that apply.)

A ❑ `clock rate 64000`

B ❑ `description WAN link`

C ❑ `encapsulation hdlc`

D ❑ `ip address dhcp`

4 Which of the following are encapsulation protocols that can be used on a serial link for a Cisco router? (Select all that apply.)

A ❑ IPX

B ❑ PPP

C ❑ PPTP

D ❑ HDLC

E ❑ RIP

5 **You need to find out if the serial port on your router is acting as the DCE device in the Point-to-Point link with another router. What command do you need to use?**

A ○ `show ip interface brief`

B ○ `show interfaces`

C ○ `show interface serial 0/0`

D ○ `show controller serial0/0`

6 **Which of the following commands is used to display a table (output shown below) indicating the IP assigned to each interface and the status of the interface?**

```
Interface       IP-Address  OK? Method Status
FastEthernet0/0  23.0.0.1    YES manual up
FastEthernet0/1  unassigned  YES manual up
Serial0/2/0      24.0.0.1    YES manual up
Serial0/3/0      unassigned  YES manual administratively down
```

A ○ `show ip interfaces`

B ○ `show ip table`

C ○ `show ip interface brief`

D ○ `show ip table brief`

7 **You use the `show interfaces` command and get the following status on your serial port. Which layer of the OSI model is there a problem with?**

```
Serial0/2/0 is up, line protocol is down
```

A ○ Layer-1

B ○ Layer-2

C ○ Layer-3

D ○ Layer-4

8 **What command can be used to modify the history size on the Cisco router?**

A ○ `R1#terminal history size 30`

B ○ `R1(config)#terminal history size 30`

C ○ `R1(config)#history size 30`

D ○ `R1#history size 30`

9 Using the output below from the `show interfaces` command, what is most likely the problem?

```
Serial0/2/0 is up, line protocol is down
```

A ○ There is no physical link.

B ○ A protocol or clock rate has not been set.

C ○ You need to configure the router as the DCE device.

D ○ You need to configure the router as the DTE device.

10 You are having trouble communicating with networks that are connected to your FastEthernet0/0 port. You use the following command to view the status of the links. What can you do to solve the problem?

```
R1>show ip interface brief
Interface       IP-Address   OK? Method Status
FastEthernet0/0 23.0.0.1     YES manual administratively down
FastEthernet0/1 unassigned   YES manual up
Serial0/2/0     24.0.0.1     YES manual up
Serial0/3/0     unassigned   YES manual administratively down
```

A ○ Configure an encapsulation protocol.

B ○ Assign an IP address.

C ○ Configure it to use DHCP.

D ○ Enable the interface.

Answers

1 **B.** The syntax to reference an interface is first the type of interface, followed by the slot/port, for example, `fastethernet 0/1`. *See "Configure IP settings for the Ethernet interface."*

2 **D.** In order to assign an IP address to an interface via DHCP, you use the `ip address` command but pass in the word `dhcp` as a parameter instead of an actual IP address. *Review "Configure IP settings for the Ethernet interface."*

3 **A, C.** When configuring a serial interface that acts as the DCE device, you need to provide the encapsulation protocol and the clock rate. *Check out "Configure other settings for the serial interface."*

4 **B, D.** You can configure the serial interfaces of a Cisco router for either the HDLC encapsulation protocol or the PPP protocol. *Peruse "Encapsulation protocol."*

5 **D.** The `show controller` command is used on an interface to display the clock rate on the link and to indicate whether the interface acts as the DTE or DCE device. *Take a look at "The show controller command."*

6 **C.** The `show ip interface brief` command displays a table listing all the interfaces and their settings. *Peek at "The show ip interface brief command."*

7 **B.** When using the `show interfaces` command, you see the status of the link shown in the format of *Serial0/2/0 is up, line protocol is down*. The `Serial0/2/0 is up` part indicates whether there is a link (layer-1), while the `line protocol down` part indicates whether the layer-2 protocol has been configured properly. *Look over "The show interfaces command."*

8 **A.** The command to increase the number of commands that are stored in the history buffer is the `terminal history size` command, which is executed from priv exec mode. *Study "Other Useful Commands."*

9 **B.** If the line protocol is down, there is a problem with the configuration of the serial link protocol or the clock rate. Also note that if the protocol has not been configured properly on the other end, the line protocol still displays as down. *Refer to "The show interfaces command."*

10 **D.** Because the status of the link shows as `administratively down`, this is an indication that you have disabled the port or have not enabled the port. You need to enable the port with a `no shutdown` command. *Examine "The show interfaces command."*

Chapter 3: Managing Cisco Devices

In This Chapter

✔ **Backing up your configuration and IOS**

✔ **Understanding CDP**

✔ **Using Telnet for remote administration**

The previous chapter introduces you to the basics of configuring your Cisco device, through a discussion of topics such as changing the hostname, configuring passwords and banners, and configuring the network interfaces. It tells you how to save your configuration from volatile memory, known as the running-config, to more permanent storage known as the startup-config (stored in nonvolatile memory).

This chapter extends your Cisco device knowledge by discussing how to back up your configuration and IOS to a central server so you can restore that configuration back to your Cisco device at any point in time. You also find out more about two popular protocols used in the Cisco world — Telnet for remote administration, and the Cisco Discovery Protocol (CDP), which you can use to discover information about Cisco devices on the network.

Quick Assessment

1   (True/False). CDP is used to remotely connect to a device.

2   A _____ server stores uploaded configuration and IOS files.

3   The _____ command is used to back up the device configuration.

4   (True/False). You can use Telnet to remotely connect to a device.

5   The IOS is stored in _____ memory.

Answers

1 *False*. See "CDP overview."

2 *TFTP*. Review *"Backing Up Your Configuration and IOS."*

3 *Copy*. Check out *"Backing up your configuration."*

4 *True*. Peruse *"Telnet overview."*

5 *Flash*. Take a look at *"Backing up your IOS."*

Backing Up Your Configuration and IOS

The configuration for your Cisco routers and switches is stored in two places by default. The configuration is stored in the running-config file and the startup-config file (if you have saved your running-config to the startup-config). It is important to also back up this configuration to a location off the Cisco device in case the configuration files are erased by accident or you decide to replace the device. In the case where you replace the device, it is possible for you to restore the configuration from the central location to the new device — saving you time because you will not need to configure settings, such as the hostname and the IP addresses on the interfaces, manually on the new device.

You can back up the Cisco router or switch configuration to a *Trivial File Transfer Protocol* (TFTP) server, which is a special server designed for transferring small files over UDP port 69. When looking at protocols that transfer files, TFTP is more basic compared to FTP. For example, it does not support authentication, while FTP (File Transport Protocol) does, but TFTP has less overhead than FTP — so it is more efficient.

It is important to back up the configuration of all of your Cisco devices so that you can restore the configuration when needed. I have talked to a number of administrators who have a base configuration stored in a file on a TFTP server; when they receive a new Cisco device for production, they download the base configuration from the TFTP server — which contains items such as passwords, encryption, and banner information — and then they tweak it from there.

Installing TFTP software

When looking to back up your Cisco device configuration to a central location, the first thing you need is a TFTP server. For this discussion, I use the 30-day trial version of WinAgents TFTP Server software that you can download and install on most versions of Windows, including Windows XP, Windows Vista, and Windows 7. The 30-day trial should be good enough to experiment with backing up your configuration but note that if you plan on using the software past the trial period you will need to purchase it.

To install and configure your own TFTP server, follow these steps:

1. **Download a trial version of WinAgents TFTP Server software from** `www.tftp-server.com`.

2. **Run the downloaded executable (most likely named `tftpserver-setup.exe`).**

3. **In the welcome screen that appears (see Figure 3-1), click Next.**

**Book II
Chapter 3**

**Managing Cisco
Devices**

Figure 3-1:
Installing
WinAgents
TFTP
Server.

   4. **Select the I Accept the License Agreement option and click Next.**

   5. **On the Select Installation Type screen, select Complete, and then click Next.**

   The WinAgents TFTP Server setup opens ports on your Windows firewall to allow communication to the TFTP server. Notice that UDP port 69, the TFTP port, is opened. (See Figure 3-2.)

   6. **Click Next.**

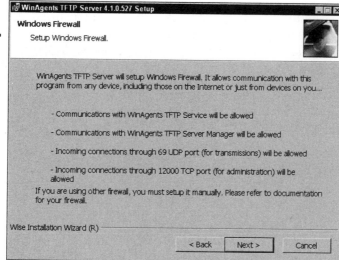

Figure 3-2:
WinAgents
TFTP
Server's
installation
configures
the
Windows
firewall
to allow
TFTP traffic
to pass
through the
firewall.

7. On the next screen, click Next to begin the installation.

8. When the installation completes, click Finish.

9. To verify that the TFTP Server software is running, choose Start⇨All Programs⇨WinAgents TFTP Server 4⇨TFTP Server Manager.

10. As the TFTP Server Manager program launches, you are asked which TFTP server you wish to connect to. (See Figure 3-3.)

    Notice that the defaults are the local server (your system).

11. Click OK.

    You are notified that the TFTP service is not running and asked if you would like to start the service.

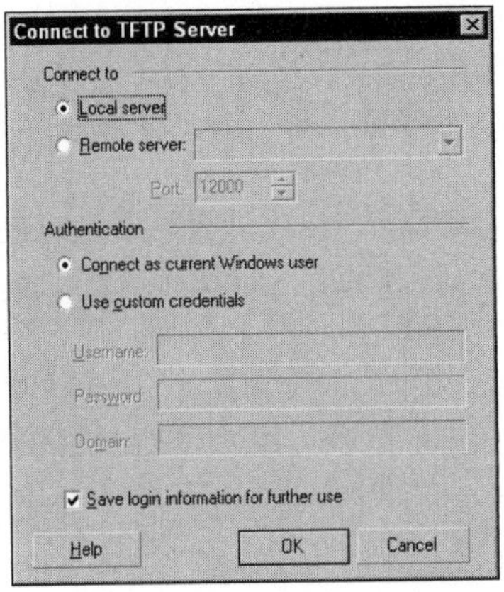

Figure 3-3:
Connecting the TFTP Server Manager to your local TFTP server.

12. You want the service running in order to be able to upload configuration files to the TFTP server, so click Yes.

    When the WinAgents TFTP Server Manager program launches, you see a screen similar to that shown in Figure 3-4. The top-left pane (the Folder List) is the folder structure on the TFTP server, while the top-right pane (the File List) displays the files located in the selected folder. At the bottom of the screen (the Transfer Log), you see status messages of file uploads and downloads.

    With the TFTP server installed, you can now back up your router and switch configurations to the TFTP server.

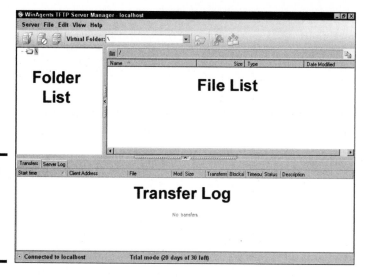

Figure 3-4:
Identifying
the TFTP
Server
Manager
screen.

Backing up your configuration

In Book II, Chapter 1, you find out that you can use the copy command to copy the running-config to the startup config. The following code reviews this syntax:

```
Copy running-config startup-config
```

To break down the syntax for the copy command, you always start with the word copy followed by the source of what you are copying, and then you specify the destination. The syntax may be better displayed as

```
Copy <source> <destination>
```

The exciting point about the copy command is that you can use it to copy your configuration — or even your IOS — from many different sources to many different destinations. In order to copy your running-config to a TFTP server, you use the following command:

```
Copy running-config tftp
```

After you enter this command, the Cisco IOS prompts you for the IP address of the TFTP server and asks what you would like to call the destination configuration file when it copies the running-config to the server.

```
NY-R1#copy running-config tftp
Address or name of remote host []? 192.168.5.100
Destination filename [ny-r1-confg]? ny-r1-confg-May272010
!!
1664 bytes copied in 4.344 secs (383 bytes/sec)
```

In the code here, you see that I use the `copy` command on router NY-R1 and specify a destination of `tftp`. The IOS has prompted me for the IP address of the TFTP server, and I have supplied an address of `192.168.5.100`. The IOS then asks me for the name of the destination file. Notice in square brackets that the IOS has a default filename to use. If you want to use that filename, you can simply press the Enter key or type a different filename like I did. I chose to include the date that the configuration was saved in the filename.

Once the file is saved, you receive confirmation of how many bytes were saved in how much time. If you navigate back to TFTP Manager (see Figure 3-5), you see the new file in the File List (the top-right pane) and also see the file transfer information (including the IP address of the system or device that performed the transfer) in the Transfer Log at the bottom of the screen.

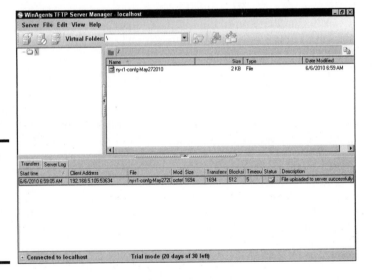

Figure 3-5:
The TFTP Server Manager displays upload activity.

Restoring your configuration

Once your configuration is backed up to a TFTP server, you can then restore that configuration at any point in time to your Cisco device. To restore the configuration, you use the `copy` command, but this time you flip the source and destination parameters around so that the source is the TFTP server and the destination is the running configuration, as shown here:

```
Copy tftp running-config
```

To test this command, you can change the name of the router from NY-R1 to NY-R1b. After the restore operation is complete, you should have the old router name applied from the configuration file stored on the TFTP server.

```
NY-R1>enable
NY-R1#config term
NY-R1(config)#hostname NY-R1b
NY-R1b(config)#exit
```

After you have changed the name of the router, you can use the `copy` command to copy the configuration from the TFTP server to your running configuration. The Cisco IOS will prompt you for the IP address of the TFTP server and the name of the configuration file to download.

```
NY-R1b#copy tftp running-config
Address or name of remote host []? 192.168.5.100
Source filename []? ny-r1-confg-May272010
Destination filename [running-config]?
Accessing tftp://192.168.5.100/ny-r1-confg-May272010...
Loading ny-r1-confg-May272010 from 192.168.5.100 (via
    FastEthernet0/0): !
[OK - 1664 bytes]

1664 bytes copied in 9.492 secs (175 bytes/sec)
NY-R1#
```

Notice at the end of the preceding code that the router name is restored to the original name that has been backed up to the configuration file. This is a quick way to validate that the changes have been applied from the configuration file on the TFTP server, but understand that any settings in the configuration file are restored, including old passwords.

For the CCENT certification exam, be sure you are familiar with backing up your router and switch configuration to a TFTP server, and also know how to restore the configuration back to the device from the TFTP server.

Backing up your IOS

It is important to back up your configuration, but you should also back up the Cisco IOS from your router to the TFTP server, just in case the IOS is corrupted on your device. In the case where the IOS is corrupt on your device, you can restore the IOS from the TFTP server — as long as you have backed it up to the TFTP server.

In order to back up the IOS, you need to know the filename of the IOS that is stored in the flash memory you wish to back up. To view a list of files in flash memory, you use the `show flash` command. The IOS file is a file stored in flash that has a `.bin` extension and most likely has a filename that symbolizes the series of the device you are working with. The following code uses the `show flash` command on my Cisco 2811 router:

Book II
Chapter 3

Managing Cisco
Devices

```
NY-R1#show flash
-#- --length-- -----date/time------ path
1     29774888 Sep 01 2006 19:02:14 +00:00 c2800nm-
   entservicesk9-mz.123-14.T7.bin
2         1823 Jun 01 2006 15:56:38 +00:00 sdmconfig-2811.cfg
3      4734464 Jun 01 2006 15:57:08 +00:00 sdm.tar
4       833024 Jun 01 2006 15:57:22 +00:00 es.tar
5      1052160 Jun 01 2006 15:57:42 +00:00 common.tar
6         1038 Jun 01 2006 15:57:58 +00:00 home.shtml
7       102400 Jun 01 2006 15:58:14 +00:00 home.tar
8       491213 Jun 01 2006 15:58:32 +00:00 128MB.sdf
10         720 Nov 30 2006 02:37:04 +00:00 vlan.dat

195948544 bytes available (60559360 bytes used)
```

Notice in the code that the first file in flash memory (displayed with a 1 on the left) is 29,774,888 bytes in size (29MB), was created on September 01, 2006, and has the filename of c2800nm-entservicesk9-mz.123-14. T7.bin. Notice that the filename has the series number specified in the filename (c2800) — this is useful so that you know what devices you can apply this IOS to. You want to make sure that you have enough space on the TFTP server to accommodate the size of your IOS file.

After you note the filename of the IOS file that is stored in flash memory, you use the copy command to back up this file to the TFTP server. The syntax to use the copy command is copy flash tftp; the source of the copy is flash memory, and the destination is the TFTP server.

```
NY-R1#copy flash tftp
Source filename []? c2800nm-entservicesk9-mz.123-14.T7.bin
Address or name of remote host []? 192.168.5.100
Destination filename [c2800nm-entservicesk9-mz.123-14.
   T7.bin]? <press enter>
!!!!!!!!!!!!!!!!!!!!!!!!!!!!!!!!!!!!!!!!!!!!!!!!!!!!!!!!!!!!!!!!!!
!!!!!!!!!!!!!!!!!!!!!!!!!!!!!!!!!!!!!!!!!!!!!!!!!!!!!!!!!!!!!!!!!!
!!!!!!!!!!!!!!!!!!!!!!!!!!!!!!!!!!!!!!!!!!!!!!!!!!!!!!!!!!!!!!!!!
29774888 bytes copied in 79.828 secs (372988 bytes/sec)
NY-R1#
```

In the code here, I use the copy flash tftp command, and the Cisco IOS prompts me for the name of the file in flash memory that I want to copy to the TFTP server. It then prompts me for the IP address of the TFTP server. Lastly, the IOS prompts me for the name of the destination file to create on the TFTP server. I recommend keeping the default name by pressing the Enter key. (The default name is shown in square brackets.) As the file copies to the TFTP server, the progress of the copy operation is displayed with exclamation points. When the copy completes, the IOS reports how many bytes have been copied and how long it took.

Upgrading the Cisco IOS

You upgrade your Cisco IOS on the Cisco device by copying the IOS from the TFTP server to flash memory on your Cisco device. This means that you first need to have the IOS on the TFTP server. You can obtain a new version of the IOS for your device from the Cisco Web site (www.cisco.com) and then copy the IOS to the TFTP server for downloading to the device.

If you do not have enough flash memory on the destination device to store the current IOS image and the new image being copied from the TFTP server, the existing IOS image is deleted from flash memory to make space. Be sure to back up your existing IOS to the TFTP server before copying a new IOS image to the device. You can use the show flash command to view how much memory is available in flash memory.

Once the IOS is on the TFTP server, you use the copy command to upgrade your IOS in flash memory. The syntax to copy the new IOS is copy tftp flash, and once again, the Cisco IOS prompts you for the TFTP server address and the filename to download to flash memory. The following example downloads an IOS from my TFTP server to flash memory:

```
NY-R1>enable
NY-R1#copy tftp flash
Address or name of remote host []? 192.168.5.100
Source filename []? c2800nm-entservicesk9-mz.123-14.T7.bin
Destination filename [c2800nm-entservicesk9-mz.123-14.
    T7.bin]? <press enter>
%Warning:There is a file already existing with this name
Do you want to over write? [confirm] <press enter>
Accessing tftp://192.168.5.100/c2800nm-
    entservicesk9-mz.123-14.T7.bin...
Loading c2800nm-entservicesk9-mz.123-14.T7.bin from
    192.168.5.100 (via FastEthernet0/0):
!!!!!!!!!!!!!!!!!!!!!!!!!!!!!!!!!!!!!!!!!!!!!!!!!!!!!!!!!!!!!!
!!!!!!!!!!!!!!!!!!!!!!!!!!!!!!!!!!!!!!!!!!!!!!!!!!!!!!!!!!!!!!
!!!!!!!!!!!!!!!!!!!!!!!!!!!!!!!!!!!!!!!!!!!!!!!!!!!!!!!!!!!!!!
[OK - 29774888 bytes]

29774888 bytes copied in 112.796 secs (263971 bytes/sec)
```

Notice in the preceding code that after the copy tftp flash command is used the IOS prompts for the IP address of the TFTP server. It then asks for the filename to download and what to call the file at the destination (flash memory). To accept the default filename (which is shown in square brackets), you press Enter. In my example, the IOS filename is already present, so it asks me if it is okay to overwrite the file. If you are prompted to overwrite and wish to do so, ensure that you have a backup of the existing IOS file on a TFTP server first. This helps you recover the old IOS file if something does

Book II
Chapter 3

Managing Cisco Devices

go wrong with the overwrite operation. As the file downloads, the progress is indicated with a number of exclamation points. After the copy operation is successful, the IOS reports how many bytes have been copied and how long it took.

Boot system command

After you copy the new IOS image from the TFTP server to the device, you can specify which IOS the router is to use (when you have multiple IOS images in flash memory) by using the `boot system` command. When using the `boot system` command, you specify where the IOS is coming from and what the IOS filename is. The following commands show how to display the contents of flash memory and then specify an IOS image filename to use as the IOS image:

```
NY-R1#show flash
System flash directory:
File   Length    Name/status
  1    50938004  c2800nm-advipservicesk9-mz.124-15.T1.bin
[50938004 bytes used, 13078380 available, 64016384 total]
63488K bytes of processor board System flash (Read/Write)

NY-R1#config term
NY-R1(config)#boot system flash c2800nm-
    advipservicesk9-mz.124-15.T1.bin
```

If you want your Cisco router to boot from the IOS image file stored on the TFTP server, you can do that as well! When booting your router off an IOS image located on the TFTP server, the image is not downloaded to flash memory on the device — instead, when the device is started it contacts the TFTP server and boots the IOS from the TFTP server.

The advantage of loading the IOS from a TFTP server on bootup is that you do not have to add the IOS to all of your routers! This gives you a central location to update your IOS without having to run around to all your routers and upgrade the IOS.

The huge disadvantage of loading the IOS from the TFTP is that if the TFTP server goes down, then you will be unable to boot any of your routers! This central point of failure is a huge disadvantage and one that makes loading the IOS from a TFTP something I cannot recommend. However, if you are still interested in loading the IOS from the TFTP server, you can use the `boot system tftp <image filename>` command in global configuration mode:

```
boot system tftp c2800-advipservicesk9-mz.124-15.T1.bin
```

In Book II, Chapter 1, you read about the Cisco boot process and the fact that the Cisco device has a mini-IOS (known as *RX-Boot*) stored in ROM that you can use when you are unable to boot an IOS normally. If you want to boot your Cisco device to this mini-IOS, you can use the `boot system rom` global configuration command. Once you boot to the mini-IOS, you can configure and enable an interface and copy an IOS from a TFTP server.

Understanding CDP

In this section, you find out about the *Cisco Discovery Protocol* (CDP) and how you can use it to identify neighboring Cisco devices on the network. Output for the `show cdp` commands can tell you which devices are connected to a device, how often CDP information is sent, and how long CDP information is stored. With `show cdp` commands, you can also find a device's ID, the port that it connects to, its model or series, and its IP address. In this section, I also tell you how to disable CDP.

Book II
Chapter 3

Managing Cisco
Devices

You are most definitely going to see a CDP question or two on the CCENT certification exam, so be sure to know this topic well.

CDP overview

The *Cisco Discovery Protocol* (CDP) is a protocol that Cisco designed for its devices to help you gather information about neighboring devices. (A *neighboring device* is a device that your router or switch is directly connected to.)

Each Cisco device sends CDP advertisement messages to each interface every 60 seconds by default. These advertisement messages identify information about the devices, such as the type of device (for example, whether the device is a switch or router), the model number of the device, the version of the IOS that the device is running, and the IP address assigned to the device.

Figure 3-6 displays the network topology you can use to understand the concepts of CDP. Notice that there are two routers, named NY-R1 and BOS-R1. Each router is connected to a switch for its network. The switches are named NY-SW1 and BOS-SW1.

I focus on CDP from the context of NY-R1, but understand that CDP is running on all devices by default — so this discussion applies to all devices. The NY-R1 router sends out CDP messages every 60 seconds (known as the *CDP timer*), identifying the information about NY-R1. The CDP packet is sent out to all interfaces (see Figure 3-7) in this example; the packet is sent out of the serial port and the Fast Ethernet port and reaches the devices — the BOS-R1 (via the serial interface) and the NY-SW1 (via the Fast Ethernet interface) — at the other end of those links.

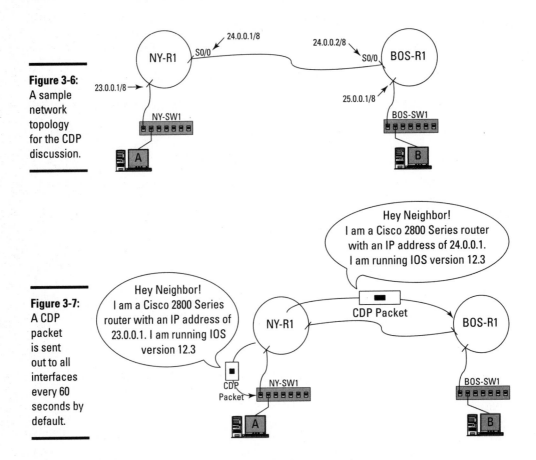

Figure 3-6:
A sample network topology for the CDP discussion.

Figure 3-7:
A CDP packet is sent out to all interfaces every 60 seconds by default.

When the BOS-R1 router and the NY-SW1 switch receive the CDP packet from NY-R1, they store the CDP information about the NY-R1 locally for 180 seconds by default. This is known as the *CDP hold timer* value. When you use the CDP commands (more on those in a minute) on BOS-R1 or NY-SW1 to view information about neighboring devices, the information is retrieved from the local device indicating that there is a neighboring device out there called NY-R1 and providing all related information about the device, such as the type of device, the model, the version of the IOS it is running, and the IP address.

For the CCENT certification exam, know that the *CDP timer* is how frequently CDP packets are sent out and is set to 60 seconds by default. Also know that the *CDP hold timer* is how long CDP information is stored on the local device and is set to 180 seconds by default.

As a Cisco administrator, you can view the setup of CDP on your system with the show cdp command:

```
NY-R1>show cdp
Global CDP information:
    Sending CDP packets every 60 seconds
    Sending a holdtime value of 180 seconds
    Sending CDPv2 advertisements is enabled
```

Notice in the preceding code that NY-R1 is sending CDP packets every 60 seconds (the cdp timer) and that the holdtime value is set to 180 seconds. If you want to change the CDP timer value (cdp timer) or the holdtime value, you use the cdp timer and cdp holdtime global configuration commands:

Book II
Chapter 3

```
NY-R1(config)#cdp timer 90
NY-R1(config)#cdp holdtime 240
NY-R1(config)#exit
NY-R1#show cdp
Global CDP information:
        Sending CDP packets every 90 seconds
        Sending a holdtime value of 240 seconds
        Sending CDPv2 advertisements is  enabled
```

Managing Cisco Devices

Remember that you can use the help feature in the Cisco IOS at any point in time to understand these commands. For example, if you want to find out what commands are supported by CDP, you can use the following:

```
NY-R1(config)#cdp ?
  advertise-v2       CDP sends version-2 advertisements
  holdtime           Specify the holdtime (in sec) to be sent
  log                Log messages generated by CDP
  source-interface   Insert the interface's IP in all CDP
  timer              Specify the rate CDP packets are sent
  run
```

Notice that holdtime and timer are parameters used with the cdp command. If you want to view help on these commands, you can use syntax similar to the following:

```
NY-R1(config)#cdp holdtime ?
  <10-255> Length  of time  (in sec) that receiver must keep
    this packet
```

Using CDP

Now that you understand the purpose of CDP, I want to show you how you can use CDP on your devices to gather information about neighboring devices on the network.

The show cdp neighbors command

The first command to talk about is a very popular command used to display neighboring devices — the show cdp neighbors command. Figure 3-8 displays the output of the show cdp neighbors command from router NY-R1.

Figure 3-8:
Using the show cdp neighbors command to view information about other Cisco devices.

```
NY-R1>show cdp neighbors
Capability Codes: R - Router, T - Trans Bridge, B - Source Route Bridge
                 S - Switch, H - Host, I - IGMP, r - Repeater, P - Phone
Device ID     Local Intrfce     Holdtme    Capability    Platform    Port ID
NY-SW1        Fas 0/0           177            S          2960        Fas 0/1
BOS-R1        Ser 0/2/0         121            R          C2800       Ser 0/2/0
NY-R1>
```

Here's how to read each column of the show cdp neighbors output in Figure 3-8:

+ **Device ID:** Indicates, in this example, that there are two device IDs present — NY-SW1 and BOS-R1; these are the names of neighboring devices to the NY-R1 router.

+ **Local Intrfce:** Stands for local interface. Lists the port on NY-R1 that each device is connected to. For example, notice that the Serial 0/2/0 interface on NY-R1 is the local interface connected to BOS-R1.

+ **Holdtme:** Stands for hold time. The value in this column tells how long, in seconds, this information is stored on the NY-R1 router.

+ **Capability:** Shows a code, such as *R* for router and *S* for switch; this is how you identify the type of neighboring device.

+ **Platform:** Displays (you guessed it) the platform; the platform identifies the model or series of the device you have as a neighbor. For example, notice in Figure 3-8 that the switch is a 2960 model switch, but the router is a 2800 series router. The difference between a model and a series is that there are many different models in a series. For example, Cisco has a 2900 series of switches and each model in the series provides something unique; there are 2924, 2950, and 2960 model switches in the 2900 series.

✦ **Port ID:** Identifies the port on the neighboring device. For example, the NY-R1 FastEthernet0/0 local port (see the Local Intrfce column) is connected to the FastEthernet0/1 port on the switch.

The show cdp neighbors detail command

If you need to collect a little more information on the neighboring devices on the network, you can use the `show cdp neighbors detail` command. This command displays information similar to what you get with the `show cdp neighbors` command, but you get additional information such as the IP addresses of the device and the IOS version that is running on each device. The following output shows the results of the `show cdp neighbors detail` command being executed on NY-R1:

```
NY-R1>show cdp neighbors detail

Device ID: NY-SW1
Entry address(es):
Platform: cisco 2960, Capabilities: Switch
Interface: FastEthernet0/0, Port ID (outgoing port):
   FastEthernet0/1
Holdtime: 135

Version :
Cisco IOS Software, C2960 Software (C2960-LANBASE-M), Version
   12.2(25)FX, RELEASE SOFTWARE (fc1)
Copyright (c) 1986-2005 by Cisco Systems, Inc.
(output cut for briefness)
-------------------------

Device ID: BOS-R1
Entry address(es):
  IP address : 24.0.0.2
Platform: cisco C2800, Capabilities: Router
Interface: Serial0/2/0, Port ID (outgoing port): Serial0/2/0
Holdtime: 135

Version :
Cisco IOS Software, 2800 Software (C2800NM-
   ADVIPSERVICESK9-M), Version 12.4(15)T1, RELEASE SOFTWARE
   (fc2)
Technical Support: http://www.cisco.com/techsupport
(output cut for briefness)
```

Notice in the preceding code that, as the router administrator on NY-R1, you can see the version of the IOS running on both NY-SW1 and BOS-R1 (the neighboring devices to NY-R1) and determine any IP addresses assigned to the devices.

Book II

Chapter 3

Managing Cisco Devices

Be sure to know how to collect information about network devices using the `show cdp neighbors` and `show cdp neighbors detail` commands. You are sure to see a question on the exam asking you to identify the model devices and IOS versions of routers and switches on the network.

The show cdp entry command

One of my personal favorite commands is the `show cdp entry` command, which you can use after using the `show cdp neighbors` command to identify more detail on a specific device. For example, looking back at Figure 3-8 you can see there is a switch with a device ID of NY-SW1. If you want to find more information about that specific entry, you use the `show cdp entry` `<ID>`; the `<ID>` is replaced by the device ID obtained from the `show cdp neighbors` command — in this case, NY-SW1:

```
NY-R1>show cdp entry NY-SW1
Device ID: NY-SW1
Entry address(es):
Platform: cisco 2960, Capabilities: Switch
Interface: FastEthernet0/0, Port ID (outgoing port):
   FastEthernet0/1
Holdtime: 129

Version :
Cisco IOS Software, C2960 Software (C2960-LANBASE-M), Version
   12.2(25)FX, RELEASE SOFTWARE (fc1)
Copyright (c) 1986-2005 by Cisco Systems, Inc.
(output cut for briefness)
```

It is important to note two things about the device ID. First, you can use an * as the device ID to display information on all devices. The second thing is that the ID is case sensitive! This means you have to type the device ID the way it displays in the `show cdp neighbors` command output in order for it to work.

There are a lot of really cool options on the `show cdp entry` command. For example, you can use the `show cdp entry *` command to display information on all devices, and you can use the `show cdp entry * protocol` command to view protocol information (such as the IP address) for all devices. Here's how:

```
NY-R1>show cdp entry * protocol

Protocol information for NY-SW1 :
  IP Address:
--------------------------

Protocol information for BOS-R1 :
  IP Address: 24.0.0.2
```

In the preceding code, you see that NY-SW1 has no IP address assigned, but an IP address is assigned to BOS-R1.

Disabling CDP

Because the CDP protocol is a protocol used for device discovery, you may choose to disable it on your network devices for security reasons. Disabling CDP on your network devices prevents someone from being able to discover your device details from neighboring routers or switches.

You can disable CDP two different ways — at the device level or at the interface level. If you disable CDP at the device level, it will no longer send CDP packets out on the network stating details about the device. If you disable CDP at the interface level, it is disabled only for that one interface but may run on other interfaces.

Disabling CDP globally

In order to disable CDP for the device *globally* — meaning disabling the protocol on the device and all the interfaces — you navigate to global configuration mode on the device and use the no cdp run command, as follows:

```
NY-R1>enable
NY-R1#config term
Enter configuration commands, one per line.  End with CNTL/Z.
NY-R1(config)#no cdp run
NY-R1(config)#exit
NY-R1#show cdp
% CDP is not enabled
```

In the preceding code example, you see that CDP is disabled from global configuration mode, and then, when you display the status of CDP with the show cdp command, it reports that CDP has been disabled. If you wish to enable CDP again, you use the cdp run command from global configuration mode.

```
NY-R1(config)#cdp run
NY-R1(config)#exit
NY-R1#show cdp
Global CDP information:
     Sending CDP packets every 60 seconds
     Sending a holdtime value of 180 seconds
     Sending CDPv2 advertisements is enabled
```

Disabling CDP on an interface

To disable CDP on a specific interface, you first need to navigate to that interface and then use the no cdp enable command as shown in the code that follows:

```
NY-R1#config term
NY-R1(config)#interface serial 0/2/0
NY-R1(config-if)#no cdp enable
```

CDP is now disabled on that interface. If you decide at a later time that you want to enable CDP on that interface, you can use the `cdp enable` command once at the interface prompt again.

Using Telnet for Remote Administration

Up to this point in the book, I discuss connecting to your router using the console port. Connecting to the console port for administration is great, as long as you can get physical access to the router. This may not always be possible, such as when you are at a different site. So, what do you do if you are at another location and need to make a change to a router?

The answer: You use a protocol such as Telnet to remotely connect to the router by its IP address, and then you can make the changes. This section discusses the concept of Telnet and how to use it to remotely administer a Cisco device.

Telnet overview

Telnet is an application-layer protocol (remember the OSI model discussion? If not, check out Book I, Chapter 4) that is designed to allow you to remotely connect to a device or system and run a program from that device. In the case of router administration, you can Telnet into the router (or switch) and issue the appropriate Cisco commands through the Telnet session to manage the device.

The Telnet protocol uses TCP port 23. If you expect to be able to Telnet into the router, you need to ensure that the firewall has TCP port 23 open to allow the Telnet traffic to pass through the firewall.

Also note that if you Telnet into a switch from another network, the switch needs to have its default gateway setting configured so it knows how to send data off the network back to your system running the Telnet client software. (See Figure 3-9.) You find out how to modify the default gateway setting on a switch in Book III, Chapter 4.

Notice in Figure 3-9 that an administrator sitting at ComputerA is Telneting into switch BOS-SW1. The traffic is sent through NY-R1, then to BOS-R1, and then to the switch. The important point is that the switch has to send a reply back to ComputerA, and the reply must pass through the BOS-R1 router to do that. In this example, if the switch is not configured for a default gateway of 25.0.0.1, the switch will not be able to send the reply back to the administrator.

Figure 3-9:
A switch
must be
configured
with a
default
gateway
if an
administrator
is going
to Telnet
into the
switch from
a remote
network.

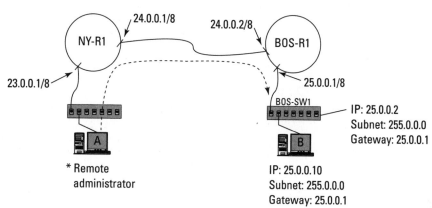

Using Telnet features

Actually Telneting into a Cisco device is a very simple process. The first
thing you need to make sure of is that you have a Telnet password assigned
to the device. (For security reasons, you cannot Telnet into a device that
does not have a password. See the preceding chapter if you need to know
how to configure a Telnet password.)

In order to Telnet into a Cisco device, use the `telnet` command and then
type the IP address of the device you wish to Telnet into. The following code
example Telnets into BOS-R1 from NY-R1 router:

```
NY-R1>telnet 24.0.0.2
Trying 24.0.0.2 ...

User Access Verification
Password:
BOS-R1>
```

When connecting to another device using Telnet, you need to specify the
Telnet password; if the password you supply is correct, you are allowed
access to the device and can administer it. After you make the changes that
are needed to the device, you can then disconnect from the device using the
`exit` command. Notice in the following code that after typing the `exit`
command at the BOS-R1 prompt, you are then disconnected and placed back
on the original router.

```
BOS-R1>exit

[Connection to 24.0.0.2 closed by foreign host]
NY-R1>
```

Be sure to remember for the exam that if you do not have a Telnet password and a privilege exec mode password or enable secret, you will be unable to Telnet into a device. This is a preventative step that Cisco has taken so that if you do not have passwords set on your Cisco router, no one can connect to the router.

Suspending and disconnecting a session

Once you connect to a router via Telnet, you can then make the changes you need to make to the device. If you decide that you need to temporarily disconnect — but you don't actually want to disconnect because you are going to come right back to the Telnet session — you can *suspend* your Telnet session. A suspended Telnet session runs in memory on the router and can be resumed at any point in time.

In order to suspend a Telnet session, you use a very strange set of keystrokes — press Ctrl-Shift-6, and then release all keys and press the X key. See the following code for the results:

```
NY-R1>telnet 24.0.0.2
Trying 24.0.0.2 ...

User Access Verification
Password:

BOS-R1>enable
Password:
BOS-R1# <I pressed ctrl-shift-6, then x to suspend>
NY-R1>
```

Notice the prompts in the preceding code. After I press Ctrl-Shift-6 and then X at the BOS-R1# prompt, I am automatically placed back on my original router (NY-R1). The reason I suspended the session was because I had some work to do on the NY-R1 router. I suspended my Telnet session and wham — I'm back on the NY-R1 router!

Imagine that after you perform some work on the NY-R1 router, you decide to see if you have any suspended Telnet sessions that you can connect to once again. (It is easy to forget about suspended sessions.) You can use the show sessions command to view a list of suspended Telnet sessions, as shown in Figure 3-10.

Notice the asterisk (*) symbol beside the only session that is suspended. The * represents your most recent session; simply pressing the Enter key allows you to resume that connection. Alternatively, you can resume *any* of the sessions shown in the show sessions output by using the resume command and specifying the connection number:

```
NY-R1>resume 1
[Resuming connection 1 to 24.0.0.2 ... ]

BOS-R1>
```

Figure 3-10:
The show sessions command displays any suspended Telnet sessions that you can reconnect to.

```
NY-R1>show sessions
Conn Host                    Address            Byte   Idle Conn Name
*   1 24.0.0.2               24.0.0.2              0      8 24.0.0.2
NY-R1>
```

When the router displays the resuming connection message, press the Enter key to activate the connection.

When you use the show sessions command and you see a suspended session that you have forgotten about and no longer need, you can disconnect from that session without resuming it by using the disconnect command and specifying the connection number, as shown in Figure 3-11.

Figure 3-11:
You can close a suspended Telnet session with the disconnect command.

```
NY-R1>show sessions
Conn Host                    Address            Byte   Idle Conn Name
*   1 24.0.0.2               24.0.0.2              0      6 24.0.0.2
NY-R1>disconnect 1
Closing connection to 24.0.0.2 [confirm]

NY-R1>show sessions
% No connections open
NY-R1>
```

If you are currently in the Telnet session, you can type exit to close the Telnet session, but if you have suspended the Telnet session and are not currently in it, you need to use the disconnect command.

Monitoring connections

As a router administrator, you want to keep a close eye on who is connected to the router. The show users command displays any connections to the router, including Telnet and local connections, using the console port. In Figure 3-12, you (as the router administrator) can see two connections to router BOS-R1; one is at the console, and the other is a Telnet session (displayed with vty).

Figure 3-12:
You can monitor connections to the Cisco router with the show users command.

```
BOS-R1>show users
      Line        User      Host(s)              Idle       Location
*   0 con 0                 idle                 00:00:00
   67 vty 0                 idle                 00:00:18 24.0.0.1

   Interface   User                    Mode         Idle     Peer Address
BOS-R1>
```

Chapter Summary

This chapter introduces you to a number of concepts that are important to managing Cisco devices. The following are some key points to remember for the CCENT certification exam:

✦ You back up your router configuration to a TFTP server using the copy running-config tftp command.

✦ You back up your IOS to a TFTP server using the copy flash tftp command.

✦ You upgrade your IOS using the copy tftp flash command.

✦ You use the boot system flash command to specify a particular IOS file in flash memory that you want to use when the router boots up.

✦ CDP is a Cisco protocol that can help you discover neighboring devices and information about them.

✦ The show cdp neighbors command shows you a list of neighboring devices, while the show cdp entry command displays information about a specific device. You can view detailed information about all neighboring devices with the show cdp neighbors detail command.

✦ You disable CDP on your Cisco router by using the no cdp run command. You can also disable CDP on a specific interface by using the no cdp enable command at an interface prompt.

✦ You Telnet into another Cisco device using the `telnet` command. Once you Telnet into another device, you can suspend that connection by using the Ctrl-Shift-6 keystroke and then pressing X.

✦ You can view a list of suspended Telnet sessions using the `show sessions` command, and you can then reconnect to a session using the `resume` command.

✦ In order to Telnet into a Cisco device, the Cisco device must have a password assigned to the Telnet (`vty`) ports, and it must have an enable password or enable secret.

Lab Exercises

This chapter introduces you to concepts related to managing Cisco devices. You discover how to back up and restore your configuration and IOS to a TFTP server. You also find out how to use CDP to discover information about a Cisco device and how to Telnet into a device. The following labs help you get familiar with backing up and restoring your configuration, working with CDP, and using Telnet.

These labs build off of each other, so be sure to complete the labs in order.

Lab 3-1: Backing up and restoring your configuration

In this lab, you install a TFTP server on your system and then back up your router configuration to the TFTP server. You end the lab by restoring the configuration back to your router.

To install and configure your own TFTP server, follow these steps on a Windows computer on your test lab network:

1. **Download a trial version of WinAgents TFTP Server software from www.tftp-server.com.**

2. **Run the downloaded executable (most likely `tftpserver-setup.exe`) by double-clicking the executable.**

3. **When the welcome screen displays, click Next.**

4. **Select the I Accept the License Agreement option and click Next.**

5. **On the Select Installation Type screen, select Complete, and then click Next.**

6. **Click Next to accept the Windows Firewall options.**

7. **Click Next to begin the installation.**

8. **When the installation completes, click Finish.**

9. To start the TFTP server, choose Start⇨All Programs⇨WinAgents TFTP Server 4⇨TFTP Server Manager.

10. Choose to connect to the local server (your system) and click OK.

11. Click Yes to start the service.

12. Leave the TFTP Server Manager window open.

13. Now that you have the TFTP server installed, you can back up your router configuration to the TFTP server. Connect to the router with HyperTerminal and type the following command:

```
router#copy running-config tftp
```

14. Answer the questions by supplying your computer's IP address as the IP address of the TFTP server, and create a destination file named lab3_1_confg.

15. When the backup completes, change the name of your router with the following command:

```
router#config term
router(config)#hostname Rout_back
```

16. Test a restore of the configuration on the TFTP server by typing the following command:

```
Rout_back(config)#exit
Rout_back#copy tftp running-config
```

17. When prompted for the IP address of the TFTP server, supply the IP address of your computer running the TFTP server software and specify that the file to download is lab3_1_confg.

18. After the copy command is complete, you should notice that your router name is back to the original router name; the router name should now be router#.

Lab 3-2: Using CDP to discover the network

In this lab, use CDP to discover other Cisco devices on the network. For this lab, you need to ensure that you have a router connected to other devices, such as another router and a switch.

1. Console into the router from HyperTerminal, if you are not connected to the router already.

2. From priv exec mode, use the show cdp neighbors command to view a list of devices connected directly to your router:

```
router>enable
router#show cdp neighbors
```

As you view the list of devices, answer the following questions:

a. *Do you see the neighboring router?*

b. *What is the device ID of the router?*

c. *What is the platform of the router?*

d. *Do you see the neighboring switch?*

e. *What is the device ID of the switch?*

f. *What is the platform of the switch?*

Notice in the output of the `show cdp neighbors` command that you do not know the IP address of these devices.

3. **To find out the IP addresses of the devices, use the following command:**

```
router#show cdp neighbors detail
```

As you view the IP addresses of the devices, answer the following questions:

a. *What is the IP address of the router?*

b. *What is the IP address of the switch?*

Lab 3-3: Using Telnet for remote administration

Now that you have the IP address of your neighboring Cisco devices, Telnet into the device so you can change the hostname of that router to router2.

1. **Console into the router from HyperTerminal, if you are not connected to the router already.**

2. **To Telnet into your neighboring router, type this:**

```
telnet <ip_of_neighboring_router>
```

3. **Once you Telnet into the router, change the hostname of the router to router2:**

```
router>enable
router#config term
router(config)#hostname router2
router2(config)#
```

4. **Suspend the Telnet session by using the Ctrl-Shift-6, then X, key sequence.**

You are now back on your original router.

5. **To display a list of disconnected sessions, use the `show sessions` command.**

6. **Write down the session ID of your last session.**

7. **Reconnect to the session you recorded in Step 6 by using the `resume` `<ID>` command.**

   You should be on the second router now.

8. **End the Telnet session by typing `exit`.**

Prep Test

1 What is the command to back up your running configuration to a TFTP server?

A ○ `backup running-config tftp`

B ○ `copy running-config tftp`

C ○ `backup tftp running-config`

D ○ `copy tftp running-config`

2 What is the command to back up your IOS to a TFTP server?

A ○ `backup flash tftp`

B ○ `copy tftp flash`

C ○ `backup tftp flash`

D ○ `copy flash tftp`

3 You need to identify other Cisco devices on the network; which Cisco protocol do you use?

A ○ Spanning Tree Protocol

B ○ Point-to-Point Protocol

C ○ Cisco Discovery Protocol

D ○ Discovery Device Protocol

4 You wish to view *only* the IP addresses of neighboring devices; what command do you use?

A ○ `show cdp entry * protocol`

B ○ `show cdp neighbors`

C ○ `show cdp neighbors detail`

D ○ `show cdp`

5 How do you suspend your Telnet session?

A ○ suspend

B ○ pause

C ○ Ctrl-Shift-6, then X

D ○ Ctrl-Alt-Del

6 You have suspended a Telnet session and wish to reconnect to that session again; what command do you use?

A ○ reconnect <IP Address>

B ○ resume <Device ID>

C ○ reconnect <Device ID>

D ○ resume <IP Address>

7 What command do you use to determine if you have any suspended Telnet sessions?

A ○ show sessions

B ○ show users

C ○ show suspensions

D ○ show suspended users

8 What command do you use to disable CDP on the serial interface?

A ○ disable cdp

B ○ cdp disable

C ○ no disable cdp

D ○ no cdp enable

9 What command do you use to determine the model number of a switch called NY-SW1?

A ○ show cdp entry NY-SW1

B ○ show cdp

C ○ show cdp NY-SW1

D ○ show cdp protocol NY-SW1

10 You wish to disable CDP on your router; what command co you use?

A ○ disable cdp

B ○ no cdp run

C ○ no cdp enable

D ○ no disable cdp

Answers

1 **B.** In order to back up your configuration, such as the running-config, or your IOS, you can use the `copy <source> <destination>` command. *See "Backing up your configuration."*

2 **D.** The `copy` command backs up the Cisco IOS. Because the IOS resides in flash memory and you are sending the copy to the TFTP server, you need to use the `copy flash tftp` syntax. *Review "Backing up your IOS."*

3 **C.** The Cisco Discovery Protocol (CDP) identifies neighboring Cisco devices and gives you information about each device, such as its platform and IP address. *Check out "CDP overview."*

4 **A.** The `show cdp entry * protocol` command shows all devices, and only the IP address of the devices. You can use the `show cdp neighbors detail` command to view all devices and their IP addresses, but you receive more information than just the IP address (which makes this an incorrect choice). *Peruse "The show cdp entry command."*

5 **C.** You can temporarily suspend a Telnet session with the Ctrl-Shift-6, and then X keystroke. *Take a look at "Suspending and disconnecting a session."*

6 **B.** In order to resume a suspended Telnet session, you use the `resume` command and specify the device ID as a parameter. *Peek at "Suspending and disconnecting a session."*

7 **A.** The `show sessions` command displays a list of suspended Telnet sessions. *Look over "Suspending and disconnecting a session."*

8 **D.** To disable CDP on an interface, you need to navigate to that interface and use the `no cdp enable` command. *Study "Disabling CDP on an interface."*

9 **A.** To display details about a specific neighboring device, use the `show cdp entry` command with the device ID. This displays information about the device, such as the device ID, IP address, and the platform (model). *Refer to "The show cdp entry command."*

10 **B.** To disable CDP on the router and not just on an interface, use the `no cdp run` command. *Examine "Disabling CDP globally."*

Chapter 4: Advanced Router Topics

In This Chapter

✔ **Implementing network services**

✔ **Understanding password recovery procedures**

✔ **Using the Security Device Manager (SDM)**

*O*nce you have configured the basic settings — such as passwords, IP addresses on the interfaces, and login banners — on a router, you will then want to look at implementing additional services, such as name resolution on the router or maybe DHCP.

You need a method of assigning IP addresses to all the clients on the network. This chapter shows you how you can configure your Cisco router as a DHCP server. You also learn how to configure additional services, such as *network address translation* (NAT). Finally, the chapter discusses the very important topic of password recovery, including instructions on what you need to do when you have forgotten your router passwords.

Quick Assessment

1   (True/False). DHCP is responsible for translating the private address of an outbound packet to a public address.

2   Static _____ maps a single private IP address to a single public address.

3   The hostname _____ is a listing of names and IP addresses.

4   (True/False). 0x2102 is the default configuration register.

Answers

1 *False.* See "Configuring DHCP services."

2 *NAT.* Review "Examining two types of NAT."

3 *Table.* Check out "Configuring hostname tables."

4 *True.* Peruse "Configuration registers."

Implementing Network Services

A *network service* is responsible for providing some form of functionality to the network. In this section, you find out about three different network services that help systems on the network communicate: hostname resolution, DHCP services, and Network Address Translation. I also review the concept of each service and then focus on how you can configure Cisco devices with those services.

Understanding hostname resolution

The first network service to discuss is *name resolution,* which allows us to connect systems or devices by name instead of the IP address of the device. This means that you do not have to memorize all of the different addresses of devices — you simply remember the name and the name gets converted to an IP address.

Most companies have a DNS (domain name service) server on the network that handles name resolution for all the systems on the network. You can configure your Cisco device to be a DNS client that resolves names by sending queries to the company DNS server, or you can build your own hostname table on the Cisco device. I tell you how to do both methods in the sections that follow.

Configuring hostname tables

Let's first take a look at how to configure a hostname table on your Cisco router to do name resolution.

In this chapter, the example topology I use is shown in Figure 4-1.

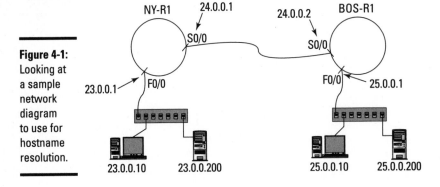

Figure 4-1: Looking at a sample network diagram to use for hostname resolution.

You see two routers, NY-R1 and BOS-R1, in Figure 4-1. For this discussion, let's say that you are the administrator for the New York branch and want to be able to Telnet into the BOS-R1 router by its name. To do this, you need to configure a hostname table with the names and corresponding IP addresses of systems you want to connect to by name.

First, verify that you cannot connect to the BOS-R1 router by name; try communicating with it using the name with the `ping` command, as shown in the following code:

```
NY-R1>ping BOS-R1
Translating "BOS-R1"...domain server (255.255.255.255)
% Unrecognized host or address or protocol not running.
```

Book II
Chapter 4

In order to communicate with the device by name, you need to add an entry to the hostname table on your router. To do that, you use the `ip host` command from global configuration mode and supply the name and IP address as parameters to the command:

Advanced Router Topics

```
NY-R1>enable
NY-R1#config term
Enter configuration commands, one per line.  End with CNTL/Z.
NY-R1(config)#ip host BOS-R1 24.0.0.2
```

Now verify that the entry has been added to the hostname table by using the `show hosts` command from priv exec mode.

```
NY-R1(config)#exit
NY-R1#show hosts
Default Domain is not set
Name/address lookup uses domain service
Name servers are 255.255.255.255

Codes: UN - unknown, EX - expired, OK - OK, ?? - revalidate
       temp - temporary, perm - permanent
       NA - Not Applicable None - Not defined

Host        Port  Flags       Age Type  Address(es)
BOS-R1      None  (perm, OK)  0   IP    24.0.0.2
NY-R1#
```

Notice in the preceding code that the entry in the hostname table for BOS-R1 is flagged as a permanent entry (`perm`), with an IP address of 24.0.0.2. A *permanent entry* is an entry that has been manually added by you and is stored there permanently. The opposite of a permanent entry is a *temporary entry*, which is placed in the hostname table as a result of a DNS query and then cached in the hostname table so future queries do not have to occur. They call it a temporary entry because it is only cached in the hostname table for a limited amount of time (72 hours from last use by default).

Now that the entry is added to the hostname table, try to communicate with the Boston router by its name.

```
NY-R1#ping BOS-R1

Type escape sequence to abort.
Sending 5, 100-byte ICMP Echos to 24.0.0.2, timeout is 2
    seconds:
!!!!!
Success rate is 100 percent (5/5), round-trip min/avg/max =
    15/25/32 ms
```

Notice in the preceding example that I was able to ping the router by name this time because the router looks to the hostname table to figure out the IP address of BOS-R1.

If you decide that you need to remove an entry from the hostname table, you can negate the command with the no keyword at the beginning of the command. The following code removes the Boston router's name from the hostname table:

```
NY-R1#config term
Enter configuration commands, one per line.  End with CNTL/Z.
NY-R1(config)#no ip host BOS-R1
```

Verify that the entry has been deleted by using the show hosts command again and you should notice that the entry has been removed.

For the CCENT certification exam, be sure to know how to view the hostname table and how to add and remove entries from the hostname table.

Configuring domain name service

If you would rather not configure a name table on your Cisco device, you can configure your Cisco router to point to the DNS (domain name service) server on your network to do the hostname resolution for the device.

In order to configure your Cisco device to perform DNS lookups, you use the ip domain-lookup command first. Actually, ip domain-lookup is a default command, so you do not have to use the command unless you have disabled domain lookups with the no ip domain-lookup command.

```
NY-R1(config)#ip domain-lookup
```

Once you enable domain name lookups, you must then specify the IP address of the DNS server to which you wish to send DNS queries (the lookups). To configure your router for a specific DNS server, use the `ip name-server` command, as follows:

```
NY-R1(config)#ip name-server 23.0.0.200
```

Once you configure your router to send DNS queries to a specific name server, you can set the optional setting of your domain name. This domain name is automatically appended to any hostnames that you use, to create a fully qualified domain name (FQDN). (Review Book I, Chapter 3 for more details on FQDN.) To set the domain name on the router, use the following command:

```
NY-R1(config)#ip domain-name gleneclarke.com
```

That is it! Once you use these few commands on your router, the router sends hostname (DNS) queries to the DNS server you specify. The following summarizes the commands used:

```
NY-R1>enable
NY-R1#config term
NY-R1(config)#ip domain-lookup
NY-R1(config)#ip name-server 23.0.0.200
NY-R1(config)#ip domain-name gleneclarke.com
```

Now when you try to communicate with a system by name, your router queries the DNS server for the IP address of the hostname you are trying to communicate with. Once the DNS server sends the address to your router, your router *caches* the address by storing the hostname and IP address in the hostname table as a temporary address (versus a permanent address). The benefit is when you communicate with that hostname a second time, the name is resolved from the hostname table (if the temporary address has not timed out) and not by querying the DNS server. This cuts down on traffic to the DNS server. The temporary entry stored in the hostname table is removed after 72 hours of not being used by default.

For the CCENT certification exam, make sure you are familiar with how to configure your device to query a DNS server.

If you need to verify that you have configured your router for DNS name resolution to a name server, you can use the `show hosts` command. When looking at the results of the `show hosts` command, notice that, above the hostname table, there are settings displaying other name resolution configuration settings, as shown in the following example:

```
NY-R1#show hosts
Default Domain is gleneclarke.com
Name/address lookup uses domain service
Name servers are 23.0.0.200

Codes: UN - unknown, EX - expired, OK - OK, ?? - revalidate
       temp - temporary, perm - permanent
       NA - Not Applicable None - Not defined

Host      Port  Flags        Age Type  Address(es)
BOS-R1    None  (perm, OK)   0   IP    24.0.0.2
```

 Although you can create a hostname table on each router on your network, it is more practical to use your DNS server on the network for name resolution. If you are using a DNS server, when you add or modify any names on the DNS server, the entire network is aware of the change, including all routers that point to the DNS server. This gives you a central point of administration, whereas working with the hostname table on each router is a decentralized approach.

Configuring DHCP services

A very popular network service is *Dynamic Host Configuration Protocol* (DHCP), which is responsible for assigning IP addresses to systems on the network.

Most companies install and configure DHCP on their Windows or Linux server, allowing it to assign IP addresses to systems on the network. The great thing about your Cisco router is that it can act as the DHCP server if you want to use it as a backup plan if something were to go wrong with your Windows or Linux DHCP feature. You can even use the DHCP feature on your Cisco router when you need to bring your Windows server down for maintenance.

The first step to configuring DHCP on your router is to create a DHCP address pool and give it a name. A *pool* is a list of addresses that the DHCP server is allowed to give out to DHCP clients on the network. The following command creates a pool:

```
NY-R1(config)#ip dhcp pool NY_Network
NY-R1(dhcp-config)#
```

Notice in the preceding code that I created a pool named NY_Network, and when the command executes, I am moved into the DHCP prompt. You can identify the DHCP prompt by the (dhcp-config).

After you specify that you wish to create a DHCP pool, your next step is to specify the network range of IP addresses that the DHCP server is to use when handing out addresses. The following command configures the router to give out addresses for the 23.0.0.0 network:

```
NY-R1(dhcp-config)#network 23.0.0.0 255.0.0.0
```

After you specify the network range of addresses that the DHCP-configured router is allowed to give out, you then specify additional settings, such as the *default gateway address* (the router address) and the DNS server that the DHCP server is to hand out to clients. Configuring these options on the DHCP server ensures that the clients point to the DNS server for name resolution and point to the router as the default gateway after receiving an address from the DHCP pool. You can also specify the domain name for the clients through the DHCP settings. To configure these settings, use the following commands:

```
NY-R1(dhcp-config)#default-router 23.0.0.1
NY-R1(dhcp-config)#domain-name gleneclarke.com
NY-R1(dhcp-config)#dns-server 23.0.0.200
```

Book II
Chapter 4

Advanced Router Topics

After configuring the default gateway and DNS server settings, you next specify the length of the lease period for the addresses. When a client receives an IP address from the DHCP server (or in this case, the DHCP-enabled router), it receives the address for a limited amount of time (known as the *lease duration*). As the administrator, you determine what the lease duration time is with the following command:

```
NY-R1(dhcp-config)#lease 7 0 0
```

When specifying the lease duration with the lease command, you have three parameters — you can specify the number of days, then hours, and finally minutes. In the preceding code example, I have specified a lease time of seven days. (The default is one day if you do not specify a lease time.)

Once you configure the lease time, the next setting you will most likely configure is the one that excludes addresses. An *excluded address* falls into the network range that you do not want the DHCP server to give. There are many reasons you may not want some addresses given out — some addresses might be statically assigned to a server, printers, or network devices such as routers and switches. The following commands exclude the first 15 addresses on the 23.0.0.0 network so that I can use most of those for the server, switches, and printers.

```
NY-R1(dhcp-config)#exit
NY-R1(config)#ip dhcp excluded-address 23.0.0.1 23.0.0.15
NY-R1(config)#
```

Notice in the preceding code example that to exclude addresses in a range, you don't use a (dhcp-config) prompt command — you need to exit out and go back to global configuration mode and specify the excluded addresses as an option on the ip command.

The following code summarizes all of the commands that enable the DHCP server feature on your Cisco router:

```
NY-R1(config)#ip dhcp pool NY_Network
NY-R1(dhcp-config)#network 23.0.0.0 255.0.0.0
NY-R1(dhcp-config)#default-router 23.0.0.1
NY-R1(dhcp-config)#domain-name gleneclarke.com
NY-R1(dhcp-config)#dns-server 23.0.0.200
NY-R1(dhcp-config)#lease 7 0 0
NY-R1(dhcp-config)#exit
NY-R1(config)#ip dhcp excluded-address 23.0.0.1 23.0.0.15
```

Once you configure DHCP on your router, you can use the `show ip dhcp binding` command to view the list of addresses your router has given out to clients on the network. Notice in the output below that you can see the MAC address of the client that has received a particular address.

```
NY-R1>show ip dhcp binding
IP address    Client-ID        Lease expiration   Type
23.0.0.16     0009.7C57.5674   --                 Automatic
```

In order for the router to hand addresses over to clients via the DHCP service, the DHCP service needs to be running. The service should be running by default, but when troubleshooting DHCP, make sure that it has been enabled — use the `service dhcp` command. You can disable DHCP at any point in time with the `no service dhcp` command.

When troubleshooting DHCP, you can use the `show ip dhcp binding` command to display the list of addresses that the service has given out. You can also use the `show ip dhcp server statistics` command to display the number of DHCP-related messages sent and received by the DHCP server.

If you need more help troubleshooting DHCP, you can enable debugging on DHCP-related events with the `debug ip dhcp server` command.

Implementing Network Address Translation

One of the most popular network services is *Network Address Translation* (NAT). The purpose of NAT is to allow you to use your own IP scheme, such as a private address range, inside the network and have those systems access the Internet using the public IP address on the NAT-enabled router. Let's look at the network diagram in Figure 4-2 to understand NAT.

When looking at Figure 4-2, notice that the FastEthernet0/0 interface (known as F0/0) is connected to the Internet and has the IP address of `24.138.20.10`. Notice that the FastEthernet0/1 interface (known as F0/1) is connected to the `10.0.0.0` network and has a private address of `10.0.0.1`. All systems on the LAN are in the `10.0.0.0/8` private network range and have a default gateway set to the `10.0.0.1` address of the router.

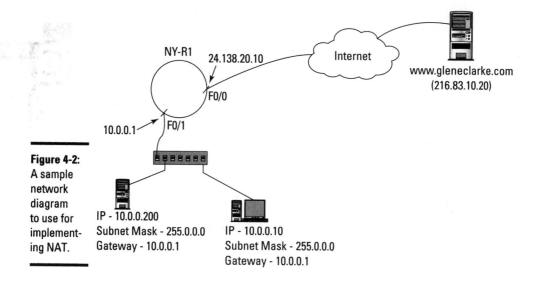

Figure 4-2:
A sample
network
diagram
to use for
implement-
ing NAT.

From a terminology point of view, the F0/0 interface connected to the
Internet is known as the *public interface,* or *outside interface,* because it is
connected to a public network (the Internet). The F0/1 interface is known
as the *private interface,* or *inside interface,* because it is connected to the
private internal network.

Understanding how NAT works

The concept of NAT is that a system on the network sends the packet to
the NAT-enabled router (default gateway) when the system tries to connect
to the Internet. The NAT device removes the source IP address from the
packet, places its public address (24.138.20.10, in this case) in the source
IP field of the packet, and then sends the packet out on the Internet.

The benefit of using NAT is that all the systems on the network connect
to the Internet using one public address — this gives you a cost benefit
because you do not need to purchase multiple public addresses. The other
benefit is seen from a security point of view; anyone on the Internet who
views the packet believes the originator of the packet is the NAT device.
If a hacker tries to attack the source of the packet, he is attacking the NAT
device and not the system inside the network. By using NAT, you are
essentially hiding the internal structure of your network.

After the NAT device removes the private address from the source IP
address field and places the public address of the NAT device in its place, it
stores this information in its *translation table* (a table in memory that stores
the private-to-public address mappings). This way, when the destination
system on the Internet sends a reply, the NAT-enabled router can translate
and send the information back. Let's look at how this works.

When reading this example, compare Figure 4-2 with the information displayed in Table 4-1. When the client using the `10.0.0.10` address sends traffic to a Web site on the Internet (say `www.gleneclarke.com`), the packet reaches the NAT-enabled router. As mentioned earlier, the NAT-enabled router strips out the source IP address and places the IP address of the public interface in its place. (This is known as the *translated IP.*) Most implementations of NAT also replace the original source port in the packet with a new, unique port value (called the *translated port*) tracked by the NAT-enabled router. The NAT device then stores this information in the translation table on the NAT device so that when a reply message comes back from the Internet, the NAT device knows which system to send the reply to.

Table 4-1		NAT Translation Table on a NAT Device			
Source IP	*Translated Source IP*	*Source Port*	*Translated Source Port*	*Destination IP*	*Destination Port*
10.0.0.10	24.138.20.10	1037	5001	216.83.10.20	80
10.0.0.200	24.138.20.10	1037	5002	216.83.10.20	80

Looking at Table 4-1, you see that two different IP addresses are surfing the same Web site (destination port 80 on destination IP `216.83.10.20`). The NAT device translates the source IP addresses of each of those outbound packets to use the public interface IP address (`24.138.20.10`). The important part to remember here is that the NAT device takes the source port in the packet (in this case, the port number that the browser uses) and translates it to a unique source port number. This way, when the Web site replies back to port 5001, the NAT device looks in the translation table and asks itself, "Who has port 5001? That is who I need to send this reply back to."

NAT overloading (see the next section) is possible because of *Port Address Translation* (PAT), which is a form of NAT that translates not only the source address but the source port address as well.

The NAT device finds out from the translation table that the system with the IP address of `10.0.0.10` is the one that the reply needs to go to, so it translates all of the addresses back on the reply message.

Examining two types of NAT

The example in the previous section is a very popular implementation of NAT, but it is not the only type of NAT. The example in the previous section is based on the concept that all network clients are using the one public IP address to connect to the Internet. This is known as *overloading*. Most NAT devices, such as D-Link or Linksys home routers and most network servers that implement NAT, use overloading. The benefit of overloading is all systems use the one IP address, so you are required to have only one public IP address.

Another form of NAT is known as *static NAT*. With static NAT, you map one internal address to one public address on the NAT device. If you want to allow ten inbound connections to ten systems on the network, you need to have ten public addresses and statically assign each public address to one of the private addresses.

For the CCENT certification exam, understand that *static NAT* is mapping one public IP address to one private address, while *NAT overloading* is mapping all private addresses to the one public address.

Implementing NAT overloading

Using the earlier Figure 4-2 as the example, if you want to enable NAT on router NY-R1, the FastEthernet0/0 interface with the IP address of 24.138.20.10 will be the public interface that is *overloaded* (meaning multiple clients will translate to that one address) and the FastEthernet0/1 interface will act as the internal interface.

To configure NAT, the first thing you need to do is create an *access list* containing the range of addresses that are allowed to use NAT. This is typically the IP range that the internal network uses — in this example, it is the 10.0.0.0 network range.

```
NY-R1(config)#Access-list 1 permit 10.0.0.0 0.255.255.255
```

Here is what you need to know about the preceding code:

✦ The `access-list` command creates an access list.

✦ You can use access lists in many different features within the Cisco world, so realistically, you create many access lists on the router.

✦ Each access list needs a unique number — in this example, I created access list 1.

✦ The word `permit` in the code allows the address range to do something. (We do not know what we are allowing until we use the access list.)

✦ The address range is specified by the network range (in this case, 10.0.0.0) and then a wildcard mask (not a subnet mask, which I discuss in Book I, Chapter 4).

✦ The *wildcard mask* (in this case, 0.255.255.255) identifies which parts of the address you supplied that you actually want the router to verify. If a wildcard mask octet has a 0, it means you want Cisco to verify that octet in the source IP address of the packet against the octet in the rule. If an octet has a 255, that means you want Cisco not to worry about the value of that octet when checking the source address of the packet. In the example here, you want to ensure that the entire 10.0.0.0 network can use NAT, so 0.255.255.255 means *verify the octet against the rule. ignore this octet.ignore this octet.ignore this octet.*

The CCENT certification exam does not cover access lists; therefore, you do not need to know about them for the exam. I mention them here only because access lists are used with NAT and a quick explanation is needed to understand the code. Access lists can get pretty complicated. They are actually done at the *bit level* and not the octet level, as I describe in the preceding text — just makes for an easier explanation! You will need to know access lists, however, for your CCNA exam!

After you create the access list, which permits the IP range to perform an action, you need to list that group of addresses as being a list of valid source addresses that can use NAT. Here's how you do that:

```
NY-R1(config)#ip nat inside source list 1 interface
    FastEthernet 0/0 overload
```

To better understand the command in the preceding code, I recommend breaking it into these three parts:

✦ **ip nat:** Enables NAT on the router.

✦ **inside source list 1:** Flags access list 1 as a valid list of source addresses that can use NAT.

✦ **interface FastEthernet 0/0 overload:** Specifies that you want to overload the FastEthernet0/0 interface.

Once you configure the NAT with the ip nat global configuration command, you then need to navigate to each interface and specify its role in the NAT scenario — whether the interface is the inside interface or the outside interface. The following commands configure the two Fast Ethernet interfaces for NAT:

```
NY-R1(config)#interface FastEthernet0/0
NY-R1(config-if)#ip nat outside
NY-R1(config-if)#interface FastEthernet0/1
NY-R1(config-if)#ip nat inside
```

The following summarizes the commands needed to configure NAT in the example shown in Figure 4-2:

```
NY-R1(config)#Access-list 1 permit 10.0.0.0 0.255.255.255
NY-R1(config)#ip nat inside source list 1 interface
    FastEthernet 0/0 overload
NY-R1(config)#interface FastEthernet0/0
```

```
NY-R1(config-if)#ip nat outside
NY-R1(config-if)#interface FastEthernet0/1
NY-R1(config-if)#ip nat inside
```

Once you configure NAT, the router translates the source address of all packets sent from the 10.0.0.0 network to use the public address assigned to interface FastEthernet0/0.

You can view the NAT address translation table with the show ip nat translations command in priv exec mode!

Understanding Password Recovery Procedures

The next topic that I discuss in this chapter covers the procedures you use to recover passwords on Cisco devices. The procedures are a little different with each router and switch model, but the general concepts are always the same. This section discusses the concepts involved with password recovery and gives you the steps to recover passwords on two different router models.

Configuration registers

Configuration registers on a Cisco device are an important concept to understand. A *configuration register* is a 16-bit value stored in NVRAM, and it is responsible for controlling how your Cisco device boots. In Book II, Chapter 1, you find out about the boot process of a Cisco device, and you discover that the IOS is loaded from flash memory before the startup configuration is loaded from NVRAM — this is all because the configuration register is configured to tell the device which boot process to follow.

The configuration register has a default value of 0x2102, which tells the device to boot the IOS from flash memory and load the startup configuration. Here's a breakdown of where the 0x2102 value comes from: The first thing to identify is the 0x at the beginning of the value; the 0x signifies that the value is a hexadecimal value. For this discussion, I remove the 0x and just work with the 2102, but understand that when you use the commands to configure the configuration register, you must supply the 0x. Figure 4-3 displays the 16 bits of a register and highlights some of the important bits for this discussion.

Notice in Figure 4-3 that the 16 bits are labeled 0 through 15 from right to left, with each bit representing a certain feature that controls the boot process. For example, bit 8 disables break mode, while bit 6 is used to ignore the contents of NVRAM when enabled.

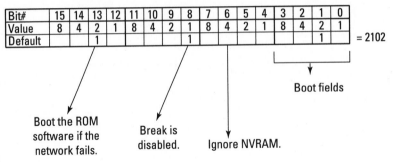

Bit#	15	14	13	12	11	10	9	8	7	6	5	4	3	2	1	0
Value	8	4	2	1	8	4	2	1	8	4	2	1	8	4	2	1
Default			1					1							1	

= 2102

Boot fields

Boot the ROM software if the network fails.

Break is disabled.

Ignore NVRAM.

Figure 4-3:
Identifying popular bits in the configuration registers that control how the Cisco device boots up.

Boot Fields	
Value	**Meaning**
0	Boot ROMMON.
1	Boot mini-IOS from ROM.
2 to F	Boot file from flash to load.

Also notice that the 16 bits are divided into four, 4-bit blocks — each 4-bit block is a *nibble*. Yes, 8 bits makes a byte, while 4 bits is only a nibble! The values associated with each of the four bits in a nibble are as follows:

✦ **The far-right bit in a nibble has a value of 1.**

Referencing Figure 4-3 and using the nibble of bits 15 through 12 as an example, bit 12 has a value of 1.

✦ **The next bit to the left has a value of 2.**

Referencing Figure 4-3 and using the nibble of bits 15 through 12 as an example, bit 13 has a value of 2.

✦ **The third bit to the left has a value of 4.**

Referencing Figure 4-3 and using the nibble of bits 15 through 12 as an example, bit 14 has a value of 4.

✦ **The final bit to the right in a nibble has a value of 8.**

Referencing Figure 4-3 and using the nibble of bits 15 through 12 as an example, bit 15 has a value of 8.

After enabling the different bits to turn on the boot features you want, you then convert each nibble to a decimal value by adding the values of the enabled bits. For example, in Figure 4-3 you can see that bits 13, 8, and 1 are enabled. So when you convert that to decimal, the first nibble is 2; the second nibble is 1; the third nibble has no bits enabled, so it has a decimal value of 0; and the last nibble on the right has a decimal value of 2. This gives you a configuration register value of 2102.

Bit meanings

Although you do not have to be familiar with all the different configuration register bits for the CCENT certification exam, Table 4-2 is a quick description of the different bits. If a bit is missing from the list, that means you combine other bits to get that value and combine the meaning of those bits.

Table 4-2	Configuration Registers
Bit Number	**Description**
0–3	Boot field
6	Ignore NVRAM contents
7	Disable boot messages
8	Break disabled
10	IP broadcast with all zeros
5, 11, 12	Console line speed
13	Boots default ROM software if network boot fails
14	IP broadcasts do not have net numbers
15	Enables diagnostic messages

Boot field

The first four bits on the far-right side (refer to Figure 4-3) are important to stress, as these bits represent the boot field. The *boot field* controls how the IOS is loaded on the device during boot up.

✦ **0:** If the boot field has a value of 0, the Cisco device boots to ROM Monitor mode *(ROMMON)* which troubleshoots issues with your Cisco device and performs tasks such as changing the configuration registers or downloading an IOS image file. When booted to ROM Monitor mode, the prompt displays rommon>. The configuration register in this example is 2100.

✦ **1:** If the boot field is set to 1, the Cisco device boots the mini-IOS image stored in ROM, known as *RX-boot*. When the device is booted to this mini-IOS, the prompt changes to router(boot)>. The configuration register in this example is 2101.

✦ **2 to F:** If the boot field has a value from 2 to F, it references an IOS image file from flash memory. The configuration register in this example is in the 2102 to 210F range.

Working with the registers

To view the current configuration value, you use the show version command or watch for the value on startup. In both cases, the configuration register is shown at the end of the output, as you can see here:

```
NY-R1>show version
Cisco IOS Software, 2800 Software (C2800NM-
    ADVIPSERVICESK9-M), Version 12.4(15)T1, RELEASE SOFTWARE
    (fc2)
Technical Support: http://www.cisco.com/techsupport
(Output cut for briefness)

2 FastEthernet/IEEE 802.3 interface(s)
2 Low-speed serial(sync/async) network interface(s)
239K bytes of NVRAM.
62720K bytes of processor board System flash (Read/Write)
```

Configuration register is 0x2102

At the bottom of the output for the show version command, you see the current configuration register value. I highly recommend that you make a note of it (write it down) before making a change to the configuration register so that you can switch it back to its original value when needed.

In order to change the configuration register, you use the config-register command and supply the new value with the 0x at the beginning of the value to indicate a hexadecimal address:

```
NY-R1>enable
NY-R1#config term
NY-R1(config)#config-register 0x2101
```

Once you change the configuration register, if you use the show version command again you will notice that you are currently still using the old configuration value until you reboot.

```
NY-R1(config)#exit
NY-R1#show version

cisco 2811 (MPC860) processor (revision 0x200) with
    60416K/5120K bytes of memory
Processor board ID JAD05190MTZ (4292891495)
M860 processor: part number 0, mask 49
2 FastEthernet/IEEE 802.3 interface(s)
2 Low-speed serial(sync/async) network interface(s)
239K bytes of NVRAM.
62720K bytes of processor board System flash (Read/Write)
```

Configuration register is 0x2102 (will be 0x2101 at next reload)

In order to have the new value take effect, you need to type the `reload` command to reboot the router.

For the CCENT certification exam, you need to know the default configuration register is 2102 and that you can change the configuration register with the `config-register` command. You can also view the current configuration register with the `show version` command.

Password recovery

Now that you are familiar with the configuration register, let's talk about password recovery. Again, the details of password recovery are a little different with each different Cisco device model, so this discussion is designed to give you a general idea of the process to take.

Book II
Chapter 4

Advanced Router
Topics

When you forget your password that you set on your Cisco device, you need to boot the Cisco device without loading the startup configuration because that is where the password information is stored. The startup configuration is stored in NVRAM, so you need to enable bit 6 in the configuration register because that is the "ignore NVRAM" setting (as you see in Table 4-2 earlier in the chapter). This way, when you boot the router it will not try to load NVRAM and, as a result, you will not have passwords in effect! The following outlines the steps to reset a password on a Cisco router:

1. **Make a note of the current configuration register value (see the previous section), and then reboot the router.**

   The configuration register is most likely 0x2102.

2. **When you boot the router, press Ctrl-Break right away.**

   This interrupts the boot process and sends you to the ROM Monitor (ROMMON) prompt, where you can alter the configuration register.

3. **Enable bit 6 in the configuration register, which gives you a value of 0x2142.**

   Remember, bit 6 configures the router to skip loading the startup configuration.

4. **Type `reset` to reboot the router. When the router reboots type `no` when prompted to continue with the configuration dialog.**

5. **When the router reboots, copy the startup-config to the running-config so you have a workable copy of the configuration; to do this, type** `copy startup-config running-config`.

6. **View the running-config file to see the passwords that are set.**

   You will be unable to view the secret because it is encrypted, so you are going to have to reset it.

7. **Change any passwords that need changing.**

For example, because you cannot view the secret, you can change it with the `enable secret <newvalue>` command.

8. **Change the configuration register back to the original value.**

9. **Before you reboot your router, copy the running-config to the startup-config.**

   You need to do this because the new passwords are in the running-config, and you need the device to be in the startup-config so that when you reload the router the new passwords are in effect.

10. **Reboot the router with a `reload` command.**

Before I leave this topic, I want to take the general steps in the preceding list and convert them to specific steps for popular router models. I first review the steps on the older 2500-series routers, and then the newer 2600-series routers.

Recovering passwords on 2500-series routers

The following are the detailed steps to recover a password when you are locked out of your Cisco 2500-series router:

1. **Make a note of the current configuration register value, and then reboot the router.**

   The configuration register is most likely 0x2102.

2. **When you boot the router, press Ctrl-Break right away to interrupt the boot process.**

   The prompt should display with a >.

3. **To change the configuration register so that NVRAM is skipped, type** `o/r 0x2142` **after >.**

   The line of code should look like >`o/r 0x2142`.

4. **To reload the router, type** `i` **after the >.**

   The line of code should look like >`i`.

5. **Navigate to priv exec mode, and copy the startup configuration to the running configuration.**

   ```
   Router>enable
   Router#copy startup-config running-config
   ```

6. **View the running-config to see the passwords that are set.**

   You will be unable to view the secret because it is encrypted, so you have to reset it.

7. Change any passwords that need changing.

```
NY-R1#config term
NY-R1(config)#enable secret <new_value>
```

8. Change the configuration register back to the original value.

```
NY-R1(config)#config-register 0x2102
```

9. Before you reboot your router, copy the running-config to the startup-config.

You need to do this because the new passwords are in the running-config. You need it to be in the startup-config so that when you reload the router, the new passwords are in effect.

```
NY-R1(config)#exit
NY-R1#copy running-config startup-config
```

10. Reboot the router with a `reload` command.

Recovering passwords on 2600-series routers

The following are the detailed steps to recover passwords on a Cisco 2600-series router:

1. Make a note of the current configuration register value, and then reboot the router.

The configuration register is most likely 0x2102.

2. When you boot the router, press Ctrl-Break right away to interrupt the boot process.

You should be placed in the ROM monitor prompt, which appears as rommon 1>.

3. Change the configuration register so that NVRAM is skipped — type `confreg 0x2142` after `rommon 1>`.

The line of code should look like rommon 1>confreg 0x2142.

4. To reload the router, type `reset`.

5. When the router reloads, choose no to the configuration dialog and navigate to priv exec mode. Copy the startup configuration to the running configuration.

```
--- System Configuration Dialog ---

Continue with configuration dialog? [yes/no]: no
Router>enable
Router#copy startup-config running-config
```

6. **View the running-config to see the passwords that are set.**

   You will be unable to view the secret because it is encrypted, so you have to reset it.

7. **Change any passwords that need changing.**

   ```
   NY-R1#config term
   NY-R1(config)#enable secret <new_value>
   ```

8. **Change the configuration register back to the original value.**

   ```
   NY-R1(config)#config-register 0x2102
   ```

9. **Before you reboot your router, copy the running-config to the startup-config.**

   You need to do this because the new passwords are in the running-config. You need it to be in the startup-config so that when you reload the router, the new passwords are in effect.

   ```
   NY-R1(config)#exit
   NY-R1#copy running-config startup-config
   ```

10. **Reboot the router with a `reload` command.**

Using the Security Device Manager

The Cisco *Security Device Manager* (SDM) is a Web-based graphical interface you can use to configure most settings on your Cisco router. This section is designed to expose you to the SDM and give you the step-by-step instructions to perform popular configuration tasks with the SDM. This section is *not* designed to give you details on each of the topics as you have already found out about the topics in the appropriate chapters. Think of this section as a guided tour of the very cool Cisco feature — the Security Device Manager!

Configuring Security Device Manager

To enable SDM on your router you need to do a little prep work first. You must configure the router to support Web applications (enable the HTTP and HTTPS services) and authentication through the Web application (Web site). You must also create a user account that has administrative access to the router (known as *privilege level 15*), and then configure console, Telnet, and SSH access to the router using the local accounts on the router. Let's get started!

1. **Ensure that the HTTP and HTTPS servers are running and access to the Web server can be gained by using an account in the local user account database on the router by using the following commands:**

```
NY-R1(config)#ip http server
NY-R1(config)#ip http secure-server
NY-R1(config)#ip http authentication local
```

2. **Create a user account that has privilege access to the router.** *Privilege access* **is the term for having full access to the router. The following commands are used to ensure that you have a privilege account you can log on to the SDM site with:**

```
NY-R1(config)#username glen privilege 15 password 0
    glenpass
```

The command creates an account called glen that has the highest level of privileges (privilege level 15) with a password of glenpass. The 0 in front of glenpass specifies that the password is not encrypted.

**Book II
Chapter 4**

**Advanced Router
Topics**

3. **With the privilege level user account create, you now specify that the account can be used for console access and Telnet (or SSH) access if you like. The following commands are used to configure the console port and Telnet ports for local authentication:**

```
NY-R1(config)#line con 0
NY-R1(config-line)#login local
NY-R1(config-line)#exit
NY-R1(config)#line vty 0 4
NY-R1(config-line)#privilege level 15
NY-R1(config-line)#login local
NY-R1(config-line)#transport input telnet ssh
NY-R1(config-line)#exit
```

4. **Connect to SDM from a Web browser by typing** https://<ip_ address_of_router> **in your browser.**

5. **You may receive a security alert letting you know that the certificate on the site is untrusted and does not match the name of the site. You are only getting this message because you have created your own secure site with the** ip http secure-server **command. You can choose Yes to continue.**

6. **The SDM software starts loading and may take a few minutes (see Figure 4-4).**

7. **You are then prompted for a username and password to access the site — use the username and password you created in Step 2.**

8. **After logging in, the SDM interface loads in the browser and you are ready to configure your router with SDM (see Figure 4-5).**

It is important to note that while there are a wealth of settings you can change through the SDM, this chapter is focused on giving you the basic steps to use the SDM for configuration changes required by the CCENT certification exam.

Figure 4-4:
Loading
the SDM
software.

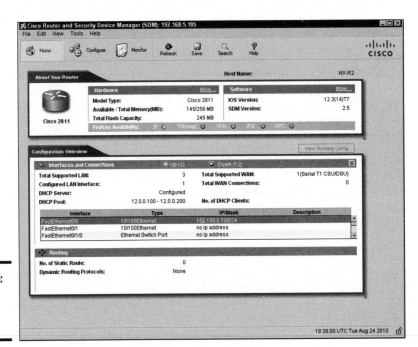

Figure 4-5:
The SDM
user
interface.

Cisco Privilege Levels

One of the topics not covered by the CCENT certification exam — but one I want to make note of — is the privilege levels on Cisco devices. There are 16 levels of privileges within the Cisco IOS numbered 0–15, with privilege level 15 being the highest level. The higher the privilege level an administrator has, the more administrative rights to the device the administrator has.

Most network administrators are aware of two privilege levels without really knowing it — level 1 and level 15. *Level 1* is the privilege level you receive when in user exec mode, while *level 15* is the privilege level you receive when you are in priv exec mode. This is why you need to be in priv exec mode to make changes — you have privilege level 15 in that mode and can perform any administrative functions.

The cool point to make is that when you create your user accounts on the Cisco device you can assign the account a privilege level. Once the account has been assigned the privilege level, that user can execute any commands associated with that level (commands have levels associated with them as well). The command to create a user account and assign a privilege level to that account is:

```
NY-R1(config)#username myadmin
    privilege 3 password mypass
```

You can also change the privilege level required by a command by using the `privilege exec` command. For example, if I want to require privilege level 3 to execute the `show startup-config` command I use the following command:

```
NY-R1(config)#privilege exec
    level 3 show startup-config
```

One last note I want to make is that you can view the privilege level you have with the `show privilege` command. There is a lot more to privileges on Cisco devices so spend some time researching the topic and experimenting!

Basic router configuration using SDM

Now that you have the SDM running, this section shows you how to use the SDM to configure a serial port, Ethernet port, and to change the hostname of your router.

Configuring a serial interface

You can configure a serial interface in much the same way as configuring an Ethernet interface. The following steps outline how to use the SDM to modify the serial interface.

1. **If you are not connected to the SDM, launch SDM by connecting to your router through a Web browser.**

2. **Within the SDM, click the Configure button at the top and then select Interfaces and Connections on the left.**

3. To configure a Serial port, select Serial (PPP,HDLC, or Frame Relay) and then click the Create New Connection button at the bottom of the screen (see Figure 4-6).

4. A wizard displays summarizing the actions needed to configure the interface; click Next.

5. When presented with a list of interfaces, choose the Serial interface you wish to configure from the drop-down list and then click Next.

6. Choose the encapsulation protocol to use over the serial link (in this example I am using the High-Level Data Link Control; see Figure 4-7) and then click Next.

7. Assign an IP address and subnet mask to the interface (see Figure 4-8) and then click Next.

8. You are then asked if you want to configure a static router or use NAT; you can skip these settings for now by clicking Next.

9. On the summary page, click Finish to complete configuring the Serial interface.

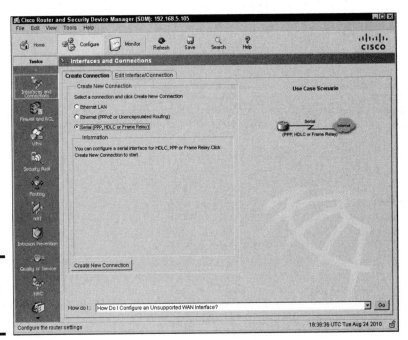

Figure 4-6: Configuring a serial interface.

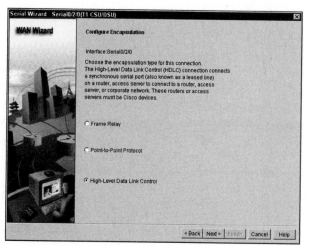

Figure 4-7:
Choosing
HDLC as the
encapsulation
protocol.

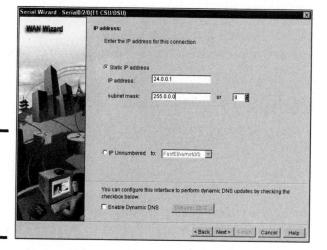

Figure 4-8:
Assigning
an IP
address to
the serial
interface.

Configuring an Ethernet interface

The following steps outline how to configure an Ethernet port on your router
using the SDM:

1. **If you are not connected to the SDM, launch SDM by connecting to
   your router through a Web browser.**

2. Within the SDM, click the Configure button at the top and then select Interfaces and Connections on the left.

3. To configure an Ethernet port, select Ethernet LAN and then click the Create New Connection button at the bottom of the screen (see Figure 4-9).

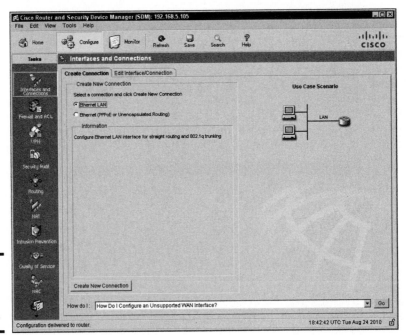

Figure 4-9:
Creating an Ethernet connection.

4. A wizard appears summarizing the actions needed to configure the interface. Click Next.

5. When presented with a list of interfaces, choose the Ethernet interface you wish to configure from the drop-down list and then click Next.

6. Select the Configure this Interface for Straight Routing option and then click Next (see Figure 4-10).

7. Assign an IP address and subnet mask to the interface and then click Next (see Figure 4-11).

8. Choose No to configuring a DHCP server and then click Next.

9. On the summary page, click Finish to complete configuring the Ethernet interface.

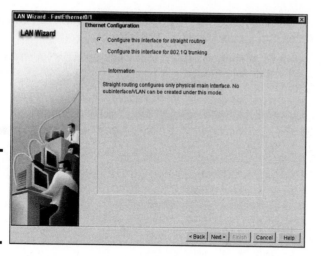

Figure 4-10:
Configuring
routing
on the
interface.

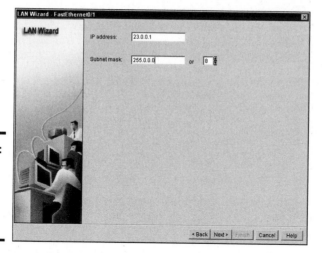

Figure 4-11:
Assigning
an IP
address
to the
interface.

Viewing interface status

Once you configure your interfaces on the Cisco router you can use the SDM to view the status of the interfaces and change their settings without running through the wizard a second time. The following steps demonstrate how to view and modify the settings on an interface.

1. **If you are not connected to the SDM, launch SDM by connecting to your router through a Web browser.**

2. Within the SDM, click the Configure button at the top and then select Interfaces and Connections on the left.

3. To view the status on the interfaces click the Edit Interface/Connection tab (see Figure 4-12).

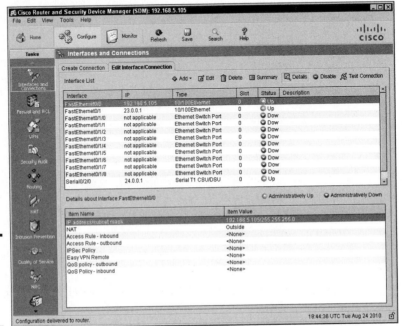

Figure 4-12:
Viewing
the status
on the
interfaces.

4. On the Edit Interface/Connection tab you can see the settings on each interface and whether the interface is up or down. To modify the settings on an interface simply double-click on the interface.

5. Make your changes.

6. Click OK to complete the changes on the interface.

Configuring hostname

Another example setting you can modify on the router through the SDM is the hostname of the router. The following outlines the steps to modify the hostname on the router:

1. If you are not connected to the SDM, launch SDM by connecting to your router through a Web browser.

2. Within the SDM, click the Configure button at the top and then select Additional Tasks on the left.

3. In the Additional Tasks window, select the Router Properties node at the top of the window and you should see the device properties (such as hostname) display on the right side of the screen.

4. To modify the device properties click the Edit button on the right side of the screen.

5. Modify the property you wish to change and then click OK to complete the changes.

Configuring DHCP using SDM

As you found out earlier in this chapter you can configure your router with a DHCP service that allows it to assign IP addresses to client systems on the network. The following outlines the steps to configure DHCP on your router using the SDM:

1. If you are not connected to the SDM, launch SDM by connecting to your router through a Web browser.

2. Within the SDM, click the Configure button at the top and then select Additional Tasks on the left.

3. From the Additional Tasks listing, expand the DHCP folder and choose DHCP Pools.

4. Click the Add button on the right-hand side to add a DHCP pool (the range of addresses your router is to hand out to clients).

5. In the Add DHCP Pool window that appears, fill in the following information:

   • *DHCP Pool Name:* Give a friendly name to the DHCP pool such as Priv_LAN.

   • *DHCP Pool Network and Subnet mask:* Specify the network ID and subnet mask for the DHCP pool.

   • *Starting IP and Ending IP address:* Specify the starting IP address and ending IP address for the range of addresses the router is to hand out to clients.

   • *Lease Length:* Specify how long clients are allowed to use the IP address.

   • *DHCP Options:* You can configure additional IP settings for the DHCP service to hand out, such as the default router address or DNS server settings.

6. When you finish filling in the dialog box, click OK.

Configuring RIP using SDM

In Book III, Chapter 2, you find out about RIP as a routing protocol and how to configure RIP with the CLI. Although you have not read about RIP yet, I thought I would place the steps for configuring RIP through the SDM here so that all SDM tasks are located in the same area of the book. This step-by-step will make more sense once you read about RIP — so come back to it after reading Book III, Chapter 2.

To configure RIP through the SDM use the following steps:

1. **If you are not connected to the SDM, launch SDM by connecting to your router through a Web browser.**

2. **Within the SDM, click the Configure button at the top and then select Routing on the left (see Figure 4-13).**

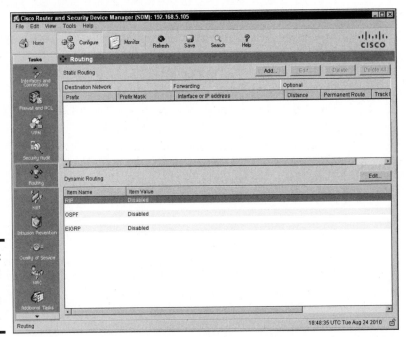

Figure 4-13: Configuring routing through the SDM.

3. **Notice the Dynamic Routing section at the bottom of the screen — click the Edit button that appears on the right side of this section.**

4. **In the Edit IP Dynamic Routing dialog box, choose to enable RIP and specify the version of RIP you would like to use (see Figure 4-14).**

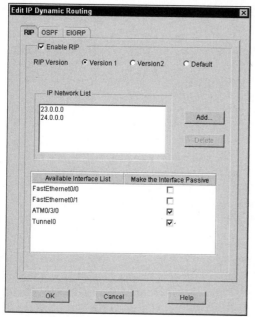

Figure 4-14:
Enabling RIP
version 1
through the
SDM.

5. **In the IP Network List section, click the Add button to add the network IDs that RIP is to broadcast knowledge of.**

6. **In the Available Interface List section, ensure any interfaces you wish to have RIP messages sent out have the Make the Interface Passive check box cleared.**

    A passive interface does not send RIP messages out the interface — a great option for the interface that is connected to the Internet.

7. **Click OK.**

Configuring NAT using SDM

This chapter has shown you how to configure NAT through the CLI, so now I want to show you the steps to configure NAT through the Security Device Manager. The following steps outline how to configure NAT through the SDM:

1. **If you are not connected to the SDM, launch SDM by connecting to your router through a Web browser.**

2. **Within the SDM, click the Configure button at the top and then select the NAT option on the left (see Figure 4-15).**

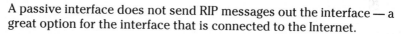

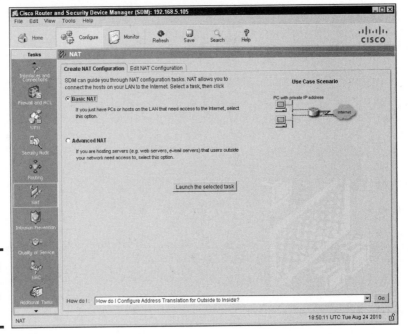

Figure 4-15:
Configuring
NAT via the
SDM.

3. **On the Create NAT Configuration tab you are prompted for whether you wish to configure Basic NAT or Advanced NAT; select Basic NAT and then click the Launch the Selected Task button.**

   Basic NAT allows you to configure the Internal list of systems that are to receive Internet access through the router (using NAT) while Advanced NAT helps you configure the NAT system for some rules that allow computers on the Internet to access systems in your DMz.

4. **A wizard appears summarizing the goals of Basic NAT. You are required to choose an interface that is your Internet connection (which will be shared) and then choose the network IDs of system that can use that shared Internet connection. Make your selections and click Next.**

5. **The Sharing Internet Connection screen appears in the wizard (see Figure 4-16) where you make the following selections:**

   • At the top of the screen, choose the interface that has the Internet connection you wish to share.

   • At the bottom of the screen, choose the networks that can use that Internet connection by selecting the check box next to the network range.

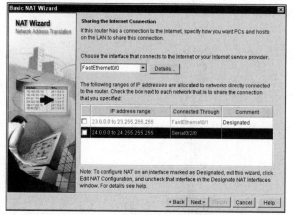

Figure 4-16:
Choosing
the shared
Internet
connection
and allowed
networks.

6. **Click Next.**

7. **A summary screen appears letting you know that you have success-
fully configured NAT; click Finish.**

Chapter Summary

This chapter illustrates a number of advanced topics, such as implementing
network services and recovering passwords. The following are some key
points to remember when preparing for the CCENT certification exam:

✦ You can resolve names you use on the router by either the hostname
table on the router or by querying DNS.

✦ Use the `ip host` command to add a hostname to the hostname table on
the router.

✦ To view the hostname table, use the `show hosts` command.

✦ You can use the `ip name-server <IP of DNS server>` command
to configure your router to query a DNS server for hostname resolution.

✦ To configure DHCP on your router, you need to use the `ip dhcp pool`
command to create an address pool. After you create the address pool,
you specify the network range of addresses to give out, with the `network`
command.

✦ Be sure to configure additional settings for the DHCP-enabled router
to give out on the network. These settings include the default router,
domain name, and the address of the DNS server.

◆ You use the `show ip dhcp binding` command to view the IP addresses assigned to clients.

◆ There are two types of NAT — static NAT and overloading. *Static NAT* associates a single public address to a single private address, while *overloading* is the concept that all private addresses use the one public address.

◆ When configuring NAT, you need to create an access list that includes all the addresses to use as the inside source list.

◆ The configuration register is a 16-bit value used to control how the Cisco router boots.

◆ You can bypass the loading of the startup config by changing the configuration register to 0x2142 and then rebooting the router, after which you can display or modify the passwords for the router.

Lab Exercises

This chapter introduces a number of different network services — such as hostname resolution, DHCP, and network address translation — and also addresses password recovery. The following labs provide you with the opportunity to get some hands-on experience with the knowledge you have gained.

Lab 4-1: Configuring hostname resolution

In this exercise, add two hostnames to the hostname table, and then configure your router to query DNS.

1. **Connect to your router's console port and add two hostnames to the hostname table using the `ip host` command:**

   ```
   NY-R1>enable
   NY-R1#config term
   NY-R1(config)#ip host TOR-R1 28.0.0.2
   NY-R1(config)#ip host TOR-R2 28.0.0.3
   ```

2. **Display your hostname table with the following commands:**

   ```
   NY-R1(config)#exit
   NY-R1#show hosts
   ```

   Do you see the two entries in the table?

3. **To configure your router to query a DNS server, use the following commands:**

```
NY-R1#config term
NY-R1(config)#ip domain-lookup
NY-R1(config)#ip name-server 28.0.0.200
NY-R1(config)#ip domain-name lab4.com
```

4. **Use the `show hosts` command again.**

```
NY-R1(config)#exit
NY-R1#show hosts
```

Do you see the DNS server information displayed at the top of the hostname table?

Lab 4-2: Configuring DHCP on a Cisco router

In this lab, configure your router to assign IP addresses to clients through the FastEthernet0/0 port. Connect your Fast Ethernet port to a switch that has a few clients connected, and then plan the commands you would use to configure NY-R1 as a DHCP server for the 192.168.3.0 network. Be sure to give the address of the router and DNS server as part of DHCP address assignment to the client. Ensure that you reserve 192.168.3.1 to 192.168.3.10 and 192.168.3.254.

1. **In the lines below, plan the commands you would use to configure NY-R1 as a DHCP server.**

_____

_____

_____

_____

_____

_____

_____

_____

_____

_____

2. **Configure DHCP on your router with the configuration you came up with in Step 1.**

   The commands you should have used to configure DHCP in this example are

   ```
   NY-R1(config)#ip dhcp pool NY_Network
   NY-R1(dhcp-config)#network 192.168.3.0 255.255.255.0
   NY-R1(dhcp-config)#default-router 192.168.3.1
   NY-R1(dhcp-config)#dns-server 192.168.3.254
   NY-R1(dhcp-config)#lease 3 0 0
   NY-R1(dhcp-config)#exit
   NY-R1(config)#ip dhcp excluded-address 192.168.3.1 192.168.3.10
   NY-R1(config)#ip dhcp excluded-address 192.168.3.254
   ```

3. **Power on a client and verify that the client has received an IP address, by using the `show ip dhcp binding` command.**

Lab 4-3: Recovering passwords

In the following, implement password recovery procedures on a Cisco 2600-series router. If you have a 1700-series router or an ISR router, you can use the same steps.

1. **Find and record the current configuration register value with the `show version` command.**

2. **Power off and then power on the router.**

3. **When you boot the router, press Ctrl-Break right away to interrupt the boot process.**

   You should be placed in the ROM Monitor prompt, which appears as `rommon 1>`.

4. **Change the configuration register so that NVRAM is skipped, by typing `confreg 0x2142` after `rommon 1>`.**

   The line of code should look like `rommon 1>confreg 0x2142`.

5. **Reload the router by typing `reset`.**

6. **When the router reloads, choose no to the configuration dialog and navigate to priv exec mode. Copy the startup configuration to the running configuration.**

   ```
   --- System Configuration Dialog ---

   Continue with configuration dialog? [yes/no]: no
   Router>enable
   Router#copy startup-config running-config
   ```

7. **View the running-config to see the passwords that are set.**

You will be unable to view the secret because it is encrypted, so you have to reset it.

8. Change any passwords that need changing.

```
YOURROUTER#config term
YOURROUTER(config)#enable secret <new_value>
```

9. Change the configuration register back to the original value.

```
YOURROUTER(config)#config-register 0x2102
```

10. Before you reboot your router, copy the running-config to the startup-config.

You need to do this because the new passwords are in the running-config, and you need it to be in the startup-config so that when you reload the router the new passwords are in effect.

```
YOURROUTER(config)#exit
YOURROUTER#copy running-config startup-config
```

11. Reboot the router with a `reload` command.

Prep Test

1 **What command displays the hostname table on a router?**

A ○ `show ip hosts`

B ○ `show ip names`

C ○ `show names`

D ○ `show hosts`

2 **Which of the following implements NAT overload?**

A ○ FAT

B ○ SNAT

C ○ PAT

D ○ JAT

3 **To configure your router to query a DNS server, what command do you use?**

A ○ `ip name-server 23.0.0.10`

B ○ `name-server 23.0.0.10`

C ○ `ip dns 23.0.0.10`

D ○ `ip domain 23.0.0.10`

4 **What keystroke interrupts the boot sequence on a Cisco router in order to implement password recovery procedures?**

A ○ Ctrl-Alt-Delete

B ○ Ctrl-Break

C ○ Fn-F4

D ○ Fn-Break

5 **What command would you use to resolve the BOS-R1 router to the IP address of `15.10.0.5`?**

A ○ `host BOS-R1 15.10.0.5`

B ○ `ip BOS-R1 15.10.0.5`

C ○ `ip name BOS-R1 15.10.0.5`

D ○ `ip host BOS-R1 15.10.0.5`

6 **What type of NAT maps a single public address to all internal addresses?**

A ○ Overloading
B ○ Static
C ○ Internal
D ○ Public

7 **What is the default configuration register on most Cisco routers?**

A ○ 0x2142
B ○ 0x2100
C ○ 0x2102
D ○ 0x2202

8 **To view a list of IP addresses given to clients on the network by your Cisco router DHCP service, what command do you use?**

A ○ show binding
B ○ show ip dhcp binding
C ○ show ip translations
D ○ show ip dhcp translations

9 **When you need to recover a password, what bit number do you manipulate in the configuration register?**

A ○ 1
B ○ 4
C ○ 6
D ○ 8

10 **What is the new configuration register value after you configure it to bypass the loading of NVRAM?**

A ○ 0x2142
B ○ 0x2100
C ○ 0x2102
D ○ 0x2202

Answers

1 **D.** You can use the `show hosts` command to display the contents of the hostname table. *See "Configuring hostname tables."*

2 **C.** NAT overloading is accomplished by port address translation (PAT) along with the address translation feature of NAT. *Review "Understanding how NAT works."*

3 **A.** The `ip name-server` command configures your router to send name queries to a DNS server. *Check out "Configuring domain name service."*

4 **B.** When trying to bypass a router's password, you interrupt normal boot operations with Ctrl-Break. *Peruse "Password recovery."*

5 **D.** You resolve the name to the IP address by adding the name to the hostname table using the `ip host` command. *Take a look at "Configuring hostname tables."*

6 **A.** Overloading is a type of NAT that translates all private addresses on the network to the one public address. Overloading is achieved through port address translation (PAT). *Peek at "Examining two types of NAT."*

7 **C.** Most routers are configured for a default register of 0x2102, which specifies to load an IOS from flash memory and the startup config from NVRAM. *Look over "Configuration registers."*

8 **B.** The `show ip dhcp binding` command displays the list of addresses that have been leased to clients on the network. *Study "Configuring DHCP services."*

9 **C.** You will enable bit 6 in the configuration registers to skip loading the startup-config from NVRAM. *Refer to "Password recovery."*

10 **A.** Once you enable bit 6 to omit loading the startup-config, the new value on the configuration register will be 0x2142. *Examine "Password recovery."*

Book III

Routing and Switching

The 5th Wave   By Rich Tennant

JERRY CRAMS FOR THE EMOTICON SECTION OF THE CCENT CERTIFICATION EXAM.

Oo-I know this one! It's...uh...

C'mon Jerry. Over 800 more to go.

Contents at a Glance

Chapter 1: Static Routing

In This Chapter

✔ Understanding routing concepts

✔ Configuring static routing

✔ Viewing the routing table

✔ Configuring the gateway of last resort

*N*ow that you know how to configure aspects of the router such as the IP addresses on the network interfaces, banners, passwords, and services such as DHCP, it is time to look at the routing process. (If you are not sure about configuring aspects of a router, see Book II before continuing with the chapters in this book.)

The purpose of a router is to route, or send, data to another network by passing the data off to the router that handles traffic for the other network. This chapter discusses the concepts of the routing process and ensures that you are familiar with the concept of static routing.

Quick Assessment

1   (True/False). Static routing is the learning of routes from other routers.

2   Networks that the router knows where to send data to are stored in the _____.

3   A router is an example of a layer-_____ device.

4   (True/False). You can view your router's routing table with the `route print` command.

5   The _____ is a value that measures the trustworthiness of the connection.

Answers

1 *False*. See "Static routes."

2 *Routing table*. Review "The Routing Process."

3 Check out "Understanding Routing Concepts."

4 *False*. Peruse "Viewing the routing table."

5 *Administrative distance*. Take a look at "Viewing the routing table."

Understanding Routing Concepts

The CCENT certification exam tests you heavily on your knowledge of the communication pathway on which information travels; this includes information traveling on the LAN and also across the WAN. This chapter is designed to ensure you understand the concept of routing and the pathway that information travels.

Before I get started with the static routing content, I want to make sure you know the scenario — Figure 1-1 displays the network setup for this discussion.

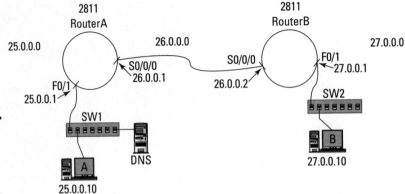

Figure 1-1:
Looking at
the network
setup.

Looking at Figure 1-1, you see there are two 2811 routers, named RouterA and RouterB. Each router has a Fast Ethernet port with an ID of F0/1, and each router has a serial port with the S0/0/0 ID.

Let's review the configuration commands needed to get this scenario up and running. (I cover basic router configuration in more detail in Book II, Chapter 2.) The following commands configure RouterA.

```
Router>enable
Router#config term

Router(config)#hostname RouterA

RouterA(config)#interface f0/1
RouterA(config-if)#ip address 25.0.0.1 255.0.0.0
RouterA(config-if)#no shutdown

10:14:19 %LINK-3-UPDOWN:  Interface FastEthernet0/1, changed
    state to up
10:14:19 %LINEPROTO-5-UPDOWN: Line protocol on Interface
    FastEthernet0/1, changed state to up
```

```
RouterA(config-if)#interface s0/0/0
RouterA(config-if)#ip address 26.0.0.1 255.0.0.0
RouterA(config-if)#encapsulation hdlc
RouterA(config-if)#clock rate 64000
RouterA(config-if)#no shutdown

10:15:10 %LINK-3-UPDOWN:  Interface Serial0/0/0, changed
    state to up
10:15:10 %LINEPROTO-5-UPDOWN: Line protocol on Interface
    Serial0/0/0, changed state to up
```

Looking at the code, you can see that you first move to privilege exec mode and then to global configuration to change the name of the router to RouterA. Once you've changed the name of the router, you then move to interface F0/1 and assign the IP address of 25.0.0.1. Notice that you bring the interface online with the no shutdown command.

After you configure the Fast Ethernet port, you then move on to the serial port, using the interface s0/0/0 command and assigning an IP address of 26.0.0.1. Remember that with serial ports, there are additional commands you need to type. For instance, you need to specify the encapsulation protocol for the link; in this example, I use HDLC. Because the serial port is the DCE device on this point-to-point link (typically used in a classroom setting), I need to specify the clock rate before bringing the interface online with the no shutdown command. Remember that in real life your router is typically the DTE device, so the clock rate is specified by the service provider.

**Book III
Chapter 1**

Static Routing

Once you have configured RouterA, it is time to move on and configure RouterB. The following commands configure RouterB in this example:

```
Router>enable
Router#config term

Router(config)#hostname RouterB

RouterB(config)#interface f0/1
RouterB(config-if)#ip address 27.0.0.1 255.0.0.0
RouterB(config-if)#no shutdown

10:21:23 %LINK-3-UPDOWN:  Interface FastEthernet0/1, changed
    state to up
10:21:23 %LINEPROTO-5-UPDOWN: Line protocol on Interface
    FastEthernet0/1, changed state to up

RouterB(config-if)#interface s0/0/0
RouterB(config-if)#ip address 26.0.0.2 255.0.0.0
RouterB(config-if)#encapsulation hdlc
RouterB(config-if)#no shutdown
```

```
10:21:55 %LINK-3-UPDOWN:  Interface Serial0/0/0, changed
    state to up
10:21:55 %LINEPROTO-5-UPDOWN: Line protocol on Interface
    Serial0/0/0, changed state to up
```

The commands to configure RouterB are very similar to configuring RouterA. Notice that the first thing you do is configure the name of RouterB with the hostname command. You then assign an IP address to the Fast Ethernet port and bring the interface online. After you bring the Fast Ethernet port online, you configure the serial port IP address and the encapsulation protocol. Notice on RouterB that the clock rate has not been set.

Once you have completed the configuration on both routers, it is time to test the configuration to see what parts of the network can communicate with other parts of the network. To test communication, ping from RouterB to the serial port on RouterA and then the Fast Ethernet port on RouterA.

Use the following code on RouterB to ping the two ports on RouterA:

```
RouterB(config-if)#exit
RouterB(config)#exit
RouterB#ping 26.0.0.1

Type escape sequence to abort.
Sending 5, 100-byte ICMP Echos to 26.0.0.1, timeout is 2
    seconds:
!!!!!
Success rate is 100 percent (5/5), round-trip min/avg/max =
    4/4/4 ms

RouterB#ping 25.0.0.1

Type escape sequence to abort.
Sending 5, 100-byte ICMP Echos to 25.0.0.1, timeout is 2
    seconds:
.....
Success rate is 0 percent (0/5), round-trip min/avg/max =
    0/0/0 ms
```

Looking at the preceding commands, the first thing you do on RouterB is move back to privilege exec mode (you cannot ping from the interface prompt) and then ping the serial interface of RouterA. The ping command sends five ICMP echo request messages, and if the system you ping sends back echo replies, you know you can communicate with the system. You can see that after the ping 26.0.0.1 command, you get ! ! ! ! !, which means that you have five received echo reply messages. (Each ! is a reply.)

After you ping the serial interface on RouterA, you then try to ping the Fast Ethernet port on RouterA with the `ping 25.0.0.1` command. Again, look to see if you receive echo reply messages with the ! symbol, but notice that you do not see ! in the output — there are five periods (.) instead. The periods mean no reply was received — this is a problem!

In order to fix this you need to know about the routing process and the fact that the routing table is populated with networks that your router is connected to, but not any other networks. You also need to know how to add static routes to solve this problem. The rest of this chapter discusses how to implement a solution that allows you to ping all networks.

The Routing Process

In order to help you understand why you cannot communicate from RouterB to RouterA in the example in the preceding section, I first discuss what happens if everything is working out great.

Look at the steps that are taken for ComputerA to send data to ComputerB. When you try to send data from ComputerA to ComputerB across a network or the Internet, you typically use a *fully qualified domain name* (FQDN), so assume that an FQDN is being used — for example, `computerb.glene clarke.com`. The following are the steps that are taken for ComputerA to send data to `computerb.gleneclarke.com`:

Book III Chapter 1

Static Routing

1. **ComputerA queries DNS.** When communicating by an FQDN, the first step is for the system to query DNS to find out the IP address of `computerb.gleneclarke.com`. ComputerA knows which system to send the DNS query to because of its TCP/IP settings. Assume that the DNS server has an entry in its DNS database and returns the IP address associated with `computerb.gleneclarke.com`.

2. **ComputerA ANDs (compares) the IP address of ComputerB.** After ComputerA receives the IP address, it then compares that against its own IP address and subnet mask to determine if ComputerB exists on the same network. (This process is called *ANDing*. To review the ANDing process see Book I, Chapter 5.) In this case, ComputerA determines that ComputerB exists on a different network because one system's network ID is different from the other's. Here's a simplified explanation of what happens in this process:

```
ComputerA IP Address:    25.0.0.10
ComputerA Subnet Mask:  255.0.0.0
ComputerB IP Address:    27.0.0.10
ANDing Result: Different Networks!
```

3. **ComputerA ARPs RouterA.** Once ComputerA knows that the system it is trying to talk to resides on a different network, it knows that it has to send the data to RouterA so that RouterA can send the data off the network. ComputerA receives the IP address of RouterA from its TCP/IP settings (in this case, it is 25.0.0.1), but in order to send the data to RouterA, ComputerA needs to know the MAC address of RouterA.

   ComputerA first checks its ARP cache for the MAC address of RouterA, and, if the MAC address is in the ARP cache, the system sends the data to that MAC address. If the MAC address of RouterA is not in the ARP cache, ComputerA has to broadcast an ARP request message out on the network to find out the MAC address of the router whose IP address is 25.0.0.1. For more information on ARP check out Book I, Chapter 4.

4. **ComputerA sends data to RouterA.** When RouterA sees the ARP request message, it replies to ComputerA with its MAC address. Once ComputerA receives the MAC address of RouterA, it stores that MAC address in the ARP cache for future reference and then sends the data destined for ComputerB to RouterA. It is important to stress that the packet being sent to RouterA at this point has a destination MAC address (layer-2 address) set to the MAC address of RouterA, but the destination IP address (layer-3 address) is set to the IP address of ComputerB. Because RouterA is a layer-3 device, it will use the layer-3 address to decide what to do with the packet.

5. **RouterA checks the routing table.** When RouterA receives the packet, it looks at the packet's destination address and sees that the packet is destined for 27.0.0.10. It then checks its routing table to see if it has an entry in the routing table for the 27.0.0.0 network. For this discussion, assume that there is an entry in the routing table for the 27.0.0.0 network, and it references RouterB as the router for that network. (I discuss routing tables in the "Viewing the routing table" section later in this chapter.)

6. **RouterA ARPs RouterB.** When RouterA knows that it has to send the data to RouterB, it needs to find out the MAC address of RouterB, so it checks its ARP cache for RouterB's MAC address. If it does not have the MAC address of RouterB in the ARP cache, it sends an ARP request (broadcast) out on the serial link for the MAC address of RouterB.

7. **RouterA sends data to RouterB.** Once RouterB receives the ARP request message, it sends an ARP reply to RouterA stating its MAC address. RouterA stores that MAC address in the ARP cache for future reference and then forwards the data on to RouterB. Again, note that the packet's destination MAC address is the MAC address of RouterB, but the destination IP address is still the IP address of ComputerB.

8. **RouterB checks the destination address.** When RouterB receives the packet from RouterA, it checks the packet's destination IP address and sees that it is destined for 27.0.0.10. RouterB checks to see if it has an entry (called a *route*) for the 27.0.0.0 network in its routing table. Again, assume that there is an entry in the routing table for the 27.0.0.0 so that RouterB knows to send the data out the Fast Ethernet port to reach that network.

9. **RouterB ARPs ComputerB.** Before RouterB can send the data to ComputerB on the Fast Ethernet port, it first must check the ARP cache for the MAC address of 27.0.0.10 (ComputerB). If the MAC address of ComputerB does not exist in the ARP cache, RouterB sends an ARP request message out the Fast Ethernet port for the MAC address of 27.0.0.10.

10. **RouterB sends data to ComputerB.** ComputerB responds to the ARP request message with an ARP reply message telling RouterB its MAC address. After receiving the MAC address, RouterB updates its ARP cache and sends the data to ComputerB. At this point, the destination MAC address in the packet is set to the MAC address of ComputerB, and the destination IP address is set to the IP address of ComputerB.

For the CCENT certification exam, it is important to be very familiar with the steps discussed here. Read through the preceding steps a few times and constantly refer to Figure 1-1 to help you visualize the steps. Also note that when ComputerA sends the data to RouterA, the layer-3 destination address is the IP address of ComputerB, but the layer-2 destination address is the MAC address of RouterA. Also understand that a reply message would need to make its way back and would follow a similar process.

**Book III
Chapter 1**

Static Routing

Configuring Routing

In the previous sections, I outline the basic steps that a router goes through to forward, or *route,* data on to the destination network. Now, let's dive a little bit deeper into the details of the routing table. This section discusses the routing table and compares connected routes with static routes. You also find out how to modify the routing table by adding and deleting your own routes.

Viewing the routing table

As I mention earlier in the chapter, a router uses what is called a *routing table* to determine where to forward a packet in order to reach the destination. Each entry in the routing table is a destination network that the router knows how to forward data to. The bottom line is if the router does not have a route to a particular destination in the routing table, it cannot forward information on to that network, and communication cannot occur.

The routing table is stored in RAM on the router and maintained through reboots by the startup-config.

Let's take a look at a routing table. To view the routing table on your Cisco router, you use the show ip route command in either user exec or priv exec mode, as shown in the code example that follows:

```
ROUTER87#show ip route
Codes: C - connected, S - static, I - IGRP, R - RIP, ...
(Additional codes omitted for briefness)

Gateway of last resort is not set
S      29.0.0.0 [1/0] via 26.0.0.2
C      26.0.0.0/8 is directly connected, Serial0/0/0
C      25.0.0.0/8 is directly connected, FastEthernet0/1
```

If you view a routing table and you do not see connected routes after you have configured your interfaces, it could be because routing has been disabled on the router with the no ip routing command. To change this, type the ip routing command in global configuration mode.

The legend in the output tells you what the codes that follow it mean. You can see that C means *connected* and an S means *static*.

You can see in the preceding output that there are three routes (*destination networks*) in my routing table. Each route in the routing table starts with a code (in this case, either an S or a C) indicating how the route got in the routing table. The output for a connected route tells you that the route appears in the routing table because you have an interface connected to that network. The output for a static route tells you that you have manually added that route to the routing table. I explain this in further detail in the sections that follow.

Connected routes

When you see C (which means *connected*) next to a route in the routing table, it means that the interface on the router is physically connected to that network. The router finds out about *connected* routes automatically once the interface has been configured with an IP address and brought online.

To the right of C in a routing table entry, you see the destination network's network ID, as shown here:

```
C       26.0.0.0/8 is directly connected, Serial0/0/0
C       25.0.0.0/8 is directly connected, FastEthernet0/1
```

Looking at the output, you see that my router has a route to the 26.0.0.0 and the 25.0.0.0 networks. The /8 portion is the CIDR notation (see Book I, Chapter 5, for more information on CIDR) for the subnet mask, which is the same thing as saying 255.0.0.0. (8 bits in the subnet mask are enabled.) You can also see that the route is known because the router is directly connected and it displays which interface is connected to that network. In my example, Serial0/0/0 is connected to the 26.0.0.0 network, and FastEthernet0/1 is connected to the 25.0.0.0 network.

Static routes

A *static* route is a route that a network administrator has manually added to the routing table. Because there are many networks on a company's *internetwork* (the multiple network segments connected together), your router will not be physically connected to all the networks. This means that your router will have entries in the routing table for networks that your router is connected to, but you will need to manually add routes for all other networks in the company's internetwork.

Looking at the output again, you can see that I configured my router for one static route that references the 29.0.0.0 network.

```
S       29.0.0.0 [1/0] via 26.0.0.2
```

Also notice, to the right of the network ID for the destination network of the route, [1/0] in the routing table — the 1 that precedes the forward slash (/) represents the *administrative distance*, which is a value that measures the trustworthiness of the route. The concept of the administrative distance is this: If there are multiple routes to the same network, the router will use the one with the lowest administrative distance. Every method that can be used to put new routes in the routing table (you can discover more ways that routes can appear in the routing table in the next chapter) has a default administrative distance value. And the lower the value, the more trustworthy the knowledge of the route is.

Table 1-1 displays the administrative distances for connected routes, static routes, and routes that are added by some of the different routing protocols. (I cover routing protocols in the next chapter.)

Table 1-1	Default Administrative Distances
Value	*Reason for the Route*
0	Route learned because of direct connection
1	Static route that was manually added
100	Route learned through the IGRP routing protocol
110	Route learned through the OSPF routing protocol
120	Route learned through the RIP routing protocol

At this point, I want to make sure you understand that there are many different types of administrative distances and that as the value increases, trust decreases. Looking at Table 1-1, you can see that a directly connected route has a lower administrative distance (0) than a static route that the network administrator added manually (1). This makes sense because you can trust the route that the router creates due to a physical connection more than a route that an administrator manually inputs — after all, the administrator is capable of making a mistake from time to time.

Be aware of the administrative distances associated with both a directly connected route and a static route. Remember that administrative distance measures the trustworthiness of the route and that routers trust a connected route over a static route.

Looking back at the static route, you know that the 1 in the [1/0] signifies the administrative distance. The 0 that appears after the forward slash (/) represents what is called the *metric,* which is a way to measure which route should be used if there are multiple routes to the destination network. The metric can be displayed as either a hop count or a cost value; routing protocols use either a hop count or a cost value as a way to measure the metric (the preferred route).

+ **Hop count:** This is the term used for the number of routers that the data has to pass through to reach the destination network. In a large network with multiple pathways to the same destination network, the lowest hop count is used. This is based on the assumption that the more routers to pass through, the greater the route distance.

+ **Cost value:** Some routing protocols base the metric off a *cost value* (which represents the *bandwidth* of the link) instead of the hop count because you may find that the pathway with the lowest number of hops does not necessarily have the most bandwidth. I tell you more about hop counts and cost values in the next chapter.

In the static route output that follows, this time notice the output (via 26.0.0.2) to the right of the administrative distance and cost value. This setting specifies where the router is to forward the data that is destined for the destination network.

```
S      29.0.0.0 [1/0] via 26.0.0.2
```

In this example, you see that if the router has any information destined for the 29.0.0.0 network, it is to forward that information on to 26.0.0.2. This is called the *nexthop,* as that router will then need to look at its routing table to decide what to do with the information.

Understanding static routes

Earlier in this chapter, you find out that a *static* route is a route that the network administrator manually adds to the routing table. There are actually three ways that a route can be added to a router's routing table:

✦ **Connected route:** The route is added automatically to the routing table as a result of the router having knowledge of the network; the router has knowledge of the network due to the fact that it is physically connected to the network.

✦ **Static route:** The administrator can manually enter additional routes in the router's routing table.

✦ **Dynamic (via routing protocol) route:** If you install a routing protocol on the router, the routers on your network can share routing tables automatically with one another. I discuss routing protocols in the next chapter.

There are a few advantages of manually adding routes to your router using static routes instead of using a routing protocol to share the routes dynamically:

✦ **No bandwidth consumption:** Static routing does not use up the network bandwidth like dynamic routing does. Dynamic routing protocols send the routing table information from one router to the next on a continuous basis by sending the information over the network, which uses up bandwidth.

✦ **Control over routes:** By not using routing protocols, the network administrator is responsible for statically configuring each route. This gives the administrator full control over communication and, as a result, can control which networks communicate with other networks.

There is a major disadvantage to static routing — the administrative burden of adding all the routes for all the networks to each of the routers. This takes time to set up, but it also takes time to manage. What if six months down the road a new network is added in your company? Then you have to once again update all of the routing tables on the routers. With static routing, you also run the risk of human error.

Adding a static route

Now that I have highlighted some of the advantages and disadvantages of static routing, let us get back to the network diagram from the beginning of the chapter (shown in Figure 1-2). Earlier in the chapter, we identified that after configuring each of the interfaces on RouterA and RouterB, I was unable to ping the Fast Ethernet port (25.0.0.1) on RouterA from RouterB. Let's find out why!

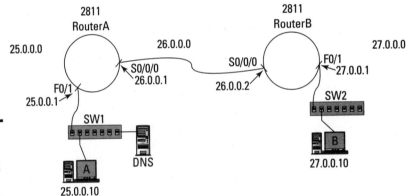

Figure 1-2:
Revisiting
the network
setup.

To troubleshoot this situation, go to RouterB and view the routing table. Use the show ip route command, as follows:

```
RouterB>show ip route
Codes: C - connected, S - static, I - IGRP, R - RIP, ...
(Additional codes omitted for briefness)

Gateway of last resort is not set
C     27.0.0.0/8 is directly connected, FastEthernet0/1
C     26.0.0.0/8 is directly connected, Serial0/0/0
```

Do you see the problem? RouterB knows how to reach the 26.0.0.0 and 27.0.0.0 networks, but it does not know how to reach the 25.0.0.0 network, which is where the 25.0.0.1 IP address exists.

To give knowledge of the 25.0.0.0 network to RouterB, you add a static route to the router. To add a static route for the 25.0.0.0 network on RouterB, use the following syntax:

```
ip route destination_network subnet_mask next_hop hop_count
```

The following list gives a description of the options you specify with the ip route command:

✦ **<destination_network>:** The network ID of the destination network that you are adding to the routing table.

✦ **<subnet_mask>:** The subnet mask of the destination network you are adding to the routing table.

✦ **<next_hop>:** This is the tricky part — you have to look at Figure 1-2 and ask yourself where RouterB needs to send information it has for the 25.0.0.0 network. The key point to remember is that whatever you specify as the <next hop> portion has to be an address that the router can already communicate with.

   Looking at Figure 1-2, you see that if RouterB needs to send information to the 25.0.0.0 network, it needs to forward that information to the next hop of 26.0.0.1. Once the information is received on RouterA, RouterA looks at its routing table and sees the route for the 25.0.0.0 network and can forward the information on.

✦ **<hop count>:** This indicates how many networks away the destination network is. This parameter is optional but allows you to customize the hop count.

So the command you need to type on RouterB to add a route to the 25.0.0.0 network is

```
RouterB>enable
RouterB#config term
RouterB(config)#ip route 25.0.0.0 255.0.0.0 26.0.0.1
```

After you add the route, you can view the routing table by going back to priv exec mode and using the show ip route command. Looking at the routing table that follows, you see that the route has been added and that it is a static route. (The entry has a code of S, meaning *static*.)

```
RouterB(config)#exit
RouterB#show ip route
Codes: C - connected, S - static, I - IGRP, R - RIP, ...
(Additional codes omitted for briefness)
```

```
Gateway of last resort is not set
S      25.0.0.0 [1/0] via 26.0.0.1
C      27.0.0.0/8 is directly connected, FastEthernet0/1
C      26.0.0.0/8 is directly connected, Serial0/0/0
```

If you try to ping the 25.0.0.1 address from RouterB at this point, you get a reply, but if ComputerB tries to ping 25.0.0.1, there will be no reply. The reason? RouterA now needs a route added to its routing table so that it can forward information to the 27.0.0.0 network. The following code shows the routing table on RouterA based off the configuration in the example in this chapter.

```
RouterA>show ip route
Codes: C - connected, S - static, I - IGRP, R - RIP, ...
(Additional codes omitted for briefness)

Gateway of last resort is not set
C      26.0.0.0/8 is directly connected, Serial0/0/0
C      25.0.0.0/8 is directly connected, FastEthernet0/1
```

You can see that you need to add a route to the 27.0.0.0 network on RouterA. To do this, use the ip route command and have the router forward data for that network to the next hop of 26.0.0.2:

```
RouterA>enable
RouterA#config term
RouterA(config)#ip route 27.0.0.0 255.0.0.0 26.0.0.2
```

To verify that the route has been added to the routing table on RouterA, use the show ip route command from priv exec mode.

```
RouterA(config)#exit
RouterA#show ip route
Codes: C - connected, S - static, I - IGRP, R - RIP, ...
(Additional codes omitted for briefness)

Gateway of last resort is not set
S      27.0.0.0 [1/0] via 26.0.0.2
C      26.0.0.0/8 is directly connected, Serial0/0/0
C      25.0.0.0/8 is directly connected, FastEthernet0/1
```

To add a static route to a Cisco router you use ip route *destination_ network subnet_mask next_hop* as the command. To view the routing table you use the show ip route command.

To see a demonstration on adding static routes to a Cisco router, check out the Static Routes video on the companion CD-ROM.

Deleting a static route

If you decide that you want to remove a static route from your routing table after you have added it, you can do that! There are many reasons why you may want to (or have to) remove a route — you may have a mistake in the configuration and, as a result, have to remove it, or you may decide that communication to a particular network is not allowed.

Whatever the reason, you remove the static route by negating the command you use to add the route with the word no in front of it. For example, the following is the command to remove the static route to the 27.0.0.0 network from RouterA:

```
RouterA>enable
RouterA#config term
RouterA(config)#no ip route 27.0.0.0 255.0.0.0 26.0.0.2
```

After making any changes to the router, always view the configuration to ensure the change has worked as expected. In this case, you verify the route has been removed with the show ip route command.

For the CCENT certification exam, make sure that you know how to view the routing table, and be able to identify missing entries from the routing table. Also know how to add and delete a static route from the routing table.

Configuring the gateway of last resort

When looking at the routing table on RouterA and RouterB with the show ip route command, you notice the statement that says Gateway of last resort is not set.

```
RouterA#show ip route
Codes: C - connected, S - static, I - IGRP, R - RIP, ...
(Additional codes omitted for briefness)

Gateway of last resort is not set
S      27.0.0.0 [1/0] via 26.0.0.2
C      26.0.0.0/8 is directly connected, Serial0/0/0
C      25.0.0.0/8 is directly connected, FastEthernet0/1
```

The *gateway of last resort* (GWLR) is a way for you to configure your router to forward all packets for unknown destinations to another router. For example, your company may have a few small branch offices where data can route between offices (because each router has a route to each office in the routing table). But because the routers do not have routes to networks on the Internet, you can set the branch office routers' GWLR feature to the router in the head office. This means that the branch offices will forward all Internet traffic to the head office router, which then forwards the traffic to the Internet. (See Figure 1-3.)

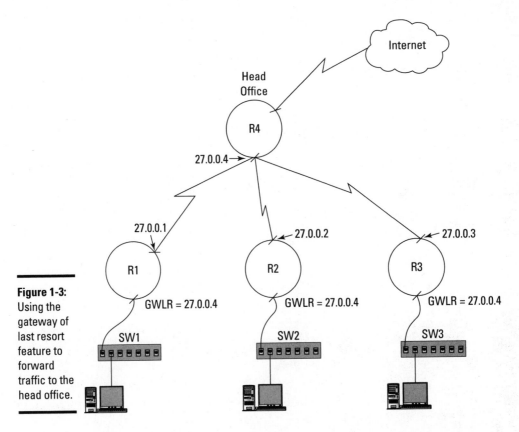

Figure 1-3:
Using the gateway of last resort feature to forward traffic to the head office.

You see in Figure 1-3 that each router in the branch offices is configured for a gateway of last resort address of 27.0.0.4. To configure the routers for gateway of last resort in this scenario, you add a route to the routing table to no particular destination network (known as a *default route*) with the following command:

```
R1>enable
R1#config term
R1(config)#ip route 0.0.0.0 0.0.0.0 27.0.0.4
```

Once you add the route with no destination network and no subnet mask and set the next hop address to the 27.0.0.4 address, the GWLR feature is enabled. Let us take a look at how this changes the routing table.

```
RouterA#show ip route
Codes: C - connected, S - static, I - IGRP, R - RIP, ...
(Additional codes omitted for briefness)

Gateway of last resort is 27.0.0.4 to network 0.0.0.0
S*  0.0.0.0 [1/0] via 27.0.0.4
C      27.0.0.0/8 is directly connected, Serial0/0/0
C      31.0.0.0/8 is directly connected, FastEthernet0/1
```

You see in the routing table that the GWLR is set to the 27.0.0.4 address, and you also see a static route to the 0.0.0.0 network in the routing table; this is the GWLR entry and is indicated with the asterisk (*).

For the CCENT certification exam, be familiar with the *gateway of last resort (GWLR)* feature and know how to configure your router for GWLR.

Chapter Summary

This chapter gives you background information about the routing process and tells you how to configure your router with static routes. The following are some key points to remember for the CCENT certification exam regarding static routing:

✦ Routers use the routing table that is stored in memory on the router to determine where to forward data.

✦ Routes are added to the routing table via connected routes, static routes, or routes that are dynamically added with routing protocols.

✦ A static route is one that is manually added to the router's routing table.

✦ You add a route to the router using ip route command.

✦ You delete a route from the routing table using the no ip route command.

✦ You view the routing table with the show ip route command.

✦ The gateway of last resort (GWLR) feature can be configured on your router so that your router will forward all packets that it has no destination route for to a particular router.

Lab Exercises

This chapter introduces to you some very important concepts regarding how a router forwards information to another network. The following labs are designed to help you practice the routing concepts.

Lab 1-1: Planning routes

In this lab, use the network diagram in Figure 1-4 and plan the routing tables of each router in the network diagram.

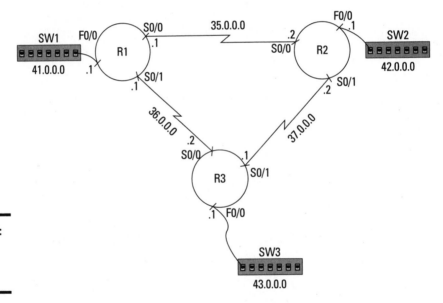

Figure 1-4:
Lab 1-1
network
diagram.

1. **Record the routes that router R1 knows about by default.**

_____

_____

_____

_____

2. Record the routes that router R2 knows about by default.

   _____

   _____

   _____

   _____

3. Record the routes that router R3 knows about by default.

   _____

   _____

   _____

   _____

4. Record the commands to add the missing routes for router R1 as static routes.

   _____

   _____

   _____

   _____

5. Record the commands to add the missing routes for router R2 as static routes.

   _____

   _____

   _____

   _____

6. Record the commands to add the missing routes for router R3 as static routes.

   _____

   _____

   _____

   _____

Lab 1-2: Configuring static routes

In this lab, you need three routers and three network switches to configure the network diagram you planned in Lab 1-1. If you do not have access to physical devices, you may want to look online for a Cisco simulator that you can use to practice router commands. For example, you could purchase the *Network simulator for CCENT* from www.certexams.com.

1. Connect the physical devices together.

2. Configure each network interface on the routers, as shown in Figure 1-4.

3. After configuring each network interface, verify your configuration by viewing your running-config.

4. View your routing table to ensure that the connected routes for each network exist.

5. Add the static routes you planned in Lab 1-1 to each router.

6. After you add the static routes, view your routing tables to ensure you see all static routes.

7. Verify that you can ping from R1 to R2 and R3.

Lab 1-3: Configuring the gateway of last resort

In this lab, configure routers R2 and R3 from Lab 1-2 for a gateway of last resort (GWLR) of R1.

1. Looking at R2, plan your command to add a GWLR with a default route pointing to router R1. What is the command you would type?

   _____

2. Looking at R3, plan your command to add a GWLR to have a default route pointing to router R1. What is the command you would type?

   _____

3. Now that you have planned the commands, go to router R2 and add the GWLR command to reference the IP address on R1 of 35.0.0.1.

4. Go to router R3 and configure the GWLR feature to point to 36.0.0.1.

Prep Test

1 **What type of memory stores the routing table on Cisco routers?**

A ○ ROM

B ○ NVRAM

C ○ Flash

D ○ RAM

2 **What command is used to view your routing table?**

A ○ `ip route show`

B ○ `show ip route`

C ○ `show route table`

D ○ `table route show`

3 **What routes exist by default on your router?**

A ○ Static routes

B ○ Dynamic routes

C ○ Connected routes

D ○ Gateway of last resort route

4 **Which of the following describes the gateway of last resort?**

A ○ It is the address of the device on the network that converts FQDNs to IP addresses.

B ○ The address that your router will forward a packet to when it does not have a route for that packet.

C ○ It is the address of the device that translates private addresses to public addresses.

D ○ It is the address of the router that shares routing table information on the network.

5 **What is the command to delete a static route?**

A ○ `no ip route`

B ○ `route delete`

C ○ `delete route`

D ○ `ip route delete`

6 **What is the administrative distance of a connected route?**

A ○ 1

B ○ 100

C ○ 120

D ○ 0

7 **What does the following entry in the routing table signify?**

```
S*   0.0.0.0 [1/0] via 56.0.0.1
```

A ○ DNS server

B ○ Gateway of last resort

C ○ NAT-enabled router

D ○ Address of the DHCP enabled router

8 **What is the administrative distance of a static route?**

A ○ 1

B ○ 100

C ○ 120

D ○ 0

9 **What command adds a static route?**

A ○ ip route 35.0.0.0 22.0.0.1

B ○ route add 35.0.0.0 255.0.0.0 22.0.0.1

C ○ route add 35.0.0.0 22.0.0.1

D ○ ip route 35.0.0.0 255.0.0.0 22.0.0.1

10 **The router will use the route which has the _____ administrative distance.**

A ○ highest

B ○ lowest

Answers

1 **D.** The routing table is stored in VRAM memory and is retained through reboots because it is rebuilt from the startup-config. *See "Viewing the routing table."*

2 **B.** The command to view your routing table is the `show ip route` command. *Review "Viewing the routing table."*

3 **C.** Connected routes exist by default in your routing table and are routes that are there because the router is connected to those networks. *Check out "Connected routes."*

4 **B.** The gateway of last resort is a default route that you can add to the router so that it forwards all packets for unknown destinations to a particular router that will then forward the packet on using its routing table. *Peruse "Configuring the gateway of last resort."*

5 **A.** You delete a static route using the `no ip route` command. Most Cisco commands can be negated by placing the word `no` in front of the command. *Take a look at "Deleting a static route."*

6 **D.** The administrative distance of a connected route is the lowest (0), as it is the most trustworthy type of route. *Peek at "Static routes."*

7 **B.** The gateway of last resort shows as an entry in the routing table with the destination network ID of `0.0.0.0`. *Look over "Configuring the gateway of last resort."*

8 **A.** A static route has an administrative distance of 1, the second-lowest administrative distance next to a connected route, which has a value of 0. *Study "Static routes."*

9 **D.** In order to add a static route to the routing table, you use the `ip route` command and then specify the destination network ID, destination subnet mask, and the next hop where the router is to forward information for that network. *Refer to "Adding a static route."*

10 **B.** The route with the lowest administrative distance is always used. If there are two routes with the same administrative distance that could be used, the metric value is used. *Examine "Static routes."*

Chapter 2: Dynamic Routing Protocols

In This Chapter

✔ Introduction to dynamic routing protocols

✔ Types of routing protocols

✔ Configuring RIP and RIPv2

*I*n the previous chapter, you find out how to configure routes on your router using static routes, but this places a lot of administrative burden on you as the network administrator. A less time-consuming approach is to load a *routing protocol,* which is responsible for sharing the routing table with other routers on the network, on your router. The end result is that all routers share their routing table with each other, meaning that all routers have knowledge of all the networks on your internetwork.

This chapter is designed to introduce you to routing protocols and how to configure the Routing Information Protocol (RIP), which is required knowledge to pass the CCENT certification exam.

Quick Assessment

1   (True/False). Dynamic routing protocols are layer-4 protocols.

2   A _____ routing protocol is a routing protocol that knows only how many hops away a network is.

3   OSPF is an example of a _____ routing protocol.

4   (True/False). RIPv1 is an example of a classless routing protocol.

Answers

1   *False*. See "Introduction to Dynamic Routing Protocols."

2   *Distance vector*. Review "Distance vector."

3   *Link state*. Check out "Link state."

4   *False*. Peruse "Routing Information Protocol (RIP)."

Introduction to Dynamic Routing Protocols

Knowing how to add static routes to the routing table is a very important aspect of understanding routing and being able to manage and troubleshoot your router, but managing static routes can be a very time-consuming job! As a result, you may want to look at loading a dynamic routing protocol on your router. A *dynamic routing protocol* is a layer-3 protocol you enable on the router that is designed to share the routing table *entries* (the routes) on your router with other routers on the network. This process also allows your router to receive routing table entries from other routers as well. Let's look at how dynamic routing works.

Looking at Figure 2-1, you see two routers, router R1 and router R2. Each router has a serial interface and Fast Ethernet port configured. The two routers are connected to a common network of 36.0.0.0, but each has its own LAN network. R1 is connected to the 35.0.0.0 LAN via the F0/1 Fast Ethernet port, and R2 is connected to the 37.0.0.0 LAN via its F0/1 Fast Ethernet port. Notice that the serial interfaces that are connected to the 36.0.0.0 network have a .1 and a .2 beside them — this is shorthand for the IP addresses assigned to those interfaces. This means the serial interface on R1 has the IP address of 36.0.0.1, while the serial interface on R2 has the IP address of 36.0.0.2.

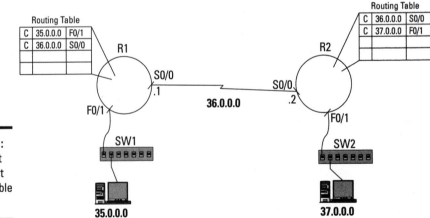

Figure 2-1:
Looking at the default routing table entries.

You see the default routing table entries that are created due to the fact that the routers have interfaces connected to those networks. R1 has routes to the 35.0.0.0 and 36.0.0.0 networks, while R2 has routes to the

36.0.0.0 and 37.0.0.0 networks by default. Notice that the R1 router does not have a route to the 37.0.0.0 network, so it is not possible for any systems on the 35.0.0.0 network to communicate with the 37.0.0.0 network. Also, R2 is missing a route in its routing table for the 35.0.0.0 network, so it is not possible for the systems on the 37.0.0.0 network to communicate with the 35.0.0.0 network.

You know from the preceding chapter that you can create static routes on the routers to give knowledge to them of the networks they are missing, but that places an administrative burden on you as the network administrator. To avoid this burden, you can use a dynamic routing protocol to have the routers share their routing tables with one another automatically.

Looking at Figure 2-2, you see that once you install a routing protocol on the routers, they start to share their routing tables with one another and, as a result, they gain knowledge of all of the networks on the internetwork.

The message that is sent from one router to another informing it of the entries in the routing table is called a *routing table update message*. When a router receives a routing table update message from another router, it adds that route to its routing table (if it is not aware of the route already) and records the metric of that route (the hop count or the bandwidth, depending on the protocol). Figure 2-3 displays the routers with updated routing tables after the routing protocol has shared the routes.

**Book III
Chapter 2**

**Dynamic Routing
Protocols**

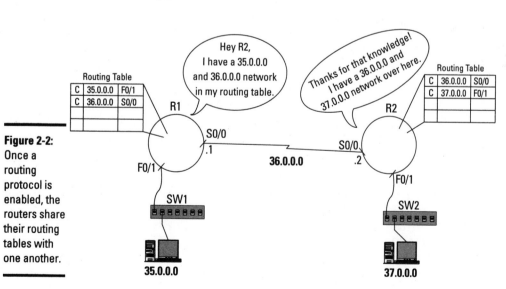

Figure 2-2:
Once a routing protocol is enabled, the routers share their routing tables with one another.

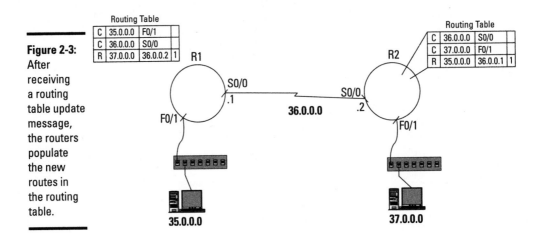

Figure 2-3: After receiving a routing table update message, the routers populate the new routes in the routing table.

Looking at Figure 2-3, you see that router R1 has a new entry in its routing table. The entry starts with the code R (because the route was learned through the RIP routing protocol; more on RIP in a bit) instead of a C (which means the route was learned due to a directly connected network). The new route also shows the destination network ID of 37.0.0.0 and the next hop address (which is where this router needs to forward information to reach that network) of 36.0.0.2, which is the IP address of the serial interface on router R2. In this example, the routing table also stores how many hops away that network is, meaning that it answers the question, how many routers do we have to pass through to reach that network? In this case, it is one router, or one hop.

In the previous chapter, you find out that the *hop count* is the metric used to measure which pathway is the best pathway. For example, if there were a third router that shared knowledge of the 37.0.0.0 network but had a hop count of 2, R1 would know that the "best" pathway is the route given by R2 (because the hop count is 1). The concept is that there is less distance involved if the traffic passes through fewer routers.

Notice in Figure 2-3 that router R2 has an updated routing table as well; it knows about the 35.0.0.0 network. When looking at that entry in the routing table, you see that the router learned the entry because of RIP (the code is R) and that if R2 has information for the 35.0.0.0 network it needs to forward that information to the address of 36.0.0.1, which is one hop away.

Now that you have the general idea of what a routing protocol is designed to do, let's take a look at the different types (classes) of routing protocols and their features. After that, I tell you about specific routing protocols that fall into those categories.

Types of routing protocols

There are different types of routing protocols (actually, they are known as *classes* of routing protocols) and each type of protocol is designed to work in a different way. This section gives you the basics on the different types of routing protocols.

Distance vector

The first type of routing protocol to talk about is the *distance vector* routing protocol, which decides on the best route (when there are multiple routes to the same destination) to use by choosing the route with the lowest hop count (the *distance*). The term *vector* implies the direction — distance vector routing protocols track the direction by the *next hop address*, which is the address of the next router to forward the traffic to.

Routers running a distance vector routing protocol are designed to share their routing table with neighboring routers only. A *neighboring router* is a router within the same broadcast domain, which is a router that has an interface connected to the same network as another router — they are neighbors. For example, looking at Figure 2-3 earlier in the chapter, you see that R1 and R2 are neighboring routers, as they share a link by their serial ports. By being on the same network, this places both routers in the same broadcast domain, so as the routing table updates are broadcasted on the network link, the neighboring router receives that broadcast.

Distance vector routing protocols typically send their entire routing table to neighboring routers at regular intervals or when an update is made. (It depends on the protocol, though.) Once a router receives an update, it compares the routes in the update message with the routes in its own routing table, and if there are any new routes that need to be added, the receiving router adds those routes. If the update message has routes that are already in the routing table but they have better metrics (like a lower hop count), those routes are also added to the routing table, as they are more preferred routes than the ones that already exist.

Once a router updates its routing table with routes that it receives from a router, it then sends the new routes within an update message to its neighboring routers at the next update interval. This continues from one router to another until all routers have knowledge of all routes on the internetwork. The network is considered *converged* when all routing tables are up to date.

TIP

Because distance vector routing protocols share routes they learn from one neighbor to other neighbors, this is sometimes referred to as *routing by rumor*.

For the CCENT certification exam, be sure to know that a distance vector routing protocol sends the entire routing table to *only* neighboring routers and not to *all* routers on the network.

The following are the advantages of using a distance vector routing protocol:

+ **Less work:** Using a distance vector routing protocol is a lot less work than manually adding static routes to each router. Once the routing protocol is loaded on the router, the routers share their routing tables to neighbors automatically.

+ **Dynamic:** The routing protocol is dynamic in the sense that if a new route is added to a router, that router will then share the route with its neighbors, who then share the route with their neighbors.

Distance vector routing protocols are designed to be simple, and as a result, they do have some pitfalls. The following are some disadvantages of using distance vector routing protocols:

+ **Bandwidth usage:** Distance vector routing protocols normally send the entire routing table at regular intervals to its neighbors; as a result, additional bandwidth is used on the network.

+ **Convergence time:** Because distance vector routing protocols send the routing table information to only its direct neighbors, it can take time before the entire internetwork is aware of *all* the routes (because one router passes the knowledge over to another router, which passes it on to the next router).

For the CCENT certification exam, know that RIP and IGRP are examples of distance vector routing protocols. You find out more on these protocols in the "Identifying popular routing protocols" section later in this chapter.

One of the major problems with distance vector routing protocols is they accommodate for distance only and do not consider the bandwidth of the links in order to choose the best route for a packet to take. For example, looking at Figure 2-4, you see three routers — R1, R2, and R3. There is a 64 Kbps link between R1 and R3, and there is a much faster T1 link (1.544 Mbps) between R1 and R2, and then R2 to R3.

When sending information from R1 to R3, the preference is to have your traffic follow the fastest route possible, which is the route from R1 to R2, and then from R2 to R3, as that route has the faster links. But if you use a distance vector routing protocol, the path with the smallest number of hops is always selected, which in this case is from R1 to R3 directly (even though that is the slower route).

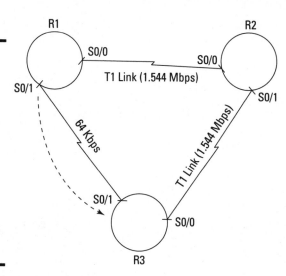

Figure 2-4: Distance vector routing protocols choose the route with the lowest hop count, which sometimes may not be the fastest route.

Link state

Distance vector routing protocols send updates to only neighboring routers because the routers do not have knowledge of all of the other routers that exist on the network. The next type of routing protocol is known as a link state routing protocol. *Link state* routing protocols have many benefits over distance vector routing protocols. The first benefit is that a link state routing protocol knows about the entire network topology; meaning it knows about all routers on the internetwork and not just neighboring routers!

The link state routing protocol knows about the entire network topology because it maintains multiple tables in memory and not just the routing table, as in the case of distance vector routing protocols. The following are three tables that the link state routing protocols use:

✦ **Neighbors:** Contains a list of the directly connected neighbors.

✦ **Topology:** Has an entry for each router on the internetwork. Link state routing protocols use the list of routers in this table to decide whom to send the routing table to.

✦ **Routing table:** This is the normal routing table.

Link state routing protocols maintain a listing of all the networks and the state of the links for each of the networks. An advantage of a link state routing protocol is it tracks different characteristics about the routes, such as the bandwidth available and whether the route is up and running. Distance vector routing protocols do not track the availability of the link or the bandwidth, so a lower hop count route will always be selected, even though it may have less bandwidth than a higher hop count pathway.

Figure 2-5 looks at the same example from the earlier Figure 2-4 but uses a link state routing protocol. Notice in Figure 2-5 that the best pathway from router R1 to router R3 is the through router R2 and not the direct 64 Kbps link.

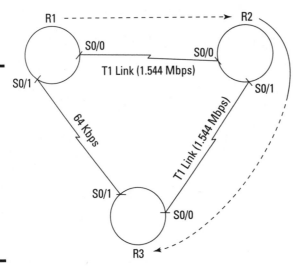

Figure 2-5: Link state routing protocols choose the best route using the bandwidth of the link and the availability of the link.

For the CCENT certification exam, know that OSPF is an example of a link state routing protocol. You find out more on this protocol in the "Identifying popular routing protocols" section later in this chapter.

Hybrid

A *hybrid* routing protocol combines features of distance vector routing protocols and link state routing protocols. An example of a hybrid routing protocol is the EIGRP routing protocol, which you read about in the next section.

Identifying popular routing protocols

Now that you are familiar with the different classes of routing protocols, let's take a look at some of the popular routing protocols that fall into those different classes. The CCENT certification exam requires you to know how to configure RIP and RIPv2, but all you need to know about the other protocols is whether they are a link state or distance vector routing protocol.

Let us start the discussion by looking at examples of *distance vector routing protocols*.

Routing Information Protocol (RIP)

The *Routing Information Protocol* (RIP) is an old industry-standard distance vector routing protocol many different vendors support — not just Cisco devices. Because it is a distance vector routing protocol, RIP chooses the route with the lowest hop count, and if there are two routes to a destination with equal hop counts, RIP load-balances between those links. *Load balance* means that RIP toggles back and forth the link it uses, essentially splitting the workload so that all the bandwidth on one link is not being used.

The RIP routing protocol has some features that make it an undesirable protocol to use on a large network, such as the fact that it sends the entire routing table out to neighboring routers every 30 seconds. The RIP routing protocol is also limited to 15 hops, so for a large internetwork, this may not be enough hops.

One of the other limitations of RIP is that it is a *classful* routing protocol, meaning it follows the rules of class addressing. (Refer to the class A, B, and C discussion in Book I, Chapter 4.) Classful routing protocols do not send subnet mask information with the routing updates. As a result of not sending subnet mask information with the routing table, the receiving router assumes that the default subnet mask of the address is being used. This also means that the protocol cannot support variable-length subnet masks (VLSM) and that all networks must use the same subnet mask when subnetted. With today's network requirements on custom address schemes, this is a huge limitation.

For more information on VLSM, check out Book I, Chapter 5.

Remember that classful routing protocols do not support VLSM.

Book III
Chapter 2

Dynamic Routing Protocols

Routing Information Protocol v2 (RIPv2)

As I mention in the previous section, RIP, also known as *RIP version 1* (RIPv1), is an old industry-standard routing protocol and has many limitations; because of this, the protocol was revamped to *RIP version 2* (RIPv2). RIPv2 works the same way as RIP but with some improvements:

✦ **Classless:** RIPv2 is a *classless* routing protocol, meaning it does support variable-length subnet masks (VLSM) by sending the subnet mask information with the routing table update message.

✦ **Updates:** RIPv1 sends out the routing table updates as broadcast messages every 30 seconds. RIPv2 makes better use of the bandwidth by *multicasting* (sending to a group of addresses) the updates.

✦ **Authentication:** RIPv2 has a bit more security, as it supports authentication, whereas RIPv1 does not.

Outside of these improvements, the two protocols are very similar — they are both industry-standard distance vector routing protocols and have an administrative distance of 120.

Interior Gateway Routing Protocol (IGRP)

RIP and RIPv2 are examples of open standard distance vector routing protocols, but Cisco decided to create its own distance vector routing protocol known as the *Interior Gateway Routing Protocol* (IGRP). Because RIP is an industry-standard protocol, it is available on various router manufacturers, but because IGRP is a Cisco protocol, it is available only on Cisco devices.

The purpose of IGRP was to overcome some of the limitations of RIP, such as the updates being sent every 30 seconds and the limited maximum-supported hop count of 15 hops. IGRP sends routing table updates every 90 seconds by default and has a maximum hop count of 255. IGRP has an administrative distance value of 100.

IGRP uses what is known as an *autonomous system* (AS) to control which other routers the router shares its routing table information with. The AS is a number which creates a logical grouping of routers that share routing table information. The following code example shows how to enable IGRP:

```
Router>enable
Router#config term
Router(config)#router IGRP 10
Router(config-router)#network 37.0.0.0
```

The commands above move you to global configuration, where the `router` command is used to move into the router config prompt and enables IGRP with an AS of 10. In this example, the router will send out updates on the `37.0.0.0` network.

IGRP has one huge drawback by today's standards — and that is the fact that it is a classful routing protocol. As a result, it does not support variable-length subnet masks (VLSM).

For the CCENT certification you are required to know only of RIP and RIPv2, but I mention the other protocols to give you a bit more background. However, you should be familiar with which protocols are distance vector and which are link state.

Enhanced Interior Gateway Routing Protocol (EIGRP)

Cisco has made some improvements to the IGRP routing protocol and as a result a lot of new versions of the Cisco IOS do not support IGRP. Cisco now wants you to use *Enhanced Interior Gateway Routing Protocol* (EIGRP) — the big brother of IGRP!

EIGRP is a classless routing protocol supporting variable-length subnet masks by sending the subnet mask information with the routing table updates. Like IGRP, EIGRP uses an autonomous system (AS) to logically group routers, and it sends the routing table information to other routers in the AS.

EIGRP is an example of a hybrid protocol, as it incorporates features of both the distance vector with link state routing protocols. This means that EIGRP is aware of the state of the link, including the bandwidth of a link. Like IGRP, EIGRP has a maximum hop count of 255.

The following commands show you how to enable EIGRP by moving to the RouterA(config) prompt and using an AS of 15. Once you are in the router prompt, you specify on which networks you wish to enable EIGRP by using the network command.

```
RouterA>enable
RouterA#config term
RouterA(config)#router eigrp 15
RouterA(config-router)#network 25.0.0.0
RouterA(config-router)#network 26.0.0.0
```

Remember that EIGRP is an example of a hybrid routing protocol.

Open Shortest Path First (OSPF)

The *Open Shortest Path First* (OSPF) routing protocol is an industry-standard link state routing protocol. The fact that it is an industry-standard protocol means that many different router manufacturers support it — so it is great when you have a mix of routers from different vendors.

OSPF is a classless routing protocol that supports VLSM and uses a complex algorithm to choose the best route when there are multiple routes to the same destination. OSPF is designed for large networks; it minimizes the traffic generated to update routing tables across the network.

Configuring RIP

For the CCENT certification exam, you are required to be familiar with RIPv1 and RIPv2 routing protocols, so be sure to carefully read over the following sections that describe them. For the exam, you are required to know not only a few facts about the two versions of RIP, but you are also required to know how to configure the RIP routing protocol. Let's see how to configure RIP!

In the text that follows, I tell you how to configure both RIPv1 and RIPv2, and then I give you some tips on troubleshooting those configurations.

Configuring RIPv1

Configuring RIP on the routers is a fairly straightforward task. You see in Figure 2-6 two routers: RouterA and RouterB. RouterA is connected to the 25.0.0.0 network and the 26.0.0.0 network, while RouterB is connected to the 26.0.0.0 network and the 27.0.0.0 network. All of the interfaces have been configured.

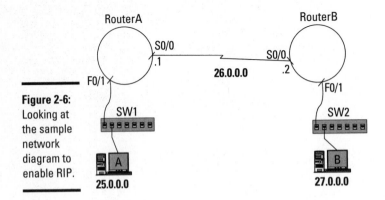

Figure 2-6: Looking at the sample network diagram to enable RIP.

To configure the RIP routing protocol on RouterA, the first thing you do is navigate to the router prompt for the RIP protocol by typing the following commands:

```
RouterA>enable
RouterA#config term
RouterA(config)#router rip
RouterA(config-router)#
```

Notice that after typing the `router rip` command you are in the router prompt and ready to enable RIP on the different network interfaces. To enable RIP on the different network interfaces, use the following commands:

```
RouterA(config-router)#network 25.0.0.0
RouterA(config-router)#network 26.0.0.0
```

Using the `network` command and specifying the network ID is required to enable RIP on the interface for that network. This configures the interface to listen for RIP update messages on the interface, and to advertise any routes out of that network interface as well.

When using the `network` command, you need to use only a classful address, and not the subnetted addresses. For example, if you have subnetted the `25.0.0.0` network into two networks — let's say `25.1.0.0/16` and `25.2.0.0/16` — you are required to specify only the 25.0.0.0 network and not the subnet IDs that have been created.

This means that if you do not want to enable both subnets for RIP, you are out of luck. Well, not really — you can use another command to stop sending RIP messages from a specific interface! If you decide that you do not want to send RIP messages from a specific interface, you can use the `passive-interface` command shown here. Keep in mind that you will still receive RIP messages on the interface, but you will not send RIP messages from that interface.

```
RouterA(config-router)#passive-interface serial 0/0
```

Be sure to know for the CCENT certification exam how to enable RIP on the different network interfaces. Also, when given a scenario where you do not want RIP messages sent from an interface, know that you can use the `passive-interface` command.

Note in Figure 2-6 that I want RIP messages sent from the serial port, so I am not going to add the `passive-interface` command. Also note that you would use the following commands to configure RIP on RouterB:

```
RouterB>enable
RouterB#config term
RouterB(config)#router rip
RouterB(config-router)#network 26.0.0.0
RouterB(config-router)#network 27.0.0.0
```

To see a demonstration on configuring RIPv1 on a Cisco router, check out the Configuring RIP video on the accompanying CD.

Configuring RIPv2

Configuring RIP on a Cisco router is a fairly straightforward task, and configuring RIPv2 is just as easy. In order to configure RIPv2 on RouterA, shown earlier in Figure 2-6, you type the following commands:

```
RouterA>enable
RouterA#config term
RouterA(config)#router rip
RouterA(config-router)#network 25.0.0.0
RouterA(config-router)#network 26.0.0.0
RouterA(config-router)#version 2
```

Notice that the only new command in the code is the `version 2` command, which specifies that you would like to use RIPv2!

Troubleshooting RIP

Once you enable RIP or RIPv2, you will want to verify that it is running and sharing routing table information. There are a few commands you should know for the CCENT certification exam when it comes to troubleshooting RIP.

The first thing you want to do is verify that the routes are added to the routing table when you receive RIP updates from other routers. The following command is used on RouterA to verify that I have a `27.0.0.0` entry added to the routing table:

```
RouterA>show ip route
Codes: C - connected, S - static, I - IGRP, R - RIP, ...
(Additional codes omitted for briefness)

Gateway of last resort is not set
R    27.0.0.0 [120/1] via 26.0.0.2, 00:00:20, Serial0/0/0
C    25.0.0.0/8 is directly connected, FastEthernet0/1
C    26.0.0.0/8 is directly connected, Serial0/0/0
```

Looking at the preceding output, you see that RouterA has a route to the `27.0.0.0` network that it has learned through RIP (code `R`). You can see the administrative distance is 120 with a hop count of 1 (by the `[120/1]`). You also see that the `27.0.0.0` network can be reached by way of `26.0.0.2`, which can be reached by sending the data out the serial port. The `00:00:20` is showing the last time a RIP update was received for that route. Remember that RIP messages are sent every 30 seconds, so this number should never be higher than 30 (displayed as `00:00:30`).

If for some reason you did not have any new entries in your routing table learned from RIP, you might have to troubleshoot using some other commands. You can use the `show ip protocols` command to display information about routing protocols that have been enabled on your router.

```
RouterA>show ip protocols
Routing Protocol is "rip"
  Sending updates every 30 seconds, next due in 3 seconds
    Invalid after 180 seconds, hold down 180, flushed after 240
  Outgoing update filter list for all interfaces is not set
  Incoming update filter list for all interfaces is not set
  Redistributing: rip
  Default version control: send version 1, receive any
    version
    Interface          Send  Recv  Triggered RIP  Key-
    chain
    Serial0/0/0         1     1 2
    FastEthernet0/1     1     1 2
```

```
Automatic network summarization is in effect
Maximum path: 4
Routing for networks:
  26.0.0.0
  25.0.0.0
Routing information sources:
  Gateway          Distance        Last Update
  26.0.0.2          120            00:00:27
Distance: <default is 120>
```

I have applied boldface to the preceding entries that you should make note of. The first line to note is at the top, where it mentions that the routing protocol "rip" has been enabled, and the output lets you know that updates are sent every 30 seconds. (This is known as the *update timer.*) You can also see that the entries are invalid after 180 seconds, which is how long the router waits before removing a route if it has not received an update within that period. (This is known as the *invalid timer.*) The flushed after setting specifies the length of time after a route has been deemed invalid that it is removed from the routing table (known as the *flush timer*). All of these values are measured in seconds.

You can also see that RIPv1 is being used to send RIP routing updates, but the router can receive RIPv1 and RIPv2 messages on each of the interfaces. Looking at the output, you also see that RIP has been enabled for the 25.0.0.0 and 26.0.0.0 networks — this is definitely a setting to watch for when troubleshooting RIP to ensure you have enabled broadcasting of the right networks! The last setting to note in the output is that at the bottom — you see the administrative distance is 120.

The final thing I want to mention when troubleshooting RIP is that you can turn on debugging for RIP by using the debug ip rip command. The debug ip rip command allows you to view the RIP messages that are sent and received at the router console! To enable RIP debugging, use the debug ip rip command as shown in the output that follows:

```
RouterA>enable
RouterA#debug ip rip
RIP protocol debugging is on
RouterA#
*Apr  19 11:43:52.354: RIP: sending v1 update to
    255.255.255.255 via Serial0/0/0 (26.0.0.1)
*Apr  19 11:43:52.354: RIP: build update entries
*Apr  19 11:43:52.354:      subnet 25.0.0.0 metric 1
*Apr  19 11:43:52.432: RIP: sending v1 update to
    255.255.255.255 via FastEthernet0/1 (25.0.0.1)
*Apr  19 11:43:52.432: RIP: build update entries
*Apr  19 11:43:52.432:      subnet 26.0.0.0 metric 1
*Apr  19 11:43:53.025: RIP: received v1 update from 26.0.0.2
    on Serial0/0/0
*Apr  19 11:43:53.025:       27.0.0.0 in 1 hops
```

```
*Apr  19 11:43:53.025:        26.0.0.0 in 1 hops
*Apr  19 11:44:22.369: RIP: sending v1 update to
    255.255.255.255 via Serial0/0/0 (26.0.0.1)
*Apr  19 11:44:22.369: RIP: build update entries
*Apr  19 11:44:22.369:    subnet 25.0.0.0 metric 1
*Apr  19 11:44:22.369: RIP: sending v1 update to
    255.255.255.255 via FastEthernet0/1 (25.0.0.1)
*Apr  19 11:44:22.369: RIP: build update entries
*Apr  19 11:44:22.369:    subnet 26.0.0.0 metric 1
```

In the preceding output, you see that debugging is enabled for the RIP routing protocol. You can also see at the top of the output that a RIPv1 update was sent from the serial port and then another RIPv1 update was sent from the Fast Ethernet port. More importantly, at 11:43:53.025, you see that I received a RIPv1 update from 26.0.0.2 (the serial interface of RouterB), and that the update includes the routes of 26.0.0.0 and 27.0.0.0, with each being one hop away.

One last point I want to make is that you should enable debugging only when troubleshooting, and then disable debugging as soon as possible, as it puts load on your router. To disable RIP debugging, you use the no debug ip rip command, or you can disable all debugging with the no debug all command.

```
*Apr  19 11:53:22.614: RIP: build update entries
*Apr  19 11:53:22.614:    subnet 26.0.0.0 metric 1
RouterA#no debug all
All possible debugging has been turned off
```

For the CCENT certification exam, be familiar with the show ip protocols command and the debug ip rip command. Also be able to interpret the output to help determine if the protocol is sending and receiving updates. In addition, know the commands to disable debugging, for the exam!

Chapter Summary

The chapter introduces you to the concept of dynamic routing protocols and shows you how to configure the RIP routing protocol. Be sure to know the following points when preparing for the CCENT certification exam:

✦ There are two major classes, or routing protocols; distance vector and link state routing protocols.

✦ Distance vector routing protocols send the entire routing table in an update at regular intervals.

✦ Distance vector routing protocols use the hop count metric, while link state uses the availability of the link and bandwidth.

✦ To enable RIPv1, you use the `router rip` command to navigate to the router prompt and then enable RIP on each network interface with the `network` command.

✦ To enable RIPv2, you use the same commands as RIPv1 but you add the `version 2` command at the router prompt.

✦ To display your routing table, use the `show ip route` command.

✦ To view routing protocol details, you use the `show ip protocols` command.

✦ When troubleshooting RIP, you can turn on RIP debugging with the `debug ip rip` command.

✦ Be sure to turn off all debugging, when you finish troubleshooting, with the `no debug all` command.

Lab Exercises

This chapter introduces you to the concept of dynamic routing protocols and how to configure the RIP routing protocol. The following lab helps you gain more understanding of RIP by configuring a network topology and enabling RIP on the routers.

Lab 2-1: Enabling RIP

1. **Using Figure 2-7 as your guide, configure each of the network interfaces with the appropriate settings.**

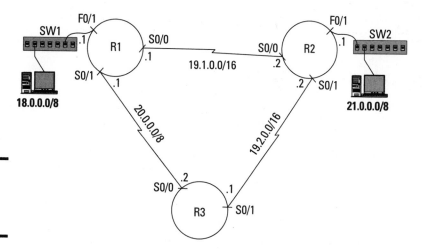

Figure 2-7:
Lab 2-1 network diagram.

**Book III
Chapter 2**

Dynamic Routing Protocols

You should have configured routers R1, R2, and R3 with the following commands:

Router R1

```
Router>enable
Router#config term
Router (config)#hostname R1

R1(config)#interface f0/1
R1(config-if)#ip address 18.0.0.1 255.0.0.0
R1(config-if)#no shutdown

R1(config-if)#interface s0/0/1
R1(config-if)#ip address 20.0.0.1 255.0.0.0
R1(config-if)#encapsulation hdlc
R1(config-if)#clock rate 64000
R1(config-if)#no shutdown

R1(config-if)#interface s0/0/0
R1(config-if)#ip address 19.1.0.1 255.255.0.0
R1(config-if)#encapsulation hdlc
R1(config-if)#clock rate 64000
R1(config-if)#no shutdown
R1(config-if)#
```

Router R2

```
Router>enable
Router#config term
Router (config)#hostname R2

R2(config)#interface s0/0/0
R2(config-if)#ip address 19.1.0.2 255.255.0.0
R2(config-if)#encapsulation hdlc
R2(config-if)#no shutdown

R2(config-if)#interface s0/0/1
R2(config-if)#ip address 19.2.0.2 255.255.0.0
R2(config-if)#encapsulation hdlc
R2(config-if)#clock rate 64000
R2(config-if)#no shutdown

R2(config-if)#interface f0/1
R2(config-if)#ip address 21.0.0.1 255.0.0.0
R2(config-if)#no shutdown
```

Router R3

```
Router>enable
Router#config term
Router(config)#hostname R3
```

```
R3(config)#interface s0/0/0
R3(config-if)#ip address 20.0.0.2 255.0.0.0
R3(config-if)#encapsulation hdlc
R3(config-if)#no shutdown

R3(config-if)#interface s0/0/1
R3(config-if)#ip address 19.2.0.1 255.255.0.0
R3(config-if)#encapsulation hdlc
R3(config-if)#no shutdown
```

2. **With each router now configured, view the routing tables on each router with the `show ip route` command and verify that you have all the connected routes on each router.**

3. **Configure RIPv2 on router R1 using the appropriate commands. (Refer to the "Configuring RIPv2" section earlier in the chapter if you need to.)**

   The following commands configure RIPv2 on router R1:

   ```
   R1>enable
   R1#config term
   Enter configuration commands, one per line.  End with
       CNTL/Z
   R1(config)#router rip
   R1(config-router)#network 18.0.0.0
   R1(config-router)#network 19.0.0.0
   R1(config-router)#network 20.0.0.0
   R1(config-router)#version 2
   ```

4. **Configure RIPv2 on router R2 using the appropriate commands. (Refer to the "Configuring RIPv2" section earlier in the chapter if you need to.)**

   The following commands configure RIPv2 on router R2:

   ```
   R2>enable
   R2#config term
   R2(config)#router rip
   R2(config-router)#network 19.0.0.0
   R2(config-router)#network 21.0.0.0
   R2(config-router)#version 2
   ```

5. **Configure RIPv2 on router R3 using the appropriate commands. (Refer to the "Configuring RIPv2" section earlier in the chapter if you need to.)**

   The following commands configure RIPv2 on router R3:

   ```
   R3>enable
   R3#config term
   R3(config)#router rip
   R3(config-router)#network 20.0.0.0
   R3(config-router)#network 19.0.0.0
   R3(config-router)#version 2
   ```

**Book III
Chapter 2**

**Dynamic Routing
Protocols**

6. **View the routing table on each router with the `show ip route` command and verify that you can see the new routes.**

   The following shows the routing table on R1.

   ```
   R1>show ip route
   Codes: C - connected, S - static, I - IGRP, R - RIP, ...

   Gateway of last resort is not set

        21.0.0.0/8 is subnetted, 1 subnets
   R      21.0.0.0 [120/1] via 19.1.0.2, 00:00:20, Serial0/0/0
        19.0.0.0/16 is subnetted, 2 subnets
   R      19.2.0.0 [120/1] via 19.1.0.2, 00:00:20, Serial0/0/0
   C      19.1.0.0 is directly connected, Serial0/0/0
   C      18.0.0.0/8 is directly connected, FastEthernet0/1
   C      20.0.0.0/8 is directly connected, Serial0/0/1
   R1>
   ```

7. **Verify the RIP configuration with the `show ip protocols` command on each router. Verify that RIPv2 is enabled by analyzing the output.**

8. **Enable RIP debugging with the `debug ip rip` command and view the RIP messages as they appear on the screen.**

Prep Test

1 Which of the following protocols are distance vector routing protocols supported by multiple vendors and not just Cisco?

A ○ OSPF

B ○ RIP

C ○ IGRP

D ○ EIGRP

2 Which of the following protocols are link state routing protocols? (Select all that apply.)

A ❑ EIGRP

B ❑ RIP

C ❑ IGRP

D ❑ OSPF

3 You have three interfaces on the router: one configured for the `27.0.0.0/8`, while the other two interfaces are configured with `29.1.0.0/16` and `29.2.0.0/16`. If you want to use RIPv2, which of the following represents the least number of commands you would need to use?

A ○ Use the following commands:

```
RouterA>enable
RouterA#config term
RouterA(config)#enable rip
RouterA(config)#network 27.0.0.0
RouterA(config)#network 29.0.0.0
RouterA(config)#version 2
```

B ○ Use the following commands:

```
RouterA>enable
RouterA#config term
RouterA(config)#router rip
RouterA(config-router)#network 27.0.0.0
RouterA(config-router)#network 29.1.0.0
RouterA(config-router)#network 29.2.0.0
```

C ○ Use the following commands:

```
RouterA>enable
RouterA#config term
RouterA(config)#router rip
RouterA(config-router)#network 27.0.0.0
RouterA(config-router)#network 29.1.0.0
RouterA(config-router)#network 29.2.0.0
RouterA(config-router)#version 2
```

D ○ Use the following commands:

```
RouterA>enable
RouterA#config term
RouterA(config)#router rip
RouterA(config-router)#network 27.0.0.0
RouterA(config-router)#network 29.0.0.0
RouterA(config-router)#version 2
```

4 **What command enables RIP debugging?**

A ○ `rip debug`
B ○ `debug rip`
C ○ `debug ip rip`
D ○ `enable debug`

5 **You want to disable sending RIP messages on interface serial 0/1. Which of the following commands would you use?**

A ○ `RouterA(config)#passive-interface serial 0/1`
B ○ `RouterA(config-router)#passive-interface serial 0/1`
C ○ `RouterA#passive-interface serial 0/1`
D ○ `RouterA>passive-interface serial 0/1`

6 **You wish to see how RIP has been configured on the router. What command would you use?**

A ○ `RouterA#show ip config`
B ○ `RouterA#show protocols`
C ○ `RouterA#show rip protocols`
D ○ `RouterA#show ip protocols`

7 **What is the default administrative distance for RIP?**

A ○ 90
B ○ 100
C ○ 120
D ○ 150

8 When looking at the routing table, how do you know which entries have been learned through RIP?

A ○ The entry with code R

B ○ The entry with code C

C ○ The entry with code RIP

D ○ The entry with code 1

9 When RIP has multiple routes to a destination with the same hop count, what will it do?

A ○ RIP uses the one with the administrative distance of 120.

B ○ RIP will load-balance the links to that destination.

C ○ RIP uses the second route in the table.

D ○ RIP uses the first route in the table.

10 What version of RIP supports VLSM?

A ○ RIPv1

B ○ RIPv2

C ○ RIPv8

D ○ RIPv9

Answers

1 **B.** RIP is an open standard distance vector routing protocol that is supported by many different router manufacturers. *See "Routing Information Protocol (RIP)."*

2 **A, D.** OSPF and EIGRP are examples of link state routing protocols. OSPF is an open standard link state protocol, while EIGRP is a Cisco protocol that uses link state. *Review "Identifying popular routing protocols."*

3 **D.** When specifying the networks for the RIP routing protocol, you need to specify only the classful addresses, even when the address space has been subnetted. *Check out "Configuring RIPv2."*

4 **C.** You can enable debugging for RIP to view the RIP–related messages, as they are sent and received, to help troubleshoot RIP. *Peruse "Troubleshooting RIP."*

5 **B.** To disable sending RIP update messages, you can use the `passive-interface` command at the router prompt. *Take a look at "Configuring RIPv1."*

6 **D.** To view the current RIP configuration after RIP has been enabled, you can use the `show ip protocols` command. *Peek at "Troubleshooting RIP."*

7 **C.** RIP uses a default administrative distance of 120. *Look over "Routing Information Protocol v2 (RIPv2)."*

8 **A.** RIP entries found in the routing table display with a code of `R`. *Study "Troubleshooting RIP."*

9 **B.** When multiple routes to the same destination exist, with RIP the router will load-balance the multiple routes. *Refer to "Routing Information Protocol (RIP)."*

10 **B.** RIPv2 supports VLSM, which allows the use of different-size subnets. *Examine "Routing Information Protocol v2 (RIPv2)."*

Chapter 3: Introduction to Switching

In This Chapter

✔ Introduction to Cisco switches

✔ Understanding switch functionality

✔ Understanding data flow

✔ Basic switch configuration

The focus of this minibook so far has been on routing concepts and routing protocols, but another very important network device to know about for the CCENT certification exam is the network switch. This chapter is designed to overview the features of a Cisco switch and ensure that you understand the flow of data before introducing you to some basic switch configuration.

Quick Assessment

1   (True/False). A switch filters traffic based on the destination IP address.

2   The _____ determines how a switch processes the frame.

3   A switch is an example of a layer-_____ device.

4   (True/False). A flashing green light on a port means there is a problem with the port.

5   The layer-2 term for the data that passes through the switch is a _____.

Answers

1   *False.* See "Switch overview."

2   *Operation mode.* Review *"Switch operation modes."*

3   *2.* Check out *"Switch overview."*

4   *False.* Peruse *"Status mode."*

5   *Frame.* Take a look at *"Switch overview."*

Introduction to Cisco Switches

Cisco switches are unlike Cisco routers; when you purchase a new router, you are required to connect the router to the network and configure the router for operation. Cisco switches do not require any configuration to perform their job — you can simply take the switch out of the box, connect some systems to the switch, and it will function!

When looking at a Cisco switch, you will notice that it looks different from a router because it has a lot more interfaces. Most routers have three or four interfaces, but the switches have dozens of interfaces on them that you can use to connect computers and devices to the network.

Looking at Figure 3-1, you see a picture of a Cisco catalyst switch. Let's take a few minutes to talk about the different LEDs that are located on the front of the switch, along with their associated modes. Keep in mind that your switch model may have different LEDs with slightly different meanings, but the general idea is all the same.

System LED

The first LED you see on the front-left side of the switch (the top-left LED in Figure 3-1) is the *system LED*, which gives information on the state of the *system,* or switch. You can use the system LED to help troubleshoot a problem.

If the system LED is not lit up at all, there are problems with the switch receiving power, or it is simply not plugged in! If the system light is a solid green, the switch is receiving power and functioning without any problems. If the system light is amber, the switch has experienced problems during POST on boot up.

If the system LED is not lit up, you may have power issues, while a system LED with an amber light indicates that you most likely have POST issues.

RPS LED

The *redundant power supply* (RPS; a system that supports multiple power supplies so that if one fails you still have power) LED uses a different color to indicate the functionality of the RPS. The following outlines the different RPS LED colors:

+ **Green:** If the LED is lit green it means that you have redundant power supplies in the device and they are functioning properly (meaning they are ready to provide backup power).

+ **Blinking Green:** Means that the redundant power supply is unavailable because it is providing power to another device at the time.

✦ **Amber:** An amber light on the RPS LED indicates you do have redundant power supplies but there is a failure in redundancy.

✦ **Blinking Amber:** Means that the internal power supply has failed and is running of the redundant power supply.

✦ **Not lit:** If you do not have redundant power supplies, the LED is not lit up at all.

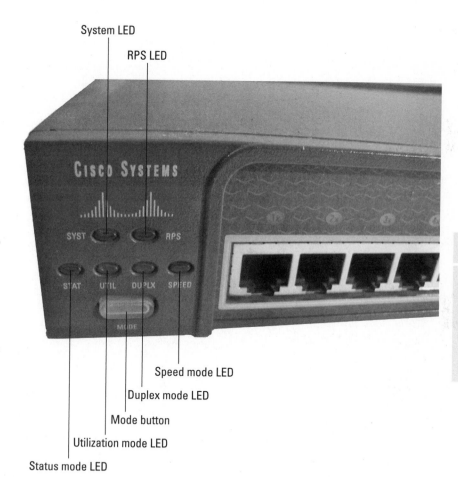

System LED

RPS LED

Figure 3-1: Looking at the LEDs on a Cisco catalyst switch.

Speed mode LED

Duplex mode LED

Mode button

Utilization mode LED

Status mode LED

Switch display modes

When you look at the front-left side of your Cisco switch, you will also notice that there are four LEDs, labeled STAT, UTIL, DUPLX, and SPEED. (These are in the second row of LEDs back in Figure 3-1.) These four LEDs are called *display modes,* and they control the meaning of each LED that is displayed with each port on the switch. The mode LED that is lit up indicates the display mode you are currently viewing, and you change the display mode you are viewing by pushing the Mode button on the front-left side of your Cisco switch.

Status mode

The default mode is STAT, or *status mode,* which indicates the status of each of the ports. When your switch is in status mode, each port LED has one of the following states:

✦ **Off:** If the LED on a port is not displaying any light while in status mode, it means there is no link to that port.

✦ **Solid green:** If the LED on a port displays a solid green, it means there is a connection to the port, known as a *link,* but that there currently is no traffic passing through the port.

✦ **Flashing green:** If the LED on a port is flashing green, it means that there is a link to the port and traffic is passing through the interface.

✦ **Amber:** If the LED on a port is amber, the port is disabled due to the administrator disabling the port, because STP placed the port in a blocking state (a CCNA topic), or it has been disabled automatically via port security (an address violation).

It is important to note that the meaning of the LEDs in status mode can change slightly from one model switch to the other. It is best to check the documentation for your model switch on the meaning of the LEDs.

Utilization mode

The UTIL, or *utilization mode,* displays the bandwidth utilization on each port. All the port LEDs together are used as a meter (see Figure 3-2) when you are in utilization mode:

✦ If *all* the port LEDs display a solid green, the bandwidth is 50 percent utilized or more.

✦ If all the port LEDs are green *except for the last port* (meaning the last port is turned off and emits no light), the network utilization is between 25 and 49 percent.

✦ If all the port LEDs are green *except for the last two,* the bandwidth utilization on the switch is less than 25 percent.

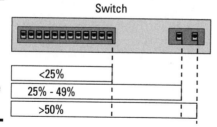

Figure 3-2:
Bandwidth
utilization
can be
determined
by using the
UTIL mode.

Duplex mode

If you switch to duplex mode by pressing the Mode button, each of the LEDs on the ports take a different meaning. The following lists the meaning of the port LEDs when you have switched to duplex mode:

✦ **Off:** If you are in duplex mode and the lights are off on a port, it means that the port is running in half-duplex mode. Remember from Book I, Chapter 3, that half-duplex means you can send and receive data but only in one direction at a time.

✦ **Green:** If you are in duplex display mode and the LEDs on a port are a solid green, the port is running in full-duplex mode. Full-duplex mode allows you to send and receive at the same time.

Speed mode

When you are in speed mode, the LED on each port helps identify what speed the port has been configured for. The following summarizes the state of the ports when speed mode is used:

✦ **Off:** If the LED on the ports is off when you are in speed mode, the port is running at 10 Mbps.

✦ **Green:** If the LED is a solid green when you are in speed mode, the port is running at 100 Mbps.

✦ **Flashing Green:** If the LED is a flashing green, the port is running at 1 Gbps.

Understanding Switch Functionality

Now that you understand the different light indicators on a Cisco switch, let's talk about the purpose and functionality of a switch. In this section, you discover how a switch filters traffic using the destination MAC address of a frame, and you also find out some of the core services that a switch offers. I go on to discuss the different operation modes supported by Cisco switches in this section.

**Book III
Chapter 3**

Introduction to
Switching

Switch overview

The purpose of the network switch is to act as a connectivity point for systems to connect to the network. Once the systems have connected to the network, they can then transmit and receive information with other networking devices and systems on the network.

Switches run at layer 2 of the OSI model (unless you have a layer-3 switch, which can also perform routing functions). As a result, they work with the data frames on the network.

The basic concept of a switch is this: The switch receives a frame from a system connected to it, looks at the destination address of that frame, and tries to find that MAC address in the MAC address table stored in memory on the switch. The *MAC address table* is a table that lists all the MAC addresses of devices connected to the switch and tells which port on the switch that MAC address is connected to.

When the switch locates the MAC address in the MAC address table, it then forwards that frame to the port that is associated with that MAC address in the MAC address table. (See Figure 3-3.)

Figure 3-3:
A switch uses the MAC address table to filter the traffic by sending the data to only the port where the destination MAC address resides.

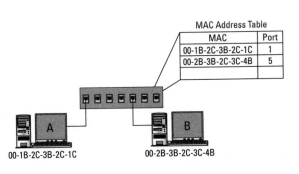

For example, looking at Figure 3-3 you see that the MAC address table on the switch has the MAC addresses of ComputerA and ComputerB. When ComputerA sends data to ComputerB, the frame travels out the network card of ComputerA and up the cable to port 1 on the switch. The switch receives the frame and looks at the destination MAC address stored in the frame. In this example, because the frame is destined for ComputerB, the frame will have a destination address of 00-2B-3B-2C-3C-4B. The switch then looks in the MAC address table to see which port that MAC address resides on — in this case, it is port 5. The switch then forwards the frame out port number 5 so that the data can reach ComputerB.

You can view the MAC address table on a switch by using the show mac-address-table command within priv exec mode on the switch. The following code displays the result of the show mac-address-table command:

```
Switch>enable
Switch#show mac-address-table
          Mac Address Table
-------------------------------------------

Vlan    Mac Address      Type       Ports
----    -----------      --------   -----

   1    0009.7c57.5674   DYNAMIC    Fa0/2
   1    0010.11d9.d001   DYNAMIC    Fa0/1
   1    00d0.bc8a.2766   DYNAMIC    Fa0/12
```

When looking at the output of the show mac-address-table command, you can see the three MAC addresses associated with the three different ports. The type *dynamic* means that the switch learned the addresses automatically as traffic passed through the switch.

Core switch services

There are three core services offered by switches — they are address learning, filtering and forwarding, and loop avoidance. This section introduces you to each of the three services.

Address learning

The first task that a switch has to do is to learn all the MAC addresses of all the systems connected to the switch and populate those MAC addresses in the MAC address table.

One of the ways that the switch learns the MAC addresses of the systems is dynamically as traffic hits the switch. For example, looking at Figure 3-4, when ComputerC sends a piece of data to ComputerA or ComputerB, the switch sees the source MAC address of the frame and then records the port that the frame was received on in the MAC address table.

The entries are stored in the MAC address table for 300 seconds after the last time the MAC address is used. (This is known as the *aging-time*.) You can modify the aging-time by using the mac-address-table aging-time <value> command to set the aging timeout to a larger value if you like. Although not recommended because it can cause communication issues in the long run, you can turn off aging and not have the entries time out of the MAC address table by setting the aging time to 0.

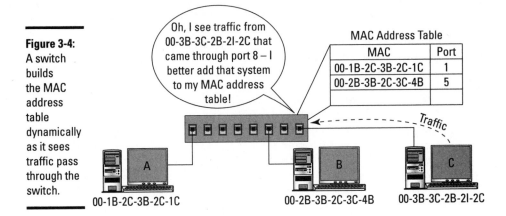

Figure 3-4:
A switch builds the MAC address table dynamically as it sees traffic pass through the switch.

Filtering and forwarding

After a switch learns the MAC addresses of all the systems, it then starts to forward traffic to only the port that the destination MAC in the frame resides at. This is an important feature of a switch, as it is filtering traffic by sending only the frames to the port that should be receiving the frame. This is unlike a hub device that forwards the information to all ports on the hub no matter what.

The fact that the switch filters traffic by forwarding the traffic to only the port that the destination system resides on gives a huge security benefit and also improves network performance. The security benefit is that the data is not sent to all systems (like a hub does), which takes away the opportunity for someone undeserving to see the information. The performance benefit is that you are not sending the data to all systems for them just to discard the frame (because it is not for them).

I typically have a number of students ask me what happens when the frame is destined for a MAC address that has not been added to the MAC address table. The answer is the switch floods the frame to all ports on the switch. *Frame flooding* is different from broadcasting because with flooding, the destination MAC address in the header of the frame references the one MAC address that is the destination of the frame.

Because the switch does not have the MAC address in its table, it has no choice but to flood the frame to all ports. The important point is that all systems connected will receive the frame but discard it if they are not the destination system of the frame. The system that is actually using the MAC address contained in the destination MAC address field of the frame will process the information and send a response.

A *broadcast message* is a message that is actually destined for all systems by having the destination MAC address in the frame set to FF-FF-FF-FF-FF-FF (the broadcast address). Any frames with the destination address of the frame set to the broadcast address will be processed by *all* systems on the network. For more on broadcast messages see Book I, Chapter 4.

Be sure to know the difference between frame flooding and the concept of a broadcast message. A broadcast message is destined for, and will be processed by, all systems. A flooded frame is a frame that is destined for only one system, and will be processed by that system, but is sent to all ports because the location of that system is unknown.

An important point to make is that when you have two switches connected together — let's say SwitchA is connected to SwitchB — all of the systems that are on SwitchB will have their MAC addresses associated with the same port on SwitchA. This is because when SwitchA has data for those systems, it will reach all of those systems through the same port — the port that is connected to SwitchB.

Loop avoidance

A *network loop* is a bad thing, and it happens when you connect switches together to create a complete circle, like the one is shown in Figure 3-5. There are many different reasons why creating a loop with your switches is bad, and one of those reasons is it creates instability in the MAC address table.

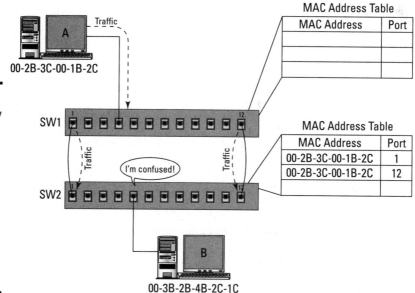

Figure 3-5:
Accidentally creating a loop on the network can cause instability in the MAC address table and bring the network down.

Let's look at how instability in the MAC address table occurs. Looking at Figure 3-5, you see that a loop has been created between two switches by connecting port 1 to port 1 and by connecting port 12 to port 12.

When ComputerA sends ComputerB some data, the frame leaves ComputerA and travels the cable to reach switch SW1. Switch SW1 then looks at the destination MAC address in the frame, which is destined for ComputerB's MAC address, and looks up the MAC address in the switch's MAC address table. As you can see in Figure 3-5, the MAC address table is empty — so the switch must flood the frame to all ports on the switch in order to locate ComputerB.

When the frame is flooded to all ports on SW1, the frame travels the network cable connecting port 1 on SW1 to port 1 on SW2. When the frame is received on port 1 at the SW2 switch, the switch stores in its MAC address table the fact that ComputerA can be found out port 1.

The problem is that, looking back to switch SW1, the frame will also travel out port 12 because the frame was flooded to all ports. When the frame is received at port 12 on switch SW2, the switch goes to add an entry in the MAC address table for ComputerA being at port 12. The problem is the switch has already learned that ComputerA exits from port number 1! This creates instability in the MAC address table.

The solution is to prevent the loop from occurring by placing one of the ports that creates the loop into a *blocking* state. A blocked port is different from a disabled port in the sense that if a port is disabled, the administrator has to enable the port when she needs to use the port — which is administrative overhead. A blocked port is unblocked automatically when the switch needs the port to function again!

It is important to understand that the opposite of a blocked port is a port that is in a forwarding state. A port in a *forwarding* state is a port that can be used to send frames, while a blocked port cannot be used to send any traffic.

Here's the big question: How does the Cisco switch decide which port to place in a blocking state in order to prevent the loop? The answer is that Cisco switches use a protocol called *Spanning Tree Protocol* (STP), which is a layer-2 protocol that uses an algorithm designed to prevent loops on a network.

In the example back in Figure 3-5, when switch SW1's ports 1 and 12 are connected to switch SW2's ports 1 and 12, the STP protocol decides to place one of those ports in a blocking state. The STP protocol uses different methods to decide on which port to place in a blocking state, but one of those methods is the bandwidth of the port — the lower bandwidth port is placed in a blocking state.

The reason why network administrators may have the two connections between the two switches is to create a *fault-tolerant* link so that if one link goes down, the other link is available between the two switches. Let's assume that port 12 is placed in a blocking state when the fault-tolerant links are put in place. If for some reason the link on port 1 becomes unavailable, the STP protocol changes port 12 from a blocking state to a forwarding state automatically — still allowing communication between the two switches!

Switch operation modes

Your network switch runs in one of three different operation modes, with each operation mode processing frames a little differently. The following outlines the differences in the three operation modes.

Store-and-forward

Store-and-forward is the default operation mode on most Cisco switches. The *store-and-forward* operation mode involves the switch receiving an entire frame (store) before it decides where it needs to forward the frame to.

Store-and-forward has the downfall of taking more time to process the frame, as it has to wait until the entire frame has been received off the network. The switch stores the frame in memory until it is ready to forward the frame on to the destination system. Again, the downfall here is the wait time to receive the entire frame before making a decision on what to do with the frame.

The advantage of store-and-forward is that after waiting for the entire frame to be received, the switch then performs an error check on the frame to decide if the frame is corrupt. If the frame is corrupt, it will not bother forwarding the frame on to the destination.

The switch does the error check by looking at the checksum value stored in the trailer of the frame — known as the *frame check sequence* (FCS) — and then calculating its own checksum on the frame. After the switch calculates its own checksum, it compares it to what is in the trailer — if the two values are the same, the data is not corrupt and the frame can be forwarded on to its destination.

Cut-through

Due to the time it takes to receive an entire frame off the network and perform an integrity check, Cisco decided to create a different operation mode that you can use — cut-through. *Cut-through processing* means that as soon as the switch receives the destination address of a frame, it can start forwarding the frame on to the destination.

Cut-through processing is designed to improve switch performance, as you have little wait time when a frame is received; the switch can start sending the frame data as it receives the information, instead of storing the bits in memory until all bits have been received (like with store-and-forward).

The downfall of cut-through is that because the switch forwards the frame bits as they are received, there is no way to do an integrity check to make sure that the frame has not been damaged. This means when a system receives the frame from a switch, the frame could be unreadable and need to be retransmitted. So, you gain performance but lose integrity with cut-through processing.

Fragment-free

Fragment-free is the switch operation mode that sits in between store-and-forward and cut-through. It has been found that the first 64 bytes of a frame is what normally contains errors, so Cisco designed *fragment-free* to wait to receive the first 64 bytes, perform an integrity check on those 64 bytes, and then, if everything is fine, start forwarding the frame data on to the destination.

It is important to note that cut-through and fragment-free were created to help speed up the processing on older switches. Today's switches can process frame data a lot faster than in the past, and that is why store-and-forward is a good default — you can do full error checking, and the switch's speed makes up for the wait time.

Understanding Data Flow

A big part of the CCENT certification exam is understanding communication and the pathway that information takes on a network. This section is designed to describe the pathway that information takes on a LAN (known as *local communication*), and how information travels between two networks (known as *remote communication*).

Local communication

Local communication is the term we use for two systems, or devices, that are communicating with each other and are within the same network. Looking at Figure 3-6, let's break down the steps for ComputerA to send data to ComputerB by using the IP addresses.

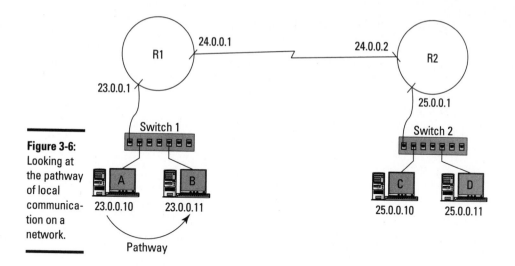

Figure 3-6:
Looking at the pathway of local communication on a network.

1. **ANDing:** When ComputerA decides it needs to send data to the 23.0.0.11 system (ComputerB), the first thing it does is compare the two IP addresses to see if the two systems are on the same network. In this case, they are on the same network (as they have the same network ID of 23.0.0.0). This decision is actually made by the IP protocol running on ComputerA.

2. **ARP request:** Once ComputerA decides that the system it is trying to communicate with exists on the same network, it knows not to bother the router for this communication. ComputerA now sends out an ARP broadcast message (known as an *ARP request;* see Book I, Chapter 4, for more on ARP requests) asking, "Whoever has the IP address of 23.0.0.11, could you send me your MAC address?"

3. **ARP reply:** ComputerB sees the ARP request message and sends a reply to ComputerA indicating its MAC address.

4. **Sending data:** Now that ComputerA has the MAC address of ComputerB, it can now send the data to ComputerB. If you were to capture this communication, you would see that the packet header has the source IP address of 23.0.0.10 and ComputerA's MAC address as the source MAC address. Notice, also, that the destination IP address is set to 23.0.0.11, and the destination MAC address is the MAC address of ComputerB.

**Book III
Chapter 3**

Introduction to
Switching

Remote communication

Remote communication occurs when two systems that are communicating reside on different networks. The pathway of remote communication is a little different from what we saw for local communication in the previous section. Using Figure 3-7, let us take a look at how ComputerA talks to ComputerC.

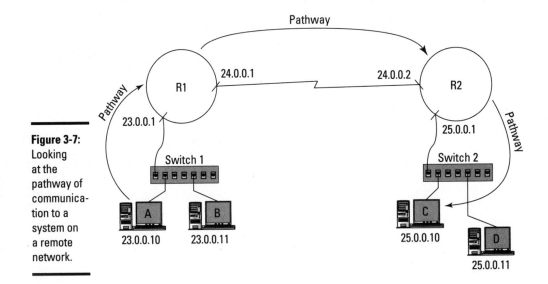

Figure 3-7:
Looking at the pathway of communication to a system on a remote network.

1. **ANDing:** When ComputerA decides it needs to send data to the 25.0.0.10 system (ComputerC), the first thing it does is compare the two IP addresses to see if the two systems are on the same network. In this case, the IP protocol on ComputerA decides the two systems are on different networks because they have two different network IDs. (ComputerA has a 23.0.0.0 network ID, and ComputerC has a 25.0.0.0 network ID.)

2. **ARP the router:** Once ComputerA decides that the two systems are on different networks, it knows that it has to involve the router in the communication. ComputerA looks at its default gateway setting (23.0.0.1) and then attempts to find out the MAC address of that default gateway IP address by ARPing the address. ComputerA sends out an ARP broadcast message (known as an *ARP request)* asking, "Whoever has the IP address of 23.0.0.1, could you send me your MAC address?"

3. **ARP reply:** Router R1 sees the ARP request message and sends a reply to ComputerA, indicating its MAC address.

4. **Sending data to router:** Once ComputerA has the router's MAC address, it sends the data to the router. The important point to stress here is what the fields in the packet header are set to:

   - *Source IP Address:* 23.0.0.10
   - *Destination IP Address:* 25.0.0.10
   - *Source MAC Address: MAC_of_ComputerA*
   - *Destination MAC Address: MAC_of_router_R1*

5. **Have route?:** Once router R1 receives the packet, it looks at the packet's destination IP address and compares that to the routing table to determine if it has a route to the destination network. Assume that router R1 has a route to the 25.0.0.0 network, so the router sees that it must send the data to 24.0.0.2 — but it needs the MAC address of that address.

6. **Router R1 ARPs R2:** At this point, router R1 sends an ARP broadcast message out asking, "Whoever has the address of 24.0.0.2, could you send me your MAC address?"

7. **R2 sends ARP reply:** Router R2 sees the ARP request message and replies with its MAC address. Router R1 then sends the data to router R2. Again, it is important to note the source and destination addresses of the packets at this point:

   - *Source IP Address:* 23.0.0.10
   - *Destination IP Address:* 25.0.0.10
   - *Source MAC Address: MAC_of_router_R1*
   - *Destination MAC Address: MAC_of_router_R2*

8. **R2 sends data to ComputerC:** When router R2 receives the packet, it looks at the destination IP address to decide whether it has a route to the destination. Router R2 sees that it does have an entry in its routing table for the 25.0.0.0 network, so it ARPs the destination IP address of 25.0.0.10 (ComputerC). ComputerC then replies with its MAC address, and router R2 sends the data to ComputerC. At this point, the packet header has the following field values:

   - *Source IP Address:* 23.0.0.10
   - *Destination IP Address:* 25.0.0.10
   - *Source MAC Address: MAC_of_router_R2*
   - *Destination MAC Address: MAC_of_ComputerC*

Book III
Chapter 3

Introduction to
Switching

The CCENT certification exam tests your knowledge on communication because it helps you understand how to troubleshoot communication problems. Be sure to be familiar with the steps listed above (and in the previous "Local communication" section) and compare the steps to the diagram so you understand each step during communication. Notice in the steps above that the source and destination IP address do not change, but the MAC address does change with each step.

Basic Switch Configuration

Now that you understand the basic concepts of a switch, let's take a look at how to configure popular settings on the switch. Understand that the basic configuration concepts of a router (see Book II, Chapter 2) apply here as well, so I don't discuss the different configuration modes, setting passwords, and navigating to an interface — all of these concepts are the same. In the next two chapters, you find out about configuration settings that are unique to the switch. But here, I tell you about configuring the device name, the IP address, and the default gateway.

Configuring the device name

The first thing to do is set a unique name on the network switch by using the `hostname` command. Assigning a name to the device is a simple first step to make sure that when you connect to the device, you know which network device you are connected to.

Configuring a name on the switch is similar to configuring a name on your router — use the following commands to configure a name on your network switch:

```
Switch>enable
Switch#config term
Switch(config)#hostname NY-SW1
NY-SW1(config)#
```

In the preceding code, you see that you configure the switch's name in global configuration mode. Once you're in global configuration mode, you use the `hostname` command to set the name on your switch. In the example here, I have changed the name to NY-SW1 to indicate that it is the first switch in the New York office.

Configuring the IP address

Another important setting you may want to configure on your network switch is an IP address. Keep in mind that you do not need to assign an IP address to your switch in order for it to do its normal job of acting as a switch — a switch works fine without having an IP address assigned to it.

So what is the purpose of assigning an IP address to the switch? You may want to assign an IP address to the switch so that you can remotely administer it. For example, after an IP address is assigned to the switch, you can Telnet into the switch and then remotely administer it. If you have no intention of remotely administering the switch, it may be better to not assign an IP address to the switch, as this will prevent a hacker from connecting to that IP.

Remember for the exam that an IP address is not needed on the switch, but if you want to be able to remotely administer the switch, you will need to assign IP address assigned to it.

To assign an IP address to the switch, you navigate to the default VLAN (Virtual Local Area Network) of VLAN1 and then assign the IP address to VLAN1. (You find out more on VLANs in the next chapter.) The following commands assign an IP address to the switch:

```
NY-SW1>enable
NY-SW1#config term
NY-SW1(config)#interface vlan1
NY-SW1(config-if)#ip address 23.0.0.25 255.0.0.0
NY-SW1(config-if)#no shutdown
```

Notice that with a switch you do not navigate to one of the Ethernet ports to assign the IP address — the reason is each system that connects to those ports has its own IP address. When assigning an IP address to the switch, Cisco had to come up with a way for the *switch* to get the IP address and not one of the ports. Cisco decided to assign the IP address to the VLAN, which they expose as a *virtual interface*.

Remembering to configure the default gateway setting

Once you configure the IP address on the switch, you can connect to that switch from anywhere on the network and administer the device. Unfortunately, you cannot connect to the switch from a different network because the switch does not know how to send data back to you; the switch cannot send data back to you because it would have to use a router to reach the other network and you have not configured it for a default gateway. (See Figure 3-8.)

Looking at Figure 3-8, assume you are sitting at ComputerC and you want to Telnet into switch SW1. In order for switch SW1 to send data back to ComputerC, it would have to pass the data to router R1. This means that the default gateway setting on switch SW1 needs to be 23.0.0.1.

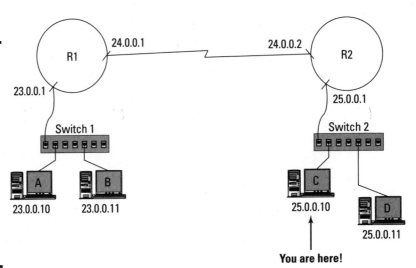

To configure the switch for a default gateway, you use the `ip default-gateway` command and reference the IP address of the router that the switch is to use to send data off the network. The following code shows how to configure the default gateway setting on the switch:

```
NY-SW1>enable
NY-SW1#config term
NY-SW1(config)#ip default-gateway 23.0.0.1
```

Notice that to configure the default gateway on the switch, you simply navigate to global configuration and use the `ip default-gateway` command.

Be sure to remember for the exam that if you do not have a default gateway setting assigned to the switch you cannot remotely administer the switch from a different network. This is because the switch does not know how to send data off the network if it has not been configured for a default gateway.

Chapter Summary

This chapter introduces you to the concept of Cisco switches and explores the basic services offered by a switch. The following are some key points to remember about a Cisco switch:

✦ Cisco switches do not need to be configured in order to function; you simply plug them in and connect systems to the switch.

✦ Switches are considered layer-2 devices, unless you are working with a layer-3 switch, which can act as a router as well.

✦ Switches offer three core services — address learning, filtering and forwarding, and loop avoidance.

✦ Switches filter traffic by storing the MAC addresses of all the systems and the port number they reside on in the MAC address table. As a frame enters the switch, the switch looks up the destination address in the MAC address table and then forwards the frame to the appropriate destination port.

✦ The *Spanning Tree Protocol* (STP) is a loop-avoidance protocol that is responsible for placing a port in a blocking state if it creates a redundant path.

✦ There are three switch operation modes — store-and-forward, cut-through, and fragment-free. Each mode processes a frame a little bit differently.

✦ The Mode button on the front of the switch toggles between the different display modes. Each display mode identifies different characteristics of the ports on a switch.

Lab Exercises

**Book III
Chapter 3**

This chapter discusses different features of a Cisco switch. The following lab exercise helps you apply basic configuration settings on the switch including changing the hostname, setting the IP address, and assigning a default gateway on the switch.

Introduction to Switching

Lab 3-1: Configuring a switch

1. Connect your system to the console port on the switch and console into the switch, using HyperTerminal.

2. Connect a few workstations to your switch and assign the IP addresses of 23.0.0.10 to the first workstation and 23.0.0.11 to the second workstation.

3. Ping from one workstation to another workstation in order to generate network traffic.

4. On the switch, display the MAC address table using the following command:

```
Switch>enable
Switch#show mac-address-table
```

5. **Record the MAC addresses and ports that each MAC resides on:**

MAC address   *Port*

_____

_____

_____

_____

_____

6. **To change the switch's name, use the following commands:**

```
Switch>enable
Switch#config term
Switch(config)#hostname LasVegas-SW1
LasVegas-SW1(config)#
```

7. **To assign an IP address and default gateway address to the switch, use the following commands:**

```
LasVegas-SW1>enable
LasVegas-SW1#config term
LasVegas-SW1(config)#interface vlan1
LasVegas-SW1(config-if)#ip address 23.0.0.2 255.0.0.0
LasVegas-SW1(config-if)#exit
LasVegas-SW1(config)#ip default-gateway 23.0.0.1
```

Prep Test

1 **Which switch operation mode waits to receive the first 64 bytes of the frame before forwarding the frame on to its destination?**

A ○ Store-and-forward

B ○ Cache and deliver

C ○ Fragment-free

D ○ Cut-through

2 **Your manager has asked you to Telnet into one of the switches in the Las Vegas office, but you cannot seem to connect. You can Telnet into the switch when you are in the Las Vegas office, but you cannot seem to Telnet when you are on a remote network. What could be the problem?**

A ○ No Telnet password assigned to the switch

B ○ No default gateway address assigned on the switch

C ○ No default gateway address assigned on your router

D ○ No Telnet password assigned on your router

3 **Bob calls complaining that he cannot access the network. When you look at the switch, you notice the port he is connected to is displaying an amber light. What does this mean?**

A ○ The IP address on the switch is incorrect.

B ○ The default gateway setting on the switch is incorrect.

C ○ The default gateway setting on Bob's station is incorrect.

D ○ The port has been disabled.

4 **Which switch operation mode waits until the entire frame is received before forwarding the frame on to its destination?**

A ○ Store-and-forward

B ○ Cache and deliver

C ○ Fragment-free

D ○ Cut-through

5 **What does a switch do with a frame it receives that is destined for a MAC address that is not stored in the MAC address table?**

A ○ Broadcast the frame.

B ○ Floods the frame.

C ○ Send the frame to the address of `FF-FF-FF-FF-FF-FF`.

D ○ Store it until the destination MAC is in the MAC address table.

6 **You wish to display your MAC address table. What command do you use?**

A ○ `Switch(config)# show mac-address-table`

B ○ `Switch(config-if)# show mac-address-table`

C ○ `Switch# view mac-address-table`

D ○ `Switch# show mac-address-table`

7 **Which of the following commands assigns a default gateway address to your switch?**

A ○ `Switch(config-if)# ip default-gateway 24.0.0.1`

B ○ `Switch# ip default-gateway 24.0.0.1`

C ○ `Switch(config)# ip default-gateway 24.0.0.1`

D ○ `Switch(config)#default-gateway 24.0.0.1`

8 **When a packet is sent from a system on your network to a system on another network, which of the following is true of the packet as it is passed to your router from your system?**

A ○ Destination IP Address: *your_router* / Destination MAC Address: *your_router*

B ○ Destination IP Address: *the_remote_system* / Destination MAC Address: *your_router*

C ○ Destination IP Address: *your_router* / Destination MAC Address: *the_remote_system*

D ○ Destination IP Address: *the_remote_system* / Destination MAC Address: *the_remote_system*

9 **Which switch operation mode starts forwarding the frame off to its destination as soon as the destination MAC address is received?**

A ○ Store-and-forward

B ○ Cache and deliver

C ○ Fragment-free

D ○ Cut-through

10 **Which of the following are considered core services offered by a switch? (Select three.)**

A ❑ Filtering and forwarding

B ❑ Loop avoidance

C ❑ Address translation

D ❑ IP address assignment

E ❑ Address learning

F ❑ Name resolution

Answers

1 **C.** Fragment-free is the switch operation mode that processes frames by waiting to receive the first 64 bytes before forwarding the frame on. *See "Fragment-free."*

2 **B.** If the switch has not been configured for a default gateway address, it cannot send data off the network. *Review "Remembering to configure the default gateway setting."*

3 **D.** If the port has been disabled by an administrator (or automatically shut down through a feature such as port security), the port displays an amber light when a system is connected to the port. You will need to enable the port before you can use it. *Check out "Status mode."*

4 **A.** The store-and-forward operation mode processes a frame by waiting till the entire frame has been received before forwarding the frame on to its destination. *Peruse "Store-and-forward."*

5 **B.** The frame is flooded when the switch is unsure what port to forward the frame to. A flooded frame is destined for a specific MAC address but was sent to all ports on the switch because the location of that MAC address is unknown. *Take a look at "Filtering and forwarding."*

6 **D.** You use the `show mac-address-table` command from priv exec mode to display the MAC address table. *Peek at "Switch overview."*

7 **C.** The `ip default-gateway` command is used to configure your switch for a default gateway address. Note that this command is executed from global configuration mode. *Look over "Remembering to configure the default gateway setting."*

8 **B.** This is an important question. When the packet is sent from your system to your router the destination IP address is set to the remote system you are trying to talk to, but the destination MAC address is set to the MAC address of your router. *Study "Remote communication."*

9 **D.** The cut-through operation mode is used to start forwarding the frame as soon as possible. *Refer to "Cut-through."*

10 **A, B, E.** The three core services of a switch are address learning, filtering and forwarding, and loop avoidance. *Examine "Core switch services."*

Chapter 4: Basic Switch Configuration

In This Chapter

✓ Configuring port speed and duplex settings

✓ Disabling ports

✓ Port security

✓ Understanding VLANs

The previous chapter discusses the basic functions of a Cisco switch, which is probably one of the most popular network devices found on networks today because it is required to allow all of the systems to communicate with one another. In this day and age, you want to be able to configure some basic settings on the switch, including the speed to use on each port, the duplex settings, and features such as port security.

This chapter continues with the discussion of switches by discussing port configuration settings such as the port speed and duplex setting, how to secure a port with port security, and discusses the concepts of VLANs and how to configure them on your switches. You are most certain to get questions on these topics on your CCENT certification exam!

Quick Assessment

1   (True/False). A VLAN creates a broadcast domain.

2   Configuring the port speed to _____ allows the switch to negotiate the speed.

3   A switch is an example of a layer-_____ device.

4   (True/False). Broadcast messages are sent to all VLANs on the switch.

5   The port _____ feature allows you to control which system can connect to the switch.

Answers

1 *True*. See "VLAN concepts."

2 *Auto*. Review "Choosing port speed."

3 *2*. Check out "Configuring port security."

4 *False*. Peruse "VLAN concepts."

5 *Security*. Take a look at "Port security."

Configuring Switch Ports

In this section, you discover some of the popular settings that you can configure on a switch port, such as the port speed and duplex setting, and I tell you how to configure security features such as disabling the port and port security. I also tell you how to view the port configuration and understand the information it gives.

Adding a port description

Assigning a description to each port serves as a reminder of the purpose of each port on your switch. It is fairly straightforward to add a description to the port, also known as an *interface,* and the description displays when you are using other commands to view your configuration. You can use the following commands to assign a description to a port:

```
Switch>enable
Switch#config term
Switch(config)#interface f0/5
Switch(config-if)#description File Server Port
```

In this case, I add a description that tells me that this is the file server port. But you can add any description that will help you when you're administering the switch. The number of characters supported by the description setting can vary between models, but my 2950 switch can support up to 240 characters in the port description.

Choosing port speed

The speed of the port is normally decided through *auto negotiation,* which means that when a system connects to the switch, the switch negotiates with the system what the speed will be. If the system connecting supports the fastest speed supported by the port on the switch, both the switch and the system will use that speed. If not, that's where auto negotiation comes in.

For example, let's say that the port on the switch supports speeds of 10, 100, and 1000 Mbps. If you connect a system to the port and the system has a network card that supports 1000 Mbps, the port runs at 1000 Mbps. If the card in the system supports only 100 Mbps, the port auto negotiates to 100 Mbps.

You may find that your switch port is not running at the maximum speed, even though the system connecting to the port supports a faster speed. In this case, you want to manually configure the port for a particular speed to force it at that speed.

To configure a port for a speed, you use the `speed` command once in the interface prompt for a particular interface (port). The following commands show you how to change the speed of a port:

```
Switch>enable
Switch#config term
Switch(config)#interface f0/5
Switch(config-if)#speed 100
```

To view a list of speeds supported by the port, you use the ? after the `speed` command, as shown here:

```
Switch(config-if)#speed ?
  10    Force 10 Mbps operation
  100   Force 100 Mbps operation
  auto  Enable AUTO speed configuration
```

If you want to configure the switch port back to auto negotiate, you use the following command:

```
Switch(config-if)#speed auto
```

Take note that when you configure ports on a switch, you do not have to configure each port individually. You can use the `range` parameter on the `interface` command to select a range of ports, and then use the `speed` command to set the speed on all ports within that range.

```
Switch(config)#interface range f0/5 - 12
Switch(config-if-range)#speed 100
```

Looking at the preceding code, you see that you can use the `range` parameter to select a number of ports, such as ports 5–12. Notice that the prompt changes to include the word `if-range` to indicate that you have multiple ports selected and any new commands will apply to a range of ports. In this example, I set the speed of those ports to 100 Mbps.

You can use the `interface range` command to configure a group of ports in one step.

Adjusting the duplex setting

In Book I, Chapter 3, you find out some things about duplex settings such as simplex, half-duplex, and full-duplex. The following list reviews the differences in the three:

✦ **Simplex:** Devices supporting simplex communication can only send or receive information, but not both.

✦ **Half-duplex:** These devices can send and receive, but only one direction at a time. With Ethernet networking that is half-duplexed, the data is sent and received on the same pair of wires, so you can only send or receive one way at a time without collisions.

✦ **Full-duplex:** Full-duplex communication supports sending and receiving data at the same time. Ethernet environments support full-duplex communication by sending data over one pair of wires and receiving over another pair of wires.

If you want to view the duplex settings supported on your switch, you use the ? after the `duplex` command on a switch port as shown below:

```
Switch(config)#interface f0/4
Switch(config-if)#duplex ?
  auto  Enable AUTO duplex configuration
  full  Force full duplex operation
  half  Force half-duplex operation
Switch(config-if)#duplex full
```

The preceding code example configures port 4 on the switch for full-duplex mode after viewing the help on the `duplex` command.

Disabling and enabling ports

When managing switches, it is important to disable any unused ports on a switch in order to prevent unauthorized individuals from connecting to the switch and gaining network access.

A disabled port displays on the switch with an amber light letting you know that the port is disabled. In order to disable a port on the switch, you use the `shutdown` command on the interface, as shown in the following code example:

```
Switch(config)#interface f0/3
Switch(config-if)#shutdown
```

You can select multiple ports at once by using the `range` parameter on the `interface` command. The following commands disable ports 6–12 on the switch:

```
Switch(config)#interface range f0/6 - 12
Switch(config-if-range)#shutdown
```

When the time comes and you wish to connect a system to a port that has been disabled, you will need to enable the port. In order to enable the port on the switch, you can negate the shutdown command with the no shutdown command.

```
Switch(config)#interface f0/6
Switch(config-if)#no shutdown
```

Viewing port configuration

There are different ways you can view your current port settings to verify that your settings are taking effect. One of the ways to verify the port settings is to use the show interfaces command and view the port information of the port you are troubleshooting.

```
FastEthernet0/5 is administratively down, line protocol is down (disabled)
   Hardware is Lance, address is 0002.1604.3605 (bia 0002.1604.3605)
   Description: File Server Port
   MTU 1500 bytes, BW 100000 Kbit, DLY 1000 usec,
      reliability 255/255, txload 1/255, rxload 1/255
   Encapsulation ARPA, loopback not set
   Keepalive set (10 sec)
   Half-duplex, 100Mb/s
   input flow-control is off, output flow-control is off
   ARP type: ARPA, ARP Timeout 04:00:00
(output has been omitted for briefness)
```

Looking at the output of the show interfaces command, you see that the interface (port) is *administratively down*. This means that you, as the administrator, have disabled the port. If the port was down because of a configuration error and not because you disabled the port, the status would simply say down instead of administratively down.

You also see in the preceding output that the description of the port is set and that the port is running at half-duplex with a speed of 100 Mbps.

Port security

Port security is a feature on the Cisco switch that allows you to limit which systems can connect to the port even though the port is enabled. With the port security feature, you limit which systems can connect to the port by the MAC address of the system.

Configuring port security

To configure port security, you first need to navigate to the port interface prompt for the port you wish to configure (or the range of ports you wish to

Book III
Chapter 4

Basic Switch Configuration

configure). After navigating to that interface, you need to configure the port for *access* mode — which allows a system such as a server or workstation to connect to the port. The following code shows you how to configure the port for access mode:

```
SW1>enable
SW1#config term
SW1(config)#interface f0/5
SW1(config-if)#switchport mode access
```

If you use the IOS help features, you will notice that three major port modes are supported by the ports on your switch — you can place each port in access mode, trunk mode, or dynamic mode.

```
SW1(config-if)#switchport mode ?
  access    Set trunking mode to ACCESS unconditionally
  dynamic   Set trunking mode to dynamically negotiate access
   or trunk mode
  trunk     Set trunking mode to TRUNK unconditionally
```

The following is a quick description of each mode:

+ **Access mode:** Configures the port to allow a system, such as a server or workstation, to access the network through this port.

+ **Trunk mode:** Configures the port as a *trunk port,* which is a port that connects to another switch and carries VLAN traffic between the two switches. (*VLAN* stands for virtual local area network; see the "VLAN concepts" section, later in this chapter, for more on VLANs.)

+ **Dynamic mode:** Allows the switch to negotiate with the device that connects to the port to determine which mode should be used.

After you set the port for access mode, you then enable the port security feature with the switchport port-security command. Once you've enabled port security, you can then configure the port for a specific MAC address by using switchport port-security mac-address *MAC_address_of_system*.

If you do not want to manually input the MAC address, you can use the sticky option, which tells the switch to learn the MAC address of the system connected and then configure port security to use that MAC address. The following commands enable port security and use the sticky option:

```
SW1(config-if)#switchport port-security
SW1(config-if)#switchport port-security mac-address sticky
```

Be prepared for a question on the sticky option and the port security feature on your CCENT certification exam. Also, remember that switches are layer-2 devices and, as a result, work with layer-2 addresses.

After you enable port security and configure the MAC address for the port, you want to limit the port so it allows for only one MAC address in the MAC address table for that port. If you do not limit the MAC address table for this port to one MAC address, the port could dynamically learn multiple addresses and associate those address with the port in the MAC address table automatically — thus allowing anyone to still connect to the port and we do not want that! The following command specifies that a maximum of one MAC address is to exist for the port in the MAC address table:

```
SW1(config-if)#switchport port-security maximum 1
```

After specifying the maximum number of MAC addresses, you then specify what happens when a system with a MAC address other than the one configured connects to the port — this is known as the *action* to take when a violation occurs. If a violation occurs, you can configure the port to any of the following:

✦ **Shutdown:** If you specify shutdown as the action upon violation, the switch disables the port when an unauthorized system connects to the port.

✦ **Protect:** The action of protect sends an alert to an administrator if a frame is received on the port from an unauthorized system.

✦ **Restrict:** The final option for action is a pretty cool setting, and that option is to set the action to restrict. When the action is set to restrict, the switch allows frames from only the specified MAC address to enter the network. This means that the port will work as long as the correct system is plugged into the port, but the second an unauthorized system is plugged into the port, the switch no longer forwards the frames.

The following command configures the port to disable if an unauthorized MAC address tries to use the port:

```
SW1(config-if)#switchport port-security violation shutdown
```

The following is a complete listing of our commands to configure port number 6 for the port security feature. The commands use the sticky option to learn the MAC address of the system and disable the port if a different system ever connects to the port.

```
SW1>enable
SW1#config term
SW1(config)#interface f0/6
SW1(config-if)#switchport mode access
SW1(config-if)#switchport port-security
SW1(config-if)#switchport port-security mac-address sticky
SW1(config-if)#switchport port-security maximum 1
SW1(config-if)#switchport port-security violation shutdown
```

For the CCENT certification exam, know how to configure port security and especially be familiar with the `sticky` option, which configures the switch to use the MAC address of the system connected to the port and saves you the trouble of finding out the MAC of the station.

Viewing port security

After configuring port security, you need to ensure that you have configured it correctly by viewing the configuration of the system.

To view the ports that you have configured for port security, you use the `show port-security address` command. In the output for this command (see the code that follows), you see the MAC address that has been configured for each of the secure ports.

```
Switch#show port-security address

              Secure Mac Address Table
------------------------------------------------------------
Vlan    Mac Address       Type               Ports
----    -----------       -----              ------
1       1111.2222.3333    SecureConfigured   FastEthernet0/6
------------------------------------------------------------
(output has been omitted for briefness)
Switch#
```

Do not confuse viewing the port security address table with viewing the regular MAC address table. You view the MAC address table with the `show mac-address-table` command, which displays a listing of all MAC addresses and their associated ports. The port security address table displays to you any ports you have configured with the port security feature and what the MAC address of the allowed systems are that can connect to the port. Think of it this way — the MAC address table is a "who is connected?" table while the port security address table is a "these are the systems who are allowed to connect" table.

One of my favorite commands for viewing port security information on a port is the `show port-security interface` command. This command displays a listing of settings that indicate what port security features have been enabled on the interface.

```
Switch#show port-security interface f0/6
Port Security                 : Enabled
Port Status                   : Secure-down
Violation Mode                : Shutdown
Aging Time                    : 0 mins
Aging Type                    : Absolute
SecureStatic Address Aging    : Disabled
Maximum MAC Addresses         : 1
Total MAC Addresses           : 1
```

```
Configured MAC Addresses   : 1
Sticky MAC Addresses       : 0
Last Source Address:Vlan   : 0000.0000.0000:0
Security Violation Count   : 0
```

In the preceding output, you can see that port security has been enabled and the violation mode is set to shutdown. Also notice that the maximum number of MAC addresses that can be associated with the port is one. You can also see that there is a *security violation count* as well — this indicates how many packets have been received from systems other than the MAC specified.

Understanding VLANs

Now that you understand how to configure basic port configuration settings on the switch, let us take a look at how to configure virtual LANs (VLANs) on the Cisco switch! Keep in mind that VLANs is more of an ICND2 exam topic for the CCNA exam, so this is just a quick introduction to the VLAN topic. I am presenting this material to you in this CCENT book because VLANs are an important part of everyday networking and can be used as a great tool to control which systems can communicate with one another on the network. You may receive a question on the exam that requires you to know what a VLAN is, but you do not need to know the details of how to configure a VLAN for the CCENT certification exam. I expand on the topic in this chapter because, as a network administrator, you should be familiar with VLANs.

VLAN concepts

The term *virtual LAN* comes from the concept that in the past, if your manager wanted you to build two different networks that could not communicate with one another, you would have had to purchase two switches and connect the appropriate systems to the switch for their network. Because you would not have connected the switches together, no communication would have been able to occur between the two networks. (See Figure 4-1 and the explanation that follows.)

Figure 4-1:
In the past,
to segment
network
communica-
tion, you
would
use two
switches
with no
connection
points.

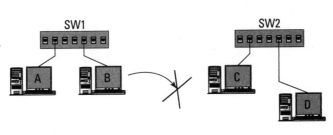

In this example, the company would have had to purchase two switches to get two different networks that could not communicate with one another. One reason a company may want to do this is they may have a department that works with sensitive information, and from a security point of view, they need to ensure that no other systems can communicate with the systems in that department.

Virtual LANs (VLANs) are a way to create multiple networks on a single switch by grouping ports on a switch into a VLAN. The important thing to note about VLANs is that by default a system connected to one VLAN cannot communicate with systems in another VLAN. The reason I say *by default* is that you can configure a router to route between the two VLANs — but save that discussion for your CCNA studies.

Looking at Figure 4-2, you see a switch that has the first four ports in VLAN1 and the last five ports placed in VLAN2. The VLANs create a communication boundary that does not allow a system in one VLAN to talk to another VLAN. This communication boundary also includes broadcast messages! As you find out in Book I, Chapter 3, VLANs are a method used to create broadcast domains. A *broadcast domain* is a group of systems that can receive one another's broadcast messages. If ComputerA sends a broadcast message out on the network, no other systems except for those in the VLAN see the broadcast message.

Figure 4-2:
Using
VLANs to
control
communication.

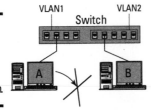

The reason that only systems in the VLAN see the broadcast messages is that when the packet leaves ComputerA, it reaches port 2 on the switch. The switch looks at the port the packet is received on and says, "What VLAN is this port a member of?" The switch checks the configuration and notes that port 2 is a member of VLAN1, so it tags the packet as a member of VLAN1. The switch then forwards the packet to all ports that are in VLAN1. (See Figure 4-3.)

Figure 4-3:
Broadcast messages are sent to other ports within the same VLAN because a VLAN creates a broadcast domain.

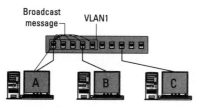

Although you should not see much in the way of VLANs on the CCENT exam, be aware that a VLAN creates a broadcast domain. When you get questions asking what methods are used to create broadcast domains, the answer is a router or VLANs.

Basic VLAN configuration

Now that you understand that a VLAN is a way to control which network devices can communicate with one another and that a VLAN is another method of creating a broadcast domain, let us take a look at the commands to configure VLANs.

Here is my example scenario: Say you want to create two VLANs for a company, one for the executives' systems and one for the developers. In this example, you navigate to the VLAN database and create VLAN2 (named Executives) and VLAN3 (named Development).

Note that by default all ports are in VLAN1.

Use the following commands to create the two VLANs:

```
Switch>enable
Switch#vlan database
Switch(vlan)#vlan 2 name Executives
```

```
VLAN 2 added:
    Name: Executives
Switch(vlan)#vlan 3 name Development
VLAN 3 added:
    Name: Development
Switch(vlan)#exit
APPLY completed.
Exiting....
```

After creating the two VLANs, take a look at the newly created VLANs with the show vlan command.

```
Switch#show vlan

VLAN   Name              Status      Ports
----   ---------------   ---------   -------------
1      default           active      Fa0/1, Fa0/2,
                                     Fa0/3, Fa0/4
                                     Fa0/5, Fa0/6,
                                     Fa0/7, Fa0/8
                                     Fa0/9,
                                     Fa0/10, Fa0/11, Fa0/12
                                     Fa0/13, Fa0/14, Fa0/15, Fa0/16
                                     Fa0/17, Fa0/18, Fa0/19, Fa0/20
                                     Fa0/21, Fa0/22, Fa0/23, Fa0/24
                                     Gig1/1, Gig1/2
2      Executives        active
3      Development       active
(output has been omitted for briefness)
```

When looking at the output of the show vlan command, you can see three VLANs configured on the switch, with all the ports still in the first VLAN. The next step is to place the appropriate ports into the appropriate VLANs. In this example scenario, you want to place ports 6–9 in the Executives VLAN and ports 10–12 in the Development VLAN. The following commands accomplish this goal:

```
Switch>enable
Switch#config term
Switch(config)#interface range f0/6 - 9
Switch(config-if-range)#switchport access vlan 2
Switch(config-if-range)#interface range f0/10 - 12
Switch(config-if-range)#switchport access vlan 3
Switch(config-if-range)#exit
Switch(config)#exit
```

In the commands here, you first navigate to the interface prompt for the interfaces you wish to place in a different VLAN. You will notice that I use the interface range command to select interfaces 6–9 in one command. I then place those interfaces in VLAN2 by using the switchport command. Ports 10–12 are then placed in VLAN3.

To verify that the ports have been placed in the appropriate VLANs, you can use the show vlan command. Notice in the output that follows that ports 6–9 are in the Executives VLAN, while ports 10–12 are in the Development VLAN.

```
Switch#show vlan

VLAN Name          Status   Ports
---- ----------    ------   ------
1    default       active   Fa0/1, Fa0/2, Fa0/3, Fa0/4
                            Fa0/5, Fa0/13, Fa0/14, Fa0/15
                            Fa0/16, Fa0/17, Fa0/18, Fa0/19
                            Fa0/20, Fa0/21, Fa0/22, Fa0/23
                            Fa0/24, Gig1/1, Gig1/2
2    Executives    active   Fa0/6, Fa0/7, Fa0/8, Fa0/9
3    Development   active   Fa0/10, Fa0/11, Fa0/12
(output has been omitted for briefness)
```

Once you place the different ports into the different VLANs, you can then start connecting the systems to the ports. In the example scenario, if you were to connect a system into port 7 (which resides in the Executives VLAN) and then connect a system into port 11 (which resides in the Development VLAN), those systems would be unable to ping one another.

Chapter Summary

This chapter discusses a number of different switch configuration settings that deal with configuring the ports on a switch. This chapter also demonstrates the commands you need to be familiar with to answer the related questions on the CCENT certification exam. The following are some key points to remember about configuring switches:

✦ A port can be disabled with the shutdown command and enabled with no shutdown command.

✦ You change the duplex setting on an interface to full-duplex by using the duplex full command.

✦ You modify the speed of the port with the speed 10/100/1000 command once at the interface prompt.

✦ You modify multiple interfaces at one time by first selecting a range of interfaces with the interface range command.

✦ *Port security* is a way to limit which systems can connect to a switch by their MAC addresses.

✦ You use the show port-security interface command to view the port security setup on a particular interface.

✦ When using the `show interfaces` command, an interface that displays as `administratively down` message is an interface that you have explicitly disabled with the `shutdown` command.

✦ VLANs are used to create multiple virtual networks on a switch (or between switches). A VLAN is a communication boundary and is also a way to implement multiple broadcast domains on a switch.

Lab Exercises

This chapter introduces you to a number of configuration options for ports on a switch. These labs are designed to help you practice configuring ports on a switch.

Lab 4-1: Configuring ports

1. Boot up your switch, connect to the console port, and HyperTerminal into the switch if you need to.

2. Your manager wants you to disable ports 10–12 on the switch; do so by entering the following commands:

```
Switch#config term
Switch(config)#interface range f0/10 - 12
Switch(config-if-range)#shutdown
```

3. Your manager now wants the Web server connected to port 9 on the switch; change the description of that port to Web Server by using the following commands:

```
Switch(config)#interface f0/9
Switch(config-if)#description Web Server
```

4. Finally, your manager wants to ensure that port 8 is using full-duplex and a speed of 100 Mbps; use the following commands to configure port 8:

```
Switch(config)#interface f0/8
Switch(config-if)#duplex full
Switch(config-if)#speed 100
```

Lab 4-2: Configuring port security

1. Boot up your switch, connect to the console port, and HyperTerminal into the switch if you need to.

2. **Configure port 6 for a MAC address of 0050.56C0.0001 and ensure that no other systems other than that MAC address can connect to the port.**

   The following commands configure port security on port 6:

   ```
   Switch>enable
   Switch#config term
   Switch(config)#interface f0/6
   Switch(config-if)#switchport mode access
   Switch(config-if)#switchport port-security
   Switch(config-if)#switchport port-security mac-address 0050.56C0.0001
   Switch(config-if)#switchport port-security maximum 1
   Switch(config-if)#switchport port-security violation shutdown
   ```

3. **Use the `sticky` option to configure port security on port 7.**

   The following commands configure port security with the `sticky` option on port 7:

   ```
   Switch>enable
   Switch#config term
   Switch(config)#interface f0/7
   Switch(config-if)#switchport mode access
   Switch(config-if)#switchport port-security
   Switch(config-if)#switchport port-security mac-address sticky
   Switch(config-if)#switchport port-security maximum 1
   Switch(config-if)#switchport port-security violation shutdown
   ```

4. **Connect a workstation to port 7 and try to ping another system on the network.**

   Were you successful? _____

5. **Connect your workstation to port 6 and try to ping another system on the network.**

   Were you successful? _____

6. **View your port security settings with the `show port-security address` command.**

   Do you see both port 6 and port 7 in the table? _____

7. **Use the `show port-security interface f0/6` command to view the status of port 6.**

   Do you see the MAC address that caused the address violation? _____

   _____

Lab 4-3: Configuring VLANs

1. Boot up your switch, connect to the console port, and HyperTerminal into the switch if you need to.

2. Create a VLAN called Web Servers to place all the Web servers into.

   To configure the VLAN and place ports 3, 4, and 5 in the VLAN, use the following commands:

   ```
   Switch>enable
   Switch#vlan database
   Switch(vlan)#vlan 2 name Web Servers
   VLAN 2 added:
       Name: Web Servers
   Switch(vlan)#exit
   APPLY completed.
   Exiting....

   Switch#config term
   Switch(config)#interface range f0/3 - 5
   Switch(config-if-range)#switchport access vlan 2
   ```

3. Use the **show vlan** command to verify the VLAN has been created and that ports 3, 4, and 5 are in the VLAN.

4. Connect a system to port 3 and connect another system to port 8.

5. Try to ping from one system to another.

   Are you able to ping from one system to another? _____

   Why or why not? _____

Prep Test

1 What command shows you MAC addresses associated with each port on the switch?

A ○ `show vlan`

B ○ `show port-security addresses`

C ○ `display mac-address-table`

D ○ `show mac-address-table`

2 You wish to view the VLAN configuration on the switch. What command do you use?

A ○ `show port-security addresses`

B ○ `show vlan`

C ○ `show mac-address table`

D ○ `show interfaces`

3 What option allows you to configure a static MAC address on the switch by using the MAC of the connected system?

A ○ `static`

B ○ `dynamic`

C ○ `sticky`

D ○ `usemac`

4 Which command modifies the port speed?

A ○ `switch(config)#speed 100`

B ○ `switch#speed 100`

C ○ `switch>speed 100`

D ○ `switch(config-if)#speed 100`

5 Which of the following actions disables the port when an address violation occurs?

A ○ `disable`

B ○ `shutdown`

C ○ `disconnect`

D ○ `restrict`

6 What mode must you place the interface into before you are able to configure port security on the interface?

A ○ Access

B ○ Trunk

C ○ Dynamic

D ○ Workstation

7 You are having trouble with a system connecting to port 5 on the switch. You want to see if the port has been configured for port security. What command do you use?

A ○ `show mac-address-table`

B ○ `show vlan`

C ○ `show port-security interface f0/5`

D ○ `show running-config`

8 When you connect the workstation to port 6, you can ping three other systems on the network, but you cannot seem to connect to the file server. You verify that others can connect to the file server, but you cannot connect to those other systems as well. What could be the problem?

A ○ Wrong default gateway address.

B ○ NAT is misconfigured.

C ○ The port used by the workstation is disabled.

D ○ You are in a different VLAN than the file server.

9 You have a workstation connected to port 10 on the switch, but for some reason you cannot ping any other system on the network. You view the configuration of the port with the following command. What is likely the problem?

```
FastEthernet0/10 is administratively down, line protocol is down (disabled)
  Hardware is Lance, address is 0002.1604.3605 (bia 0002.1604.3605)
  Description: File Server Port
  MTU 1500 bytes, BW 100000 Kbit, DLY 1000 usec,
     reliability 255/255, txload 1/255, rxload 1/255
  Encapsulation ARPA, loopback not set
  Keepalive set (10 sec)
  Half-duplex, 100Mb/s
  input flow-control is off, output flow-control is off
  ARP type: ARPA, ARP Timeout 04:00:00
(output has been omitted for briefness)
```

A ○ You are using the wrong IP address.

B ○ The port is disabled.

C ○ The speed is 100 Mbps.

D ○ ARPA is not being used.

10 **What are the three actions that you can configure when an address violation occurs?**

A ❑ restrict

B ❑ disable

C ❑ shutdown

D ❑ disconnect

E ❑ protect

Answers

1 **D.** To display the MAC addresses associated with each port on the switch, you view the MAC address table, which resides in memory on the switch. Use the `show mac-address-table` command. *See "Viewing port security."*

2 **B.** To view a list of VLANs and the ports associated with the different VLANs, use the `show vlan` command. *Review "Basic VLAN configuration."*

3 **C.** The `sticky` option is important when configuring port security. It allows you to configure a port to allow traffic only from the current or first MAC address (assuming you set the maximum addresses to 1). *Check out "Configuring port security."*

4 **D.** To modify the port speed on a switch, you first need to navigate to the port interface of the port you wish to configure and then use the `speed` command. *Peruse "Choosing port speed."*

5 **B.** Shutdown is the action you can configure on the switch that tells the switch to disable the port if there is an address violation. *Take a look at "Configuring port security."*

6 **A.** Before you can configure port security on a port, you must first put the port in access mode by using the `port-security mode access` command. *Peek at "Configuring port security."*

7 **C.** To view the port security settings on a port, you use the `show port-security interface` command. *Look over "Viewing port security."*

8 **D.** If you find that you can communicate with some systems on the network but not with others, it is possible that you are connected to a port that is part of a VLAN — meaning that you will not be able to communicate with others that are in a different VLAN unless a router is being used. *Study "VLAN concepts."*

9 **B.** When looking at the interface, if you notice that it says `administratively down`, you have most likely disabled the port with the `shutdown` command. You will need to enable the port before it can be used. *Refer to "Disabling and enabling ports" and also "Viewing port configuration."*

10 **A, C, E.** When configuring port security, you can configure one of three actions to be taken upon address violation — `restrict`, `shutdown`, or `protect`. *Examine "Configuring port security."*

Chapter 5: Troubleshooting Network Communication

In This Chapter

✔ Understanding troubleshooting utilities

✔ Troubleshooting connectivity issues

✔ Using show commands to view configuration

✔ Using debug commands

*W*ithin Books II and III, you discover how to configure many different settings on a Cisco router and switch. This chapter is designed to show you how to troubleshoot a device that is not working the way that it should by using some of the different troubleshooting features and commands available on a Cisco device.

This chapter is very important from a CCENT certification exam point of view because the exam simlets test heavily on troubleshooting problems with different Cisco devices. This means you have to be very comfortable with the different ways to identify what the problem is, either in the configuration or with the physical aspects of the network such as the network links.

Quick Assessment

1   (True/False). CDP can be used to locate the IP addresses that neighboring devices use.

2   The _____ command is used to test connectivity to a device.

3   Use the `show` _____ command to view the status of your network interfaces.

4   (True/False). You can disable all debugging with the `no debug all` command.

Answers

1   *True*. See "Viewing network topology."

2   *ping*. Review "The ping command."

3   *interfaces*. Check out "The show interfaces command."

4   *True*. Peruse "Disabling debugging."

Understanding Troubleshooting Utilities

Most operating systems give you a number of commands or troubleshooting utilities that help you diagnose connectivity issues on the network, and the Cisco IOS is no different! In this section, you find out about some of the different IOS commands you can use to troubleshoot connectivity issues with Cisco devices. For your own information (not for the exam), I also tell you how to use some troubleshooting commands on Windows computers on the network. (And I even throw in a few Linux commands, for good measure.)

Before getting started, I want to make sure that you understand the example network topology I am using for this chapter. It is a simple network setup similar to other network topologies used within the book. Figure 5-1 displays the example network layout with the New York and Boston offices connected in a network.

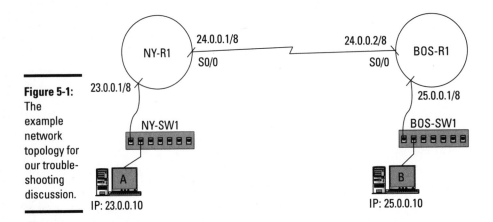

Figure 5-1: The example network topology for our trouble-shooting discussion.

Notice in Figure 5-1 that the NY-R1 router has a serial connection to the BOS-R1 router and that each of the networks has a switch and workstation.

As you find out about the different commands in this chapter, constantly refer back to Figure 5-1 so you understand the scenario.

Using Cisco commands to troubleshoot

The Cisco IOS has a number of commands that are similar to some of the Windows commands you may have used to troubleshoot connectivity issues.

Be sure to be very familiar with the commands in this section, as they are used quite often in the real world and on the exam!

The ping command

The first command to discuss is the `ping` command. Ping stands for *Packet InterNet Groper* (PING) and is a popular command-line utility that you can use to send test messages from one system to another in hopes that you receive replies. If you receive replies, you know the communication link and configuration of the devices is fine, but if there is no reply, you know that there is a problem — and you need to start troubleshooting!

The `ping` command uses the *Internet Control Messaging Protocol* (ICMP) and works by sending ICMP *echo request* messages from a source to a destination in hopes that an ICMP *echo reply* message is received as a response. Remember from my TCP/IP discussion (see Book I, Chapter 4) that ICMP is a network-layer protocol in TCP/IP and is responsible for status information and error reporting.

To ping from the NY-R1 router across the WAN link, you use the following command:

```
NY-R1>ping 24.0.0.2

Type escape sequence to abort.
Sending 5, 100-byte ICMP Echos to 24.0.0.2, timeout is 2
    seconds:
!!!!!
Success rate is 100 percent (5/5), round-trip min/avg/max =
    31/31/32 ms
```

When using the `ping` command, notice that you supply the IP address of the device you are trying to ping; in this example, I am pinging the serial interface on BOS-R1. The Cisco device sends out five ICMP echo messages in hopes of receiving replies. You can see that five replies are received because you see five exclamation points (!); each exclamation point represents an echo reply received. If a reply is not received, the command displays a period (.) with each missing reply message, as shown in the following output:

```
NY-R1>ping 24.0.0.5

Type escape sequence to abort.
Sending 5, 100-byte ICMP Echos to 24.0.0.5, timeout is 2
    seconds:
.....
Success rate is 0 percent (0/5)
```

In the preceding code, I am pinging an IP address that is not being used on the network, so no reply comes back. Notice that the ping command has a timeout set to two seconds, which means that it will wait two seconds after each echo request message is sent before determining that a reply is not coming back.

When troubleshooting communication issues, you should ping each IP address along the pathway of the communication to see where the failure is occurring.

The traceroute command

The ping command is very popular, but it indicates only whether the IP address you are pinging is up and running. The ping command does not display the pathway the ping packets are taking. When troubleshooting network communication and the configuration of your router, you want to be able to determine the pathway that information is taking, and you do this by using the traceroute command.

The traceroute command uses ICMP as a protocol as well, but it recieves a reply back from each router it hits along the path to the address being tested. For example, to test traceroute, I am going to traceroute from NY-R1 to 25.0.0.10 (the workstation on the Boston network). Note that in order to reach the 25.0.0.10 system, I have to pass through the BOS-R1 router by sending through the IP address of 24.0.0.2.

```
NY-R1>traceroute 25.0.0.10
Type escape sequence to abort.
Tracing the route to 25.0.0.10

  1   24.0.0.2        31 msec    31 msec    31 msec
  2   *      94 msec  94 msec
NY-R1>
```

In the preceding code, you see that I am using the traceroute command to the 25.0.0.10 system. The traceroute command comes back with a list of *hops,* which are the routers it passes through to reach that destination. The first hop is the 24.0.0.2 address, which is the address of the BOS-R1 router, while the second hop is the packet reaching the workstation itself. This command would be more exciting with a larger network, as you would see more hops — one hop for each router the traceroute packet passes through.

Using the traceroute feature is a great way to verify the pathway that a packet is taking. If you find that network performance is degrading, it may be because a direct link between two networks has gone down and your traffic is taking an indirect, less-preferred route. The traceroute feature helps you identify whether the traffic is taking an undesired pathway.

The telnet command

Another very popular command you can use when troubleshooting is the `telnet` command, which you can use to remotely connect to and fix a configuration problem on the router. For more information on how to use the `telnet` command to Telnet into a Cisco device, check out Book II, Chapter 3.

The `telnet` command is also useful when troubleshooting problems on servers such as e-mail or Web servers. When troubleshooting problems with servers such as SMTP servers, you use the `telnet` command to Telnet into the port of the server and issue related commands. For example, from a Windows or Linux machine, you can type `telnet ip_address 25` in a command prompt to Telnet into port 25 (the SMTP port) to connect to the SMTP server of a system.

Viewing the ARP cache

When troubleshooting communication problems, you can view your ARP cache (which stores the ARP replies your device has received) on a Cisco router to ensure that the *logical address* (IP address) is resolved to a *physical address* (MAC address). You use the `show ip arp` command to view the local ARP cache of a Cisco router:

```
NY-R1>show ip arp
Address          Age (min)    Hardware Addr    Interface
23.0.0.1              -        0010.11D9.D001   FastEthernet0/0
23.0.0.10            4         0011.9520.8c27   FastEthernet0/0
23.0.0.100          10         0006.d6ab.a040   FastEthernet0/0
(Protocol and type columns have been removed for briefness)
```

In the preceding code, you see that the IP address is displayed with the corresponding MAC address (`Hardware Addr`). There is also an age limit that indicates how long the entry will stay in the ARP cache before it expires. In addition, an Interface column indicates the interface that communicates with the device using that address.

For the CCENT certification exam, know that you can use both the `show arp` and the `show ip arp` commands to display the ARP cache on a Cisco router.

Troubleshooting commands in Windows

Although you are not tested on Windows commands on the CCENT certification exam, I do want to mention a few of the same commands for the Windows environment. The reason is that when you troubleshoot communication problems on the network, you may sometimes have to troubleshoot from the computers on the network.

The ipconfig command

When troubleshooting communication issues from the client systems, you may need to verify that the IP address, subnet mask, and default gateway settings are correct. To view the TCP/IP settings on a Windows system, you can use the ipconfig command:

```
C:\>ipconfig
Windows IP Configuration
Ethernet adapter Local Area Connection:

        Connection-specific DNS Suffix  . :
        IP Address. . . . . . . . . . . . : 23.0.0.10
        Subnet Mask . . . . . . . . . . . : 255.0.0.0
        Default Gateway . . . . . . . . . : 23.0.0.1
```

On a Linux system, you can view your TCP/IP settings with the ifconfig command. The ifconfig command stands for *interface configuration,* and it displays or temporarily modifies settings on your network card.

Windows' ping command

In the code example in the previous section, the router that the client uses to get off the network is 23.0.0.1 (the default gateway), so if you are having trouble with this client system communicating over the Internet or WAN link, you use a ping of 23.0.0.1 to verify that the client can communicate with the router.

```
C:\>ping 23.0.0.1

Pinging 23.0.0.1 with 32 bytes of data:

Reply from 23.0.0.1: bytes=32 time=1ms TTL=255
Reply from 23.0.0.1: bytes=32 time<1ms TTL=255
Reply from 23.0.0.1: bytes=32 time<1ms TTL=255
Reply from 23.0.0.1: bytes=32 time<1ms TTL=255

Ping statistics for 23.0.0.1:
    Packets: Sent = 4, Received = 4, Lost = 0 (0% loss),
Approximate round trip times in milli-seconds:
    Minimum = 0ms, Maximum = 1ms, Average = 0ms
```

The tracert command

Windows and Linux systems also support a traceroute feature that sends a reply back from every router the traceroute packet passes through along the pathway to the address you traceroute. In Windows, the traceroute command is actually called tracert, but it works the same way as on a Cisco router:

```
C:\>tracert 25.0.0.10

Tracing route to 25.0.0.10 over a maximum of 30 hops:

   1    13 ms      9 ms       7 ms      23.0.0.1
   2    13 ms     13 ms       8 ms      24.0.0.2
   3    19 ms     18 ms      23 ms      25.0.0.10

Trace complete.
```

In the preceding code example, I perform a traceroute, using the `tracert` command in Windows, from the workstation on the New York network (ComputerA). Notice that the packet goes through the `23.0.0.1` router first before passing through `24.0.0.2`, which is then passed on to the destination system of `25.0.0.10`.

In Linux, you can do a traceroute using the `traceroute` command instead of the `tracert` command found in Windows.

Looking at the ARP cache

The computers on a network also have an ARP cache that stores recent IP addresses you have communicated with and their corresponding MAC addresses. Like on the Cisco device, if you wish to view the ARP cache, you can, but the command is a little different. To view the ARP cache on a Windows or Linux system, you use the `arp -a` command:

```
C:\>arp -a

Interface: 23.0.0.10 --- 0x4
   Internet Address      Physical Address       Type
   23.0.0.19             00-11-95-20-8c-27       dynamic
   23.0.0.45             00-17-e0-c9-b7-b0       dynamic
```

Be sure to focus on the *Cisco commands* for the CCENT certification exam and not the Windows commands. You should be familiar with the Windows commands for the real world.

Troubleshooting Connectivity Issues

Now that you know about popular commands to use on the Cisco device to help troubleshoot or identify communication problems, let us take a look at some of the causes of communication failures. We will first look at popular issues dealing with the physical aspect of the network (such as cabling), and then take a look at the logical aspect of the network (such as IP addressing).

Identifying physical issues

When troubleshooting problems on the network, you first want to look to the simple stuff like the cabling. This section discusses popular issues with the cables and then looks at how to diagnose a problem based on the LED indicators on the router or switch.

Cables and connectors

The first thing to do when troubleshooting communication failures is to make sure that all the cables are connected properly to the router or the switch. When troubleshooting a router (or an interface on the router), be sure that all network cables and communication links are connected firmly in the ports.

You can use the LED on the port to help you identify whether there is connectivity at either end of the line. (See Book III, Chapter 3, for more about the port LEDs.) The interface link light, also known as a *port LED,* should display a green light if there is a link; remember that you need to verify that the cable is connected at either end in order for communication to occur.

Wrong port

After verifying the cable is seated properly in the port, you should then triple-check that you have the cable connected to the correct port. I do not know how many times I thought I had connected the cable to FastEthernet 0/0, only to find out it was connected to FastEthernet 0/1.

Wrong cable type

Another common problem is connecting the wrong type of cable between two points (or devices). This, unfortunately, is a common mistake with junior network technicians, as they may not understand when to use a crossover and when to use a straight-through cable.

A general rule is to use crossover cable when you are connecting similar devices. For example, if you are connecting a switch to another switch, you use a crossover cable; if you are connecting a router to another router, you use a crossover cable; and if you are connecting two computers together, you use a crossover cable. It is important to note that if you connect a computer directly to a router (which is unlikely, but possible), you use a crossover.

You use a straight-through cable when connecting a switch to a computer or a router to a switch.

For the CCENT certification exam, be sure to know when to use a crossover cable and a straight-through cable when connecting different network devices to one another.

For more details on which cables to use, see Book I, Chapter 2.

Port shutdown

If you have verified that you are using the correct cable and you have confirmed that the cable is connected properly, communication could be failing because of a configuration problem. It could be that the port was never enabled with the no shutdown command. View the running-config to display the configuration settings on the router to determine if there is a configuration issue. (For more details on how to do this, see Book II, Chapter 2.)

If the port has been disabled for any particular reason, it will display an amber light on the port LED.

LED indicators

It is important to keep a close eye on the LEDs on each of the ports on routers and switches when troubleshooting connectivity issues.

See Book III, Chapter 3, for more about the ports LEDs.

When the link light, or LED, on the interface is a solid green, it indicates that the physical cable is attached (layer 1) and that the layer-2 communication protocol at either end of the link is established. If you are unable to get a link light, then you want to ensure that both of these conditions are met. For an Ethernet interface, the layer-2 protocol is Ethernet and is configured automatically, but for a serial link, you must specify a data link (layer-2) protocol such as HDLC or PPP.

For the CCENT certification exam, know that a link light appearing on a port indicates that a layer-2 protocol is established at either end of the link and that there is a layer-1 medium (such as a cable) making contact the two points.

When the light on the interface, or port, flashes green, it means that traffic is passing through the interface and everything is okay. If the port displays an amber light, it means the port has either not been enabled or has been disabled either manually by the administrator or automatically through a feature such as port security. In this case, you should check the status of the port to see if it has been disabled, and if so, you need to enable the port with the no shutdown command.

**Book III
Chapter 5**

Troubleshooting
Network
Communication

Identifying logical issues

Checking the physical (layer-1) aspects of the devices is only the first step to troubleshooting interface issues. Once you verify the cables are connected, you are using the correct cable types, and that you have the appropriate layer-2 protocol enabled on the interfaces (for example, Ethernet, PPP, or HDLC), it is time to check some of the logical aspects of the configuration.

TCP/IP settings

When troubleshooting connectivity issues, you need to take the time to verify that the correct IP address (layer-3) information is assigned to each interface on the router. You can view your running configuration to see the addresses assigned, or you can use the `show interfaces` command to view the settings applied to each interface on the router.

When checking for IP addressing problems, be sure to check for the following issues:

+ **Address in network range:** Ensure that the address assigned to an interface on a router, switch, or computer is within the network range for the network or subnet.

+ **Correct subnet mask:** Ensure that the subnet mask is the correct subnet mask for the address being used.

+ **Correct default gateway:** Ensure that the default gateway assigned to switches and computers is the correct IP address for that network or network segment. The default gateway address assigned to systems or devices must be an address on the subnet.

The CCENT certification exam will have network scenarios describing situations where communication fails. In these scenarios, always watch for misconfiguration in the IP addresses of the devices or computers involved. Also watch for IP addresses assigned to a system or device that is outside the range of the subnetted network, wrong subnet masks being used, and referring to the wrong default gateway.

For more information on IP addressing and subnetting, check out Book I, Chapters 4 and 5 — very important chapters for the CCENT certification!

Routing table

After you verify that all of the involved interfaces are configured with the correct IP addresses, you should check that there is a route to the destination network in the routing table when troubleshooting communication problems.

By default, the Cisco device adds a route for each of the networks that it is connected to, and it is up to you to add any additional routes. You can manually add static routes for additional networks that your router needs to know about, or you can load a routing protocol that shares routing table information with other routers. Either way, there must be a route to any networks you wish to communicate with.

To find out more about routing and the routing table, refer back to Book III, Chapters 1 and 2.

Name resolution

If you are experiencing communication problems when trying to connect to other systems via a fully qualified domain name (FQDN), you need to ensure that your systems and devices can resolve the name. To resolve names of other devices or systems that you connect to by name, you can add the names and matching IP addresses to the hostname table, or configure your router to send DNS queries to a DNS server if you expect to use FQDN on the router.

If you suspect that name resolution is the problem, connect to the device or system you are trying to communicate with by the IP address instead of the FQDN. If name resolution is the problem, communication should occur when using the IP address.

You can use the `show hosts` command to display the local hostname table on a Cisco device.

To read more about name resolution check out Book II, Chapter 4.

Book III
Chapter 5

**Troubleshooting
Network
Communication**

Using Show Commands to View Configuration

Now that you understand some of the areas where problems can occur, it is important to review the Cisco IOS commands you can use to help identify the physical and logical connectivity issues. Throughout this book, you find out about many commands you can use to display your configuration, but I want to make sure that I summarize those commands here in the troubleshooting chapter. I first review how to look at the configuration files, then give you some guidelines for using commands in layer-1 and layer-2 troubleshooting, and then cover troubleshooting layer 3. After that, I remind you how to discover neighboring network devices.

You will be tested on these commands heavily on the CCENT certification exam, so be sure you understand what to look for with each command.

Viewing configuration files

When you are troubleshooting problems on routers and switches, the first commands I tend to use are the show commands to display configuration files — the show running-config and the show startup-config commands. Here is an example:

```
NY-R1#show running-config
Building configuration...
version 12.4
no service password-encryption

hostname NY-R1

ip ssh version 1

interface FastEthernet0/0
 ip address 23.0.0.1 255.0.0.0
 duplex auto
 speed auto

interface Serial0/2/0
 ip address 24.0.0.1 255.0.0.0
 clock rate 64000

ip classless
ip route 25.0.0.0 255.0.0.0 24.0.0.2

line con 0
line vty 0 4
 login
```

Using the show running-config command displays the commands that were used to configure the device, and most times it will lead you to the cause of the problem.

The CCENT certification exam will give you many simlets where you need to determine a problem in the configuration of the router. One of the approaches you can use to determine the problem is to show the running configuration and look for a mistake in a command. Eventually, Cisco will not allow you to use the show running-config command, so you will need to know other show commands to identify what the problem is!

Viewing router configuration

It is important to know how to view your running configuration, as it displays the commands used to configure the Cisco device, but using a number of other show commands can display status information that can better help you understand the cause of a problem.

Layer-1 and layer-2 troubleshooting

You find out earlier in this chapter that when troubleshooting communication problems, you should confirm the correct cables are used to make the connection and verify the cables are connected properly to the device. This is how you troubleshoot layer 1 of the OSI model — the physical layer.

You can use some Cisco device commands to view the status of layer-1 and layer-2 information regarding the network communication. For example, when troubleshooting, you want to know if there is a link and if a data link protocol is configured. The following sections discuss commands that you can use to answer these questions.

The show interfaces command

You are introduced to the show interfaces command in Book II, Chapter 2, and it is a very popular command to use when troubleshooting why communication cannot occur. When you are using the show interfaces command and you wish to verify that the connection and layer-2 protocol are configured properly, you look for the typical Interface is up, line protocol is up status on the interface, as shown here:

```
NY-R1>show interfaces
FastEthernet0/0 is up, line protocol is up
   Hardware is Lance, address is 0010.11d9.d001 (bia
   0010.11d9.d001)
   Internet address is 23.0.0.1/8
   MTU 1500 bytes, BW 100000 Kbit, DLY 100 usec, rely 255/255,
   load 1/255
   Encapsulation ARPA, loopback not set
   ARP type: ARPA, ARP Timeout 04:00:00,
   (output cut for briefness)
FastEthernet0/1 is administratively down, line protocol is
   down
   Hardware is Lance, address is 0010.11d9.d002 (bia
   0010.11d9.d002)
   MTU 1500 bytes, BW 100000 Kbit, DLY 100 usec, rely 255/255,
   load 1/255
   Encapsulation ARPA, loopback not set
   (Output has been cut for briefness)
Serial0/2/0 is up, line protocol is up
   Hardware is HD64570
```

```
Internet address is 24.0.0.1/8
MTU 1500 bytes, BW 128 Kbit, DLY 20000 usec, rely 255/255,
  load 1/255
Encapsulation HDLC, loopback not set, keepalive set (10
  sec)
(Output has been cut for briefness)
```

In the preceding code, I have bolded the relevant portions of the output. The line that says FastEthernet 0/0 is up, line protocol is up is the status on the physical link (the interface) and the layer-2 protocol, which allows the communication to occur. It is important to understand how to read the interface status — if the link is down, the protocol will never be up, so the problem is physical in nature and not due to the wrong protocol being loaded. If the interface is up, but the protocol is down, you have a mistake in the protocol configuration at either end of the link — so that should be your focus.

In the code here, you can also see the layer-2 protocol that is used on each of the interfaces. The layer-2 protocol is known as the *encapsulation protocol.* The Fast Ethernet interfaces use an encapsulation protocol of *ARPA,* meaning that Ethernet is the layer-2 protocol, but the serial link should show a different protocol, such as HDLC or PPP. This is important to note when viewing the configuration because both ends of the link must use the same encapsulation protocol for communication to occur.

The show interface serial 0/0 command

Instead of using the show interfaces command to view all status information on all interfaces, you can just view the status of a particular interface by using the show interface *type* command, like this:

```
NY-R1>show interface serial 0/2/0
Serial0/2/0 is up, line protocol is up
  Hardware is HD64570
  Internet address is 24.0.0.1/8
  MTU 1500 bytes, BW 128 Kbit, DLY 20000 usec, rely 255/255,
    load 1/255
  Encapsulation HDLC, loopback not set, keepalive set (10
    sec)
  (Output has been cut for briefness)
```

The show ip interface brief command

A great command to use when troubleshooting is the show ip interface brief command. This command displays a table-like view that lists the status of each of the interfaces. Again, you can identify the problem as being layer 1 or layer 2 by looking at the output — a layer-1 problem means there is a physical problem with the cable, while layer-2 issues are related to the protocol. (See Figure 5-2.)

Figure 5-2:
The
`show ip`
`interface`
`brief`
command
displays
status
information
about the
interfaces
in a table
format.

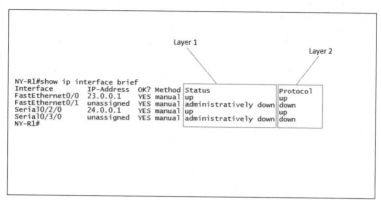

The show controllers serial 0/0 command

The last command I want to mention that relates to troubleshooting layer 1 and layer 2 is the `show controllers serial` *slot/port* command. This command has the benefit of displaying whether the serial interface acts as the DCE or DTE device, and it also displays the clock rate.

```
NY-R1#show controllers serial0/2/0
Interface Serial0/2/0
Hardware is PowerQUICC MPC860
DCE V.35, clock rate 64000
(output has been cut for briefness)
```

In the preceding code, you can replace any interface types and numbers with the interface that you are troubleshooting.

Layer-3 troubleshooting

When troubleshooting layer 3 of the OSI model, you are moving away from the physical aspect of networking and into the logical area. As mentioned earlier in this chapter, when you are troubleshooting layer 3, you are dealing with the IP protocol and features of IP such as logical addressing and routing.

IP addresses

When troubleshooting the IP addresses assigned to the interfaces, you can verify the addresses by using the same commands you use when troubleshooting layer 1 and layer 2, including the `show interfaces` and the `show ip interface brief` commands.

Book III
Chapter 5

Troubleshooting Network Communication

The reason you can use these commands to troubleshoot IP-related issues is that these commands show the layer-3 address that is configured on each of the interfaces as well. Use these commands to verify that you do not have a typo in the addressing.

Routing

After verifying the IP address (see the previous section), you next need to check that routing is configured properly. You do this by checking the routing table with the show ip route command to ensure that all destination networks exist in the routing table.

```
NY-R1>show ip route
Codes: C - connected, S - static, I - IGRP, R - RIP, M -
    mobile, B - BGP, D - EIGRP, EX - EIGRP external,
    (output cut for briefness)

Gateway of last resort is not set

C    23.0.0.0/8 is directly connected, FastEthernet0/0
C    24.0.0.0/8 is directly connected, Serial0/2/0
S    25.0.0.0/8 [1/0] via 24.0.0.2
```

If you are missing any routes, you may have to add them manually. Another reason you might be missing routes is a routing protocol used to share routing table information is not running on your router. To verify information about routing protocols such as the Routing Information Protocol (RIP) or Interior Gateway Routing Protocol (IGRP), use the show ip protocols command, as shown here:

```
NY-R1>show ip protocols
Routing Protocol is "rip"
Sending updates every 30 seconds, next due in 10 seconds
Invalid after 180 seconds, hold down 180, flushed after 240
Outgoing update filter list for all interfaces is not set
Incoming update filter list for all interfaces is not set
Redistributing: rip
Default version control: send version 1, receive any version
  Interface            Send  Recv  Triggered RIP  Key-chain
  FastEthernet0/0       1     2 1
  Serial0/2/0           1     2 1
Automatic network summarization is in effect
Maximum path: 4
Routing for Networks:
    23.0.0.0
    24.0.0.0
Passive Interface(s):
Routing Information Sources:
  Gateway          Distance      Last Update
  24.0.0.2              120       00:00:17
Distance: (default is 120)
```

You need to know RIP for the CCENT certification exam, and for this reason, I have loaded RIP on the router and displayed the output of the `show ip protocols` command. To find out more about RIP, see Book III, Chapter 2.

There are a few points to note about the preceding code. First, notice at the top of the code that the routing protocol is RIP. If one of your other routers is configured for a different protocol (maybe EIGRP), this would be the reason the routers are not sharing routing table information — they need to use the same protocol!

You can also see that the version of RIP messages sent here is RIPv1, but I can receive any version of RIP messages (version 1 or version 2). In addition, notice that RIP has been configured to advertise networks 23.0.0.0 and 24.0.0.0. This is important because if other routers are not receiving knowledge of your 24 network, it might mean that you forgot to list it as a network to advertise. This setting shows that you did not forget to configure network 24.0.0.0 as a network to advertise.

The last point to note in the output is the passive interface setting. You can configure RIP not to send RIP messages out an interface, such as the one connected to the Internet. If you find that a network is not receiving RIP messages, you might have configured the passive interface by mistake. This setting verifies that!

Viewing network topology

On the CCENT certification exam, you will be required to know how to document what type of routers and switches are used across the network. You can use the CDP (Cisco Discovery Protocol) commands that are discussed in Book II, Chapter 3, to discover neighboring network devices and information such as the IP addresses of the devices, the type of device (router or switch), and the model of the device (2900 or 2800).

The following list reviews some of the CDP commands, but be sure to go back and read over CDP in Book II, Chapter 3 for a complete review:

+ **show cdp neighbors:** Displays basic information about all neighboring devices, such as the name of the device (known as the *device ID*), the type of device, and the model. You do not see the IP address of the devices with this command.

+ **show cdp neighbors detail:** Displays all information about each device, including the name of the device, type of device, model, and the IP address of the device!

+ **show cdp entry *device_ID*:** Displays all information for a particular device by supplying the name of the device.

Be prepared for questions that expect you to know all of the different show commands discussed in this chapter. You will be allowed to view the running-config in some questions, but in other questions, Cisco disables that command, which forces you to know the other show commands!

Using Debug Commands

If you configure your Cisco router and the features that have been configured do not work as expected, what can you do, other than view the configuration? What you can do is use the debugging feature built into Cisco devices to give you detailed information about different events as they occur! This section discusses the purpose of debugging, and it also tells you how to enable and disable debugging.

Knowing how to use debugging efficiently

Debugging is a feature that you can enable on the Cisco router to display detailed information about different events as they occur. For example, if you are troubleshooting to find out why you are not getting the RIP routing table entries in your routing table, it could be because you are not receiving the RIP messages. Without a feature such as debugging, it is hard to determine if you are actually sending and receiving RIP updates. It is easy to determine the entries are not in the routing table, but challenging to determine why.

Debugging is one of those troubleshooting features you enable to help you diagnose a problem, but because it is resource-intensive (puts a heavy load on the CPU on the router), it is important to enable it to troubleshoot. You should then disable it as soon as possible; I do not recommend leaving debugging running for long periods of time.

You can reduce the load that debugging places on your Cisco device by enabling debugging for only the IOS feature you are troubleshooting. There are dozens of debugging options, and you want to debug only the features you need to troubleshoot. For example, if you are troubleshooting RIP on the router, you enable debugging of only the RIP protocol and do not enable debugging of all features on the router.

Debugging is resource-intensive; therefore, you should enable debugging for only the feature you are troubleshooting, and then disable debugging as soon as possible.

Looking at a debugging example

Let's look at an example of debugging. Let's assume you are having trouble with the NY-R1 router: The RIP routing table entries from other routers are not appearing in NY-R1's routing table. You decide that you need to enable RIP debugging. To do that, you use the debug command and then specify ip rip as parameters:

```
NY-R1#debug ip rip
RIP protocol debugging is on
```

In the preceding code, RIP debugging is enabled with the debug ip rip command. The Cisco IOS enables RIP debugging and then gives you confirmation that RIP debugging has been enabled.

After you enable debugging, you start to receive messages at the console as RIP messages are sent or received by the router. This is what debugging is all about — displaying information about packets or events that occur on the router!

The following code displays some of the messages that are then displayed at the console when RIP messages are sent or received by the router. Notice that you can see the version of RIP being used to send or receive the update (version 1). For messages received, you see who the sender is, and on what interface the message was received on. You also see RIP messages sent and on what interface the message is sent with. Eventually, you see that the updates are applied to the router.

```
NY-R1#RIP: received v1 update from 24.0.0.2 on Serial0/2/0
      25.0.0.0 in 1 hops
RIP: sending  v1 update to 255.255.255.255 via
    FastEthernet0/0 (23.0.0.1)
RIP: build update entries
      network 24.0.0.0 metric 1
      network 25.0.0.0 metric 2
RIP: sending  v1 update to 255.255.255.255 via Serial0/2/0
    (24.0.0.1)
RIP: build update entries
      network 23.0.0.0 metric 1
```

As I mention earlier, you can enable debugging on a number of different types of events. The following is a listing of priv exec commands that enable debugging for popular events to troubleshoot on the Cisco router.

**Book III
Chapter 5**

**Troubleshooting
Network
Communication**

✦ **debug all:** Enables debugging of all events.

I do not recommend enabling all debugging, as it places a heavy processing load on the router.

✦ **debug eigrp:** Permits debugging of the EIGRP routing protocol.

✦ **debug ppp:** Facilitates debugging of the Point-to-Point Protocol used for communication over a serial link.

✦ **debug ip icmp:** Allows debugging of ICMP messages sent by the router. The following is an example of the result of enabling ICMP debugging:

```
NY-R1#debug ip icmp
ICMP packet debugging is on
NY-R1#
ICMP: echo reply sent, src 24.0.0.1, dst 24.0.0.2
ICMP: echo reply sent, src 24.0.0.1, dst 24.0.0.2
ICMP: echo reply sent, src 24.0.0.1, dst 24.0.0.2
ICMP: echo reply sent, src 24.0.0.1, dst 24.0.0.2
ICMP: echo reply sent, src 24.0.0.1, dst 24.0.0.2
```

✦ **debug ip nat:** Enables debugging of Network Address Translation. This allows you to see packets that are passing through the NAT device and includes translated address information.

✦ **debug ip ospf:** Permits debugging of the OSPF routing protocol and viewing information about OSPF-related events.

✦ **debug ip rip:** Facilitates debugging of RIP, as you saw earlier in this section.

✦ **debug ip packet:** Displays information about all packets that are sent and received on the router. Information displayed includes the source and destination IP address of the packet:

```
R1#debug ip packet
Packet debugging is on
R1#
IP: s=24.0.0.2 (Serial0/2/0), d=24.0.0.1 (Serial0/2/0), len 0, rcvd 3
IP: tableid=0, s=24.0.0.1 (local), d=24.0.0.2 (Serial0/2/0), routed via
    RIB
IP: s=24.0.0.1 (local), d=24.0.0.2 (Serial0/2/0), len 0, sending
IP: s=23.0.0.1 (local), d=255.255.255.255 (FastEthernet0/0), len 0,
    sending broad/multicast
IP: s=24.0.0.1 (local), d=255.255.255.255 (Serial0/2/0), len 0, sending
    broad/multicast
```

Once you have enabled debugging, the debug information goes to the console by default. This becomes an issue if you Telnet into the router — you want the debug information to go to your Telnet session window. To configure debug information to be sent to the Telnet terminal session, use the terminal monitor command from privilege exec mode.

Disabling debugging

After you troubleshoot the problem you are facing on the router, gather the debugging information, and solve the problem, you need to disable debugging on the router.

The first command to disable debugging is to place the `no` keyword in front of the command you used to enable debugging. For example, to disable RIP debugging you use the `no debug ip rip` command:

```
R1#no debug ip rip
RIP protocol debugging is off
```

Notice in the preceding code that after RIP debugging is disabled, the IOS reports back to you that RIP debugging has been turned off. The problem with disabling a specific debugging feature is that you may have enabled debugging of multiple types of events, but you have turned off only one debugging event. It is therefore a best practice to disable all debugging with the `no debug all` command once you have completed troubleshooting.

```
R1#no debug all
All possible debugging has been turned off
```

Notice that after you use the `no debug all` command, the feedback displayed lets you know that all debugging has been turned off (versus just turning off RIP debugging, as seen in the previous example).

It is a best practice to disable all debugging with the `no debug all` command once you have finished troubleshooting! This ensures that you have not forgotten about a debugging feature that was enabled.

Chapter Summary

This chapter focuses the discussion on troubleshooting communication problems and using commands to diagnose problems. The following are some key points to remember for the real world and when preparing for the exam:

✦ Troubleshoot layer-1 and layer-2 characteristics of the network first when you're having connectivity issues.

✦ When troubleshooting layer 1, ensure that you are using the correct cables and that they are properly connected to the ports.

✦ When troubleshooting layer 2, ensure that the data link protocol is set (either Ethernet, PPP, or HDLC) and verify related settings such as the clock rate.

✦ After verifying the physical aspect of the network, you can then move on to checking the logical aspect of that network, such as the network layer, also known as layer 3.

✦ When troubleshooting layer 3, verify the IP address configuration and routing table information.

✦ When preparing for the exam, be sure to review the different show commands discussed in this chapter.

✦ When answering troubleshooting-type questions on the CCENT certification exam, view the running-config first and then use some of the show commands to identify the problem.

✦ Debugging is a great troubleshooting feature that writes detailed event messages, providing information on activity that is occurring on the router.

✦ You can use the debug command to enable different levels of debugging. Avoid using the debug all command, as it places a heavy load on the router.

✦ Be sure to disable debugging with the no debug all command as soon as you are done troubleshooting.

Lab Exercises

This chapter covers a number of concepts and commands related to troubleshooting connectivity issues. The following labs are designed to help you put the concepts to practice.

Lab 5-1: Identifying connectivity issues

In this lab, review Figure 5-3 and identify causes for communication problems. Read the problem and analyze the network diagram to identify the cause of the problem and propose a solution. You can assume the serial ports are configured properly and are functioning for this discussion.

Problem: The network services manager located in the Boston office complains that she is unable to Telnet into the switch in the New York office.

Solution: _____

_____

_____

_____

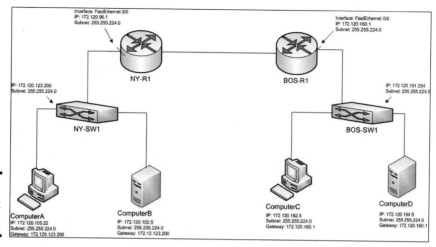

Figure 5-3:
Lab network
topology.

Problem: The Boston systems cannot communicate with the computers in New York.

Solution: _____

_____

_____

_____

Problem: No computer or device can communicate with ComputerD.

Solution: _____

_____

_____

_____

Lab 5-2: Using the show commands

In this lab, practice using the different show commands to view the configuration on your router.

1. **Connect to the console port and use HyperTerminal to connect to your router.**

2. Move into priv exec mode by typing `enable`.

3. Find out if all of the interfaces are up and running and have IP addresses assigned, by using the `show ip interface brief` command. Record your interface information below.

_____

_____

_____

4. Determine if your serial port is the DCE or DTE device, by typing `show controllers serial 0/0`. (Use your serial port numbers.)

Is the serial port the DCE or DTE device? _____

5. Determine if there is a problem with any of your interfaces, by checking the state of the physical connection and the data link protocol with the `show interfaces` command.

Record the state of your serial ports and Ethernet ports in the format of *Serial0/2/0* `is up, line protocol is` *up*.

_____

_____

_____

6. Using the list you created in the previous step, record if each of the links are fine, you see a layer-1 problem, or you see a layer-2 problem.

_____

_____

_____

7. Use the `show ip protocols` command to display any routing protocols that are running on the router.

Record the routing protocol being used (if any): _____

8. Display your routing table to verify the different destination networks by typing the `show ip route` command and recording your routing table entries below.

_____

_____

_____

_____

_____

Lab 5-3: Troubleshooting configuration

In this lab, look at parts of sample configuration files and identify issues with the configuration.

1. **Review the code listing and identify potential issues related to why this serial interface is not up:**

   ```
   interface Serial0/2/0
    ip address 24.0.0.1 255.0.0.0
    encapsulation ppp
   ```

   _____

   _____

   _____

2. **Review the code below and identify any issues related to the configuration:**

   ```
   line con 0
    password conpass
   line vty 0 15
    password telnet
   ```

   _____

   _____

   _____

Lab 5-4: Enabling debugging

In this lab, look at enable debugging on your router that is running the RIP routing protocol. This lab requires that you have two routers connected, with RIP enabled on both routers.

1. **Connect to the console port on the first router and navigate to priv exec mode by typing** `enable`.

2. **Once you are in priv exec mode, enable debugging of ICMP traffic with the** `debug ip icmp` **command.**

   You should see a message that says ICMP debugging has been turned on.

3. **Go to your second router and ping the IP address of the router with ICMP debugging by using the** `ping ip_address` **command.**

4. **Go back to your first router that has debugging turned on, and you should see messages on the console that indicate your router has sent ICMP replies to a system; record the details of the message below.**

   Source address: _____

   Destination address: _____

5. Disable ICMP debugging with the `no debug ip icmp` command.

6. Enable debugging of the RIP routing protocol by typing the `debug ip rip` command while in priv exec mode.

7. Wait for up to 30 seconds to see if you receive any messages that indicate RIP updates have been sent or received; once you receive RIP debugging information, record the details below.

   Version of RIP update received: _____

   Update received from what IP address? _____

   Network ID of the route being received: _____

8. Disable all debugging on the router by using the `no debug all` command while in priv exec mode.

Prep Test

1 You receive the following output when looking at the `show interfaces` command. What should you check?

```
Serial0/2/0 is down, line protocol is down
```

A ○ Check the physical aspects of the link, such as the cable.

B ○ Check that the IP address is set.

C ○ Check that the data link protocol is configured.

D ○ Verify that a route is defined to the remote network.

2 What command do you use to view whether your serial port is the DCE or DTE device?

A ○ `show interface serial 0/0`

B ○ `show controllers serial 0/0`

C ○ `show ip protocols serial 0/0`

D ○ `show serial 0/0`

3 You receive the following output from the `show interfaces` command. What should you check?

```
Serial0/2/0 is up, line protocol is down
```

A ○ Check the physical aspects of the link, such as the cable.

B ○ Check that the IP address is set.

C ○ Check that the data link protocol is configured.

D ○ Verify that a route is defined to the remote network.

4 Which of the following commands is recommended to disable debugging?

A ○ `no debug ip all`

B ○ `no debug ip nat`

C ○ `no debug ip rip`

D ○ `no debug all`

5 Which of the following commands can you use to figure out the IP address of a neighboring router?

A ○ `show cdp neighbors`

B ○ `show cdp neighbors detail`

C ○ `show cdp`

D ○ `cdp run`

6 You are troubleshooting communication problems on a network on the other side of the country. What command do you use to identify at what point in the communication pathway there is a failure?

A ○ `show ip arp`
B ○ `ping ip_address`
C ○ `telnet ip_address`
D ○ `traceroute ip_address`

7 If an interface shows as administratively down, what command do you use to bring the interface up?

A ○ `up`
B ○ `enable`
C ○ `no shutdown`
D ○ `no down`

8 Having a green link light indicates that which of the following conditions have been met? (Select two.)

A ❑ A layer-3 protocol has been assigned at either end of the link.
B ❑ The network media is attached at both ends of the link.
C ❑ The IP address on the interface has been configured.
D ❑ A layer-2 protocol has been loaded and configured at either end of the link.

9 How do you view your ARP cache on a Cisco router? (Select two.)

A ❑ `show ip arp`
B ❑ `arp -a`
C ❑ `arp -show`
D ❑ `show arp`

10 You are having trouble communicating with a remote network. You have checked the status of the interfaces — each interface is up, and the IP addresses look fine. What command do you use next?

A ○ `show ip route`
B ○ `show ip interface brief`
C ○ `show controllers serial 0/0`
D ○ `show cdp`

Answers

1 **A.** When an interface shows a status of down, . . . down, you should look to the physical (layer-1) components of the network because the line protocol will not be up unless the interface is up. *See "Layer-1 and layer-2 troubleshooting."*

2 **B.** When troubleshooting your serial port and wanting to verify whether you have configured the interface as the DCE or DTE device, use the show controllers serial *slot/port* command. *Review "Viewing router configuration."*

3 **C.** When the interface status displays as up, . . . down, this is an indication that the data link protocol has not been configured properly. With a serial port, check that a layer-2 protocol such as HDLC or PPP has been configured. *Check out "Layer-1 and layer-2 troubleshooting."*

4 **D.** When you disable debugging, use the no debug all command so that you can be sure that all levels of debugging are disabled. Debugging places extra processing load on the router, which means you do not want it running if it is not needed. *Peruse "Disabling debugging."*

5 **B.** Of the commands listed, only the show cdp neighbors detail command displays a list of neighboring devices and their IP addresses. *Take a look at "Viewing network topology."*

6 **D.** When trying to identify the point in the communication pathway that is failing, use the traceroute command, which sends you status information with each router that is hit on the way to the destination. *Peek at "The traceroute command."*

7 **C.** If an interface is shown as administratively down, try to bring the interface up by using the no shutdown command on the interface. *Look over "Port shutdown."*

8 **B, D.** If the link light on an interface displays green, it indicates that a physical connection is established between the two points, and a data link protocol is configured at either end. *Study "LED indicators."*

9 **A, D.** The show ip arp command and the show arp command can be used to view the ARP cache on a Cisco router. *Refer to "Viewing the ARP cache."*

10 **A.** After you have verified the physical components and the IP addresses, you should verify that there is a route in the routing table to the destination network. *Examine "Routing."*

Book IV

Advanced Topics

The 5th Wave   By Rich Tennant

Contents at a Glance

Chapter 1: Network Security Terminology

In This Chapter

✔ **Introduction to security terminology**

✔ **Identifying types of attacks**

✔ **Looking at security devices**

✔ **Mitigating security threats**

*O*ne of the most important skills to have if you are going to support networked systems or systems connected to the Internet is the ability of securing systems and networks. In order to be successful as a network professional today, you need to have a solid understanding of network security and ways to protect the network.

I remember when a close friend of mine had his Web site totally replaced by a hacker. My friend's Web site files were replaced with inappropriate content, and he wondered how on Earth someone had hacked his server. It seems amazing now, but back then (circa 1994) a lot of companies did not use firewalls because they were not aware of the risks involved in having a computer connected directly to the Internet. Back then, people thought, "I have a password on the administrator account, so I am secure."

In this chapter, you find out about the basic concepts and terminology related to information system security and network security. Be sure to read this chapter carefully, and make sure you understand the topics, as you will be tested on basic security concepts with the CCENT certification exam. Have fun with this topic area — security is a very exciting field!

Quick Assessment

1   (True/False). A packet-filtering firewall checks the state of the conversation.

2   A _____ is responsible for creating a secure tunnel over an unsecure network.

3   The term used for controlling who is allowed to access a resource is _____.

4   (True/False). A dictionary attack calculates all potential passwords.

5   A _____ virus is a self-replicating virus.

Answers

1 *False*. See "Firewalls."

2 *VPN*. Review "Virtual Private Networks."

3 *Authorization*. Check out "Authorization."

4 *False*. Peruse "Password attacks."

5 *Worm*. Take a look at "Worm."

Introduction to Security Terminology

Let me start the discussion by going over some basic security concepts and terminology. The CCENT certification exam expects you to have some background in security best practices, so this chapter is designed to expose the concepts to you. The next chapter looks at specific steps you need to take to secure your Cisco devices.

Authentication

Authentication is the process of proving one's identity to the network environment. Typically, authentication involves typing a username and password on a system, and it is then verified against an account database before you are granted access. There are different methods you can use to authenticate to a system or network — you can supply a valid username and password or maybe even use biometrics to be authenticated. *Biometrics* is the concept of using a unique physical characteristic of yourself to authenticate to the system, such as a fingerprint, a retina scan, or voice recognition to prove your identity.

Consider these three different forms of authentication, known as *authentication factors,* and their uses:

- ✦ **Something you have:** Dependent on the user having an object in her possession to prove who she is. An example of this authentication is possession of an ID card or door key.

- ✦ **Something you know:** Dependent on the user knowing a piece of information to validate who he is. Examples of this are knowledge of a password, pass code, or even a PIN (personal identification number).

- ✦ **Something you are:** Dependent on you proving your identity by something you are, such as a fingerprint or retina scan — so biometrics falls into this authentication factor.

Most authentication systems use a *two-form* authentication factor, where two of the three factors mentioned here are used. For example, it is not enough to have the ATM card in your possession to use it — you must know the PIN for that card as well.

Smart card

A popular authentication device used today in networking environments is a smart card, which is a small, ATM card–like device that contains your account information. You insert the smart card into a smart card reader that is connected to a computer, and then you enter the PIN associated with the smart card. This is an example of securing an environment by requiring the user to not only have the card, but also know the PIN — an example of two-form authentication.

Using strong passwords

A number of years ago, I had a coworker who was always trying to get me to guess his passwords. He thought I had some magical trick or program that was cracking them, but all I was doing was guessing his passwords. I remember one time he changed it, and I could not guess it — until one night when we were at a social function for work and all he talked about was the Flyers hockey team. I remember sitting there thinking, "I bet that is his password." Sure enough, the next day at work, I tried `flyers` as his password, and it worked. Now the lesson here is that he should have at least mixed the case of the word *flyers* to make something like `flYeRs`, or even better, thrown a symbol in there by replacing the *s* with a *$*. I would have had a much harder time trying to guess his password if he had used `flYeR$` instead. This is an example of a strong password.

Strong passwords

It is really hard to talk about authentication without talking about ensuring your usage of strong passwords on systems and devices. A *strong password* is a password that is very difficult for hackers to guess or crack because it contains a mix of uppercase and lowercase characters, a mix of numbers and letters, and is a minimum of six characters long.

Authorization

After someone is authenticated to a system or device, he is then granted or denied access to resources such as files and printers, or given limited privileges to a device. *Authorization* is the process of giving a person permission to access a resource or a device.

Do not confuse authentication and authorization: You must be first *authenticated* to the network; then, after authentication, you can access the resources and perform the tasks that you have been *authorized* for.

An example of authorization in the networking world is choosing to authorize a system on the network (meaning we allow it to connect to the network through a port on the switch) by its MAC address. In high-security environments, this is very popular, and in the Cisco world, this is known as *port security*.

Vulnerability

Vulnerability is the term we use for a weakness in a system or device. The vulnerability is created accidentally by the manufacturer and is typically the result of a code mistake in the software or firmware.

Hackers find out about vulnerabilities in the software and hardware devices we use by purposely testing the limitations of the device or software. Once they discover the vulnerability, they work on figuring out how they can exploit it.

Exploit

An *exploit* takes advantage of a weakness, or vulnerability, in a piece of software or a device. For example, years ago it was found that most Web servers were vulnerable to attack because the Web server did not verify the file being requested in a URL. Hackers exploited this by starting to send commands in a URL that would navigate the folder structure of the Web server and call for files other than normal Web pages. This is known as *folder traversing*, and it was a popular exploit on Web servers.

What about CIA?

When working in the security field, you will most likely run into the terms *confidentiality, integrity, availability* (CIA). These are the fundamental goals of security, and ultimately, every security control that we put in place satisfies one of the elements of CIA.

Confidentiality

Confidentiality is the concept of keeping information secret. In order to implement confidentiality, you may look to securing data with permissions, but you also have to look at encrypting the information that is stored on disk or travels across the network.

Integrity

Integrity is the veracity of the data. *Data integrity* is about ensuring that when you receive information, it is the information that was actually sent and not something that was modified in transit. *Hashing* is one of the popular methods of ensuring data integrity. With hashing, the data sender runs the data through a mathematical algorithm (known as a *hashing algorithm*), and an answer is created. When the recipient receives the information, she runs the data on the same algorithm to see if she gets the same mathematical answer. If the same answer is calculated, she knows that the data has not been altered in transit.

Availability

Availability is the concept that the data stored on the network is always accessible to the people who want the data — the people who are authorized to access it, that is. As security professionals, we need to ensure the availability of the data, and there are a number of ways to ensure availability. For example, you can do backups, use RAID volumes for storing your data, and implement high-availability solutions such as *clustering technologies* (multiple servers running the same application, or service, so if one server fails the request for the service is sent to the second server).

Identifying Types of Attacks

Now that you are familiar with some basic network security terms, let's talk about some popular attacks against businesses today. These attacks may sometimes seem far-fetched, but in reality, they happen every day! This section outlines some of the most popular types of attacks that can happen in today's networking environments.

For the CCENT certification exam, it is critical that you are familiar with the different types of attacks covered in this section. You are sure to get a few questions about types of attacks.

To me, a hacker is someone with the technical expertise to bypass the security of a network or a system. A hacker knows how to use features of a piece of software or hardware to gain access to restricted areas of a network and then use those features against you and your system. For example, an e-commerce Web site connects to a product database behind the scenes so that you can get a list of products when you visit the site. A hacker knows how to input data into the site to manipulate the database server into executing the code that the hacker wants to execute — and this happens because the hacker understands the technologies used behind the scenes.

There are two major types of hackers:

✦ **Black-hat hackers:** Break into a system or network for malicious reasons or for personal gain. The black-hat hacker could be looking for financial gain, bragging rights, or revenge.

✦ **White-hat hackers:** Try to hack into software or hardware in order to understand how to protect others from black-hat hackers. These are the good guys.

Hackers use a number of different types of attacks to hack into a network, device, or a system. Sometimes an attack lays the groundwork for a future or different type of attack: That is, the initial attack does not seem all that dangerous, but it is used in the future to gain unauthorized access.

Social engineering attacks

A *social engineering attack* occurs when a hacker tries to obtain information or gain access to a system through social contact with a user. Typically, the hacker poses as someone else and tries to trick a user into divulging personal or corporate information that allows the hacker access to a system or network.

For example, a hacker calls your company's phone number, listed in the phone book, and poses as a technical support person for your company. He tells the user who answers the phone that a new application has been deployed on the network, and for the application to work, the user's password must be reset. After the password is reset to what the hacker wants, he might "verify" with the user the credential that the user uses. A user who is not educated on social engineering might divulge important information without thinking that the caller might have malicious intent.

A social engineering attack is an attack where a hacker tries to trick a user or administrator into divulging sensitive information through social contact. After the sensitive information is obtained, the hacker can then use that information to compromise the system or network.

This example might sound unrealistic, but it happens all the time. If you work for a small company, you might not experience a social engineering attack. In a large corporate environment, though, it is extremely possible that a social engineering attack would be successful if the company does not educate its users. A large company usually stations the IT staff or management at the head office, but employees in most branch locations have never talked to IT management. The branch employees would not recognize the voices of the IT folks, so a hacker could impersonate someone from the head office — and the user at the branch office would never know the difference.

There are a number of popular social engineering attack scenarios — and network administrators are just as likely to be social engineering victims as "regular" employees, so they need to be aware. Here are some popular social engineering attack scenarios:

✦ **Hacker impersonates an IT administrator.** The hacker calls or e-mails an employee and pretends to be the network administrator. The hacker tricks the employee into divulging a password or even resetting the password.

✦ **Hacker impersonates a user.** The hacker calls or e-mails the network administrator and pretends to be a user who forgot her password, asking the administrator to reset her password for her.

✦ **Hacker e-mails a program to network users.** The hacker typically e-mails all the users on a network, telling them about a security bug in the OS. He advises users to run the `update.exe` file attached to the e-mail. In this example, `update.exe` is the attack file — it opens the computer up so that the hacker can access the computer.

When you are working as a network professional, educate your users never to run a program that has been e-mailed to them. Most software vendors, such as Microsoft, state that they will never e-mail a program to a person: Instead, they will e-mail a URL, but it is up to the person to go to the URL and download the update. A great book to find out more on the process a hacker employs to compromise a system is Kevin Beaver's *Hacking For Dummies,* 3rd edition (Wiley).

Network-based attacks

A *network-based attack* uses networking technologies or protocols to perform the attack, and they are some of the most popular types of attacks today. The following explains the terminology associated with seven important network-based attacks.

Ensure that you are familiar with the different types of network-based attacks for the CCENT certification exam.

Password attacks

A *password attack* involves the hacker trying to figure out the passwords for different accounts on a system, or a password that guards a device. The three major types of password attacks are dictionary attack, hybrid attack, and brute force attack.

With a *dictionary attack*, hackers use a program in conjunction with two text files to automatically try a number of passwords.

✦ One text file contains the most popular user accounts — such as administrator, admin, and root — found on networks. This file is termed the user account text file.

✦ The second text file contains a list of all the words in the English dictionary, and then some. Hackers can also obtain dictionary files for different languages. This file is termed the dictionary text file or password list file.

The dictionary attack program then tries to log in with every user account in the user account text file with every word in the dictionary text file, attempting to determine the password for the user account.

To protect against a dictionary attack, be sure to use strong passwords that mix letters, numbers, and symbols. This prevents the passwords from being found in the dictionary. Also, passwords are normally case sensitive, so be sure to use a mix of both lowercase and uppercase characters. Mixing the case of a password means a hacker not only has to guess the password but also the combination of uppercase and lowercase characters.

Also note that because there are dictionary files for different languages you should not use words found in *any* dictionary. This means avoiding not only English words, but also French, German, Hebrew . . . even Klingon!

A second type of password attack is known as a hybrid password attack. A *hybrid password attack* is like a dictionary attack in the sense it uses a dictionary file, but it also tries variations of the password by placing numbers on the end of the word and sometimes replacing popular characters. For example, after the hybrid attack program tries all the passwords in the dictionary file, it may then try them again by replacing any letter *a* with @ in the words.

Hackers can also perform a *brute force attack*. With a brute force attack, instead of trying to use words from a dictionary file, the hacker uses a program that tries to figure out your password by mathematically calculating all potential passwords with a certain length and set of characters. Figure 1-1 shows a popular password-cracking tool known as LC4. Tools like this are great for network administrators to audit how strong their users' passwords are.

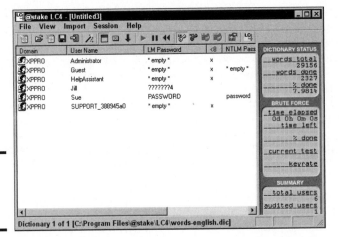

Figure 1-1:
Cracking
passwords
with LC4.

To protect against dictionary attacks, we use strong passwords, but to protect against a brute force password attack, we must implement an *account lockout policy,* where after three bad logon attempts, the account is locked and cannot be used.

If you have configured an account lockout policy to protect your account database, understand that only works if the hacker is connected to your network and attempting to hack into live systems (known as an *online attack*). If the hacker can get a copy of your account database, or hashed passwords in a configuration file, and take that away with him (known as an *offline attack*) then there is no protection against the brute force attack.

Denial of service

Another popular network attack is a *denial of service (DoS)* attack, which can come in many forms and is designed to cause a system or network device to be so busy that it cannot service a real request from a client, essentially overloading the system or device and shutting it down.

For example, say you have an e-mail server and a hacker attacks the e-mail server by flooding the server with e-mail messages, causing it to be so busy that it cannot send any more e-mails. You have been denied the service that the system was created for.

There are a number of different types of DoS attacks that have come out over the years, including the following:

✦ **Ping of death:** The hacker continuously pings your system with over-sized packets causing your system to crash.

✦ **SYN flood:** The hacker performs a partial three-way handshake with each port on the system. This uses up memory on your system and eventually crashes the system. The hacker accomplishes this by sending a SYN message to a number of different ports, but when your system replies with an ACK/SYN, the hacker does not complete the process with an ACK. As a result your system holds that partial connection in memory, waiting for the ACK. For more on the three-way handshake, SYN, and ACK, see Book I, Chapter 4.

To protect against denial of service attacks, you need to have a *firewall* (a piece of software or a hardware device that prevents someone from entering your system or network) installed, and you should also keep your systems and devices patched (apply any updates and security fixes).

Spoofing

Spoofing is a type of attack in which a hacker modifies the source address of a frame or packet. There are three major types of spoofing:

✦ **MAC spoofing:** The hacker alters the source MAC address of the frame.

✦ **IP spoofing:** The hacker alters the source IP address in a packet.

✦ **E-mail spoofing:** The hacker alters the source e-mail address to make the e-mail look like it came from someone other than the hacker.

An example of a spoof attack is the *smurf attack*, which is a combination of a denial of service *and* spoofing. Here is how it works:

1. The hacker pings a large number of systems but modifies the source address of the packet so that the ping request looks like it is coming from a different system.

2. All systems that are pinged reply to the modified source address — an unsuspecting victim.

3. The victim's system (most likely a server) receives so many replies to the ping request that it is overwhelmed with traffic, causing it to be unable to answer any other request from the network.

To protect against spoof attacks, you can implement encryption and authentication services on the network.

Eavesdropping attack

An *eavesdropping attack* occurs when a hacker uses some sort of packet sniffer program to see all the traffic on the network. Hackers use *packet sniffers* to find out login passwords or to monitor activities. Figure 1-2 shows Microsoft Network Monitor, a program that monitors network traffic by displaying the contents of the packets.

Figure 1-2: Using Network Monitor to analyze FTP logon traffic.

Notice in Figure 1-2 that the highlighted packet (frame 8) shows someone logging on with a username of `administrator`; in frame 11, you can see that this user has typed the password `P@ssw0rd`. In this example, the hacker now has the username and password of a network account by eavesdropping on the conversation!

To protect against eavesdrop attacks, you need encrypt network traffic and physically control who can connect to your network.

Man-in-the-middle

A *man-in-the-middle attack* involves the hacker intercepting the data in transit, potentially modifying the data, and then forwarding the information on to the intended recipient. Note that the intended recipient receives the information, but the hacker sees the information as well.

Man-in-the-middle attacks are popular with wireless networks at coffee shops today. The hacker poisons the ARP cache of the wireless clients so that they forward all the traffic to the hacker's system first, who then forwards the information onto the Internet. The clients are still surfing the Internet, but what they do not realize is that they are passing through the hacker's laptop first. (And the hacker is typically capturing all the traffic with a packet sniffer in hopes of capturing user passwords.)

To protect against man-in-the-middle attacks, you need to restrict access to the network and implement encryption and authentication services on the network.

Session hijacking

A *session hijack* is similar to a man-in-the-middle attack, but instead of the hacker intercepting the data, altering it, and sending it to whomever it was destined, the hacker simply hijacks the conversation by disconnecting one of the participants off the network (usually via a denial of service attack) and then impersonates that person within the conversation. The other party has no idea that he or she is communicating with someone other than the original person.

To protect against session hijacking attacks, you need to restrict access to the network and implement encryption and authentication services on the network.

Buffer overflow

A very popular type of attack today is a *buffer overflow attack,* which involves the hacker sending more data to a piece of software than the software expects. The information sent to an application is typically stored in an area of memory known as a *buffer.* When more data than expected is sent to the application, the information is stored in memory beyond the allocated buffer. It has been found that if a hacker can store information beyond the allocated buffer, he can run his own code that typically results in a remote command shell with administrative access. The reason why administrative access is gained is because the code executes in the context of the user account associated with the software that was hacked — normally an administrative account!

TIP

To protect against buffer overflow attacks, you need to keep the system, applications, and devices up to date with patches and security fixes.

Software-based attacks

Just like there are a number of different types of network attacks, there are a number of software attacks. As you can likely guess, a *software attack* comes through software that a user runs. The most popular software attacks are mentioned in the sections that follow, and you should be familiar with them for the CCENT certification exam.

SQL injection

A *SQL injection attack* occurs when the hacker sends `Transact SQL` statements (statements that manipulate a database) into an application so that the application will send those statements to the database server to be executed. If the application developer does not validate data inputted into the application, the hacker can modify the data in the underlying database or even manipulate the system.

Viruses

A *virus* is a program that causes harm to your system. Typically, viruses are spread through e-mails and are included in attachments, such as word processing documents and spreadsheets. The virus can do any of a number of things: It can delete files from your system, modify the system configuration, or e-mail all your contacts in your e-mail software. To prevent viruses, install antivirus software and do not open any unexpected file attachments that arrive in your e-mail.

Trojan horse

A *Trojan horse* is a type of virus that a user is typically tricked into running on the system, and when the software runs, it does something totally different from what the user expected it to do. For example, NetBus (an older Trojan horse virus) is an example of a Trojan horse virus sent as a file called `patch.exe`. The user receiving the file — typically through an e-mail — believes the file will fix a security issue. The problem is that `patch.exe` is a Trojan horse, and when that horse starts running, it opens the computer up to allow a hacker to connect to the system.

The hacker then uses a client program, like the one shown in Figure 1-3, to connect to the system and start messing with the computer. The hacker can do things like launch other programs, flip your screen upside down, eject your CD-ROM tray, watch your activity, and modify or delete files!

Worm

A *worm* is a virus that does not need to be activated by someone opening the file. It is *self-replicating*, meaning that it spreads itself from system to system automatically, infecting each computer. How the virus spreads depends on the virus itself — there have been worm viruses that connect across the network automatically to a vulnerable system and then infect that system. Recently, worm viruses automatically infect a flash drive that is connected to the system so that when you take the drive to the next system, the worm infects that system from the flash drive.

Figure 1-3:
Using a
Trojan virus
known as
NetBus
to control
a user's
computer.

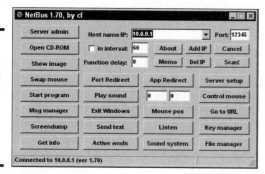

Logic bomb

A *logic bomb* is a type of virus or malicious software that was designed to wreak havoc on your system on a certain date and time. The scary thing about logic bombs is that they seem like useful software until the day the programmer decides it will become malicious!

To protect against malicious software such as a virus, Trojan horse, worm, and a logic bomb, you need to use a firewall and keep your virus definitions up-to-date.

Looking at Security Devices

When looking to secure your systems or networks, you can definitely follow best practices such as patching systems or using strong passwords, but realistically, you are going to need to use one or more popular security devices to secure your environment. In this section, I discuss popular security devices you should be familiar with for the CCENT certification exam.

Firewalls

A *firewall* is a piece of software or a device that is designed to control what traffic is allowed to enter or leave the network. Most firewalls control traffic that enters the network by analyzing the header of the packet and looking at the source IP address, destination IP address, and the source and destination port. If the packet trying to enter the network meets certain conditions, such as the destination port is 80, the packet is then allowed or denied access to the network depending on how the firewall is configured.

There are three major types of firewalls that are popular today:

✦ **Packet-filtering firewall:** A packet-filtering firewall is limited in the sense that it filters traffic by the fields in the header such as the source and destination IP address and the source and destination port numbers. It is very easy for the hacker to bypass this firewall; she can alter the fields in the header.

✦ **Stateful packet inspection firewall:** Most firewalls today are stateful packet inspection firewalls, which filter traffic by the fields in the header but also can understand the context of the conversation. For example, a stateful packet inspection firewall knows that before you can send data to a Web site you must have had a three-way handshake with the system. The firewall stores the "state" of the conversation in a state table so it can verify that the packet it is receiving should actually be occurring at this point in time.

✦ **Application-level firewall:** An application-level firewall has the benefit of not only being able to analyze the fields in the header and being stateful, but it has the added benefit of being able to analyze the application data that is stored in the packet. For example, an application-layer firewall can verify that a three-way handshake has occurred and that the destination port is 80, but it can also verify that the HTTP command in the packet is a GET and not a POST. These firewalls can limit what features of an application are allowed to be performed.

There are many different ways to implement a firewall solution, and most networks use multiple firewalls to control access to different parts of the network. Figure 1-4 shows a very popular firewall solution that uses two firewalls.

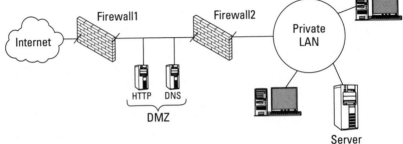

Figure 1-4: Firewalls are used to protect the internal network from unauthorized traffic.

The first firewall (Firewall1 in Figure 1-4) is connected to the Internet and controls what traffic is allowed to pass from the Internet through the firewall. You can see that the first firewall has to allow HTTP traffic and DNS server traffic through the firewall, as there are public HTTP and DNS servers behind the first firewall.

The second firewall (Firewall2 in Figure 1-4) is designed to stop all traffic from passing through that firewall in order to protect the private LAN. The area between the two firewalls is known as a *demilitarized zone* (DMZ) and is designed to allow selected traffic to enter the zone. This firewall solution is known as a *screened-subnet* as any traffic that passes into the DMZ is screened first and ensured it is authorized traffic.

Another very popular firewall solution that relates to Cisco devices is what is known as a *screened-host firewall,* shown in Figure 1-5. It is a topology that has the Internet connected to your router, which will then *filter,* or screen, what packets are allowed to pass through and reach the firewall.

Figure 1-5:
A screened-host firewall uses a router to filter which packets reach the firewall.

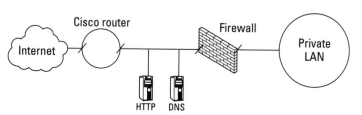

Cisco routers use *access lists* (a list of rules that determine what packets are allowed to enter or leave the network) to control what traffic is allowed to pass through the router. Access lists are beyond the scope of the CCENT certification but are required knowledge to pass the CCNA certification exam.

Intrusion detection system

An *intrusion detection system* (IDS) is a device or piece of software that monitors activity and identifies any suspicious activity on a network or system. When the IDS identifies the suspicious activity, it logs the activity and may even send notification to the administrator as an alert.

**Book IV
Chapter 1**

**Network Security
Terminology**

There are two main types of intrusion detection systems:

✦ **Host-based IDS:** This is typically software installed on the system that monitors activity on that one system. If suspicious activity is found on the system an alert is generated and the administrator is notified.

✦ **Network-based IDS:** Monitors network traffic and identifies suspicious traffic on the entire network, not just one system! The network-based IDS captures network traffic and then compares that to signatures in the IDS software. This analysis indicates what type of traffic is considered suspicious.

What action the IDS takes when suspicious activity is found depends on what class of intrusion detection system we are talking about. There are two major classes of intrusion detection systems:

✦ **Passive IDS:** A passive IDS logs suspicious activity to a file and could send an alert to the administrator if alerts have been configured. A passive IDS is normally referred to as just an *IDS*.

✦ **Active IDS:** An active IDS logs the suspicious activity, sends an alert to the administrator, and also takes corrective action such as preventing the system that is creating the suspicious activity from further accessing the network.

An active IDS is now known as an *intrusion prevention system* (IPS).

For the CCENT exam, ensure that you are familiar with the purpose of an intrusion detection system. Also, know the difference between an IDS and an IPS.

Switches

I know we talk about switches in detail within Book III, Chapters 3 and 4, but I want to make sure that I mention switches here as a security device because switches have some great features that help protect a network environment. The following are some security features to remember about a switch:

✦ **Filtered traffic:** The purpose of a switch is to filter traffic by sending the traffic to only the port where the destination MAC address of the frame is connected to the switch. This aids in security, as someone else connected to the switch cannot easily run a packet sniffer and see all traffic on the network. Because the traffic is not sent to the port of the person doing the sniffing, there is no opportunity for that person to capture and view network traffic.

✦ **Port security:** Port security is the feature on a switch that allows you to limit which systems can connect to which ports on the switch. With port security, you associate the MAC address of a system with the port, and no other system can connect to that port.

✦ **Disable ports:** For security reasons, you need to disable any ports on the switch that you are not using. This prevents someone from connecting an unknown system to the network without your knowledge.

✦ **VLANs:** Virtual LANs allow you to create communication boundaries on the switch. You can create multiple VLANs on the switch and then place different ports into different VLANs. Systems that are connected to ports in one VLAN cannot communicate with systems in another VLAN without the use of a router.

You find out how to configure security features of Cisco switches in the next chapter.

Virtual Private Networks

The final security technology I want to mention is what is known as a *virtual private network,* or VPN. A VPN is responsible for creating an encrypted tunnel across an unsecure network such as the Internet. Once the tunnel is created between the client and the VPN server, any data that is sent through the tunnel is encrypted.

Looking at Figure 1-6, you see that you are in a hotel room in Toronto and want to access some files that are in your office in New York. Normally, you would not try to access those files across the Internet because you would not want the information sent or received in plain text for someone to intercept.

Figure 1-6:
A VPN creates an encrypted tunnel over an unsecure network so that data can be sent and received securely.

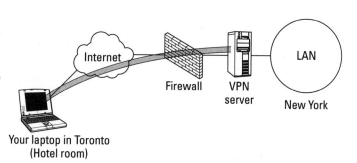

Your laptop in Toronto (Hotel room)

Firewall   VPN server   LAN   New York

As a solution, you install VPN client software on your laptop, which connects across the Internet to the VPN server in New York. After the VPN server authenticates you with your username and password, you are granted access to the network, and the encrypted tunnel is created. Now any data sent between the VPN client and the VPN server is secure, as it is encrypted in transit.

VPN protocols are responsible for encrypting the data. Examples of VPN protocols are the Point-to-Point Tunneling Protocol (PPTP) and the Layer 2 Tunneling Protocol (L2TP). Growing in popularity is SSL VPNs, which do not require VPN client software on the client systems as the Web browser makes the client connection. It should also be noted that VPNs can be created from one site to another in order to encrypt all traffic between the two sites (as opposed to the clients creating the VPN).

Mitigating Security Threats

Now that you have been introduced to some of the different types of network attacks and identified some of the popular network security appliances, let's take a look at how you can minimize potential network threats. A fancy term for minimizing the threats is *mitigating*.

Although this section is not intended to be a complete list of the steps to take to secure your environment, it is definitely a list of some of the fundamental steps you should take — and they will go a long way to helping create a secure environment.

Workstations

To help keep your desktop workstations secure, you should consider doing the following, at a minimum:

✦ **Patch your systems.** Be sure to keep your systems up to date with patches. This includes patching the operating system and all software installed.

✦ **Use antivirus software.** Ensure that you have company-approved antivirus software installed on all desktop systems.

✦ **Keep virus definitions up to date.** Make sure you are keeping the virus software definitions up to date. These definitions allow the virus-protection software to know what the current viruses are.

✦ **Limit administrative accounts.** Do not give all the users administrative capabilities to the desktop system. Ensure that most users utilize restricted accounts and limit how many people have administrative access.

✦ **Maintain user awareness.** It is important to ensure users are aware of some of the different threats that exist. Educate users on good e-mail practices and about social engineering attacks.

Servers

To help keep your servers secure you should contemplate doing the following, at a minimum:

✦ **Patch systems.** Be sure to keep your servers up-to-date with patches. This includes patching the operating system and all software installed.

✦ **Use server-class antivirus software.** Ensure that you have company-approved antivirus software that is designed to run on servers.

✦ **Keep virus definitions up-to-date.** Make sure that you are keeping the virus software definitions up-to-date. These definitions allow the virus-protection software to know what the current viruses are.

✦ **Limit administrative accounts.** Ensure that you limit how many people have administrative access to the servers. The more people making changes to a server, the more chances mistakes will happen.

✦ **Configure permissions.** Make certain that all the resources are secured with appropriate permissions.

✦ **Place server in a secure room.** Be sure that servers are placed in a locked server room, where access to that room is limited to authorized personnel.

✦ **Install a firewall.** Depending on the type of server, you may decide to limit what traffic can reach the server by installing a software firewall on the system. For example, if the system is used only as a Web server, I recommend installing a software firewall that allows only HTTP and HTTPS traffic to the system.

Network

To help create a more secure network environment, you should consider following these general steps, at a minimum:

✦ **Encrypt traffic.** Depending on how sensitive the information is that travels on your network, you may decide to encrypt all network traffic.

✦ **Use firewalls.** Use firewalls to control what type of traffic is allowed to enter and leave different areas of the network.

✦ **Use intrusion detection systems.** Be sure to configure an IDS or IPS to monitor network activity and notify you of any suspicious activity.

✦ **Place switches and routers in a secure room.** Make sure you are storing switches and routers in a locked server room where you are limiting access to the room.

✦ **Implement device security best practices.** Ensure that on your switches and routers you are following security best practices such as configuring passwords, encrypting passwords, and using other switch and router device security concepts mentioned in the next chapter!

**Book IV
Chapter 1**

**Network Security
Terminology**

Chapter Summary

This chapter covers the fundamental concepts regarding network security. It is an important topic, but understand that this chapter only scratches the surface of security concepts. For the CCENT certification, be familiar with the following facts about security:

◆ *Authentication* is proving your identity to the system.

◆ *Authorization* is granting someone access to a system or resource after he has been authenticated.

◆ *CIA* stands for confidentiality, integrity, and availability.

◆ A *social engineering attack* is when the hacker tries to trick someone into compromising security through an e-mail or phone call.

◆ A *buffer overflow attack* is when the hacker sends too much data to an application, which normally results in administrative control of the system in a command shell.

◆ There are three types of password attacks: dictionary, hybrid, and brute force.

◆ A *denial of service* (DoS) attack is when a hacker attacks a system or device by overloading it and causing it to crash or be too busy to perform its job.

◆ *Firewalls* control what traffic can enter the network.

◆ An *intrusion detection system* detects suspicious activity and alerts the administrator.

◆ A *VPN* creates an encrypted tunnel over an unsecure network such as the Internet.

Lab Exercises

This chapter introduces you to the world of security by exposing you to some popular security terms and attack types. The following labs help you review the security concepts discussed in this chapter.

Lab 1-1: Security terminology

In this lab, review basic security terms by matching the term with the appropriate description.

Term	Description
___ Vulnerability	**A.** Verifying a user's identity.
___ Packet-filtering firewall	**B.** Creates an encrypted tunnel over an unsecure network.
___ Authentication	**C.** Filters traffic by understanding the context of the conversation.
___ Mitigating threats	**D.** A weakness in a piece of software or hardware.
___ CIA	**E.** An area of the network used to place servers that are accessed from the Internet.
___ VPN	**F.** Implementing security controls to minimize the threats against a system or device.
___ DMZ	**G.** A device that identifies suspicious activity on a system or network.
___ Stateful packet inspection firewall	**H.** The fundamental goals of information security.
___ IDS	**I.** Inspects the fields in the header of the packet to decide whether to allow or deny the traffic.

Lab 1-2: Types of attacks

In this lab, review the different types of attacks by matching the term with the appropriate description.

Term	Description
___ Denial of service	**A.** Type of malicious software that the user is tricked into installing; it allows the hacker access to the system.
___ IP spoofing	**B.** Capturing network packets and being able to view information in the packets.
___ Buffer overflow	**C.** Overloading a system, which results in the system not being able to perform its job.
___ Eavesdrop attack	**D.** A type of password attack that tries dictionary words but also adds numbers to the end of each word.
___ Social engineering attack	**E.** A self-replicating virus.
___ MAC spoofing	**F.** Sending too much data input to an application.
___ Trojan virus	**G.** Altering the layer-3 source address of a packet.
___ Hybrid attack	**H.** Altering the layer-2 source address of a packet.
___ Worm virus	**I.** A hacker tries to trick you into compromising security through social contact.

Prep Test

1 What type of firewall can allow or deny traffic after inspecting the application data in the packet?

A ○ Application-level firewall

B ○ Stateful packet inspection firewall

C ○ Personal firewall

D ○ Packet-filtering firewall

2 Which of the following is a form of denial of service attack? (Select all that apply.)

A ❑ SYN flood

B ❑ Spoof attack

C ❑ Brute force attack

D ❑ Ping of death

3 What is the term used for the area of the network where you are to place servers from the Internet?

A ○ IDS

B ○ Private LAN

C ○ DMZ

D ○ Internal LAN

4 What type of attack involves the hacker contacting the victim through e-mail or a phone call?

A ○ Social engineering attack

B ○ Denial of service

C ○ E-mail attack

D ○ Contact attack

5 What type of firewall is capable of inspecting the fields found *only* in the header of the packet?

A ○ Application-level firewall

B ○ Stateful packet inspection firewall

C ○ Windows firewall

D ○ Packet-filtering firewall

6 What type of attack involves the hacker sending too much data to the application, which normally results in administrative access within a command shell?

- **A** ○ Spoof attack
- **B** ○ Buffer overflow attack
- **C** ○ Social engineering attack
- **D** ○ Denial of service attack

7 What type of attack involves the hacker modifying the source IP address of a packet in order to try to bypass the security control?

- **A** ○ Spoof attack
- **B** ○ Buffer overflow attack
- **C** ○ Social engineering attack
- **D** ○ Denial of service attack

8 What type of password attack mathematically calculates all possible password combinations?

- **A** ○ Dictionary
- **B** ○ Hybrid
- **C** ○ Brute force
- **D** ○ Calculated

9 What type of firewall knows about the context of the conversation and whether the packet is the right packet at that point in time?

- **A** ○ Spoof firewall
- **B** ○ Stateful packet inspection firewall
- **C** ○ Screened firewall
- **D** ○ Packet-filtering firewall

10 Which of the following take corrective action when suspicious activity is detected? (Select two.)

- **A** ❑ Active IDS
- **B** ❑ Passive IDS
- **C** ❑ IPS
- **D** ❑ NAT

Answers

1 **A.** Application-level firewalls can inspect the application-level data, such as what application command is executing, and either allow or deny that traffic. *See "Firewalls."*

2 **A, D.** A SYN flood attack and the ping of death attack were popular denial of service attacks years back. *Review "Denial of service."*

3 **C.** The demilitarized zone (DMZ) is where you should place public servers such as Web and DNS servers. *Check out "Firewalls."*

4 **A.** A social engineering attack is when the hacker contacts the victim and tries to trick the individual into compromising security. *Peruse "Social engineering attacks."*

5 **D.** A packet-filtering firewall is capable of inspecting only the packet header to decide if the packet should be allowed or denied. This type of firewall could be easily tricked with a spoof attack. *Take a look at "Firewalls."*

6 **B.** A buffer overflow attack involves the hacker sending too much data to the application, which typically results in administrative access to the system. *Peek at "Buffer overflow."*

7 **A.** A spoof attack is when the hacker alters the source address of a packet in order to bypass a security control such as a firewall or access control list. *Look over "Spoofing."*

8 **C.** A brute force attack mathematically calculates all potential password combinations. *Study "Password attacks."*

9 **B.** A stateful packet inspection firewall knows the context of the conversation and the order in which packets should be received. For example, the firewall knows that you can send data to a Web server without a three-way handshake. *Refer to "Firewalls."*

10 **A, C.** An active IDS takes corrective action when suspicious activity is detected. Active IDSes are now known as intrusion prevention systems (IPS). *Examine "Intrusion detection system."*

Chapter 2: Cisco Device Security Best Practices

In This Chapter

✔ The importance of physical security

✔ Cisco router best practices

✔ Cisco switch best practices

The previous chapter introduces you to a number of security terms, such as *authentication,* and a number of different types of attacks. This chapter takes a more hands-on approach to security by discussing basic configuration settings and best practices that you should follow when you are configuring your Cisco routers and switches.

From an exam point of view, you will be tested heavily on these concepts! The CCENT certification exam has a number of simulations that require you to review the configuration of a device and identify any security-related issues with the device. This chapter helps you prepare for those types of questions!

Quick Assessment

1   (True/False). The `enable password` command takes precedence over the `enable secret` command.

2   _____ is a feature that allows you to restrict which stations can connect to a port on a switch.

3   _____ security controls who gains local access to a device.

4   (True/False). SSH is used to encrypt traffic.

5   A _____ is a message displayed when the administrator connects to the router.

Answers

1 *False.* See "Configuring passwords."

2 *Port security.* Review "Configuring port security."

3 *Physical.* Check out "The Importance of Physical Security."

4 *True.* Peruse "Configuring SSH."

5 *Banner.* Take a look at "Configuring banners."

The Importance of Physical Security

Physical security is one of the first aspects of security in an organization to look at, and it is definitely one of those areas of security that is overlooked in most organizations.

Physical security deals with controlling how someone can physically gain access to your company assets, including personnel and network equipment. There are many things to consider when dealing with physical security — including preventing unauthorized persons from entering the property, moving equipment away from windows, locking rooms containing switches and routers, and adjusting workstation CMOS settings — and this section is designed to introduce you to some of the fundamental aspects of physical security.

Physical premises

The first point to make about physical security is that you need to secure the physical *premises,* or property, of the company. There are a number of ways to secure access to the premises, starting with having a barbed wire fence surrounding the perimeter of the property, with a security guard at the entrance of the premises.

The security guard watches to make sure that all persons entering the premises have a valid ID card. The guard can also be responsible for checking in any visitors and handing out temporary passes to those visitors. It is important in high-security environments that all persons wear the ID badge in a visible area so that unauthorized personnel can be identified.

As an IT professional you have a responsibility to help maintain a secure environment — not only from a technology side, but also from an organization point of view. If you see someone walking around the premises without their ID badge in plain view, remind them that it needs to be visible.

Windows and lighting

When assessing physical security within the organization, you want to always ensure the employees' safety, and that includes ensuring that you have proper lighting at the entrances and exits, especially if you have employees working late at night. You also want to ensure that you have proper lighting in the parking area and video surveillance set up to monitor those areas. As an IT professional, making decisions on these types of controls is not your responsibility but if you notice an unsafe environment then you should report it.

You also want to keep a close eye on information and equipment that is too close to windows in the building. Having a computer close to a window allows for someone to potentially view information on the computer screen. Most high-security environments audit the placement of equipment and monitors during a security assessment. Move monitors away from the windows, if possible. If you cannot move them, angle them so they are not viewable through the window.

If computer equipment and other valuables are viewable through a window, you may find that someone breaks through the window to swipe the equipment. This is something to watch for with laptops as well.

Laptops and other portable equipment should be physically secured with a lockdown cable. If you check the side of a laptop, you can see a place to insert a connector from the lockdown cable so the laptop can be secured to the desk.

Secure facility

Part of securing the facility is ensuring that server and equipment rooms are locked so that you can control who has access to the server, switches, and routers. Ensure that you are using a proven locking system, such as swipe cards and numeric keypads, on the doors to the server room. A number of key locks are too easy to pick, so try to stay away for the lock-and-key scenario.

For the CCENT certification exam, remember that servers, switches, and routers should be in a locked room where physical access to the room is controlled. Be sure to also put passwords on the switch and router's console, auxiliary, and Telnet ports.

Workstations and servers

I want to make a note about workstations and servers as related to physical security. You need to ensure that servers are locked away in the server room, where you can control access to them.

Also understand that if someone can get physical access to a system, that person can boot off a CD or DVD and bypass most of the security features of the server OS. In high-security environments, you may want to change some of the CMOS settings on the workstations and servers to prevent that. You can adjust the CMOS settings to control the boot order of the devices and disable booting from devices such as CD-ROMs, DVDs, and USB drives.

You also may want to disable external ports on the workstations to limit the likelihood that someone will take a copy of company data home with them on a thumb drive.

Cisco Router Best Practices

The main focus of this chapter is to ensure that you understand some of the fundamental steps you can take in the configuration of your Cisco devices to help create a more secure environment. In this section, you review popular tasks, such as setting passwords, configuring user accounts, creating login banners, and configuring SSH for your Cisco devices.

Configuring passwords

In Book II, Chapter 2, you find out how to configure passwords on your router so that if someone tries to move from user exec mode to priv exec mode, she is challenged for a password. Use the following commands on your Cisco router to configure passwords for navigating into privilege exec mode:

```
RouterA>enable
RouterA#config term
RouterA(config)#enable password mypass
RouterA(config)#enable secret mysecret
```

Remember the difference between the `enable password` command and the `enable secret` command: The `enable password` is stored in an unencrypted format in the device configuration files, while the `enable secret` is encrypted in the configuration. The benefit of encrypting the password, known as the secret in this example, is that if someone views your configuration file they will be unable to tell what the secret is (because it is encrypted). Note that it is a best practice to use the `enable secret` over the `enable password`. Also note that when both the `enable password` and the `enable secret` are used, you are required to use the secret when logging in to the router. This should be easy to remember, as it makes sense that the most secure method is used.

Let's take a look at the configuration after the `enable password` and the `enable secret` are set on the router.

```
RouterA(config)#exit
RouterA#show running-config

Building configuration...
(output omitted for briefness)
!
enable secret 5 $1$u76B$IOFVJ7VxfVXYVpGDrFTcI0
enable password mypass
!
(output omitted for briefness)
!
```

Notice in the preceding output that the `enable secret` has been encrypted (you cannot tell that the value is set to the word *mysecret*), but the `enable password` is stored in clear text. This is a problem, as anyone who gets physical access to the router can view the password (I show you how to encrypt all passwords in the upcoming "Encrypting passwords" section — let us get more passwords in the configuration file first).

For the CCENT certification exam, remember that the `enable secret` is encrypted in the configuration and takes precedence over the `enable password` command when both are used.

Not only do you want to set a password for when someone tries to go into privilege exec mode, but you also want to set a password on each of the different ports that someone may make a connection to in order to gain access to your router; these ports are the console port, auxiliary port, and the Telnet ports used for remote connections.

Console port password

To set the console port to prompt for a password when someone tries to make a connection through it, you use the following commands:

```
RouterA>enable
RouterA#config term

RouterA(config)#line con 0
RouterA(config-line)#password conpass
RouterA(config-line)#login
```

Looking at the preceding commands, you see that you first move to global configuration to make the change. Then you use the `line con 0` command to move into the configuration of the console port. Once you are in the line prompt, you can then specify the password you want for this port.

Make a mental note that you have to specify the `login` command after the password is set — if you do not, the router will not prompt for a password when someone makes a connection to the port. The `login` command is how you turn on authentication for that port and have the Cisco device ask for a password.

During your CCENT certification exam, you will be presented with many configuration scenarios where you see the running-configuration of a device. You will be asked to identify mistakes in the configuration — watch for things like the password on the port being set but the `login` command is missing!

Auxiliary port password

Configuring the auxiliary port for a password is similar to configuring the console port for a password. In order to configure the auxiliary port for a password, use the following commands:

```
RouterA>enable
RouterA#config term

RouterA(config)#line aux 0
RouterA(config-line)#password auxpass
RouterA(config-line)#login
```

You can see the only difference between setting a password on the console port and the auxiliary port is the line aux 0 command. Notice that the login command is supplied and enables authentication on that port.

You can disable authentication on any of the ports (and any type of port) at any time using the no login command.

Telnet password

You set the console port and auxiliary port passwords on the router to help control who can physically connect to those ports and manage the device. Administrators can also Telnet into the router in order to administer the device from a remote location. You need to configure your router for Telnet passwords if someone is going to Telnet into the router using the Telnet ports, also known as the *virtual teletype* (VTY) ports. The following commands configure passwords on the Telnet ports:

```
RouterA>enable
RouterA#config term

RouterA(config)#line vty 0 1180
RouterA(config-line)#password vtypass
RouterA(config-line)#login
```

Cisco devices require you to configure a Telnet password and a password when entering privilege exec mode on the router in order to remotely connect to the router. Cisco devices do not allow you to do remote administration without these passwords set.

Encrypting passwords

Once you have configured the passwords on your router for all the different ports you will notice that the only password that is encrypted is the secret value. This is a problem, as you want to protect all passwords from someone being able to see them when viewing the configuration. This section walks you through how to encrypt all passwords in the configuration of your Cisco switch or router.

Now that we have our passwords set on the router, let us take a look at the running-configuration to verify that the passwords are set.

```
RouterA#show running-config
Building configuration...
!
(output omitted for briefness)
!
enable secret 5 $1$u76B$IOFVJ7VxfVXYVpGDrFTcI0
enable password mypass
!
(output omitted for briefness)
!
line con 0
  password conpass
  login
line aux 0
  password auxpass
  login
line vty 0 4
  password vtypass
  login
line vty 5 1180
  password vtypass
  login
!
(output omitted for briefness)
```

When viewing the running configuration file (or the startup configuration file, for that matter), you see the passwords that have been configured on the router.

From a security point of view, it is important that all passwords are encrypted in the configuration files. In order to encrypt all passwords, you use the `service password-encryption` command, as shown here.

```
RouterA#config term
RouterA(config)#service password-encryption
```

Let's take a look at the running configuration after the passwords have been encrypted.

```
RouterA#show running-config
Building configuration...
!
(output omitted for briefness)
!
enable secret 5 $1$u76B$IOFVJ7VxfVXYVpGDrFTcI0
enable password $1$u76B$IOFVJ7VxfVXYVpGDrFTcI0
!
(output omitted for briefness)
```

```
!
line con 0
  password $1$u76B$IOFVJ7VxfVXYVpGDrFTcI0
  login
line aux 0
  password $1$u76B$IOFVJ7VxfVXYVpGDrFTcI0
  login
line vty 0 4
  password $1$u76B$IOFVJ7VxfVXYVpGDrFTcI0
  login
line vty 5 1180
  password $1$u76B$IOFVJ7VxfVXYVpGDrFTcI0
  login
!
(output omitted for briefness)
```

When looking at the preceding output, you see that all of the passwords have been encrypted.

The CCENT certification exam expects you to know how to encrypt all the passwords in the configuration files with the `service password-encryption` command. Also, know for the exam that you can turn this service off with the `no service password-encryption` command — which does not decrypt the passwords in the configuration until you set them again. In the real world you want to ensure that passwords are being encrypted so I don't recommend turning this off.

Configuring user accounts

If you want to require more than just a password in order to log in to the router, you can create individual usernames and passwords for each administrator who will connect to the router. In order to create the usernames and passwords, use the following commands:

```
RouterA>enable
RouterA#config term
RouterA(config)#username dan password danpass
RouterA(config)#username glen password glenpass
```

Once the usernames and passwords are created, you can then force those *local* usernames (meaning the accounts in the current device) to be used when logging in to the different ports, by using the `login local` command. The following command shows how to enable login access on the console port using the local user accounts that have been configured:

```
RouterA(config)#line con 0
RouterA(config-line)#login local
```

Once you configure the console port for the `login local` command, you are required to have a username and password in order to gain access to the router!

For the CCENT certification exam, know the purpose of the `login local` command and the fact that you can use it on the console, auxiliary, and Telnet ports. Also, when given example code on the exam, watch out for instances where the `login local` command is missing. It is not enough to create the usernames and passwords — you must also configure the different ports to use the local accounts for authentication, by using the `login local` command.

To see a demonstration on configuring passwords with Cisco devices, check out the Configuring Passwords video on the accompanying CD.

Configuring banners

As discussed in Book II, Chapter 2, there are a number of different types of banners that can be used on your Cisco device. To review, *banners* are used to display a message to anyone accessing the Cisco device, and it is a security best practice to give a message indicating that the device is to be accessed by authorized individuals only.

For many years, network administrators have created cute banner messages that include the word *welcome*. For legal reasons, you do not want to display warm, inviting banner messages. If you do, hackers may use this defense in court: *"Honest, your honor. I thought they wanted me to hack the system because the message said 'Welcome to my router'!"*

For the CCENT certification exam, remember that any type of banner message with the word *welcome* in it is a poor configuration choice and a violation of security. Banners should be short, simple messages indicating that unauthorized access to the system is prohibited.

Types of banners

In Book II, Chapter 2 you learned how to configure banners on the Cisco router or switch, let's review banners and then make some important points to remember for the exam!

It is important to know that there are different types of banners that you can configure. Each banner type is designed for a specific purpose and appears at a different time during the logon process:

✦ **Message of the day:** The message of the day banner, known as the MOTD, displays before the administrator is asked to log in. The initial purpose of the MOTD banner was to show a temporary notice to the person connecting, and it could change from time to time. Today, network administrators are using the MOTD banner to display disclaimers that unauthorized access to the system is strictly prohibited!

✦ **Login:** The login banner displays before the administrator is asked to log on but after the MOTD banner (if one is set). The login banner is designed to display a more permanent message, something that will not change from day to day, to the person connecting.

✦ **Exec:** The exec banner, or what I like to refer to as the user exec banner (not an official term by the way), displays after an administrator logs on and enters user exec mode. This type of banner is used to display a message you only want someone who has been authenticated to the system to view. Because the MOTD and login banner appear before a login they are viewable by anyone who connects to the system; the exec banner appears after someone logs on so you know whoever sees the message is an authorized person.

Configuring a banner

Now that you are comfortable with the different types of banners, let's take a look at how to configure the banners on a Cisco router.

You configure banners on a switch the exact same way you do for a router.

The following code is used to configure a MOTD banner on your Cisco device.

```
RouterA(config)#banner motd #
Enter TEXT message.  End with the character '#'.
This device is for authorized personnel only.
Please disconnect at once if you have not been given
    permission to access this device
#
RouterA(config)#
```

Notice that you set the MOTD banner from global configuration mode with the banner motd # command. The # symbol serves as the *delimiter* and indicates what character ends the message when you are typing the message out. Notice that I have two lines of text set as the message of the day and a third line with the # indicating I am done setting the message of the day. You can use whichever character you like as the delimiter as long as you specify it in the banner command.

The following code is used to specify the login banner. Notice that it is very similar to setting the MOTD banner but the keyword `login` is used instead of `motd` in the `banner` command.

```
RouterA(config)#banner login #
Enter TEXT message.  End with the character '#'.
*** Login Required.  Unauthorized use is prohibited ***
#
RouterA(config)#
```

You are not required to set the MOTD banner and the login banner (most companies set one or the other), but if you find that you do have the need to show a unique message on different days then you may set your normal "unauthorized access is prohibited" message as the login banner so that you can have a MOTD banner as well if and when you need it.

Notice in the output below that when someone connects to the router or switch the MOTD is displayed before the login banner:

```
RouterA Con0 is now available
Press RETURN to get started!

This device is for authorized personnel only.  Please
    disconnect at once if you have not been given permission
    to access this device

*** Login Required.  Unauthorized use is prohibited ***

User Access Verification

Password:
```

If you wish to set a user exec password you can use the `banner exec` command. Remember, this exec banner message shows after login as the individual enters user exec mode:

```
RouterA(config)#banner exec #
Enter TEXT message.  End with the character '#'.
*** Be sure to update the change log after any changes ***
#
RouterA(config)#
```

On the CCENT certification exam you are presented with many configurations where you need to identify problems with the configuration. One of the points to watch for is a configuration that involves the banner containing a message welcoming the person connecting. As a security best practice you should never have a message welcoming a connection as it could be used as an excuse by the hacker that they received authorization to access the system when the word *welcome* appeared.

Configuring SSH

In Book II, Chapter 3, you discover how to Telnet into the router or switch and remotely manage the device. Telnet runs on TCP port 23 and sends the data and authentication credentials (username and password) in clear text. This presents a huge security risk, as anyone who taps into the communication can see the username and password needed to log in to the device.

Secure Shell (SSH) is a protocol that is used to encrypt communication between two systems and is a popular replacement for Telnet as Telnet does not encrypt the traffic. You should configure your Cisco devices for SSH and use it instead of Telnet because it encrypts the communication between the client and the Cisco device, including the logon credentials.

Note for the exam that SSH uses TCP port 22.

The first thing you must do to configure SSH on your Cisco router is set your hostname and domain name. These settings are used when the encryption key is created in a future step.

If the hostname and domain name are already set on the device, you are not required to perform the following commands. You can verify these settings by show running-config.

Use these commands to set the hostname and domain name:

```
Router>enable
Router#config term
Router(config)#hostname ROUTERA
RouterA(config)#ip domain-name gleneclarke.com
```

After ensuring the hostname and domain name are set, you create a username and password for an account that will be used to log in remotely to the system via SSH.

```
RouterA(config)#username glen password glenpass
```

After configuring a username and password, you need to generate the encryption key that SSH uses to encrypt the traffic:

```
RouterA(config)#crypto key generate rsa
The name for the keys will be: R1.gleneclarke.com

Choose the size of the key modulus in the range of 360 to
    2048 for your General Purpose Keys. Choosing a key modulus
    greater than 512 may take a few minutes.
```

```
How many bits in the modulus [512]: 1024
% Generating 1024 bit RSA keys, keys will be non-
    exportable...[OK]
```

After generating the encryption key, you configure the Telnet ports to use the local user accounts for authentication (via the `login local` command) and then specify that the Telnet ports accept only SSH as a protocol for remote administration, by using the `transport input ssh` command.

```
RouterA(config)#line vty 0 4
RouterA(config-line)#login local
RouterA(config-line)#transport input ssh
```

The `transport input` command accepts the value of `ssh`, `telnet`, or `none`, or you can use the `all` keyword to support both Telnet and SSH for remote administration.

For the CCENT certification exam, remember that in order to encrypt traffic to your router, you should use SSH instead of Telnet for remote administration. Also remember that Telnet uses TCP port 23, while SSH uses TCP port 22.

Cisco Switch Best Practices

The security concepts discussed in the router sections (such as setting banners, passwords, and using SSH to encrypt traffic between the Cisco device and the system to perform remote administration) of this chapter can be applied to switches as well, so I do not repeat that discussion here. In this section, you find out about the best practices that apply specifically to network switches and their ports. I discuss a number of these concepts in Book III, Chapter 2, so this is a quick section.

Configuring port security

The first point to review about switch security is the fact that you can configure port security on your switches. Port security allows you to configure each port on the switch to allow a connection from a specific MAC address and no other system. Port security is a big part of physical security, as it limits who can physically connect to the network.

In the following code, you see that I am configuring port security for interface f0/5. After navigating to that interface, I then ensure the port is running in access mode, which allows a workstation to connect to the port.

```
SW1>enable
SW1#config term
SW1(config)#interface f0/5
SW1(config-if)#switchport mode access
```

After I place the port in access mode, I then enable the port security feature with the `switchport port-security` command. After enabling port security, I configure the port for a specific MAC address `switchport port-security mac-address MAC_Of_System`. If you do not want to manually input the MAC address, you can use the `sticky` option, which tells the switch to learn the MAC address of the system connected and then configure port security to use that MAC address. The following commands enable port security and use the `sticky` option:

```
SW1(config-if)#switchport port-security
SW1(config-if)#switchport port-security mac-address sticky
```

After you enable port security and configure the MAC address for the port, you then need to limit the port so it allows for only one MAC address in the MAC address table for that port. After that, you specify what happens when a different system connects to that port (a violation), such as having the port disabled if there is a violation. The following commands are the last two commands to configure port security:

```
SW1(config-if)#switchport port-security maximum 1
SW1(config-if)#switchport port-security violation shutdown
```

The following lists all the commands you use to configure port security on port 5 of the switch:

```
SW1>enable
SW1#config term
SW1(config)#interface f0/5
SW1(config-if)#switchport mode access
SW1(config-if)#switchport port-security
SW1(config-if)#switchport port-security mac-address sticky
SW1(config-if)#switchport port-security maximum 1
SW1(config-if)#switchport port-security violation shutdown
```

For the CCENT certification exam, know how to configure port security and especially be familiar with the `sticky` option. The `sticky` option is how you configure the switch to use the MAC address of the system connected to the port, and it saves you the trouble of finding out the MAC of the station.

Disabling ports

Once you configure port security for all the ports used on your network switch, the next step to help secure the switch is to ensure that you have disabled all unused ports. Disabling any ports that are not being used ensures that someone cannot connect to the port and gain network access without your knowledge.

The following commands disable port number 8 on a switch, with the `shutdown` command:

```
SW1>enable
SW1#config term
SW1(config)#interface f0/8
SW1(config-if)#shutdown
11:23:18 %LINK-3-UPDOWN:  Interface FastEthernet0/8, changed
    state to administratively down
11:23:18 %LINEPROTO-5-UPDOWN: Line protocol on Interface
    FastEthernet0/8, changed state to down
```

If you have a number of ports that you wish to disable at one time, you can select a group of ports with the `interface range` command. The following command selects ports 6–12 and disables the ports.

```
SW1(config)#interface range f0/6 - 12
SW1(config-if)#shutdown
```

For the CCENT certification exam, know that all unused ports should be disabled on the network switch. In order to disable ports, you use the `shutdown` command. If you wish to enable the port, you use the `no shutdown` command.

Chapter Summary

This chapter illustrates the importance of good security practices when configuring your Cisco device. These concepts are important from an exam point of view, but also for the real world:

✦ Ensure you are using complex passwords.

✦ The `enable secret` command creates an encrypted password in the configuration file that is used to enter priv exec mode. The `enable secret` command takes precedence over the `enable password` command.

✦ You can configure a console password on your router so that anyone connecting to the console port must supply a password.

✦ You should also set auxiliary and Telnet passwords so that anyone connecting through those methods must also supply a password.

✦ Remember, after setting the password for the console, auxiliary, and Telnet ports, use the `login` command so that the Cisco device prompts for login to the port.

✦ If you create usernames and passwords, you must use the `login local` command on the ports to indicate you wish to use the local accounts for authentication.

✦ Ensure that the banner messages do not contain any form of welcome message and that they notify the individual connecting to the system that authorized persons only are to connect to the system.

✦ SSH should be used instead of Telnet because the traffic is encrypted when SSH is used.

✦ Configure port security on a port so that only the system with a particular MAC address can connect to the port.

✦ Disable any unused ports on the switch so that nonauthorized systems cannot connect to the switch.

Lab Exercises

This chapter introduces a number of settings on the Cisco routers and switches that aid in the security of the devices. The following exercises are designed to help you practice implementing those best practices.

Lab 2-1: Configuring passwords

1. Connect to your router and configure the following passwords:

• *Console password:* con

• *Auxiliary password:* aux

• *Telnet password:* telnet

• *Enable password:* enable

• *Secret password:* secret

The following commands should have been used to configure the passwords on your router:

```
RouterA>enable
RouterA#config term
RouterA(config)#enable password enable
RouterA(config)#enable secret secret

RouterA(config)#line con 0
RouterA(config-line)#password con
RouterA(config-line)#login

RouterA(config)#line aux 0
RouterA(config-line)#password aux
RouterA(config-line)#login
```

```
RouterA(config)#line vty 0 1180
RouterA(config-line)#password telnet
RouterA(config-line)#login
```

2. **Once you configure the passwords, go back to priv exec mode and show your running-config.**

   Do you see the passwords in the configuration?

3. **The passwords have been stored in clear text, so in order to encrypt the passwords, go to global configuration and type the following command:**

   ```
   RouterA(config)#service password-encryption
   ```

4. **Verify the passwords are encrypted by displaying your running configuration.**

   Are the passwords encrypted?

Lab 2-2: Configuring banners

Configure a banner on your router so that anyone connecting to your router sees a notice indicating the system is to be accessed by authorized persons only.

1. **Fill in the table below identifying the purpose of the three different banner types listed:**

Banner Type	*Purpose*
Login	
MOTD	
Exec	

2. **Use the following commands to configure a MOTD banner on your router:**

   ```
   RouterA(config)#banner motd #
   Lab 2-2 - This device is for authorized personnel only.
   Please disconnect at once if you have not been given
       permission to access this device.
   #
   RouterA(config)#
   ```

3. **Disconnect from the router and then connect again.**

   Do you see the MOTD banner?

Lab 2-3: Reviewing router configuration

You have been asked to review the running-configuration of a router. Looking at the output of the show running-config command, identify any potential security issues with the configuration.

```
RouterB#show running-config

Building configuration...

(output ommitted for briefness)
service timestamps log datetime msec
no service password-encryption
!
hostname RouterB
!
ip subnet-zero
!
interface FastEthernet0/1
  ip address 27.0.0.1 255.0.0.0
  no ip directed-broadcast
!
interface Serial0/0/0
  ip address 26.0.0.2 255.0.0.0
  no ip directed-broadcast
!
router rip
 network 26.0.0.0
 network 27.0.0.0
!
banner motd
Welcome to Glen's router!  You have connected to 192.168.0.1!
!
line con 0
  password myc0nP@ss

line aux 0
line vty 0 4
  password telnet
  login
end
```

Lab 2-4: Configuring port security

1. **Ensure that only a system with the MAC address of 1111.2222.3333 can connect to port number 3 on the switch. Use the following commands to secure port number 3:**

```
SW1>enable
SW1#config term
SW1(config)#interface f0/3
SW1(config-if)#switchport mode access
SW1(config-if)#switchport port-security
SW1(config-if)#switchport port-security mac-address 1111.2222.3333
SW1(config-if)#switchport port-security maximum 1
SW1(config-if)#switchport port-security violation shutdown
```

2. **Configure port number 4 to allow only the system that is currently connected to the port to connect to that port, using the `sticky` option. Use the following command to configure port number 4:**

```
SW1#config term
SW1(config)#interface f0/4
SW1(config-if)#switchport mode access
SW1(config-if)#switchport port-security
SW1(config-if)#switchport port-security mac-address sticky
SW1(config-if)#switchport port-security maximum 1
SW1(config-if)#switchport port-security violation shutdown
```

3. **Use the following commands to disable port number 5:**

```
SW1#config term
SW1(config)#interface f0/4
SW1(config-if)#shutdown
```

Prep Test

1 **What command do you use to configure the Cisco router to prompt for a username and a password?**

A ○ router(config)#login local

B ○ router(config-line)#login local

C ○ router(config)#login

D ○ router(config)#login local

2 **What command encrypts all passwords in the configuration files?**

A ○ router#service password-encryption

B ○ router(config)#enable service password-encryption

C ○ router#enable service password-encryption

D ○ router(config)#service password-encryption

3 **What option on your Cisco switch allows you to configure port security to automatically use the MAC address of a system connected to the switch?**

A ○ SW1(config-if)#switchport port-security mac-address sticky

B ○ SW1(config-if)#switchport port-security

C ○ SW1(config-if)#mac-address sticky

D ○ SW1(config-if)#port-security mac-address automatic

4 **Which of the following commands configure a password on your console port and ensure that the router prompts for a password anytime someone connects to that port?**

A ○ RouterA(config)#password con
RouterA(config)#login

B ○ RouterA(config)#line vty 0 4
RouterA(config-line)#password con
RouterA(config-line)#login

C ○ RouterA(config)#line con 0
RouterA(config-line)#password con
RouterA(config-line)#login

D ○ RouterA(config)#line con 0
RouterA(config-line)#password con

5 **What command disables a port on the switch?**

A ○ `switch(config)#shutdown port 5`

B ○ `switch(config-if)#shutdown`

C ○ `switch(config)#port 5 shutdown`

D ○ `switch(config-if)#disable`

6 **Which of the following commands create a username and password on the router?**

A ○ `router(config)#enable user rebecca password mypass`

B ○ `router(config-if)#username rebecca password mypass`

C ○ `router(config)#create user Rebecca password mypass`

D ○ `router(config)#username rebecca password mypass`

7 **Which of the following banners is displayed last?**

A ○ Exec banner

B ○ Login banner

C ○ MOTD banner

D ○ All banners are shown at the same time.

8 **Which of the following commands do you use to ensure that remote access to the router is only through secure communications?**

A ○ `router(config)#transport input ssh`

B ○ `router(config-line)#transport input ssh`

C ○ `router(config-line)#transport input both`

D ○ `router(config-line)#transport input telnet`

9 **Which of the following port modes support the port security feature?**

A ○ secure

B ○ trunk

C ○ access

D ○ workstation

10 Which of the following code examples create a username and password that is required for Telnet access?

A ○ `RouterA(config)#username bob password pass`
   `RouterA(config)#line con 0`
   `RouterA(config-line)#login local`

B ○ `RouterA(config)#username bob password pass`
   `RouterA(config)#line vty 0 4`
   `RouterA(config-line)#login`

C ○ `RouterA#username bob password pass`
   `RouterA#config term`
   `RouterA(config)#line vty 0 4`
   `RouterA(config-line)#login`

D ○ `RouterA(config)#username bob password pass`
   `RouterA(config)#line vty 0 4`
   `RouterA(config-line)#login local`

Answers

1 **B.** The `login local` command is used on the console port, Telnet port, or auxiliary port to ensure a username and password is required. *See "Configuring user accounts."*

2 **D.** The `server password-encryption` command is used in global configuration to ensure that all passwords are encrypted. *Review "Configuring passwords."*

3 **A.** You need to use the `sticky` option on the `switchport port-security mac-address` command within the interface prompt for the interface you are configuring a MAC address for. *Check out "Configuring port security."*

4 **C.** You must set the password in the console line prompt but then ensure you use the `login` command to configure the Cisco device to require the password for authentication. *Peruse "Console port password."*

5 **B.** The `shutdown` command at the interface prompt disables a port. *Take a look at "Disabling ports."*

6 **D.** To create a username and password on the router, you can use the `username` command in global configuration mode. *Peek at "Configuring user accounts."*

7 **A.** The exec banner is the last banner of the ones listed to display. It displays after an administrator logs on and as he enters user exec mode. *Look over "Types of banners."*

8 **B.** To ensure that only secure communication is used to remotely connect to the router, you must configure SSH but also configure the vty ports to use only SSH as the transport protocol. *Study "Configuring SSH."*

9 **C.** A port must be placed in access mode before you can configure port security on it. *Refer to "Configuring port security."*

10 **D.** The username and password is created in global configuration mode, but to ensure that anyone connecting through Telnet is prompted for a username and password, you must navigate to the Telnet ports and use the `login local` command. *Examine "Configuring user accounts."*

Chapter 3: Wireless Networking

In This Chapter

✔ Looking at wireless terminology

✔ Introduction to wireless standards

✔ Understanding wireless configuration

✔ Wireless security protocols

*I*n this chapter, you find out about the different technologies and protocols surrounding building a wireless network. The CCENT certification exam expects you to have a sound understanding of the theory required to create a wireless network.

You first become familiar with wireless network concepts and terminology before identifying design considerations surrounding wireless networking. You finish the chapter by discovering the different wireless security protocols.

Quick Assessment

1   (True/False). A wireless access point is needed to have a wireless network.

2   A(n) _____ is a wireless network with a single access point that is connected to a wired network.

3   The _____ is responsible for defining the wireless standards.

4   (True/False). The SSID is the name assigned to the wireless network.

Answers

1   *False*. See "Types of wireless networks."

2   *IBSS*. Review "Basic configuration overview."

3   *IEEE*. Check out "Wireless agencies."

4   *True*. Peruse "Wireless access point."

Looking at Wireless Terminology

In this section, I start the discussion by overviewing the concept of wireless networking and the agencies that govern it. I also discuss some of the hardware that typically exists in a wireless network, including wireless access points and clients. I finish the discussion with an introduction to the two types of wireless network topology.

The CCENT certification exam expects you to know only the basics of wireless networking, so if you are comfortable with this chapter and the concepts discussed here, you should have no problem with the wireless portion of the exam!

Wireless concepts

There are a number of different wireless technologies out there, but when it comes to wireless LANS (WLANs), understand that any WLAN uses radio frequencies that travel through the air as radio waves. This means that you do not need a direct line of sight to the system you are communicating with, as the radio waves travel through walls (unlike infrared, which is line of sight).

Wireless agencies

Wireless communication and its related technologies are governed by a number of different agencies. The following is a listing of some of the popular wireless agencies to know for the CCENT certification exam:

✦ **IEEE:** The IEEE (Institute of Electrical and Electronics Engineers) is responsible for creating the different wireless networking standards such as 802.11b, 802.11g, and 802.11n. (See the "Introduction to Wireless Standards" section, later in this chapter, for more on these standards.) You can find out more about the IEEE at www.ieee.org.

✦ **Wi-Fi Alliance:** The Wi-Fi Alliance is responsible for ensuring compatibility and interoperability of wireless networking components. The organization also tests and certifies components for Wi-Fi compatibility. You can discover more about the Wi-Fi Alliance at www.wi-fi.com.

✦ **Federal Communications Commission:** The Federal Communications Commission (FCC) is a very important agency that regulates the use of wireless devices and frequencies. The FCC has defined three frequency ranges that are free for public use: the 900 MHz, 2.4 GHz, and 5 GHz frequency ranges. It is important to understand that if you are looking to implement a wireless solution outside of those frequency ranges, you must acquire a license to do so from the FCC.

+ **International Telecommunications Union:** The International Telecommunications Union (ITU) is a United Nations agency that is responsible for developing international standards and regulations surrounding the telecommunications field. The ITU works alongside the FCC to help develop international wireless standards.

For the CCENT certification exam, be sure to know that the Wi-Fi Alliance is responsible for testing and certification of Wi-Fi-compatible components, and the FCC is responsible for regulating the use of wireless devices and frequencies.

Wireless LAN frequencies

As mentioned in the previous section, the FCC has licensed three frequencies for public use: the 900 MHz, 2.4 GHz, and 5 GHz ranges. It is important to note that these are frequency ranges, and wireless components are designed to use a frequency range.

For example, the most popular frequency range for wireless networks is 2.4 GHz. This frequency range is divided into a number of different channels, with each channel running on a different 22 MHz frequency within the 2.4 GHz frequency range.

Table 3-1 outlines the different channels provided in the 2.4 GHz frequency range and the frequency range of each channel. The important thing to note is that cordless phones run at the 2.4 GHz range as well, so you may experience issues with your wireless network due to a cordless phone causing interference. What can you do about it? The answer is simple; you can change your wireless network to run on a different channel, which places the network in a different frequency and hopefully solves the interference problem with the cordless phone.

Table 3-1	The 2.4 GHz Frequency Ranges
Channel	*Frequency Range*
1	2.3995 GHz–2.4245 GHz
2	2.4045 GHz–2.4295 GHz
3	2.4095 GHz–2.4345 GHz
4	2.4145 GHz–2.4395 GHz
5	2.4195 GHz–2.4445 GHz
6	2.4245 GHz–2.4495 GHz
7	2.4295 GHz–2.4545 GHz
8	2.4345 GHz–2.4595 GHz

**Book IV
Chapter 3**

**Wireless
Networking**

(continued)

Table 3-1 *(continued)*

Channel	Frequency Range
9	2.4395 GHz–2.4645 GHz
10	2.4445 GHz–2.4695 GHz
11	2.4495 GHz–2.4745 GHz
12	2.4545 GHz–2.4795 GHz
13	2.4595 GHz–2.4845 GHz

When looking at Table 3-1, notice there is overlapping between the frequencies in most of the channels. For example, the first channel starts at frequency 2.3995 and goes to 2.4245. This is within the same frequency range of channel 2, which starts at 2.4045. Figure 3-1 visually displays the overlapping of frequencies and their associated channels.

Figure 3-1: Overlapping frequencies in the 2.4 GHz frequency range.

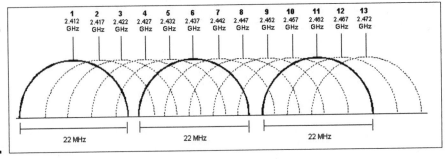

The reason I stress the overlapping of the frequencies is that when you modify the channel on your wireless network to try to eliminate the interference with the cordless phone, it is recommended to jump a few channels ahead or behind your current channel so you are in a totally different range. Also notice in Figure 3-1 the frequencies that do not overlap one another (they are the bolded lines) — these frequencies map out to channels 1, 6, and 11. If you need to configure multiple access points to run on different channels, these channels make great choices, as there should be no interference between them because they do not overlap one another.

Wireless equipment

When creating a wireless network, you will need in your possession some popular wireless equipment such as a wireless access point (depending on the type of wireless network you create — more on the types of wireless networks in a bit), and a wireless client, which is a system with a wireless network card used to connect to the wireless network.

Wireless access point

The first wireless equipment to mention is a very popular device known as a *wireless access point,* which has antennas to send and receive the wireless traffic but also normally has a network port to connect the access point to the wired network. A wireless access point allows wireless clients to connect to a wireless network and access resources on the wired network and vice versa. (See Figure 3-2.)

The wireless access point is configured with a *service set identifier* (SSID), which acts as a name for the wireless network. In order for wireless clients to connect to the wireless access point, they must specify the name of the wireless network, or SSID. This is not much of a security feature, as the SSID is broadcasted onto the network by default.

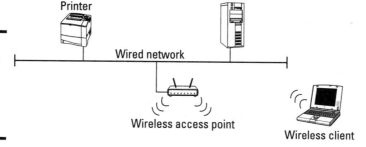

Figure 3-2: A wireless access point on the wired network.

Wireless clients

The other type of wireless equipment to discuss is *wireless clients,* which are systems that have a wireless network card installed; wireless network cards are configured to connect to the access point or even to other wireless clients directly. When a wireless client accesses a device such as a printer or server on the wired network, the information is sent to the wireless access point from the wireless client, and then onto the wired network.

Book IV Chapter 3

Wireless Networking

Types of wireless networks

When you design your wireless network you can choose from one of two different network topologies, known as *modes:* ad hoc and infrastructure.

+ **Ad hoc:** With the *ad hoc* wireless network topology, you do not have a wireless access point on the network — the wireless devices connect directly to one another in a peer-to-peer type of configuration.

+ **Infrastructure:** With *infrastructure mode,* the wireless clients and devices connect to a wireless access point by the SSID and access the wireless network through the access point.

Introduction to Wireless Standards

Wireless networking standards have been around for quite some time now, and like anything else that is technology driven, it is something that has been improving over the years. The Institute of Electrical and Electronic Engineers (IEEE) is responsible for defining networking standards, including the standards that govern wireless networking.

Wireless networking falls under the IEEE 802.11 project model. A number of different wireless standards have been developed over the years, and I discuss the most recent wireless standards in the following sections.

Table 3-2 also summarizes the different wireless standards.

Table 3-2	Wireless Network Standards			
	802.11a	*802.11b*	*802.11g*	*802.11n*
Frequency	5 GHz	2.4 GHz	2.4 GHz	2.4/5 GHz
Transfer Rate	54 Mbps	11 Mbps	54 Mbps	150 Mbps
Range	150 feet	300 feet	300 feet	300 feet
Compatibility	802.11n	802.11g/n	802.11b/n	802.11a/b/g

802.11a

The first major wireless networking standard is known as the *802.11a* network standard. It runs at 54 Mbps but uses the 5 GHz frequency range, as opposed the popular 2.4 GHz range. Wireless 802.11a devices are incompatible with 802.11b and 802.11g devices but are compatible with 802.11n devices.

802.11b

The next wireless standard is the *802.11b* wireless standard, which runs at 11 Mbps and uses the 2.4GHz frequency. Because 802.11b uses a different frequency range than 802.11a, they are incompatible with one another. For example, you cannot connect a client using an 802.11a network card to an 802.11b access point. 802.11b devices are compatible with 802.11g and 802.11n devices.

The 802.11b standard has become the Wi-Fi standard, and as future standards and technologies are developed, they will be part of the Wi-Fi standard.

802.11g

The 802.11g standard follows the Wi-Fi standard and is therefore compatible with the 802.11b wireless standard. 802.11g runs at 54 Mbps and uses the 2.4 GHz frequency that is used by 802.11b (which is one of the reasons why they are compatible). 802.11g is also compatible with 802.11n, but it is not compatible with 802.11a.

802.11n

At the time of this writing, 802.11n is the most current wireless standard, and it is compatible with 802.11a, 802.11b, and 802.11g because it can run at either the 2.4 GHz frequency or the 5 GHz frequency. 802.11n has a number of new features that help increase the transfer rate, including a feature called *channel bonding,* which allows the device to send data over multiple channels. The 802.11n standard has a transfer rate of 150 Mbps!

For the CCENT certification exam, know the differences in the 802.11a/b/g/n wireless network standards. Be familiar with the fact that 802.11b/g/n are compatible with one another.

Wireless Configuration and Troubleshooting

Now that you have an understanding of the different wireless network standards created by the IEEE, lets take a look at the basic configuration and troubleshooting of a wireless network. As I discuss in the text that follows, you can configure a wireless network with one access point, or multiple access points if you need to cover a larger area. And when you're trouble-shooting wireless network problems, you can use the steps I provide to figure out what is wrong.

Basic configuration overview

Basic Service Set, or BSS, is the term we use in the wireless world for a wireless network that uses a single wireless access point with an SSID configured. (See Figure 3-3.) If you have two access points, with each access point configured to a unique SSID, this creates two different Basic Service Sets. Also note that an access point connected to a wired network with a unique SSID is known as an *Infrastructure Basic Service Set* (IBSS).

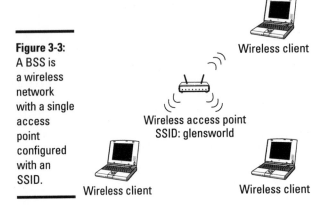

Figure 3-3:
A BSS is a wireless network with a single access point configured with an SSID.

Wireless client

Wireless access point
SSID: glensworld

Wireless client

Wireless client

For the CCENT certification exam, know that a single access point creates a *Basic Service Set* (BSS). If this access point is connected to a wired network, it creates an *Infrastructure Basic Service Set* (IBSS)

Designing a multi-access point WLAN

If you need a wireless network to cover a large area, you may need to create a wireless network with multiple wireless access points that use the same SSID. A wireless network with multiple access points using the same SSID is known as an *Extended Service Set* (ESS). Figure 3-4 displays an ESS wireless network.

When you configure multiple access points using the same SSID positioned throughout the facility, it allows clients to roam from one end of the facility to the other and not lose network connectivity. Before the roaming clients get too far from one access point, they move into the range of the next access point and are switched over to that access point without losing a network connection.

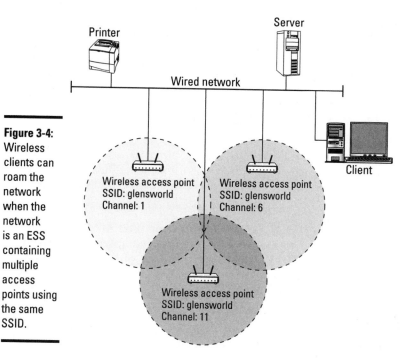

Figure 3-4: Wireless clients can roam the network when the network is an ESS containing multiple access points using the same SSID.

In order to configure an ESS wireless network that supports roaming users, the following conditions must be met:

+ **You must configure multiple access points with the same SSID.**

+ **The access points must overlap coverage areas by 10 percent or more so the wireless client does not lose a network connection.**

+ **Each wireless access point must be configured for a different channel.**

Notice in Figure 3-4 that each access point is connected to the wired network and has an SSID of glensworld configured. You also see that each access point is configured for different channels and that I have selected channels that I know do not overlap frequencies with one another.

For the CCENT certification exam, be sure to know the requirements to configure an ESS to support roaming users. You must have the same SSID set on all access points, with each access point using a different channel. The area covered by the access point must overlap by 10 percent or more.

Troubleshooting wireless networks

When you are having trouble connecting a wireless client to a wireless network, a number of things could be the cause of the problem. The following outlines some of the settings to verify when troubleshooting a client that cannot connect to a wireless network:

1. **Ensure that you have configured the client to connect to the correct SSID name.**

2. **If you are sure you have the correct SSID name, ensure that you have enabled the same encryption protocol that is configured on the access point, and ensure that you have specified the correct encryption key.**

   You can find more on this in the next section.

3. **If you have verified all the settings and you have not connected to this network in the past, it is possible that you are not authorized to connect. Most wireless networks will limit who can connect by MAC address — you will need to add your MAC address to the access point's MAC address filter list.**

If you are experiencing intermittent problems where you lose your connection with the wireless network, it could be due to interference with a device that uses the same frequency, such as a cordless phone. You can change the channel on your wireless network to use a different frequency than the phone. If you are purchasing new cordless phones, ensure you buy phones that use a different frequency than the 2.4 frequency range.

Wireless Security Practices

In this section, you find out about general practices you can take to secure your wireless network. You will also read about the different encryption protocols that you can use to encrypt wireless traffic.

General security practices

Wireless networks have a default characteristic of being unsecure by nature — this is known as *open* security. The concept of a wireless network is to allow someone who is not connected physically to the network to access network resources. This is great from a convenience point of view, but the security folks in the company do not like it! With a wireless network, you essentially lose the physical security aspect of requiring someone to be in the office to gain network access. The following are some steps you can take to help create a more secure wireless network.

Change the SSID

Most wireless access points have a default SSID, which makes it very easy for someone who wants to connect to your wireless network to do so. In order to make it harder for someone to connect to your wireless network, alter the SSID from the default value to something unique and not easily guessed. Remember, in order for someone to connect, she needs to know the SSID.

Disable SSID broadcasting

The problem with changing the SSID is that the access point is, by default, configured to broadcast that SSID name out on the network. This means that clients can browse the network to find the SSID even after you have changed it. In order to lock down the SSID a bit more, you can configure the access point to not broadcast the SSID. This means that clients will not see your wireless network when they browse for wireless networks.

Relying on changing the SSID and disabling SSID is a false sense of security. Keep in mind that wireless traffic is in the air for your wireless network, and there are tools such as Kismet that can still identify the wireless network even though you have disabled SSID broadcasting. (This just keeps the honest folks out.) You must use other forms of security in addition to disabling SSID broadcasting.

Restrict by MAC

Another step you can take to add a layer of security to your wireless network is to configure the wireless access point with a list of MAC addresses that are allowed to connect to the wireless network. Once you have configured MAC filtering on the wireless access point, any system that does not have a listed MAC address is denied access to the network when it attempts to connect.

MAC filtering by itself is not a very secure feature, as a hacker can use a program such as Kismet to view a list of clients and their MAC addresses that are connected to your network. Once the hacker sees the MAC addresses of valid clients on the network, he can then spoof the address so it looks like traffic from that system is one of those clients.

Enable encryption

A very popular technique for securing the wireless network is to implement *encryption* (converting readable text to unreadable text) on the wireless network. When you configure the access point for an encryption protocol, you specify a *pre-shared key,* or *passphrase,* that is required by anyone who wishes to connect to the wireless network. Any clients who connect with that key can access the wireless network, and all the traffic from the wireless client to the access point is encrypted traffic.

It is important to stress the two security benefits of using encryption. The first benefit is that only those who know the passphrase, or encryption key, connect. The other benefit is that those clients that have been configured with the same encryption key are sending and receiving encrypted traffic with the access point.

Encryption protocols

Most secured wireless networks use some form of encryption protocol to encrypt the traffic between the wireless client and the wireless access point. In this section, I introduce you to some of the popular wireless security protocols.

WEP

The first wireless security protocol to discuss is the *Wired Equivalent Privacy* (WEP) protocol, which is very popular with 802.11b devices. WEP uses a *pre-shared* key (meaning you must tell the client the key in order to connect) assigned on the access point and the client to encrypt and decrypt the traffic. The preshared key is required at the client in order for the client to connect to the network.

WEP supports 64-bit or 128-bit encryption and uses the RC4 symmetric encryption protocol.

WPA

The WEP encryption protocol has some flaws in how it performs the encryption, so the Wi-Fi Alliance created the Wi-Fi Protected Access (WPA) protocol. WPA uses the *Temporal Key Integrity Protocol* (TKIP), which is a protocol that changes the encryption key (known as *key rotation*) with every packet sent to try to make it harder for hackers to crack the key.

There are two different modes for WPA, with each mode providing a different level of security:

+ **Personal:** With personal mode, also known as *WPA-PSK* (the *PSK* portion stands for pre-shared key), WPA uses a shared key as a starting value and then changes it with each packet. Personal mode is popular with home networking and small-office environments.

✦ **Enterprise:** With enterprise mode, WPA uses a central server to authenticate anyone connecting to the wireless network. The central server that the wireless access point uses for authentication is known as a *Remote Authentication Dial In User Service (RADIUS) server,* which is also a popular server for Remote Access Service (RAS) authentication. RADIUS is a service that provides authentication services to many different technologies such as wireless and dial-in services (RAS services). Running your wireless network in enterprise mode and using an authentication server for network access is known as the *802.1x standard.*

WPA2

The Wi-Fi Alliance updated the WPA protocol to WPA2 and added some improvements to the protocol, such as the fact that WPA2 uses the *Advanced Encryption Standard* (AES) protocol, which has yet to be cracked. AES supports 128-bit, 192-bit, and 256-bit encryption! Like WPA, WPA2 also supports both personal and enterprise modes.

For the CCENT certification exam, know that WEP uses RC4 as the encryption algorithm, WPA uses TKIP and has a key-rotation feature, and WPA2 uses AES as the encryption algorithm.

Chapter Summary

This chapter is designed to give you the background in wireless networking needed to pass the CCENT certification exam. The following are some key points to remember when preparing for the exam:

✦ The IEEE defines the wireless standards such as 802.11a/b/g/n.

✦ The FCC regulates the use of wireless components and frequencies.

✦ The Wi-Fi Alliance is responsible for testing and certifying wireless components for Wi-Fi compatibility.

✦ Wireless networks can run in ad hoc or infrastructure mode. *Ad hoc* networks do not use a wireless access point, while *infrastructure* mode does.

✦ The *SSID* is the name assigned to a wireless network.

✦ The term used for a wireless network that has a single access point using a single SSID is *BSS,* while a wireless network with multiple access points using the same SSID is called an *ESS.*

✦ In order to allow users to roam between access points on an ESS network, you must assign the same SSID to each access point, but use different channels. You must overlap coverage 10 percent or more.

✦ Be sure to review the different wireless standards such as 802.11b/g/n.

✦ Know the difference in WEP, WPA, and WPA2 for the exam.

Prep Test

1 Which of the following are requirements for an ESS network?

- **A** ❑ Use multiple access points with different SSIDs.
- **B** ❑ Use multiple access points with the same SSIDs.
- **C** ❑ Each access point uses a different frequency range.
- **D** ❑ Each access point uses the same frequency range.
- **E** ❑ Access points must overlap by 10 percent or greater.
- **F** ❑ Access points must overlap by less than 10 percent.

2 Which wireless standard runs at 54 Mbps and is compatible with 802.11b?

- **A** ○ 802.11a
- **B** ○ 802.11x
- **C** ○ 802.11g
- **D** ○ 802.11n

3 Which agency is responsible for regulating the use of wireless and wireless frequencies?

- **A** ○ Wi-Fi Alliance
- **B** ○ IEEE
- **C** ○ IETF
- **D** ○ FCC

4 Which wireless protocol uses the TKIP protocol?

- **A** ○ WEP
- **B** ○ WPA2
- **C** ○ WPA
- **D** ○ AES

5 Which type of wireless network uses a single wireless access point with an SSID assigned?

- **A** ○ BSS
- **B** ○ ESS
- **C** ○ TKIP
- **D** ○ FCC

6 **Which WPA mode uses a RADIUS server for authentication?**

A ○ Personal

B ○ Enterprise

C ○ WPA-PSK

D ○ BSS

7 **Which wireless network standard runs at 54 Mbps and uses the 5 GHz frequency?**

A ○ 802.11a

B ○ 802.11b

C ○ 802.11g

D ○ 802.11n

8 **Which wireless encryption protocol uses AES for encryption?**

A ○ WEP

B ○ WPA2

C ○ WPA

D ○ TKIP

9 **Which agency is responsible for ensuring compatibility with wireless networking components?**

A ○ Wi-Fi Alliance

B ○ IEEE

C ○ IETF

D ○ FCC

10 **Which type of wireless network supports roaming users by having multiple access points share the same SSID?**

A ○ BSS

B ○ ESS

C ○ TKIP

D ○ FCC

Answers

1 **B, C, E.** In order to have users roam a wireless network and jump from one access point to another in the ESS, you configure multiple access points with the same SSID, each having a different frequency range (or channel), and they must overlap by 10 percent or more. *See "Designing a multi-access point WLAN."*

2 **C.** 802.11g runs at 54 Mbps and is compatible with 802.11b devices because it runs at the same frequency range of 2.4 GHz. *Review "802.11g."*

3 **D.** The FCC is responsible for regulating the use of wireless and wireless frequencies. It is the governing body that legalized public use of the 900 MHz, 2.4 GHz, and 5 GHz frequencies. *Check out "Wireless agencies."*

4 **C.** WPA uses the TKIP protocol as part of the encryption process. TKIP is responsible for changing the preshared key with each packet sent. *Peruse "WPA."*

5 **A.** The Basic Service Set (BSS) is the type of wireless network that has a single access point with an SSID assigned. *Take a look at "Basic configuration overview."*

6 **B.** WPA enterprise mode is the mode that uses a central authentication server such as a RADIUS server. *Peek at "WPA."*

7 **A.** The 802.11a wireless standard runs at 54 Mbps in the 5 GHz frequency range. *Look over "802.11a."*

8 **B.** WPA2 is the more secure encryption protocol of the three major protocols (WEP, WPA, and WPA2) and uses the Advanced Encryption Standard (AES). *Study "WPA2."*

9 **A.** The Wi-Fi Alliance is responsible for testing and certifying wireless components for Wi-Fi compatibility. *Refer to "Wireless agencies."*

10 **B.** The Extended Service Set (ESS) is the term used for a wireless network that supports roaming users by having multiple access points use the same SSID. Remember that you must configure each access point to use a different channel, and they must have overlapping coverage of 10 percent or more. *Examine "Designing a multi-access point WLAN."*

Chapter 4: Introduction to WANs

In This Chapter

✓ Introduction to WAN terminology

✓ Methods of connecting to WANs

✓ Configuring serial links

*T*he CCENT certification exam expects you to have a basic understanding of the purpose of a Wide Area Network (WAN) and the different WAN technologies that connect your network to the WAN. This chapter is designed to give you the background to answer the WAN-related questions presented to you on the CCENT certification exam and review the configuration of the serial port, which is typically used in a WAN environment.

Quick Assessment

1   (True/False). The clock rate on a serial link is set by the DCE device.

2   _____ is an example of a circuit switched network environment.

3   When configuring the serial port on a Cisco router, you need to configure the _____ protocol.

Answers

1   *True*. See "Setting the clock rate."

2   *ISDN*. Review "Circuit switching."

3   *Encapsulation*. Check out "Serial link protocols."

Introduction to WAN Terminology

The term *wide area network* (WAN) is used to define a network that is made up of two or more LANs that are geographically separated. The LANs that are connected together in a WAN environment typically have great distances between them, making it impossible for you to use normal network media to connect them. This means that you end up needing to use a service provider's network as the physical connection between the LANs in different offices, as shown in Figure 4-1.

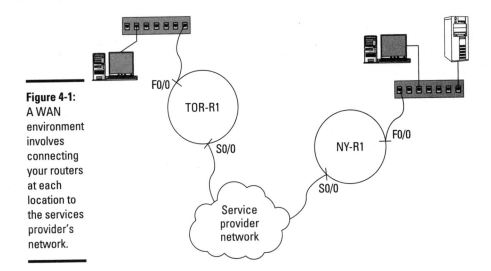

Figure 4-1: A WAN environment involves connecting your routers at each location to the services provider's network.

Looking at Figure 4-1, you see that the office in New York uses the service provider's network, such as your telco, to connect to the network environment in Toronto. When the traffic travels from New York to Toronto, the traffic leaves the WAN port on the router (in this case, it is the serial port) and enters into the service provider's network. The provider's network is made up of a number of different routers and switches. Your data travels through the service provider's network and reaches your router in Toronto via its WAN port. (Again, in this example, it is the serial port on the Toronto router.)

The service provider offers a number of different choices for this subscription service. You can purchase a not-so-permanent solution where you have to establish a network connection each time data is sent from one LAN to another, and you pay for only the time you use the connection (*circuit switching*). Alternatively, you can purchase a dedicated connection that is always there whether you use it or not (*leased line*). Or you can subscribe to a *packet-switching solution,* which sends packets along different pathways to reach the destination. The following sections identify the different types of WAN technologies, including circuit switching, leased lines, and packet switching.

Circuit switching

The concept of *circuit switching* is that when you need to send and receive data between two points, you first establish a connection between the two points, and then send and receive the information. The information travels the same pathway the entire time, and you are guaranteed to have the bandwidth along that pathway to your network — you do not share this bandwidth with any other customers of the circuit switching network.

Circuit-based networks are designed for scenarios where you have low bandwidth requirements as you pay for the bandwidth allocated and the time you are connected to the WAN.

It is important to stress that with circuit switching, you do not pay for the service when you are not connected.

Examples of technologies based on circuit switch networks are the telephone system and *Integrated Services Digital Network* (ISDN), which is a system of digital telephone connections that carry voice and data. ISDN carries data over channels known as *B-channels,* which are 64 Kbps, and the signaling information is carried over what is known as a *D-channel* (16 Kbps or 64 Kbps, depending on the implementation). There are two major types of subscriptions to ISDN:

+ **Basic Rate Interface (BRI):** With BRI, you have two, 64-Kbps B-channels and one signaling channel (D-channel) of 16 Kbps. This gives you a 128 Kbps data connection.

+ **Primary Rate Interface (PRI):** A PRI subscription uses twenty-three, 64 Kbps data channels (B-channels) and one 64-Kbps D-channel for signaling information.

Remember for the CCENT exam that the phone system and an ISDN network are examples of circuit switching technologies.

Leased lines

Companies that send information across the WAN link constantly find that circuit switching is not cost effective (as you pay while you are using it). When this is the case, it is usually more beneficial to pay the monthly fee to have a dedicated link to your service provider's network — this is known as a *leased line* or *point-to-point link.*

With a leased line, you pay the monthly fee to the service provider to allocate dedicated links with dedicated bandwidth to your company's network. For example, if you are the administrator of the network shown back in Figure 4-1 and you pay a monthly fee for a leased line between Toronto and New York, this dedicated link is a pre-established connection that has a dedicated path for the information sent between your two office locations.

A leased line typically has more bandwidth assigned than a circuit switch environment offers, and it sends voice and data. Examples of leased lines include T1 and T3 links:

+ **T1 link:** Consists of 24 channels that carry data, with each channel offering 64 Kbps of bandwidth. The total bandwidth of a T1 link is 1.544 Mbps (24 × 64 Kbps). If your company cannot afford or justify the cost of a T1 link, you can get a fractional T1, which allows the company to subscribe to a few channels and not all 24.

+ **T3 link:** Leased line that offers a total bandwidth of 44.736 Mbps. A T3 link is made up of twenty-eight T1 lines that are combined together to create the 44.736 Mbps.

Packet switching

A packet switch network is different from a circuit switch network and leased line in the sense that with a circuit switch network (and leased line), once the circuit is created, all data delivered takes the same pathway. With *packet switched networks,* the data is sent along different pathways within the provider's network and assembled at the destination. (See Figure 4-2.)

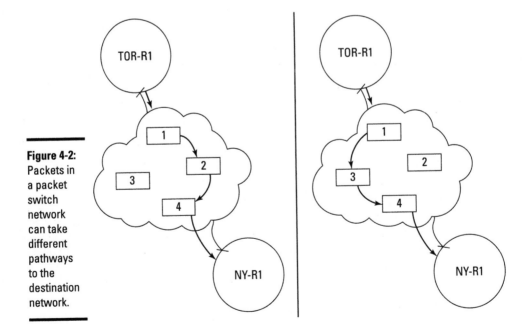

Figure 4-2: Packets in a packet switch network can take different pathways to the destination network.

Looking at Figure 4-2, you see that packets sent from Toronto to New York are sent through different pathways on the packet switched network. It is also important to note that as each router sends the data to the next router, a temporary virtual circuit is created for that stage of the transmission. The virtual circuit has bandwidth allocated to it for that phase of the communication.

Examples of packet switched network technologies include the following:

✦ **X.25:** An older packet switch network technology that uses a *packet assembler/disassembler* (PAD) device that connects to the serial port on the router, allowing the device to connect to the X.25 network. X.25 has a transfer rate of around 2 Mbps.

✦ **Frame relay:** Has replaced X.25, as it is a digital network technology that can reach up to 50 Mbps.

✦ **Asynchronous Transfer Mode (ATM):** A unique packet switched network environment in the sense that it uses a fixed-length packet size, known as a *cell,* which is 53 bytes in size. ATM is a WAN technology that sends large types of data (such as video) with a transfer rate of 622 Mbps.

For the CCENT certification exam, remember that T1 and T3 links are dedicated leased lines, and that X.25, frame relay, and ATM are packet switched environments.

Methods of Connecting to WANs

There are a number of different ways to connect your router to a WAN environment. You will most likely connect a serial interface to the WAN link, or you will have a built-in interface on the router for the WAN technology you are connecting to. The following sections discuss the different types of ports that are present on Cisco devices to connect to your WAN environment.

Serial ports

When connecting your router to a WAN environment, one of the methods you can use is to connect the serial port on the router to a WAN device such as an external CSU/DSU to get a connection to the provider's network. (See Figure 4-3.)

**Book IV
Chapter 4**

Introduction to
WANs

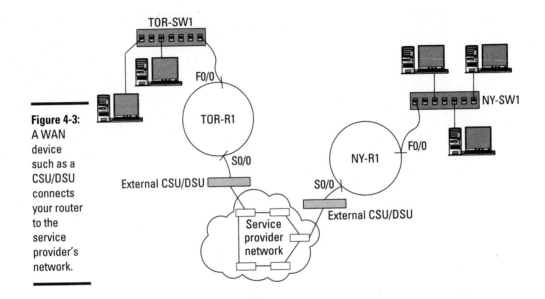

Figure 4-3:
A WAN device such as a CSU/DSU connects your router to the service provider's network.

In Figure 4-3, you see that the serial port on each router connects to an external CSU/DSU device, which is then connected to the service provider's network. In this example, the CSU/DSU is known as an *external* CSU/DSU because it is not part of the router itself and normally sits right beside (or on top of) the router. In this example, the CSU/DSU connects to a T1 link provided by the service provider. You can read more about using a CSU/DSU in Book II, Chapter 1.

You can also use the serial ports on your router to create a point-to-point link between two routers. Although this is not popular in the real world, it is a great concept for a lab environment. In order to connect two serial ports directly together, you need to obtain a DTE/DCE cable (also known as a *back-to-back serial cable*), which is similar to a crossover cable with Ethernet ports. The DCE end of the cable is connected to the router you wish to use to set the clock speed on the link. It does not really matter which router that is, but you will need to set the clock rate using the `clock rate` command on that router (see the "Setting the clock rate" section later in this chapter). Figure 4-4 displays the DTE end of a back-to-back cable being connected to a serial port on a router.

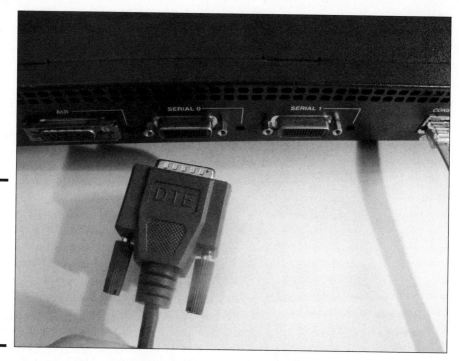

Figure 4-4:
You can use a DTE/DCE cable to create a point-to-point link between your routers.

Integrated CSU/DSU port

A number of routers may come with a built-in CSU/DSU port, known as an *integrated* CSU/DSU port. This means that the line coming from your service provider connects directly to the CSU/DSU port on the router and not to an external device that is then connected to your serial port. Figure 4-5 displays an integrated CSU/DSU port on a Cisco 2811 router, which is used to connect to a leased T1 link.

ISDN ports

Your router may also connect to a WAN environment using an ISDN connection. A number of routers have built-in ISDN ports, which are used to connect to the ISDN network. Figure 4-6 displays a built-in ISDN port on a Cisco router.

An integrated CSU/DSU port

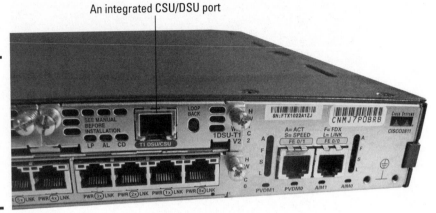

Figure 4-5:
An integrated CSU/DSU port is used to connect directly to a T1 leased line.

Figure 4-6:
An ISDN port built in to the Cisco router is used to connect to an ISDN network.

An ISDN port

Configuring Serial Links

Once you have the WAN link connected to your router, you are then responsible for configuring your router for that WAN link. The following outlines the minimal steps you need to take to configure NY-R1, shown back in Figure 4-1.

To configure the serial interface, the first thing you want to do is configure the IP address on the interface with the `ip address` command, as shown here:

```
NY-R1>enable
NY-R1#config term
NY-R1(config)#interface serial0/0
NY-R1(config-if)#ip address 24.0.0.1 255.0.0.0
```

After you configure the IP address on the serial port you next need to configure the serial port with a protocol and also a clock rate. The following sections discuss how to configure these settings on the serial port.

Serial link protocols

Once you configure the basic IP settings on the interface, you then need to configure the encapsulation protocol to carry data across the serial link. There are two major serial link protocols that you can use to send and receive data on a serial link — HDLC and PPP.

HDLC

The *High Data Link Control* (HDLC) protocol is a data link layer protocol that is an ISO standard, but each vendor has its own implementation of the protocol. This means that if you are connecting two routers with different manufacturers, you will need to use a different serial link protocol, as the two different implementations of HDLC are incompatible.

HDLC is the default serial link protocol on Cisco routers, but it has a limitation of not supporting any form of authentication. You can use HDLC on only synchronous links such as a T1 leased line.

To enable HDLC on your serial link, use the following commands in addition to assigning an IP address:

```
NY-R1(config-if)#encapsulation hdlc
```

Remember for the CCENT exam that both ends of the serial link must use the same serial link protocol. If your router has loaded the HDLC protocol on the serial link, the other end of the link must be HDLC.

PPP

The *Point-To-Point Protocol* (PPP) is an industry standard for carrying data across a serial link. PPP is supported by many different vendors and allows you to create a serial link between routers of different manufacturers.

The benefit of PPP is that you can use it on synchronous serial links such as an ISDN or T1 link, but you can also use it on an asynchronous link such as a dialup link. PPP also supports authentication to verify who is connecting across the link.

**Book IV
Chapter 4**

Introduction to
WANs

PPP supports two different authentication protocols:

✦ **PAP:** The Password Authentication Protocol is an authentication protocol that sends the username and password in clear text when a connection is made between the two hosts. Sending the password in clear text is a security vulnerability, as someone can tap into the communication and discover the username and password.

✦ **CHAP:** The Challenge Handshake Authentication Protocol is an authentication protocol that does not send the authentication information in clear text. With CHAP, a secret is known to both parties and then passed through a mathematical function (known as a *hashing algorithm*), and an answer is generated (known as the *hash value*). The hash value, not the actual secret, is sent across the link. A hash value is a unique value that can be calculated only by knowing the original data (in this case, the secret).

To configure your router for PPP authentication, you must perform the following steps on the serial links on both routers after assigning the IP address:

1. **Set the hostname on each router.**

When a router connects to another router, the hostname of the router connecting will be the username for authentication purposes.

2. **Create a username and password on each router, with the username being the hostname of the router connecting.**

Ensure the password for both ends is the same.

The following is the code sample you use on the NY-R1 router back in Figure 4-1 to configure PPP authentication:

```
NY-R1(config)#username TOR-R1 password mypass
NY-R1(config)#interface serial 0/0
NY-R1(config-if)#encapsulation ppp
NY-R1(config-if)#ppp authentication chap
```

In the preceding code, because the other router that will be connecting to this router is named TOR-R1, you need to create a username on the New York router called TOR-R1. Also note that this name is case sensitive, so watch how the hostnames are configured on your different routers.

After setting the username and password, the encapsulation protocol is set to PPP on the serial interface. After configuring PPP as the encapsulation protocol, I then configure PPP authentication to CHAP. (I could have also specified PAP.)

For the CCENT exam, know how to configure the serial link for an encapsulation protocol such as PPP, and also know how to configure PPP authentication on the routers.

Setting the clock rate

Once you have configured the IP address on the serial interface and the encapsulation protocol to either PPP or HDLC, and set any authentication requirements you may have on PPP, you are now ready to work with the clock rate on the link.

The clock rate determines the speed of the link and is controlled by the *Data Communication Equipment* (DCE). The DCE device is normally at the service provider, so you typically do not set the clock rate on your WAN connection — the service provider sets it.

If you are working in a test lab and have connected two routers together with a DCE/DTE cable, you will be required to set the clock rate from the DCE device in the configuration. The DCE device is the device connected to the DCE end of the cable. To set the clock rate on the serial link of a DCE device, use the following command:

```
NY-R1(config-if)#clock rate 64000
```

In the preceding code example, I set the clock rate to 64000 bits per second, which is a 64 Kbps link. To see a list of values that you can assign to the clock rate command, use the `clock rate ?` command.

For the CCENT exam, remember that the clock rate needs to be configured only on the DCE device and is normally set by the service provider of a WAN link.

Chapter Summary

This chapter illustrates key points of interest when dealing with WAN links on a Cisco router. The following are some key points to remember for the CCENT certification exam:

✦ *Circuit switch environments* establish a pathway (a *circuit*) that is used for the duration of the communication. But after it is disconnected and the next circuit is established, the pathway can be different.

✦ The phone system and ISDN are examples of circuit switched environments.

Book IV
Chapter 4

Introduction to WANs

♦ A *dedicated leased line* is a permanent point-to-point link that typically has more bandwidth than a circuit switched environment. T1 and T3 links are examples of leased lines.

♦ *Packet switched environments* deal with routing each packet a different way and then assembling them at the end. X.25 and frame relay are examples of packet switched networks.

♦ You can connect the serial port to an external CSU/DSU, which connects your network to a leased line such as that used by a T1 or T3 link.

♦ A router may have an internal, or integrated, CSU/DSU port, which connects directly to the leased line coming into your building from the service provider.

♦ The HDLC encapsulation protocol can be utilized when you are using Cisco devices at either end of the serial link.

♦ You can use the PPP encapsulation protocol when connecting different manufacturer routers over a serial link.

♦ PPP supports two authentication protocols — PAP and CHAP. CHAP is the more secure authentication protocol, as it does not send the username and password in clear text.

Lab Exercises

This chapter introduces you to concepts related to WAN terminology and configuring your Cisco router for WAN communication. The following labs are designed to give you the opportunity to practice these concepts.

Lab 4-1: Configuring HDLC encapsulation

In this lab, configure the serial ports on TOR-R1 and NY-R1, which are connected using a back-to-back serial cable. Use Figure 4-7 as a guideline for the configuration of these routers.

1. **Connect the two routers with a back-to-back serial cable, but connect the DCE end of the back-to-back cable to the TOR-R1 router.**

2. **Configure the following on the TOR-R1 router:**

```
Router>enable
Router#config term
Router(config)#hostname TOR-R1
TOR-R1(config)#interface f0/0
TOR-R1(config-if)#ip address 23.0.0.1 255.0.0.0
TOR-R1(config-if)#no shutdown
TOR-R1(config-if)#interface s0/0
TOR-R1(config-if)#ip address 24.0.0.1 255.0.0.0
TOR-R1(config-if)#clock rate 64000
```

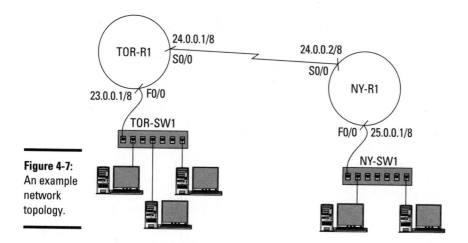

Figure 4-7:
An example
network
topology.

3. **Configure the following on NY-R1:**

```
Router>enable
Router#config term
Router(config)#hostname NY-R1
NY-R1(config)#interface f0/0
NY-R1(config-if)#ip address 25.0.0.1 255.0.0.0
NY-R1(config-if)#no shutdown
NY-R1(config-if)#interface s0/0
NY-R1(config-if)#ip address 24.0.0.2 255.0.0.0
```

4. **State the reason for using the clock rate command on the Toronto
router but not the New York router.**

_____

5. **Configure the serial link on Toronto for HDLC using the following
commands:**

```
TOR-R1(config)#interface s0/0
TOR-R1(config-if)#encapsulation hdlc
TOR-R1(config-if)#no shutdown
```

6. **Configure the New York router for HDLC using the following command:**

```
NY-R1(config)#interface s0/0
NY-R1(config-if)#encapsulation hdlc
NY-R1(config-if)#no shutdown
```

7. **Verify that you can ping across the serial link.**

**Book IV
Chapter 4**

**Introduction to
WANs**

Lab 4-2: Configuring PPP encapsulation

In this lab, change the configuration of the routers that you worked on in Lab 4-1 to use the PPP encapsulation protocol instead of HDLC.

1. **Enable PPP on the TOR-R1 router using the following commands:**

```
TOR-R1(config)#username NY-R1 password mypass
TOR-R1(config)#interface serial 0/0
TOR-R1(config-if)#encapsulation ppp
```

Why are you configuring a username of NY-R1 on the Toronto router?

_____

2. **Configure PPP authentication on the Toronto router using the following commands:**

```
TOR-R1(config-if)#ppp authentication chap
```

3. **Ensure you can ping the New York router.**

4. **Enable PPP on the NY-R1 router using the following commands:**

```
NY-R1(config)#username TOR-R1 password mypass
NY-R1(config)#interface serial 0/0
NY-R1(config-if)#encapsulation ppp
```

5. **Configure PPP authentication on the New York router using the following command:**

```
NY-R1(config-if)#ppp authentication chap
```

6. **Verify you can ping NY-R1 from the TOR-R1 router.**

Prep Test

1 Which of the following are circuit switching technologies?

A ○ T1

B ○ ISDN

C ○ X.25

D ○ Frame relay

2 What are the requirements to configure PPP authentication between NY-R1 and TOR-R1? (Choose three.)

A ❑ Set the hostname on each router to the same name.

B ❑ Set the hostname on each router to a unique name.

C ❑ Create a username on each router named PPP.

D ❑ Create a username on each router that matches the hostname of the other router.

E ❑ Enable PPP authentication on both routers and specify either PAP or CHAP as the authentication protocol.

F ❑ Enable PPP authentication on the first router configured and specify either PAP or CHAP as the authentication protocol.

3 You have configured a test lab and you want to allow communication between two routers using PPP. Review the following code and identify any reasons why the two routers cannot communicate over the serial link.

```
MTL-R1(config)#interface s0/0
MTL-R1(config-if)#ip address 24.0.0.1 255.0.0.0
```

A ○ The encapsulation protocol needs to be set.

B ○ The IP address is incorrect.

C ○ The subnet mask is incorrect.

D ○ The name of the router needs to be changed.

4 Which device on a point-to-point link needs to have the clock rate set?

A ○ The DTE device

B ○ The first device connected

C ○ The DCE device

D ○ Both devices

5 **Which of the following WAN technologies are packet switching technologies? (Select all that apply.)**

A ❑ T1

B ❑ ISDN

C ❑ X.25

D ❑ Frame relay

6 **Which of the following encapsulation protocols will allow communication with non-Cisco devices?**

A ○ PPP

B ○ HDLC

C ○ Frame relay

D ○ IPX

7 **If you want to load a Cisco proprietary encapsulation protocol over the serial link, what command do you use?**

A ○ `encapsulation ppp`

B ○ `encapsulation hdlc`

C ○ `serial link ppp`

D ○ `serial link hdlc`

8 **Which of the following technologies are dedicated leased lines?**

A ○ T1

B ○ ISDN

C ○ X.25

D ○ Frame relay

9 **Which authentication protocol with PPP is considered the most secure?**

A ○ HDLC

B ○ PPP

C ○ PAP

D ○ CHAP

10 **Which type of WAN technology dedicates the bandwidth to the communication until the connection is terminated?**

A ○ Dedicated link

B ○ Packet switch

C ○ Circuit switch

D ○ Leased line

Answers

1 **B.** ISDN is an example of a circuit switched technology where the bandwidth is allocated for the duration of the connection. *See "Circuit switching."*

2 **B, D, E.** To configure PPP authentication, you set the hostname on each router to a unique name and then create a username on each router that is the hostname of the other router. (Set the passwords to the same value.) Then you enable PPP authentication and specify the authentication protocol of either CHAP or PAP. *Review "Serial link protocols."*

3 **A.** The encapsulation protocol needs to be set to PPP. The default encapsulation protocol on a serial link is HDLC. *Check out "Serial link protocols."*

4 **C.** The DCE device is responsible for setting the clock rate. *Peruse "Setting the clock rate."*

5 **C, D.** X.25 and frame relay are examples of packet-switching technologies where each packet can take a different route. *Take a look at "Packet switching."*

6 **A.** The PPP encapsulation protocol is an industry standard available with most router manufacturers and can be used for authentication across router vendors. *Peek at "Serial link protocols."*

7 **B.** To utilize the Cisco proprietary version of HDLC, you use the `encapsulation hdlc` command. *Look over "Serial link protocols."*

8 **A.** A T1 or T3 link is considered a dedicated leased line, as the connection is always available and dedicated to your company. *Study "Leased lines."*

9 **D.** CHAP is the more secure PPP authentication protocol, as the password is not passed in clear text across the network. *Refer to "PPP."*

10 **C.** Circuit switching is responsible for creating the circuit, which is bandwidth and pathway dedicated to the communication until the connection is closed. *Examine "Circuit switching."*

Appendix A: About the CD

On the CD-ROM

✔ System requirements

✔ Using the CD with Windows and Mac

✔ Test Engine designed to help you prepare for the CCENT Certification exam

✔ Videos of the author demonstrating different configuration tasks on some Cisco routers and switches

✔ Lab Manual PDFs containing all of the labs from each chapter along with all the answers to the lab exercises

✔ Troubleshooting

This appendix is designed to give you an overview of the system requirements needed to run the software found on the accompanying CD. I also include a description of what you can find on the CD; it will help you prepare for the CCENT certification exam!

System Requirements

Make sure your computer meets the minimum system requirements shown in the following list. If your computer does not meet most of these requirements, you might have problems using the software and files on the CD. For the latest and greatest information, please refer to the ReadMe file located at the root of the CD-ROM.

✦ A PC running Microsoft Windows 2000 or later

✦ A Macintosh running Apple OS X or later

✦ An Internet connection

✦ A CD-ROM drive

If you need more information on the basics, check out these books published by Wiley: *PCs For Dummies,* 11th edition, by Dan Gookin; *Macs For Dummies,* 10th edition, by Edward C. Baig; and *Windows XP For Dummies,* 2nd edition, *Windows 7 For Dummies,* and *Windows Vista For Dummies,* all by Andy Rathbone.

Using the CD

To install the items from the CD to your hard drive, follow these steps.

1. **Insert the CD into your computer's CD-ROM drive to bring up the license agreement.**

   Note to Windows users: The interface won't launch if you have AutoRun disabled. In that case, do this:

   a. *Choose Start⇨Run.*

      For Windows Vista and Windows 7, choose Start⇨All Programs⇨ Accessories⇨Run.

   b. *In the dialog box that appears, type **D:\start.exe**.*

      Replace D with the proper letter if your CD-ROM drive uses a different letter. If you don't know the letter, see how your CD-ROM drive is listed under My Computer (XP and earlier) or Computer (Vista and 7).

2. **Click OK.**

   Note for Mac Users: The CD icon will appear on your desktop. Just double-click the icon to open the CD and then double-click the Start icon.

3. **Read through the license agreement and then click the Accept button to use the CD.**

   The CD interface appears, from which you can install the programs and run the demos with just a click of a button (or two).

What You Will Find on the CD

The following sections are a summary of the software on the CD-ROM included with this book.

Test Engine

The Test Engine is located on the CD interface's *Test Engine* tab and is designed to simulate the actual CCENT certification exam, which includes questions with multiple choice answers. The Test Engine on the CD is not adaptive, though, and it is not timed — so you might want to time yourself to gauge your speed. With each question you have the option to click the Show Answer button and then they see the correct answer and an explanation. You can also review all of your answers and the correct answers once you finish.

There are two tests included on the CD's Test Engine, and I highly recommend that you wait until after you have read the entire book, performed all of the labs, and answered all of the Prep Test questions at the end of each chapter before attempting the Test Engine. I know a lot of readers like to do the Test Engine as they study, but the problem with doing that is you learn the questions — and the answers — in the Test Engine. By the time you are done reading the book, you get 100 percent on the Test Engine, and it is not an accurate assessment of how you will do on a live test. Save the Test Engine for the end — when you say to yourself, "I think I am ready," do the Prep Test.

Videos

You will also find a *Videos* tab on the CD's interface. The Videos section contains a number of videos I recorded. These videos are designed to demonstrate some of the different tasks you need to know in order to pass the CCENT certification exam. Although you should practice on your own routers and switches, or use a simulator, the videos are there for those who do not have a router handy and still want to see the topics they read about executed on a live system.

Lab Manual PDF files

Also located on the CD's interface is a *Lab Manual* tab. The Lab Manual section contains two PDFs. The first PDF is the Lab Manual and contains all of the labs from each chapter in one central place. It may be useful to print the lab manual and work off the printout instead of writing in the book.

The second PDF is the Lab Manual Answer Key and contains all the answers to the lab exercises. You will find this most useful so that you can verify your answers to the lab exercises.

Adobe Reader

Included on the CD is a copy of Adobe Reader (for Windows and Mac) so you can view PDF files that accompany the book's content. For more information on Adobe Reader or to check for a newer version, visit Adobe's Web site at www.adobe.com.

Troubleshooting

You should not experience any problems with the CD running on your system as long as you meet the system requirements listed in the "System Requirements" section earlier in this appendix. The two likeliest problems are that you don't have enough memory (RAM) for the programs you want to use or you have other programs running that are affecting the installation or execution of a program. If you get an error message such as Not enough memory or Setup cannot continue, try one or more of the following suggestions, and then try using the software again:

+ **Turn off any antivirus software running on your computer.** Installation programs sometimes mimic virus activity and might make your computer incorrectly believe that it is being infected by a virus. Be sure to turn the virus protection back on once you have finished troubleshooting!

+ **Close all running programs.** The more programs you have running, the less memory is available to other programs. Installation programs typically update files and programs, so if you keep other programs running, the installation might not work properly.

+ **Have your local computer store add more RAM to your computer.** This is, admittedly, a drastic and somewhat expensive step. However, adding more memory can really help the speed of your computer and allow more programs to run at the same time.

If you have trouble with the CD-ROM, please call the Wiley Product Technical Support phone number at 1-800-762-2974. Outside the United States, call 1-317-572-3994. You can also contact Wiley Product Technical Support at http://support.wiley.com. Wiley Publishing provides technical support only for installation and other general quality-control items. For technical support on the applications themselves, consult the program's vendor or author.

To place additional orders or to request information about other Wiley products, please call 1-877-762-2974.

Appendix B: CCENT Exam Reference Matrix

You can use this matrix to identify which chapters to study in preparation for the CCENT certification exam. The matrix that follows helps you locate the mini-book and chapter where each of the objectives is covered.

After reading the entire book, you can use this matrix as part of your review. If you go through the objectives and find any area that you think you don't know, you can immediately turn to the appropriate mini-book and chapter for in-depth review. I recommend checking off the objectives once you feel comfortable with them so you can identify which objectives you need to work on.

Objective	Bk	Ch
Describe the operation of data networks.		
❑ Describe the purpose and functions of various network devices	1	3
❑ Select the components required to meet a given network specification	1	3
❑ Use the OSI and TCP/IP models and their associated protocols to explain how data flows in a network	1	2, 4
❑ Describe common networking applications including web applications	1	3
❑ Describe the purpose and basic operation of the protocols in the OSI and TCP models	1	2, 4
❑ Describe the impact of applications (Voice Over IP and Video Over IP) on a network	1	3
❑ Interpret network diagrams	3	1, 2, 3
❑ Determine the path between two hosts across a network	3	1, 2, 3
❑ Describe the components required for network and Internet communications	1	4
❑ Identify and correct common network problems at layers 1, 2, 3 and 7 using a layered model approach	3	5
❑ Differentiate between LAN/WAN operation and features	1	2

(continued)

Objective	Bk	Ch
Implement a small switched network		
❑ Select the appropriate media, cables, ports, and connectors to connect switches to other network devices and hosts	1	2
❑ Explain the technology and media access control method for Ethernet technologies	1	2
❑ Explain network segmentation and basic traffic management concepts	1	3
❑ Explain the operation of Cisco switches and basic switching concepts	3	3
❑ Perform, save and verify initial switch configuration tasks including remote access management	3	3
❑ Verify network status and switch operation using basic utilities (including: ping, traceroute, telnet, SSH, arp, ipconfig), SHOW & DEBUG commands	3	5
❑ Implement and verify basic security for a switch (port security, deactivate ports)	3	4
❑ Identify, prescribe, and resolve common switched network media issues, configuration issues, autonegotiation, and switch hardware failures	3	4
Implement an IP addressing scheme and IP services to meet network requirements for a small branch office		
❑ Describe the need and role of addressing in a network	1	4
❑ Create and apply an addressing scheme to a network	1	5
❑ Assign and verify valid IP addresses to hosts, servers, and networking devices in a LAN environment	1	4
❑ Explain the basic uses and operation of NAT in a small network connecting to one ISP	2	4
❑ Describe and verify DNS operation	2	4
❑ Describe the operation and benefits of using private and public IP addressing	1	4
❑ Enable NAT for a small network with a single ISP and connection using SDM and verify operation using CLI and ping	2	4
❑ Configure, verify and troubleshoot DHCP and DNS operation on a router (including CLI/SDM)	2	4
❑ Implement static and dynamic addressing services for hosts in a LAN environment	2	4
❑ Identify and correct IP addressing issues	3	5

Objective	Bk	Ch
Implement a small routed network		
❏ Describe basic routing concepts (including packet forwarding, router lookup process)	3	1
❏ Describe the operation of Cisco routers (including router bootup process, POST, router components)	2	1
❏ Select the appropriate media, cables, ports, and connectors to connect routers to other network devices and hosts	2	1
❏ Configure, verify, and troubleshoot RIPv2	3	2
❏ Access and utilize the router CLI to set basic parameters	2	2
❏ Connect, configure, and verify operation status of a device interface	2	1, 2
❏ Verify device configuration and network connectivity using ping, traceroute, telnet, SSH or other utilities	3	5
❏ Perform and verify routing configuration tasks for a static or default route given specific routing requirements	3	1
❏ Manage IOS configuration files (including save, edit, upgrade, restore)	2	3
❏ Manage Cisco IOS	2	3
❏ Implement password and physical security	2	2
	4	2
❏ Verify network status and router operation using basic utilities (including ping, traceroute, telnet, SSH, arp, ipconfig), SHOW & DEBUG commands	3	5
Explain and select the appropriate administrative tasks required for a WLAN		
❏ Describe standards associated with wireless media (including IEEE, WI-FI Alliance, ITU/FCC)	4	3
❏ Identify and describe the purpose of the components in a small wireless network (including SSID, BSS, ESS)	4	3
❏ Identify the basic parameters to configure on a wireless network to ensure that devices connect to the correct access point	4	3
❏ Compare and contrast wireless security features and capabilities of WPA security (including open, WEP, WPA-1/2)	4	3
❏ Identify common issues with implementing wireless networks	4	3

(continued)

Objective	Bk	Ch
Identify security threats to a network and describe general methods to mitigate those threats		
❏ Explain today's increasing network security threats and the need to implement a comprehensive security policy to mitigate the threats	4	1
❏ Explain general methods to mitigate common security threats to network devices, hosts, and applications	4	1
❏ Describe the functions of common security appliances and applications	4	1
❏ Describe security recommended practices including initial steps to secure network devices	4	1
Implement and verify WAN links		
❏ Describe different methods for connecting to a WAN	4	4
❏ Configure and verify a basic WAN serial connection	4	4

Index

F

M

P

Q

R

S

W

X

Wiley Publishing, Inc.
End-User License Agreement

READ THIS. You should carefully read these terms and conditions before opening the software packet(s) included with this book "Book". This is a license agreement "Agreement" between you and Wiley Publishing, Inc. "WPI". By opening the accompanying software packet(s), you acknowledge that you have read and accept the following terms and conditions. If you do not agree and do not want to be bound by such terms and conditions, promptly return the Book and the unopened software packet(s) to the place you obtained them for a full refund.

1. **License Grant.** WPI grants to you (either an individual or entity) a nonexclusive license to use one copy of the enclosed software program(s) (collectively, the "Software") solely for your own personal or business purposes on a single computer (whether a standard computer or a workstation component of a multi-user network). The Software is in use on a computer when it is loaded into temporary memory (RAM) or installed into permanent memory (hard disk, CD-ROM, or other storage device). WPI reserves all rights not expressly granted herein.

2. **Ownership.** WPI is the owner of all right, title, and interest, including copyright, in and to the compilation of the Software recorded on the physical packet included with this Book "Software Media". Copyright to the individual programs recorded on the Software Media is owned by the author or other authorized copyright owner of each program. Ownership of the Software and all proprietary rights relating thereto remain with WPI and its licensers.

3. **Restrictions on Use and Transfer.**

   (a) You may only (i) make one copy of the Software for backup or archival purposes, or (ii) transfer the Software to a single hard disk, provided that you keep the original for backup or archival purposes. You may not (i) rent or lease the Software, (ii) copy or reproduce the Software through a LAN or other network system or through any computer subscriber system or bulletin-board system, or (iii) modify, adapt, or create derivative works based on the Software.

   (b) You may not reverse engineer, decompile, or disassemble the Software. You may transfer the Software and user documentation on a permanent basis, provided that the transferee agrees to accept the terms and conditions of this Agreement and you retain no copies. If the Software is an update or has been updated, any transfer must include the most recent update and all prior versions.

4. **Restrictions on Use of Individual Programs.** You must follow the individual requirements and restrictions detailed for each individual program in the "About the CD" appendix of this Book or on the Software Media. These limitations are also contained in the individual license agreements recorded on the Software Media. These limitations may include a requirement that after using the program for a specified period of time, the user must pay a registration fee or discontinue use. By opening the Software packet(s), you agree to abide by the licenses and restrictions for these individual programs that are detailed in the "About the CD" appendix and/or on the Software Media. None of the material on this Software Media or listed in this Book may ever be redistributed, in original or modified form, for commercial purposes.

5. **Limited Warranty.**

   (a) WPI warrants that the Software and Software Media are free from defects in materials and workmanship under normal use for a period of sixty (60) days from the date of purchase of this Book. If WPI receives notification within the warranty period of defects in materials or workmanship, WPI will replace the defective Software Media.

   (b) WPI AND THE AUTHOR(S) OF THE BOOK DISCLAIM ALL OTHER WARRANTIES, EXPRESS OR IMPLIED, INCLUDING WITHOUT LIMITATION IMPLIED WARRANTIES OF MERCHANTABILITY AND FITNESS FOR A PARTICULAR PURPOSE, WITH RESPECT TO THE SOFTWARE, THE PROGRAMS, THE SOURCE CODE CONTAINED THEREIN, AND/OR THE TECHNIQUES DESCRIBED IN THIS BOOK. WPI DOES NOT WARRANT THAT THE FUNCTIONS CONTAINED IN THE SOFTWARE WILL MEET YOUR REQUIREMENTS OR THAT THE OPERATION OF THE SOFTWARE WILL BE ERROR FREE.

   (c) This limited warranty gives you specific legal rights, and you may have other rights that vary from jurisdiction to jurisdiction.

6. **Remedies.**

   (a) WPI's entire liability and your exclusive remedy for defects in materials and workmanship shall be limited to replacement of the Software Media, which may be returned to WPI with a copy of your receipt at the following address: Software Media Fulfillment Department, Attn.: *CCENT Certification All-In-One For Dummies*, Wiley Publishing, Inc., 10475 Crosspoint Blvd., Indianapolis, IN 46256, or call 1-800-762-2974. Please allow four to six weeks for delivery. This Limited Warranty is void if failure of the Software Media has resulted from accident, abuse, or misapplication. Any replacement Software Media will be warranted for the remainder of the original warranty period or thirty (30) days, whichever is longer.

   (b) In no event shall WPI or the author be liable for any damages whatsoever (including without limitation damages for loss of business profits, business interruption, loss of business information, or any other pecuniary loss) arising from the use of or inability to use the Book or the Software, even if WPI has been advised of the possibility of such damages.

   (c) Because some jurisdictions do not allow the exclusion or limitation of liability for consequential or incidental damages, the above limitation or exclusion may not apply to you.

7. **U.S. Government Restricted Rights.** Use, duplication, or disclosure of the Software for or on behalf of the United States of America, its agencies and/or instrumentalities "U.S. Government" is subject to restrictions as stated in paragraph (c)(1)(ii) of the Rights in Technical Data and Computer Software clause of DFARS 252.227-7013, or subparagraphs (c)(1) and (2) of the Commercial Computer Software - Restricted Rights clause at FAR 52.227-19, and in similar clauses in the NASA FAR supplement, as applicable.

8. **General.** This Agreement constitutes the entire understanding of the parties and revokes and supersedes all prior agreements, oral or written, between them and may not be modified or amended except in a writing signed by both parties hereto that specifically refers to this Agreement. This Agreement shall take precedence over any other documents that may be in conflict herewith. If any one or more provisions contained in this Agreement are held by any court or tribunal to be invalid, illegal, or otherwise unenforceable, each and every other provision shall remain in full force and effect.

Apple & Macs

iPad For Dummies
978-0-470-58027-1

iPhone For Dummies,
4th Edition
978-0-470-87870-5

MacBook For Dummies, 3rd
Edition
978-0-470-76918-8

Mac OS X Snow Leopard For
Dummies
978-0-470-43543-4

Business

Bookkeeping For Dummies
978-0-7645-9848-7

Job Interviews
For Dummies,
3rd Edition
978-0-470-17748-8

Resumes For Dummies,
5th Edition
978-0-470-08037-5

Starting an
Online Business
For Dummies,
6th Edition
978-0-470-60210-2

Stock Investing
For Dummies,
3rd Edition
978-0-470-40114-9

Successful
Time Management
For Dummies
978-0-470-29034-7

Computer Hardware

BlackBerry
For Dummies,
4th Edition
978-0-470-60700-8

Computers For Seniors
For Dummies,
2nd Edition
978-0-470-53483-0

PCs For Dummies,
Windows
7 Edition
978-0-470-46542-4

Laptops For Dummies,
4th Edition
978-0-470-57829-2

Cooking & Entertaining

Cooking Basics
For Dummies,
3rd Edition
978-0-7645-7206-7

Wine For Dummies,
4th Edition
978-0-470-04579-4

Diet & Nutrition

Dieting For Dummies,
2nd Edition
978-0-7645-4149-0

Nutrition For Dummies,
4th Edition
978-0-471-79868-2

Weight Training
For Dummies,
3rd Edition
978-0-471-76845-6

Digital Photography

Digital SLR Cameras &
Photography For Dummies,
3rd Edition
978-0-470-46606-3

Photoshop Elements 8
For Dummies
978-0-470-52967-6

Gardening

Gardening Basics
For Dummies
978-0-470-03749-2

Organic Gardening
For Dummies,
2nd Edition
978-0-470-43067-5

Green/Sustainable

Raising Chickens
For Dummies
978-0-470-46544-8

Green Cleaning
For Dummies
978-0-470-39106-8

Health

Diabetes For Dummies,
3rd Edition
978-0-470-27086-8

Food Allergies
For Dummies
978-0-470-09584-3

Living Gluten-Free
For Dummies,
2nd Edition
978-0-470-58589-4

Hobbies/General

Chess For Dummies,
2nd Edition
978-0-7645-8404-6

Drawing
Cartoons & Comics
For Dummies
978-0-470-42683-8

Knitting For Dummies,
2nd Edition
978-0-470-28747-7

Organizing
For Dummies
978-0-7645-5300-4

Su Doku For Dummies
978-0-470-01892-7

Home Improvement

Home Maintenance
For Dummies,
2nd Edition
978-0-470-43063-7

Home Theater
For Dummies,
3rd Edition
978-0-470-41189-6

Living the
Country Lifestyle
All-in-One
For Dummies
978-0-470-43061-3

Solar Power Your Home
For Dummies,
2nd Edition
978-0-470-59678-4

Internet

Blogging For Dummies,
3rd Edition
978-0-470-61996-4

eBay For Dummies,
6th Edition
978-0-470-49741-8

Facebook For Dummies,
3rd Edition
978-0-470-87804-0

Web Marketing
For Dummies,
2nd Edition
978-0-470-37181-7

WordPress
For Dummies,
3rd Edition
978-0-470-59274-8

Language & Foreign Language

French For Dummies
978-0-7645-5193-2

Italian Phrases
For Dummies
978-0-7645-7203-6

Spanish For Dummies,
2nd Edition
978-0-470-87855-2

Spanish
For Dummies,
Audio Set
978-0-470-09585-0

Math & Science

Algebra I
For Dummies,
2nd Edition
978-0-470-55964-2

Biology For Dummies,
2nd Edition
978-0-470-59875-7

Calculus For Dummies
978-0-7645-2498-1

Chemistry For Dummies
978-0-7645-5430-8

Microsoft Office

Excel 2010 For Dummies
978-0-470-48953-6

Office 2010 All-in-One
For Dummies
978-0-470-49748-7

Office 2010 For Dummies,
Book + DVD Bundle
978-0-470-62698-6

Word 2010 For Dummies
978-0-470-48772-3

Music

Guitar For Dummies,
2nd Edition
978-0-7645-9904-0

iPod & iTunes For
Dummies, 8th Edition
978-0-470-87871-2

Piano Exercises
For Dummies
978-0-470-38765-8

Education

Parenting For Dummies,
2nd Edition
978-0-7645-5418-6

Type 1 Diabetes
For Dummies
978-0-470-17811-9

Pets

Cats For Dummies,
2nd Edition
978-0-7645-5275-5

Dog Training For Dummies,
3rd Edition
978-0-470-60029-0

Puppies For Dummies,
2nd Edition
978-0-470-03717-1

Religion & Inspiration

The Bible For Dummies
978-0-7645-5296-0

Catholicism For Dummies
978-0-7645-5391-2

Women in the Bible
For Dummies
978-0-7645-8475-6

Self-Help & Relationship

Anger Management
For Dummies
978-0-470-03715-7

Overcoming Anxiety
For Dummies,
2nd Edition
978-0-470-57441-6

Sports

Baseball
For Dummies,
3rd Edition
978-0-7645-7537-2

Basketball
For Dummies,
2nd Edition
978-0-7645-5248-9

Golf For Dummies,
3rd Edition
978-0-471-76871-5

Web Development

Web Design
All-in-One
For Dummies
978-0-470-41796-6

Web Sites
Do-It-Yourself
For Dummies,
2nd Edition
978-0-470-56520-9

Windows 7

Windows 7
For Dummies
978-0-470-49743-2

Windows 7
For Dummies,
Book + DVD Bundle
978-0-470-52398-8

Windows 7 All-in-One
For Dummies
978-0-470-48763-1

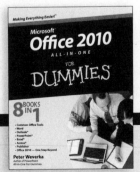

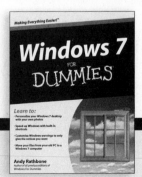